"While the world tries to redefine and redirect families, Gary Collins has written a book that will save, strengthen, and enrich families. In the midst of half-truths, this is a clear message to resolve our problems rather than reproduce them in generations to come."
Stephen Arterburn, M.Ed., Minirth Meier New Life Clinics
Author of *Hand-Me-Down Genes and Second-Hand Emotions*

"Crucial topic, landmark book, potential for doing substantial good. God is on the move, and this book follows the path he is taking. Read it!" **Larry Crabb, Ph.D.,** Institute of Biblical Counseling
Author of *The Silence of Adam*

"Here is a Holy Spirit–given resource, a practical leadership tool, as well as a personal model to help in three ways: to reinforce strong families, to stabilize families, and to rebuild broken families."
Jack W. Hayford, D.Litt., Senior Pastor, The Church on the Way
Author of *The Power and Blessing*

"*Family Shock* is not only a comprehensive look at the state of the family, but it also offers sound advice and direction to parents. The family stories are both compelling and inspiring."
Josh D. McDowell, Campus Crusade for Christ; Author of *More Than a Carpenter* and *Right from Wrong*

"As we head into the twenty-first century, Christian families seem to be increasingly affected by issues that were rare for them less than fifty years ago: divorce, sexual abuse, addictions, etc. What are our hopes for the future, and what are specific steps we can take to reclaim our families for Christ? This book gives biblically sound and practical solutions to help strengthen our families now so that we can build toward a better future for generations to come."
Frank Minirth, M.D., Minirth Meier New Life Clinics
Author of *The Father Book*

"Our world needs this hopeful voice that challenges us to reach out to help each other build solid families in shaky times. This book should be required reading for every family as we enter the twenty-first century." **Tom Landry,** Former Head Coach of the Dallas Cowboys; Author of *Tom Landry*

"Gary Collins's commitment to the stability of the family goes well beyond a commitment to the American family. *Family Shock* takes a compassionate and hopeful look at godly families around the globe. This book reminds us that we have a lot to learn from each other."
Gary Smalley, President, Today's Family; Author of Hidden Keys video series

"Gary Collins offers not just an accurate picture of the state of many families today, but a prescription for help, healing, and hope through Jesus Christ and his church. If you are a parent, you can't afford to miss *Family Shock.*" **H. Edwin Young, D.D.,** Senior Pastor, Second Baptist Church of Houston, Texas; Author of *Been There, Done That, Now What?* and *Romancing the Home*

"In a day when life is weakened by an endless array of cultural factors, the need for this book is obvious. Gary's energy and profound thoughtfulness are evident throughout."
Grace Ketterman, M.D., Crittendon Child and Family Development Center Author of *Verbal Abuse: Healing the Hidden Wound*

"As a pastor for twenty-five years, I have watched families in the pew go through tremendous change. As a pastor to pastors, the parsonage has also felt the 'shock waves.' Dr. Gary Collins has written a book that I can enthusiastically recommend to others and to my own family." **John C. Maxwell, D.Min.,** Founder, INJOY Author of *Developing the Leaders around You*

"Gary Collins has challenged us all. May godly men and women catch the vision of this book and step forward to lead and shape families through the coming decades." **Paul Meier, M.D.,** Minirth Meier New Life Clinics; Coauthor of *Happiness Is a Choice* and author of *The Third Millennium*

"As a mother of seven children, who range in age from thirty-one to eleven, and as a grandmother of seven and counting, I have experienced many of the changes Gary Collins addresses in *Family Shock: Keeping Families Strong in the Midst of Earthshaking Change.* The world that our youngest child and grandchildren are growing up in is a far different world from the one in which our oldest child grew up.

I am often overwhelmed by the changes that are taking place in our society and especially those that affect the family. At times I want to lash out, fight, stop the madness. At other times I just long to grab my little (large) family and run away and hide.

But the truth of the matter is that reality is precariously balanced somewhere between these two extremes. As I have often done before, I look to Gary Collins and his biblically based, yet very practical, wisdom to help me out.

For many years, Dr. Gary Collins has been one of my very favorite authors because of his keen sense of balance. His counsel is first of all biblically sound, based on good common sense, clothed in a delightful sense of humor, and extremely practical. Once again, thank you, Gary Collins." **Gigi Graham Tchividjian,** Author of *A Search for Serenity: Encouragement for Your Weary Days*

"Only Gary Collins could gather over fifty family experts and get them together in one place: this book. Together these voices provide solid biblical answers in a shaken world." **John Trent, Ph.D.,** President, Encouraging Words; Author of *LifeMapping*

"This volume is a vital and helpful answer to a critical and pressing need. It is factual, spiritual, and practical. I strongly advise those who value the family and who are looking for real answers to read this book." **Adrian Rogers, D.D.,** Senior Pastor, Bellevue Baptist Church; Former president of the Southern Baptist Convention

"American society is eroding at a frightening pace, and at the core of this deterioration is the disintegration of the family. Gary Collins confronts the crisis head-on and in a provocative way, challenging Christians to get off the sidelines and 'mobilize a movement.' This book is a must for those who want to participate in a cause that is worth fighting for." **Tony Evans, Th.D.,** Senior Pastor, Oak Cliff Bible Fellowship; Author of *America's Only Hope: Impacting Society in the '90s*

"Once again Gary Collins has given us a realistic appraisal of a difficult area along with a challenge to envision the impact truly Christian families can have on our culture." **Diane Langberg, Ph.D.,** Director, Diane Langberg, Ph.D., & Associates; Author of *Counsel for Pastors' Wives*

"*Family Shock* is well-named. Few of our social institutions have experienced the wrenching changes the family has undergone in the latter half of this century. Dr. Collins and the experts who speak in this book will have a major impact on public opinion regarding the crisis of the American family today. I am glad to see this authoritative and compelling work made available to families before the dawning of the twenty-first century, which will perhaps be the most critical time for families in all of human history." **D. James Kennedy, Ph.D.,** Senior Minister, Coral Ridge Presbyterian Church

FAMILY SHOCK

KEEPING FAMILIES STRONG
IN THE MIDST OF
EARTHSHAKING CHANGE

Gary R. Collins

Tyndale House Publishers, Inc.
Wheaton, Illinois

Library of Congress Cataloging-in-Publication Data

Collins, Gary R.
    Family shock : keeping families strong in the midst of earthshaking change /Gary R. Collins.
       p.   cm.
    Includes bibliographical references and index.
    ISBN 0-8423-1756-2 (alk. paper)
    1. Family—Religious life. 2. Family—United States.   I. Title.
    BV4526.2.C619   1995
    261.8'3585—dc20   95-13053

Printed in the United States of America

00 99 98 97 96 95
7   6   5   4   3   2

Whoever said that
death and taxes are
the only inevitable things in life
was overlooking
an obvious third one:

family.

WILLIAM J. DOHERTY

TO MY FAMILY

In memory of my parents
Harold A. (Bus) Collins (1910-1987)
and
Vera G. Collins (1907-1993)

With appreciation for my sister
Judith A. Swayze

With deep love and gratitude to
my wife, Julie, and
daughters, Marilynn and Jan

CONTENTS

FOREWORD

A QUARTER of a century ago, Alvin Toffler's *Future Shock* made waves with his now historic analysis of the impact of rapid and cataclysmic social change during the latter half of the twentieth century. In *Family Shock,* Gary Collins has taken Toffler's cue and followed his trajectory straight into the heart of the most fundamental of all social institutions—the family. In so doing, I believe he does more than put his finger on the most crucial questions of our time. He also identifies their sources and makes some highly plausible proposals for their ultimate resolution. And he manages to leave his reader hopeful and encouraged. It's a tall order, but Collins fills it admirably.

Gary Collins comes to his task bristling with qualifications. He's a licensed psychologist in the state of Illinois, president of the American Association of Christian Counselors, and editor of *Christian Counseling Today.* Furthermore, *Family Shock* is not his first venture as an author; he has written more than forty books and over 125 journal and magazine articles. It's an impressive record, and it attests to the esteem in which Collins is held by colleagues and readers alike. He is widely recognized and respected as an expert on subjects of concern to the family.

That in itself might be enough to explain my interest in his work. But I have other reasons for following Gary Collins's career with enthusiasm and goodwill. I have known and respected this man for more than twenty years—since before the birth of Focus on the Family! Besides, he has me in his debt: In

1970, Dr. Gary Collins was the first professional to endorse my first book, *Dare to Discipline.* He put his reputation on the line for me, and I've never forgotten it!

If you share my concern for the family and for the larger society that stands or falls on its foundation, you will want to think hard about the information in this book. But more than that, if you are an active family advocate, you need the fuel, the nourishment of the message that underlies the facts, figures, and expert analyses: The family, or more specifically God's intended design for the family, is strong and resilient enough to face, survive, and outlast the shifting winds of change. I know you'll want to discover how you can be a part of that process, and in *Family Shock,* Gary Collins will give you answers to the questions you've been asking—and some that probably haven't occurred to you yet. It's a wise, informed, and thorough piece of work that those who care about the future of the family can't afford to miss. I recommend it highly!

James C. Dobson, Ph.D.
President, Focus on the Family
Colorado Springs, Colorado

In Appreciation

LONG before the thought of this book ever entered my mind, I was having lunch one day with Tim Clinton, my colleague in the American Association of Christian Counselors. He came up with the idea of a Congress on the Family that might be cosponsored by the AACC and Focus on the Family. As we discussed this further, our enthusiasm grew. When the people at Focus on the Family agreed, I suggested that somebody should write a pre-Congress book about the current status of the family. I even had ideas about who would be good writers. When it was suggested that *I* should write the book, I resisted for several months before agreeing to tackle the project. I am grateful to Tim Clinton, Ron Beers, Ken Ogden, and Melissa Breyette, who were convinced that the project was needed and who kept pushing me, gently.

In writing this book I have been encouraged, prayed for, and assisted in many practical ways by some of the finest people imaginable. I was able to write this book, in part, because other people shared with me their expertise, skills, and gifts of insight. I have no words to express my appreciation for their support.

I want to give special thanks to the people who allowed me to tell their stories. You will meet them as you read through the book. I am also grateful to the fifty Christian leaders who agreed to write the articles that appear throughout the following pages. Every person who agreed to participate is busy, but each took time to prepare a contribution—as a gift. The book is stronger as a result.

There are others. Gary Sibcy, Bill Smith, and Lynn Collins were actively involved in helping me complete the task. With her characteristic efficiency and graciousness, my administrative assistant, Michelle Storer, protected me from interruptions and made many insightful suggestions for improving the manuscript.

My wife, Julie, has been with me through many books, always giving support and keen observations. I cannot imagine writing a book about the family without overflowing gratitude for the wife and family that God has given to me. All of these people have given valuable gifts of care, prayer, and encouragement. Thank you all.

I would like to express my appreciation to the following people, each of whom contributed to this book in some way. To any whose names I may have omitted in error, please accept my apologies.

Sandra Picklesimer Aldrich
Steve Arterburn
Gary Bauer
Roy Becke
Ronald Beers
Timothy R. Botts
Melissa and David Breyette
Robert and Beth Bridier
Stuart and Jill Briscoe
George Callendine
Lee Carter
Esly Carvalho
Edmund Chan
Reuben Chavez
Timothy E. Clinton
Jim and Sally Conway
Larry Crabb
Larry Day
Jef De Vriese
Scott and Stacey Davis
Devlin Donaldson
Ted W. Engstrom
Paul Faulkner
Joy Fea
Ronald Glendenning
Daniel R. Henderson
Adrián Hernández
Masaru Horikoshi
Antonio Hristov
Paul and Janell Jochim
Jami and Jill Jochim
Kenneth and Debbie Johansen
Jay Kesler

Grace H. Ketterman
Mark R. Laaser
Diane Langberg
Steven Largent
David and Susan Larson
H. B. London
Bill Smith
Michael Lyles
Grant L. Martin
Josh McDowell
Mark and Lisa McMinn
Paul Meier
Sergio Mijangos
David R. Miller
Frank Minirth
Nathan B. Mohr
Becky Nesbitt
Kenneth Ogden
Barbara Olsson
Leslie Parrott
Les Parrott III
Ken Petersen
Dennis Rainey
Charles R. Ridley
Carlos A. Rodriguez
Dale S. Ryan
Sue Rutz
Buddy Scott
Charles Sell
Gary Sibcy
Rahela Sokač
Patrick Springle
Miriam J. Stark

Dennis Stein
Michelle Storer
Daniel S. Sweeney
Judd and Nancy Swihart
Scott Thelander
Willy Theissen

Joseph and Suneetha Vijayam
Lynn Vanderzalm
Henry Virkler
John Warlow
Sandra Wilson
Everett Worthington, Jr.

When I first turned on my computer to start this book, I was committed to producing a volume that would give up-to-date information on the state of the family, written in a way that would be clear, interesting, carefully documented, readable, practical, inspirational, biblical, and not a rehash of what we already know. If I have succeeded, I credit the people whose names I have listed.

In one of his books, Richard Foster writes, "Like the proud mother who is thrilled to receive a wilted bouquet of dandelions from her child, so God celebrates our feeble expressions of gratitude." Our gifts of service and praise are imperfect and inclined to wilt, but they express our love and delight the Father. The image stuck in my mind, and almost every time I prayed about this book, I offered these pages to God as a gift—imperfect, but an expression of my gratitude and service. I also prayed that it would be accurate, fair, and helpful—maybe even like a gift—to any who might read the pages that follow.

I hope that this book will be encouraging and useful. I pray that God will use it to strengthen modern families, including yours.

Gary R. Collins

PART ONE

FAMILIES IN THE MIDST OF CHANGE

1

COPING WITH CHANGE

"THIS is a book about what happens to people when they are overwhelmed by change. It is about the ways in which we adapt—or fail to adapt—to the future."[1]

A quarter century ago, a writer named Alvin Toffler used these words to begin his book *Future Shock*. In what quickly became a best-seller, Toffler argued that permanence had died and that our whole society was in the midst of cataclysmic change—change that would sweep through industrialized countries "with waves of ever accelerating speed and unprecedented impact." Before the end of this century, millions of ordinary, psychologically normal people will collide abruptly with the future, Toffler predicted. We will be inundated with a flood of novelty, information overload, sensory bombardment, and a revolutionary increase in the tempo of daily life.

Of course, some people would sleepwalk through all of these changes. Even though they live in one of the most exciting periods of human history, this majority would try to hide from the change or find the novelty and new ideas so threatening that they would deny what was happening. These people would complain about the changes brought by technology or telecommunications and would call out for a return to their traditional roots. Most would not realize or admit that "all the old roots—religion, nation, community, family, or profession—are now shaking under the hurricane impact of the accelerative thrust."[2]

In the midst of all this change sits the family—stunned by the shock waves of novelty, shifting values, and information over-load, wondering how they are going to survive. "The family has been called the 'giant shock absorber' of society," Toffler wrote in his book. Home is "the place to which the bruised and battered individual returns after doing battle with the world, the one stable point in an increasingly flux-filled environment."[3] This was written before we knew about the groundswell of domestic abuse and violence that has surfaced during the past decade and has shaken many families. But Toffler correctly predicted that as change escalates and the technological revolution unfolds, the family "shock absorber" would come in for some shocks of its own.[4]

The book that you hold in your hands goes beyond Toffler and takes an end-of-the-century look at the shock waves that now threaten the stability of marriages and weaken the foundations of many homes. We will summarize scientific research and facts about families as they have unfolded during the past two or three decades. We will consider the arguments of writers who publish a stream of books about the disintegration of the family, the incompetence of politicians, the predictions of economic catas-trophes, and the abandonment of traditional values.

But we will go further. We dare not deny the dangerous reali-ties of our present world, and we mustn't close our eyes to the potential for social shake-ups in the future. Even so, it is time to quit the whining and the wallowing in the gloom and doom of those who see no hope for the family or for the future. The message of this book is different. It's a message of hope that can be stated in a few sentences:

- The whole of society is in the midst of change so powerful that it rocks every part of our lives, including our families.
- Many people fear these changes, sensing that they will tear apart our nation and our homes, so they call for a return to the nostalgic families and traditional values of the fifties.
- Change, however, is a part of life, and we cannot cope by resisting its impact, denying its reality, retreating to

the past, or withdrawing into what have been called "armored cocoons"—homes and churches that we turn into cozy bunkers where we "set up alarm systems, pull down the blinds, and imagine ourselves safe from the threats outside."[5]

- When we understand the changes that are shaking families, we can take steps to deal with the change and to undergird our homes so they can stand firm.
- The church can, and must, become a stabilizing influence that gives direction, healing, hope, and security to marriages and families that are battered by the shock waves of change.
- We can reach out from our homes to make others a part of our families, bringing them into God's family as well.

Three Forces That Shake Our Families

Polls and research reports confirm that many people today are scared, fearful about their safety, worried about their families, and lacking in hope for the future. Almost every day the newspapers and television reporters tell us about crime, abuse, uncontrolled sexuality, militant groups that push their perverted values, teenage pregnancies, poverty-stricken families, single-parent frustrations, poor schools, neglected children, and kids that kill other kids. In our own homes—including the homes of Christians—there is conflict, tension, insensitivity, communication breakdown, and probably more abuse than we dare to admit. We face endless demands that rob us of our time, pull us apart, and disrupt our hopes for family unity and stability. A host of forces shake our homes and cause our families to crumble, but three are of major impact: change, pressure, and pessimism.

Catastrophic Change

Change is an ongoing process in which one thing—event, stage in life, experience, or situation—is replaced by another. We all know that to live is to go through change, over and over again. In itself, change doesn't have to be bad; often it is good. When a child stops crawling and starts walking, everybody rejoices because of the change. When the dull exterior of a house is changed by a fresh coat of paint, the place looks brighter and more inviting. When change is expected, wanted, or not too disruptive, most of us handle it well and welcome the variations that it brings. Even when change is more dramatic and unexpected—like the onset of a serious illness or the loss of a job—we may stagger from the shock, but most of us recover, regain equilibrium, and move on with life.

The change that Toffler described is much more traumatic. He used the term *future shock* to describe the shattering stress and disorientation that come when we are subjected to too much change in too short a time. In this technological era, repeated and rapid change comes incessantly—by modems, computers, fax machines, interactive networks, television, and other media. Change comes from shifting values, fluctuating economies, vacillating politicians, and the earthshaking events that we watch on CNN. In many lives this change has made divorce more acceptable, sex more recreational, homosexuality more "natural," marriage more temporary, child rearing more confusing, family commitments more rare, and stable family relationships more impossible. Even families that want closeness and stability face so many stresses, complications, and time demands that togetherness is a rare commodity.

Toffler was right; it is hard for individuals and families to cope with the confusion and shock of swirling change. But unless we learn to adapt and to control the rate of change—in our lives, families, churches, and communities—we are set on the track of massive psychological, spiritual, physical, family, and social breakdown.

Persistent Pressure
Some people thrive on change, invigorated by the excitement of taking risks, challenged by the novelty of new opportunities, maybe addicted to their own adrenaline. Perhaps more people resist change and struggle to survive. They know about the need to persist in a fast-paced world, but they would like to disengage and be less clock-conscious or driven by the need to produce.

Have you noticed how the pace of living has picked up as

change has invaded our lives? We work longer, later, and harder but wonder why our bodies and our psyches give out. A few years ago our culture was fascinated with "downshifting"—the attempt to live life at a slower and simpler pace.[6] Some people gave up their high-stress jobs and moved with their families to smaller communities where change would be less traumatic and where they could find respite from the treadmill frenzy of their lives. Most of us are unwilling or unable to return to a downshifted lifestyle, so we live lives surrounded by devices that are supposed to make life simpler but don't.

The fax machine is an example. Only a few years ago most of us hadn't heard of this modern invention. When it became clear that it would be more convenient to send and receive faxes, I bought a machine that could be hooked to my home phone line. Whenever somebody wanted to send a message, however, I had to switch the button on my phone, and that added confusion. It wasn't long before we got a separate line, dedicated to only the fax machine.

The convenience of sending and receiving messages almost instantaneously was expected to make life easier. No longer would I have to wait for the mail. No longer would I have to worry about getting the right postage or delays because of holidays. I could send or get a fax at any time.

I soon discovered, however, that faxes need to be answered. Unlike letters that can sit in a box for a few days, the people who send faxes want quick answers. About that time, we got an answering machine for our phone so we wouldn't miss any verbal messages while we were away. But like the people who send faxes, the friends who call and leave messages expect us to respond by calling them back—soon.

One day I discovered that I had become a slave to the fax machine and the answering machine. When I get up in the morning or return to the house after an evening out, I seem to drift toward both machines to see if anybody has sent or left a message. Two laborsaving, timesaving devices have made my life more complicated and have added more demands.

It's worse for people who walk around with beepers, never leave home without the cellular phone, become slaves to call-waiting and call-forwarding, or find it impossible to be in a house with the television set turned off. Good technology designed by well-intentioned people has stolen time from our families and disrupted our relationships. For millions of us, the rarest and most precious commodity in our hectic lives is time.

Pervasive Pessimism

Is it surprising that many people are pessimistic? I found this repeatedly as I did research for this book. Surveys show that people are dissatisfied with the economy, the government, the media, and the persistence of crime, drugs, divorce, uncontrolled sexuality, and family tensions. We have tried to live on our own, running our own lives and satisfying our desires, but instead of getting fuller, life has become emptier. Many people put their hope in angels, New Age mysticism, hyperemotional religion, or twelve-step programs of recovery, but an inner emptiness remains. We don't know how to tell right from wrong, and we don't know where to turn, but we're tired of hearing about how bad things are or how things are getting worse.

So many of us plod through life without much hope or optimism for ourselves or our families. We need to shake off the dust of discouragement and get our lives and families back on track.

Getting Back on Track

Many years ago, in the palace of a Persian king named Artaxerxes, a Jewish foreigner rose to a place of prominence. We know little about his background and nothing about his family, but the man was appointed cupbearer to the king—a position that involved tasting the wine before it touched the royal lips and ensuring that the king's food and drink were not poisoned. Cupbearers were like personal valets and security agents. They were powerful and important people. Everybody knew that a king's life—and the whole of his empire—could depend on the loyalty and competence of the cupbearer.

In those days royal servants were expected to hide their feelings and to show a cheerful disposition in the presence of the king, whether or not they felt happy. Even cupbearers could lose their jobs or their heads if they moped around the palace or hinted that they weren't happy in the royal court. It isn't surprising that the cupbearer was afraid when King Artaxerxes noticed that something was wrong and asked why his servant's face looked so sad. The king surmised correctly that the cupbearer was weighted down with a "sadness of heart."

Maybe you have guessed that the sad-faced servant was Nehemiah, an Old Testament personage who was deeply saddened by changes that had taken place in his ancestral home. The walls of Jerusalem had crumbled and were in disrepair. The inhabitants were disillusioned and oppressed, "in great trouble and disgrace." The people were steeped in poverty, idolatry, squabbling, and materialism. Try as he might, Nehemiah could not hide his deep distress even in the presence of the king.

Whenever I read Nehemiah's life story, I learn again about leadership, stamina, stress management, and dependence on God. I also learn about how a believer, working in partnership with others, was able to rise above his pessimism, face the change that his hometown had encountered, and take action to make things better. I see a man whose persistence and determination can have modern relevance to people like us, people who struggle not with crumbling walls and buildings in faraway places but with disintegrating families and collapsing marriages in their own communities. Notice what Nehemiah did when he learned about the shocking changes in Jerusalem.

Nehemiah prayed (Neh. 1:5-11). What we tend to do last, when all else has failed, Nehemiah did first. He expressed his praise to God, confessed personal and community sins, remembered God's promises, and asked for help and guidance as he prepared to take action.

My wife and I have two daughters in their late twenties. We raised them in an atmosphere of prayer. We need divine guidance to be good parents even as we need God's help in building our marriage and keeping a family together and firm during times of change.

Nehemiah planned (Neh. 2:2-8). When faced with change and decay, some people sit back and think about how wonderful things were in the past. Some people pull back and think how terrible things are and how there is no hope for the future. Others get back into gear and try to decide what they can do to make things better. When King Artaxerxes asked Nehemiah what would make him happy, Nehemiah had a plan. Maybe he didn't know all the details of the plan, but he had some initial ideas about how to meet the changes that had shaken his homeland.

How do we make plans to improve our families in times of change? To answer that question, I wrote to a group of people who work with families all the time. I asked each of them to write an article suggesting how we can understand and make plans to strengthen our families. Some of these writers are well-known experts in counseling and family therapy; others offer additional insights that can help us all. These articles appear throughout the pages of this book.

Nehemiah proceeded (Neh. 2:9-12). With the king's support, Nehemiah took the first steps toward confronting the situation and trying to rebuild what was broken. The cupbearer moved ahead with confidence because he had prayed about his actions. He knew he was right in what he was determined to do, and he sensed that the hand of God was on him (Neh. 2:8, 18).

We can have similar confidence when we look to God and determine to build stronger families, strengthen biblical values, respect individual family members, and show compassion to others. The steps that Nehemiah took to build a solid wall are similar to the steps we can take to build or rebuild solid family relationships.

Nehemiah joined with others (Neh. 2:12-18). When Nehemiah reached Jerusalem, after a journey that perhaps took several months, he went on a late-night tour of the broken walls. Remember that Nehemiah was a cupbearer, not a carpenter. He knew very well that no person could rebuild a city wall without help. He surveyed the scene with a few colleagues, but then he mobilized the people to build together.

God rarely uses loners. Most often he seems to use groups of people to accomplish his purposes. Jesus had twelve disciples. Paul worked with Timothy, Barnabas, and others. Billy Graham works with a team of associates. When superstar evangelists and business tycoons try to build on their own, they often slide into pride and a smug sense of self-importance that hinder and sometimes destroy their usefulness. People—wall builders and family builders—need other people.

I wonder if some of those people in Jerusalem saw Nehemiah, the cupbearer to a Persian king, as a foreigner. I wonder if they resisted him or discounted his ideas because he wasn't one of them.

Sometimes we fall into that trap. We assume that people from other countries don't understand or can't relate to us. We assume that their insights aren't valid because they don't live in our culture. While that is an easy assumption to make, it is a false one. During the past decades I have consistently learned from my friends who live in other parts of the world. Not only do they have fresh perspectives because they live in other cultures but they often can see things in our culture that we can't see. Because the experiences of people from different cultures can be so helpful to us, I have included several of their stories in the following pages. In a real sense, these people have helped me write this book.

Nehemiah encountered opposition. Expect it! When we are committed to building families, we will face opposition. Radical feminists (but not all feminists), militant gays (but certainly not all homosexuals), some political leaders, the producers of some television programs, even a few Christian leaders, fellow believers, or your own family members will stand in your way and seek to undermine your efforts to build a strong family.

Nehemiah was hit with several types of opposition. They all sound remarkably contemporary. Some people laughed and ridiculed the efforts and determination of the rebuilders (Neh. 2:19; 4:1-3). Some plotted to undermine the rebuilding efforts (Neh. 4:7-9). Fatigue and stress threatened to undermine the project (Neh. 4:10-12). An economic crisis and squabbles among the builders threatened the project for a while (Neh. 5:5-7). Other people made deliberate attempts to distract the builders from their task (Neh. 6:4-9).

In every case, Nehemiah and his associates prayed and kept on building. When the builders disagreed, Nehemiah led with integrity, honesty, compassion, and fairness. The critics had no cause to hurl insults against their leader (Neh. 5:14-18). And eventually the cupbearer succeeded in motivating God's people to complete the task of rebuilding the wall (Neh. 6:15).

This book has a similar goal: *to acknowledge the earthshaking pressures on the family but to keep building.* To be successful we need to keep praying, planning, and moving ahead, in partnership with others and despite the opposition that naturally comes to any who dare to believe that the future of the family is bright.

A New Wave

People who have been in the midst of a serious earthquake agree that the experience is frightening. The waves of aftershocks leave individuals and families tense and vigilant for weeks afterward.

Maybe Alvin Toffler sensed some of this after his *Future Shock* book sent waves of debate and discomfort through thousands of shaken readers. A few years later he published *The Third Wave,* a book that offered a startling message of hope. "We stare in horror at the headlines," he wrote, but there are those who think the human story, far from ending, has only just begun. "In the very midst of destruction and decay, we can now find striking evidences of birth and life," Toffler argued. "If the main argument of this [new] book is correct, there are powerful reasons for long-range optimism, even if the transitional years immediately ahead are likely to be stormy and crisis-ridden."[7]

The following pages carry a similar message of hope and optimism. In this book we will steer away from speculation and dire predictions of the family's demise and look instead at the research reports, journal articles, and books that tell us what we can know about families.

We will look in detail at some families who have experienced earthshaking change and difficulties but who are surviving, some with inspiring success.

We will also look into the pages of the Bible to see how the wisdom of this ancient and God-inspired book applies to twenty-first-century families.

And we will try to avoid negativism.

When we look at the modern family, we see much that is

negative. But nothing is likely to improve if we wallow in the isn't-it-awful mentality of perpetual negativism.

Psychiatrist Karl Menninger told a story about President Jefferson. One day when Jefferson was horseback riding with a group of his companions, they came to a gushing stream that had been swollen by a spring thaw. Crossing that turbulent stream was dangerous, but several of the men made it to the other side. At that point a bystander approached Jefferson and asked for a ride across the stream. Jefferson readily agreed, took the man on the back of the horse, and rode across the swirling water.

"Why did you select the president to ferry you across?" one of the men asked when they reached the opposite bank. The wayfarer expressed surprise and answered that he had not known the identity of the man who had given the ride. "All I know is this. On some of the faces I could see the answer 'no.' On this man's face I saw the answer 'yes.'"[8]

As you go with me through the remaining pages of this book, I hope you will end your reading with a better understanding of families, including yours, and with a sense of hope. With all of the changes, pressures, and shocks, will the institution of the family survive and be strong as we move into a new century? When we look at some worried faces, even the faces of Christians, we see the answer no. I hope you will join me in looking at families with faces that say yes.

2

NINE INFLUENCES
THAT SHAPE OUR FAMILIES

CULTURES and people have always been changing, but during the twentieth century the pace has quickened. Many of us feel overwhelmed, saturated with new ideas or challenges and reeling from the impact that all of this has on our individual families. It isn't surprising that many people wonder if their families will survive and retain their continuity through the next generation or two.

Family life, with all its richness and complexity, can't be forced into some idealized picture of what all families ought to be like. Family life can't be illustrated by snapshots that capture seconds from the past and get pasted into albums. Families are more like ongoing motion pictures in full color and stereophonic sound, with plots, subplots, and lots of action. Like the dramas of Shakespeare, some families are ongoing tragedies with one crisis and conflict following another. Other family dramas are comedies. Some are exciting; many are dull. Some families live in deep relationship to God; others never bring him into their family stories at all. Some families thrive on "much ado about nothing" and a few live by the philosophy that "all's well that ends well."

Unlike the plays of Shakespeare or the movies from Hollywood, however, family dramas never end. Each one is different, and each is playing at the same time. Every script is being developed, acted out, and recorded as we live our lives and interact with others. We have few opportunities for rehearsals or reruns.

15

Your family script is different from mine and from every other family in the world. Twenty years from now, what will make our families different from the way they are now? To answer this question, we need to look at nine family influences, all of which can have practical impact on the ways in which we live and move into the twenty-first century. Let's start by thinking about the past.

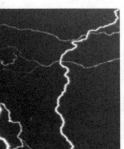

INFLUENCES THAT IMPACT OUR FAMILIES

1. Experiences and incidents from the past
2. Events and influences in the present
3. Worldviews
4. Dreams and expectations for the future
5. Our decisions and choices
6. Family stages and transitions
7. Racial and cultural uniquenesses
8. Family continuity and constant change
9. The hand of God

The Impact of the Past

Every counselor knows that to understand people and help them with their present struggles, we often need to take a long, hard look at the past. The same is true of families. Think about it: How have your life and your present family been influenced and molded by the family in which you grew up? How has your family been influenced by past events, both positive and negative?

If you grew up in poverty, as the child of a substance abuser, in a home where your parents were both too busy, or in a family that had been touched by the Holocaust, civil rights violence, failure, or a lot of fame, these influences probably have left their mark on you. And if you were raised in a stable home by parents who taught clear moral standards, you were influenced by these factors as well.

The Bible is filled with examples of the family's impact. In his father's house, young Joseph learned values that guided his life and morals in the court of Pharaoh. Centuries later, Paul wrote to young Timothy about his "sincere faith, which first lived in your grandmother Lois and in your mother Eunice" (2 Tim. 1:5). Much different, and less famous, is a man named Ahaziah, who became ruler of Israel following the reign of his father, King

Ahab, and the notoriously wicked Queen Jezebel. According to the Old Testament, Ahaziah "did evil in the eyes of the Lord, because he walked in the ways of his father and mother" (1 Kings 22:52). Other kings reacted against their past and threw off the influences of their parents.[1]

During the past decade and a half, our society has recognized the crippling influences parents can have on children. In response to this awareness, we have seen the rise of the popular recovery movement that began years earlier with Alcoholics Anonymous. The founders of AA recognized that they could get free of their compulsions to drink if they met together to encourage one another and go through a twelve-step program designed to bring about sobriety. AA was very successful in accomplishing its purposes, so it was not surprising that organizations like Gamblers Anonymous and Narcotics Anonymous soon made their appearance.

Families of addicted people formed their own groups in which relatives helped one another to live with addicted loved ones. In time we began to hear about adult children of alcoholics (ACOAs), adults who had been harmed by their troubled pasts. It wasn't long before the adult children of abusive parents and even adult children of fundamentalists formed groups of their own—each with a twelve-step program for recovery. At the height of this movement, some enthusiasts implied that everybody was an adult child of some harmful family influence and that we all needed to be in a recovery group. Many people developed a victim mentality that said, in essence, "Don't blame me for my failures or family problems. They are all caused by my parents and how they brought me up."

The recovery movement and this victim mentality showed some excesses that aroused a lot of criticism, but even critics admit that recovery programs continue to help many people. The movement has emphasized a truth that almost everybody accepts: People and families are influenced by their past experiences.

The Power of the Present
Nobody knows how many families were squeezed into the Goshen Methodist Church on Palm Sunday morning. Newspapers

17

reported that the little church was more crowded than usual because children from the congregation were presenting their pre-Easter play. At 11:30 A.M., while the young voices were singing "Jehovah Jireh"—Hebrew for "the Lord will provide"—a devastating tornado ripped into the church, tearing off the roof, shattering the windows into bits of flying glass, and toppling a wall of bricks and cinder blocks onto the worshipers, including the kids on the stage. Most people in the church were hurt, some seriously. Twenty people died, including several children and the pastor's four-year-old daughter, Hannah Clem.

"It is the most horrible thing I've ever seen," said one of the rescue workers who came to help. Pews were used to carry the injured, and dead bodies were laid in a carport across the street from the church. In the days that followed, the grief-stricken pastor began the sad task of comforting the congregation and burying the dead. Pastors from other churches and other denominations came from across the state to give help and support. On Easter Sunday, one week after the tornado struck, the remnants of the congregation gathered together in the parking lot, sat on folding chairs—or in wheelchairs—and celebrated the Resurrection.

The Clem family will never be the same, and neither will the families of that church and community. The events of one sad Sunday morning will stay with them for life. Maybe some family members will turn away from God or from each other, engulfed in anger and anguish. Others will draw nearer to the God of all comfort, seeking peace, security, and some answer to the difficult question of why this happened.

Few of us encounter tragedies so catastrophic and unexpected, but most families are forced to cope with events that shatter their dreams and disrupt their lives. Divorce, bankruptcy, loss of work, serious illness, slowly fading health, the death of a family member—all make an impact. Some families are jolted by the news that a family member has been arrested or that someone has attempted suicide. Others struggle with the reality of a relative who becomes an alcoholic, fails in a business, makes an unexpected career change, or announces plans to move in with a homosexual lover. War in the country, crime in the streets, abuse in the bedroom, instability in the government, violence and immorality on the television screen—the list of ongoing family stresses can seem endless.

Positive events also can force families to change and make adjustments. Joyful times like a birth in the family, a move to another home or town, a marriage, a child leaving for college, or a job change can trigger many changes in how our families function. Each can have an impact on how your family drama develops.

The Impact of Our Worldviews

Life dramas are also affected by each person's *worldview.* Worldviews are the assumptions that we make about the universe, about God, about human beings, about right and wrong, and about how we can know anything for certain. Each of us has a worldview that influences how we see the world, think, act, and relate to other people. Often we don't give these assumptions much thought until somebody nudges us to think about them.[2]

Think, for example, about your view of abortion. Are you pro-life, pro-choice, or something in-between? What do you think about gay marriages? What is your perspective on working women who leave their kids with baby-sitters, on fathers and mothers who share the parenting role fifty-fifty, on parents who do home schooling, on sex apart from marriage, on Christians who get involved trying to pass pro-family legislation, or on people who protest outside abortion clinics? Each of these family-related issues can arouse heated debate, and each is related to the debater's worldview assumptions. I once knew a divorced woman who didn't trust men. When I learned about her life story, about her husband's unfaithfulness and his leaving to marry another woman, I could understand this woman's perspective. It was easy to comprehend why she repeatedly warned her daughter that men could not be trusted. This woman knew many kind and caring men as she grew older, men that included her own sons, but she went to her grave convinced that males, in general, were untrustworthy. It had become a part of her worldview.

Family conflict often arises when a husband and wife or parents and children have different worldviews about emotionally laden issues such as religion, morals, lifestyle, or parenting.

When our kids were younger, my wife, Julie, and I had similar views about child rearing, but we detected early on that some of our perspectives were not shared by my parents. Sometimes when my parents came to visit, we felt tension about these different viewpoints, but to their credit, they said very little and didn't make any attempt to meddle. Apparently they had reached a conclusion all family members need to learn: Sometimes we need divine wisdom to know when to keep our views to ourselves, when to express our worldviews clearly, and how to tell the difference.

The Effects of Our Expectations for the Future

To understand families and make them better, we cannot ignore how people view the future and what they expect. Sadly, the world is filled with people who drift through life without ambition, living in families that have no hope for anything better than the boring routines and perpetual difficulties that they encounter day after day. Some of these people are lazy and need a prod to get them moving, but I suspect that most people feel trapped in dead-end careers, abusive families, difficult relationships, or endless financial struggles. Don't tell people in these families to "think positively," to "snap out of your problems," or to "make things happen"; they will know you don't understand.

Not long ago, my wife, Julie, and I visited a young missionary family in Thailand. We went sightseeing around Bangkok and ate lots of Thai food, but much of our time was spent talking about the challenges of building a marriage and raising a family in a foreign culture, far away from relatives and supportive friends.

At one point I asked the husband to tell me about his dreams and plans for the future. Apparently this question surprised him. He and his wife had been in Thailand for a year, but nobody had asked about their hopes and aspirations. The couple had heard plenty about missionaries who had failed in the past. They knew about the difficulties of reaching the Thai people with the gospel. More experienced missionaries, undoubtedly trying to be helpful, had encouraged our friends to guard against unrealistic expectations. As a result, their youthful idealism had been squelched, and their spirits were deflated. They needed fresh dreams and hope for the future.

Life is often better for people who dream about the future, are energetic, determined, and able to make some of their dreams come true. Even from the depths of prison, the apostle Paul wrote about joy, thought about opportunities for future service, and looked ahead to his eternity with Christ. Building careers, molding marriages, nurturing children, and planning for the future can be hard, but it's invigorating work for people who see prospects for change and success.

The Importance of Our Decisions

The health of our families often depends on the decisions we make, especially when difficult circumstances threaten to overwhelm us and keep us from growing together. Psychiatrist Robert Coles tells the story of a man who longed for a son to add to his family of five daughters. When the man's wife gave birth to a boy, the husband was in ecstasy until he got the news that baby Ben was mildly retarded, born with Down's syndrome.

In the weeks that followed, the family saw a steep decline in the man's spirits and a change in his entire way of life. Previously filled with energy and enthusiasm, he became lethargic and irritable. "He's heartbroken," the wife said. "We both are, only I seem to be taking it much better. I say a dozen times to myself: God's will. If the good Lord wanted to send a retarded child here, and a boy, then that's His decision. For me the church is a big help."[3] But the husband was frustrated with God and refused to go to church anymore.

One Sunday morning the wife got ready to attend a church service by herself but let her husband know that she was fed up with "all this feeling sorry for yourself." She left the house, slammed the door as hard as she could, and got into the car. Then she had second thoughts.

"I was ready to go and then I said to myself, 'Hey, stop a minute. What's more important—to go to church and sit there and fume and ask Jesus to feel sorry for you and to condemn your husband or to skip church and go back inside and sit with him and hope he'll really break down and cry and cry, so all that disappointment in him will come out, and then he can talk with me, and we can try to figure out a way that we can pick up from here.'"4

The woman left her car, went into the house to make some coffee, and sat with her husband. For a long time he sobbed, and then they talked. The wife suggested that he needed some brief times away from the family, but he didn't know where to turn. They decided against talking to the pastor, and both knew the saddened father couldn't talk to his friends. He was Mr. Confidence and Mr. Keep Busy with them. But the husband agreed to chat with their pediatrician, and a week later the two had a long talk. The doctor took the lead and told Ben's dad that he needed to have experience with older children who needed special education. With the physician's help, the father began to volunteer on weekends at a state school for retarded and disabled children.

At first he was anxious, frightened, ready to give up, and flooded with feelings of inadequacy. But before long he started to change. He got involved with several of the kids, encouraging them, challenging them to action, and learning from them. Soon they were a team—in sports, games, cleanup activities, doing routines, and helping the staff with other children. The man organized a Little League team and learned creative ways to relate to his son. He eagerly looked forward to every visit to that state school, and he talked to his friends about the choice he had made to get involved with the kids. Everybody could see that his old enthusiasm had returned.

After telling this story, Robert Coles described this father as "a man who had shown what it can mean to fall down, then to pick himself up, not through hours of psychological talk or the support of a 'group,' and not even through the healing that time offers [all of which can be helpful and often needed]. In the end, his willfulness responded to his wife's loyalty and affection and to a doctor's sensible suggestion. But in the end, also, his pain responded to the visible concrete opportunities a few children offered him. The gifts he brought on their birthdays and at Christmas signaled not only what these children had come to mean to him, but what they had enabled him to find and affirm in himself."5

This man was overwhelmed by a family disappointment, but he made some positive decisions and was able to turn his trials into a triumph.

The Effects of Family Stages and Transitions

At the end of a long, emotionally draining day, our whole family—including my sister's one-year-old grandson—sat around a group of tables pulled together in the corner of a restaurant. The dinner hour was long past, but the place was alive with Thursday-night shoppers, bustling servers, and rattling dishes. Life swirled all around us, but our thoughts were someplace else as we talked, sometimes laughed, occasionally fought back tears, and reflected on the events of the previous few hours. That morning we had gathered around a grave site as my mother's body was buried. She had stood with us at that same spot after my father died six years earlier. The names on the weathered gravemarker reminded me that several generations of my ancestors—people whom I never knew—had stood there long before me.

My mother was born seven years after the twentieth century began, and she died seven years before it ended. As a schoolgirl during World War I, she was taunted because her classmates assumed that her last name, Stanger, was German. In fact, her ancestors had come from England and had settled in southern Ontario, where my mother lived for her whole life. She and her brother were raised in a home where my godly grandmother guided her children to adulthood while also caring for one of her husband's eccentric older relatives.

When my parents were married in 1932, two years before I was born, they moved in with my grandparents, and my mother cared for her dying mother, who died before I arrived. For the next nineteen years, my grandfather lived with us and left me with indelible memories of good times together, the realities of aging, and the simmering tensions that sometimes led to verbal explosions, especially as he got older.

My parents gave me solid roots but allowed me to have wings and to fly away from home—first to the adventures of the Canadian Navy and then to study in Toronto, London, and the United States. When I married an American and we established our family away from Canada, my mother accepted the separation reluctantly. But she never stopped hoping (and maybe praying) that we would someday return to Hamilton, where most of my relatives still live.

When my father got sick, less than five years after we all had celebrated their golden wedding anniversary, my eighty-year-old mother took care of him until the day he died. The experience left her exhausted but without regrets. During her widowhood she struggled with loneliness, worry, and questions about why she continued to live when she would have preferred to be in heaven with her husband. Often she mentioned that her family was the only reason she had for living.

On the day of the funeral, her family sat together, and somebody mentioned that at last she was free of her worries and at peace in the place where she had often said she wanted to be: away from the body and at home with the Lord (2 Cor. 5:8). Later that night one of my nieces made a thought-provoking reflection about our few days together.

"This week," she said, "we all moved up one generation."

I doubt that my niece has ever heard of family cycles, but her comment pointed to another important influence on how families change: People go through cycles. Christian psychologist Everett Worthington, Jr., suggests that the family life cycle can be divided into seven stages.

- *Stage one:* marriage and life without children. A couple establishes a household, builds a satisfying marriage, and adjusts sexually.
- *Stage two:* birth of first children. A couple becomes a family and adjusts to life with children.
- *Stage three:* first child enters school and the family becomes involved with community. A couple balances roles as spouses, parents, church members, and career builders.
- *Stage four:* children become adolescents. A couple feels stress and finds marital satisfaction and fulfillment threatened.

- *Stage five:* children leave home for college, jobs, or marriage. A couple learns to turn their children loose.
- *Stage six:* all children live outside the home. A couple may be grandparents and experience the death of older family members. A couple becomes the family elders.
- *Stage seven:* retirement. A couple deals with declining health or vigor, the death of a spouse, and changing roles with their adult children.[6]

At each of these stages, the family has responsibilities and unique stresses. Families with adolescents, for example, have to adjust to individual differences in schedules, attitudes, and ideas about appropriate dress, behavior, morals, or chores. Families often have financial strains at this stage. One or both parents may be struggling with midlife insecurities. Sometimes they find themselves as part of the *sandwich generation* in which a middle-aged couple is caught between the demands and challenges of caring for both hard-to-understand teenagers and older parents who have increasing needs.[7]

Transitions
The transition periods from one family stage to another can be difficult for families.[8] Think about what happens when a couple gets married, for example. In making the transition from single-ness into marriage, they change their living arrangements, economic circumstances, and ways of relating both to each other and to their relatives. Sometimes these transitions are smooth, but they can become rocky if one or both of the spouses can't break from the original family, if the parents meddle, or if the couple discovers that they have clashing expectations about money, sex, or lifestyle. Most of us know families, maybe the one in your house, in which the wife has one idea about what the husband should do in the house, and he has a different idea. If the couple handles disagreements by arguments, power struggles, or attempts to control each other, the initial bliss of marriage won't last very long. It may take a lot of effort and perhaps some help from others before this couple settles into a more harmonious relationship. If the conflict continues, they are poorly prepared

for the transition into parenthood, when the initial problems could get worse.

Glitches

Times of transition call for extra effort, adjustment, and reorganization, but most families move into each new stage with relative ease. Sometimes, however, family cycles and family transitions run into family glitches, problems that hinder the smooth operation of families and disrupt family cycles. What happens to all these family stages, for example, if a married couple is infertile and unable to have children? What if they decide not to have children? How are the family stages interrupted by divorce, the early death or severe illness of a child, or the marriage of an older couple when one or both of the spouses already have kids?

Even poverty has an effect on the family cycle. One researcher studied poor black families and concluded that some of these have only three stages. The first involves the "unattached young adult," who may be as young as eleven or twelve years old and who is unaccountable to adults and not protected by older family members. Often these young people get pregnant, starting stage two. They become single parents who move in with their parents, grandparents, and siblings (and their children) and live together as three- or four-generation families. In time many of the women become grandmothers (stage three), often before they are forty years old, and their lives are involved in caring for the younger generations.[9]

The Influences of Racial and Cultural Distinctives

Every family is a product of culture. Think about the religious beliefs in your family, the ways people relate and show emotion, or the family's rules, attitudes, lifestyles, and ways of celebrating birthdays or Christmas. Much of this is shaped by the country or part of the country where you live and by your family's origins, income level, language, race, education, and a host of other influences. For decades we have heard about the American melting pot as if we can or should forsake our cultural differences and all blend together. This is neither possible nor desirable. We make a mistake if we try to squelch ethnic differences and rich

NEVER MISS
THE IMPORTANCE OF
GRANDPARENTS

JAY KESLER
President, Taylor University
Author of *Grandparenting:
The Agony and the Ecstasy*

Grandparents have always played an important role in providing stability and support to families. The apostle Paul begins his second letter to Timothy by reminding him of the background and heritage of his family—the faith and character of his mother, Eunice, and his grandmother, Lois. Paul encourages Timothy to imitate the examples of these godly women, who lived devout lives in the midst of a pagan society.

Biblical history reveals that the family structure of the first century was at least as tense and stressed as it is today. Infidelity, abuse, incompatibility, and divorce plagued the family structure. War, poverty, depression, epidemics, slavery, and exile threatened the stability of family life.

To meet the needs of that culture, God in his divine wisdom ordained that each child should have six adults to provide care and backup. In ancient times, because of disease and accident, life expectancy was short. Families were often broken up as fathers went off to war or mothers were sold into slavery. The involvement of the extended family, especially grandparents, was crucial to the survival of the children.

As we approach the twenty-first century, many families face similar challenges, not because of slavery but because of the breakdown of the moral and social fabric of society. This generation will meet the challenge, especially if Christians understand that this is not only a social challenge but also a spiritual battle.

In this important battle, we encourage a recommitment to Christian grandparenting. The whole weight of responsibility cannot rest on an individual set of grandparents or a single grandmother or grandfather, but we can stand in the gap in our particular situations.

cultural diversities in an attempt to blend us all into some bland mixture.

Even before I was a teenager, I wanted to travel to countries overseas. Maybe those missionary pictures had made more of an impact than I realized as a child. When I got to college I joined the reserve navy so I could "see the world." After college graduation I lived for a while in Europe. I quickly became aware of cultural and family differences that I had not read about or noticed in the multicultural neighborhood where I grew up. I learned, for example, that in North America we value individual initiative and being open about our feelings, but other cultures put more emphasis on family loyalty, hiding feelings, and not bringing disgrace on the family. I discovered that in some places people are very hospitable, open, warm, and friendly, even to strangers, but people in other places arc more reserved and cautious. Americans tend to be informal, use first names, and don't pay much attention to titles. In other countries such behavior is considered brash and disrespectful. When I worked in a predominantly African American urban environment, I discovered that family life and values there were different from those I had experienced living in the suburbs. One family counselor has expressed this with special clarity. She wrote, "What you think, how you act, even your language, are all transmitted through the family from the wider cultural context. This context includes the culture in which you live, and those from which your ancestors have come. . . . No two families share exactly the same cultural roots. . . . No matter what your family background is, it is multicultural. . . . If we look carefully enough, all of us are a hodgepodge."[10]

The Effects of Changing Demographics and Family Continuity

This hodgepodge of diversity is influenced by another factor— the constant change in the makeup of the population, or *demographics*. In four countries—Australia, New Zealand, Canada, and the United States—a baby boom began after World War II and continued for almost twenty years before leveling off in the 1960s. This generation of baby boomers are now well into middle

AFRICAN-AMERICAN FAMILIES

CHARLES R. RIDLEY, PH.D.
Associate Professor, Indiana
University
Director of Training, Counseling
Psychology Program
Author of *Overcoming
Unintentional Racism in
Counseling and Therapy:
A Practitioner's Guide to
Intentional Intervention*

Alex Haley's *Roots* is powerful and sobering. Haley recounts the life of his ancestor Kunta Kinte, a young Mandinka warrior stolen from his native Gambia in West Africa. *Roots* depicts the African's life on a plantation, marriage to a slave girl, and generations of his offspring. *Roots* is also a reminder that African-American families cannot be fully appreciated apart from the legacy of slavery.

What lessons are to be learned from this history? First, African-American families have an incredible will to survive. Against the most degrading forms of inhumanity, survival has been their strength. Descriptions of these families as a "tangle and web of pathology" disregard the social and historical context. Moreover, Negro spirituals and gospel music are clues that spirituality underlies much of their enduring strength.

Second, confronting racism is a fact of African-American family life. For instance, it is often a vital part of child-rearing practices. Racism involves any barriers that tend to block equal access and opportunity, limiting full participation in American society. The disproportionate poverty and hypertension in the African-American community are testimony to the insidious effects of racism.

Third, African-American families must accommodate two worlds— their own communities and the larger white society. Each has implicit and sometimes competing values, traditions, and norms. W. E. B. Dubois recognized this double consciousness as a particularly demanding psychological task.

Fourth, many African-American families function as extended families and kinship networks. Clearly, this is an outgrowth of family and community patterns in Africa. Family members with a variety of blood ties form a multigenerational unit for interaction and support. ◢◣

age. They have developed morals, lifestyles, values, and perspectives that continue to change. Boomers tend to be self-reliant, highly motivated, nontraditional, open to new ideas, mobile, and tolerant of diversity, including diversity in families, sexual preferences, and lifestyles. This is a generation with a microwave mentality that likes immediate gratification. They value honesty, enthusiasm, informality, and participation in almost everything they do.[11]

Boomers are followed by Generation X, sometimes known as baby busters: younger people who are overshadowed by the large numbers in the preceding generation, frequently confused and disillusioned about the future, and inclined to reject the boomer values as fickle, self-centered, and impractical.

In contrast are graybeards, the increasing number of older people, who live longer than people did a century ago. This upsurge in the elderly population—a movement that will increase when the boomers reach retirement age—has been called the most important trend of our time.[12] It is a trend that already has begun to change the nature of families. When the average life expectancy was between forty-five and fifty years, most adult years were spent working and raising children. Now, when many people live into their eighties and nineties, the majority of family relationships are between adults and no longer between parents and their young children. We have increasing numbers of transgenerational families that include four and sometimes five generations of relatives.

However, in our mobile society, family members often live great distances from each other, and continuity is difficult to maintain. A friend whose family has grown up in different parts of Eastern Europe shared some of his thoughts about family continuity. After his extended family had suffered through the devastating oppression of two world wars and the restraints of dictatorial Communist regimes, they settled together in a small German town near Frankfurt, where they live near each other and all go to the same church. As my friend has watched American families during his years in graduate school in the States, he and his wife see many contrasts between family life in North America and family life in Europe. My friend and his wife wonder

DO YOU LOVE ME?

GARY OLIVER, PH.D.
Clinical Director, Southwest
Counseling Associates
Author of *Real Men Have
Feelings Too*

When I was a boy, the cry "Come out, come out, wherever you are!" announced that the game was over and that those who were still hiding should come out. In Genesis 3:9, we read that when sin caused Adam and Eve to hide from God, he came looking for them and called out, "Where are you?"

For many years God has been in the churches and out in society, calling to men: "Where are you?"

When we respond to Christ's call, our first question is "What do you want me to do?" While that is an important question, it is far from what is most important.

When we "come out," the first thing Christ wants is an answer to the question he has been asking people for years. It's the question he asked Peter as he was fishing by the Sea of Galilee: "Do you love me?" (John 21:15-17).

Certainly Christ's call is for us to become loving husbands, wise fathers, and faithful friends. But ultimately the quality of our *horizontal* relationships is determined by the quality of our *vertical* relationship to Christ. An intimate, growing love relationship with Jesus is the greatest achievement, the most honored position, and the most valuable contribution we can make to our families.

Every day Christ asks us the same question he asked Peter. What one thing will you do today to show that your answer is a loud, resounding yes?

---

how they will fit into the larger family when they go back to Germany. "We have been through a lot of change," the young husband shared. "But despite the moves, separations, and different experiences, something holds our family together."

Often families are tied together by invisible strands that give them continuity even when the family members are far apart emotionally or geographically. My family experienced this on the day of my mother's funeral. Aunts, uncles, cousins, and more distant relatives appeared to give support and to affirm by their presence that we are all part of a family. Like almost everybody else, the people in our family have known sickness, personal problems, and conflict along with the good times. But despite the changes, a sense of continuity holds us together.

The Power of God in Families

From the beginning of recorded time, God has placed people in families. It was his idea that couples would marry, that we would all be born into families, and that we would all have family ties. The God who initiated the family surely is still interested in families, including yours and mine.

If you believe, as I do, that God is sovereign, ever present, and touched by our infirmities and struggles, you will agree that the mighty hand of God has an impact on our marriages and families. This family influence is more powerful and significant than any of the influences we have explored to this point.

Surprisingly, the Bible doesn't tell us much about how to get along in our homes. In contrast to all that is said in the New Testament about the church or about how we should live, only a few verses speak about the family. In his book *The Measure of a Family,* Gene Getz suggests that the New Testament writings about the church also apply to families. He argues that from God's perspective the family is really the church in miniature. "True, on occasions the New Testament writers zero in on special needs that are uniquely related to family living. But in the most part, what was written to believers as a whole applies directly to Christian living in the smaller context of the home."[13]

Churches and families can both be rigid, tense, and even abusive. But both can be, and often are, places of love, support, learning, hope, service, spiritual maturing, and personal growth. In the pages that follow, we will look at the church, with its weaknesses and strengths, and ponder how the body of Christ helps us understand and strengthen families. We will look, too, at these nine family influences and see how they have an impact on individual families.

Before we go any further, however, we must pause to consider an important question that isn't easy to answer. What is a family?

3

WHAT IS A FAMILY?

SEVERAL weeks before the 1992 election, the president of the United States and the prime minister of Canada were in the Rose Garden of the White House, trying to hold a press conference on matters of state. But the assembled reporters were more interested in Murphy Brown.

"Who is Murphy Brown?" the puzzled prime minister asked his host. Most American television watchers knew the answer. In the week before that White House press conference, millions had watched as Murphy, a fictional television character played by actress Candice Bergen, had given birth to a baby boy. Described by one reporter as a defiantly unmarried Madonna, Murphy made it clear that she intended to raise her child in "triumphant autonomy" as a single parent.

This might have gone unnoticed had it not been mentioned in a speech by Vice President Dan Quayle. Even his critics acknowledged that Quayle had given a serious, sensitive, "reasonably persuasive and sometimes eloquent" talk about hard work, law and order, personal responsibility, and the family. *Time* magazine noted that a number of non-Republicans and black leaders, "including Jesse Jackson, might have made the same points without controversy"; and they have.[1] A year or so after the election that sent Mr. Quayle into unwanted retirement, Bill Clinton resurrected the infamous address and said he "thought there were a lot of very good things in that speech." Would we or our society be better off if babies were born to married couples? "You bet we would," the new president said.

What had caused the original furor? Quayle had stated, "The failure of our families is hurting America deeply. . . . Children need love and discipline. They need mothers and fathers. A welfare check is not a husband. The state is not a father. . . . Bearing babies irresponsibly is, simply, wrong." Then the former vice president made the statement that sent the media into a frenzy and triggered weeks of talk-show chatter: "It doesn't help matters when prime-time television has Murphy Brown—a character who supposedly epitomizes today's intelligent, highly paid professional woman—mocking the importance of fathers by bearing a child alone and calling it just another 'lifestyle choice.'"

The debate over Murphy Brown faded as the election approached, but the issue was brought into more serious public debate when the highly respected *Atlantic* magazine took half an issue to summarize research on the state of the family. The corner of the cover showed a little boy looking at a broken toy house, but most dramatic were these words that were boldly printed on the cover: "DAN QUAYLE WAS RIGHT. After decades of public dispute about so-called family diversity, the evidence from social-science research is coming in: The dissolution of two-parent families, though it may benefit the adults involved, is harmful to many children and dramatically undermines our society."[2]

In all of the English language, perhaps there is no more confusing word than *family*. Many people, including those who work in government and the courts, use the word to define almost any group of people who live together or who in some other way are involved with one another. Two gay men who refer to themselves as a married couple, three older widows who share an apartment, an unmarried man and woman who live and sleep together, college roommates who share an apartment, a single mother who lives with three adopted children—all are considered families by at least some people in our society.

And the definition of family is getting broader. One article describes the family as "a married couple or other group of adult kinfolk who cooperate economically in the upbringing of children, and all or most of whom share a common dwelling."[3] Even

AUSTRALIANS HAVE FAMILY PROBLEMS TOO

JOHN WARLOW, M.D.
Christian Wholeness Counselling Centre
Greenslopes, Qld., Australia

Australia, "down under"! Australia is a country the size of the USA but has a population of only 19 million people. The Australian family is facing many of the same problems families in other countries face.

Types and Trends

The Australian nuclear family has changed exponentially over the last century. It is shrinking, aging, more varied, and declining.

- The family is *smaller,* now having two and a bit children (whatever the "bit" is).
- The family is *aging.* Couples are waiting longer to marry and then to have children. Teenagers are dependent on their parents for longer periods of time. Parents return the favor by living about twenty-five to thirty years longer than their great-grandparents lived a century ago. (Adolescence and retirement are recent inventions.)
- Australian families are becoming more *varied.* The "NUclear" family is becoming "UNclear." One-parent, blended, and de facto families are more prevalent. The increased number of migrant families adds to the variety.
- The family is *declining.* Now 20 percent of adults do not marry. The divorce rate has increased to over 33 percent. Marriages are lasting about 11 years on average, four years shorter than for the previous generation.

Turmoils

From start to finish the Australian family faces destructive issues. Abortion is on the rise. Australia has one of the world's worst male-adolescent suicide rates. Domestic violence and child abuse are increasing, feeding the rising problem of homeless youth. Euthanasia is openly debated.

Triumphs

The family still wins, hands down. The family is not all "down" or "under" in Australia! But with triumph comes challenge. The challenge is a turn to God. Spiritual renewal will revive moral foundations. This will enhance the basic cell of society, which remains the family.

broader is the definition of a Manhattan man who describes a family as "any group of people who opt to live together and who should be nurturing each other in one way or another." When a word is defined so broadly that it applies to everything or to everybody, the word no longer has any meaning. In time, it disappears from the language.[4]

Is the word *family* about to disappear? Probably not. Despite the dire predictions of those who foresee the family's demise, families are not about to fade.

Someone has suggested that becoming a father may take only a few minutes, and a mother must carry her baby for nine months, but raising kids right takes a lifelong commitment from both parents. Unlike any other institution, the family surrounds us from the cradle to the grave, shapes our minds and values, largely determines what we look like, remains an emotional presence wherever we go, and gives generous portions of joy and frustration.[5] We can ignore the debates and magazine articles about the state of the family, but we cannot ignore the importance of the family.

Three Types of Families
The books that counselors write, the words of media psychologists and talk-show hosts, the messages in many sermons and college classrooms, the speeches from politicians and professors, the stories we hear in our counseling sessions—all seem to give a similar message: The modern family is in a mess, and it is changing drastically. Writer William J. Doherty believes that these changes began at the start of the twentieth century and have been going on ever since.[6] During the past ten years, he suggests, we have seen three types of families. We might call these institutional families, individualist families, and diverse families.

Institutional Families
In the first two or three decades of the century, most American and Canadian families were glued to the idea of *responsibility*. When a couple married, they planned to stay together for life. Families were built around commitment, communities, and kin-

ship ties. The father was the authority and the major wage earner, while the mother usually stayed home with the kids. Family traditions, loyalty, solidarity, support, and partnerships were all important. Families experienced unfaithfulness, divorce, and probably a lot of hidden problems, of course, but they were committed to family responsibilities. Irresponsible behavior was harder to ignore in an era when most of the relatives lived in the same community and when people didn't travel as they do today. Everybody agreed that the institution of the family was needed for support and for economic survival.

Individualistic Families

In the 1920s, sociologists began to write about a shift away from traditional institutional families and noted that people were becoming more mobile, more focused on the nuclear family of a married couple and their children, and less tied to communities and to all the aunts, uncles, cousins, and other relatives. Unlike the institutional families with their commitment to responsibility, the newer individualistic families were built on a desire for personal satisfaction and the fulfillment of individual family members. There still were generational and gender differences: Everybody assumed that the younger generation would respect those who were older, and the male was given special privileges. Sometimes those males even became "organization men" who were married to their careers and without much concern for their families.

Of course, many people didn't fit this suburban picture. The poor, many city dwellers, numerous people in minority groups, and most of those in the working class, for example, were stuck in communities with limited opportunities for improvement. Even so, people still had hope in the great American dream of poor boys becoming famous, powerful, and successful.

Then came the turbulent 1960s, when families, like individuals, were uprooted by the social changes in Europe and America. Women began to achieve more independence. In the eyes of many young people, the sexual revolution made marriage less necessary for sexual fulfillment. People began leaving their unhappy marriages and what feminist Betty Friedan called the "uncomfortable concentration camp" of traditional family life. Commitment and responsibility were replaced with concerns about individual rights expressed in the slogan "If it feels good, do it!" A generation of adolescents and young adults started to see themselves as deserving more from and owing less to their families or to society.

This emphasis on self-fulfillment and individualism has moved to the core of American culture and much of Western culture. We applaud individual accomplishments and build careers around individual attainments. We flock to therapists who help us cope with individual hang-ups, and we attend seminars or read self-help books to find meaning, internal peace, and personal fulfillment. When people consider religion, they often look to see "if there's anything in it *for me*," and churches across the land cater to this search for significance and satisfaction of needs.

Does all of this mean that families are being sacrificed in our personal pursuits of self-satisfaction? The answer depends on the family. Many people still value family commitment and have a healthy fear about what will happen if these meaningful commitments don't last.[7] We have all seen families breaking up, and we have noticed a change in the way many people look at families. The age of diverse families has arrived.

Diverse Families

Despite the fact that some people who talk about tolerance are relatively intolerant, our culture has embraced diversity as an important value. As a result, many people—including individuals, legislative bodies, courts, employers, some insurance managers, and religious leaders—are willing to accept a variety of "family" arrangements, including dual-career families, never-married families, single-parent families, postdivorce families, stepfamilies, and even families headed by gay or lesbian couples.

Most of us still claim to believe in the old values of responsibility and commitment, and most would accept the idea that family life should be satisfying and fulfilling. Surveys indicate that a lot of us still believe that the stable, two-parent family is the best environment for raising children.[8] But the chief value in this era of diverse families is *flexibility*. By accepting the idea that individuals and families are likely to change over the course of life, many people are concluding that there should be freedom to change family styles. This fits "American social life of the late 20th century, where the pace of life requires quick adjustments and where respect for diversity is a paramount civic virtue."[9] According to this modern thinking, if one type of family isn't fulfilling, then we should feel free to get out and try another.

This tolerance for different family styles can leave us all feeling insecure. Families can't be very stable when more and more family members feel free to change their living arrangements over the course of life. The diversity and flexibility mind-set also leads to confusion whenever people talk about family values or about the state of the family. It's tough to build secure marriages and stable families when values change and people disagree about what is and is not appropriate family behavior.

But before we give up in frustration, we should recognize a positive side to this tolerance for diversity. As an example, consider the story of Gus.

Gus

Sue Rutz is middle-aged, white, hardworking, Christian, and never married.[10] She is also the mother of three adopted kids. Public speaking makes her nervous, but when she was asked to tell her fellow church members about Gus, she agreed.

Sue didn't say much about her background that morning, but she told us that Gus's biological mother was a seventeen-year-old high school dropout whose family was so abusive and dysfunctional that the young girl was the only stability holding them together. When she got pregnant, the teenaged mother decided to carry the baby to term and to arrange for an adoption. She was able to find a doctor who knew a family that wanted a child, so the needed arrangements were made.

But the deal fell through when the girl mentioned that the baby's father was an African American. The adoptive family backed out, and so did the doctor. He told his pregnant patient that if she did not find another family within twenty-four hours, she would have to have an abortion. In desperation she turned to the lawyer who had made the arrangements. He called Sue.

Did she want another child? Was she willing to have a biracial baby? When Sue answered yes to both questions, the lawyer expressed his concern that the birth mother might not want her child to go into a single-parent family. After the birth mother mulled over the options and remembered her own negative experiences with men, she thought that her baby would have a good chance in a home headed by a single mom.

As Sue shared some of this with her church congregation, she was interrupted by her adopted son, who was five at the time. We all waited while he whispered into her ear. Then a smile came over her face. "Gus wants me to tell you something," she said. "He wants you to know that he was not aborted before he was born!"

The little boy had arrived nine weeks premature. For three days the young mother kept him at her side or in her arms. According to the amazed nurses who watched, she tenderly talked to the child over and over again. She told him that she loved him but that she couldn't raise him herself because she wasn't able to give him a stable home. She told him about his new mom and explained why it was better for him to be adopted.

When the doctor arrived to take Gus for circumcision, the birth mother refused for a reason that surfaced several weeks later. In the midst of her immaturity and insecurity, she was afraid that the doctor who had wanted Gus to be aborted might now try to castrate him. So the young girl called the lawyer and then took her tiny son from the hospital. Several hours later, in a conversation area of a suburban mall, in front of Marshall Field's department store, the birth mother handed Gus to his new mother.

For the next four months Sue and the birth mother kept in contact. Then the birth mother decided that she wanted Gus to have a life of his own and that she would not contact Sue until Gus reached his eighteenth birthday. Sue hasn't heard from her since.

"That young woman has a lot of guts," Sue said admiringly. But Sue Rutz also has a lot of guts and so do her parents, who came from families that tended to be racially biased. Gus has become a part of the family, and his grandfather has become a stable and admired male role model.

This relationship began almost immediately after Gus was born. His grandfather held Gus in his arms day after day, reading aloud to him. Since the older man didn't have any children's books, he read from *National Geographic* and from the stock market reports in the business section of the *Chicago Tribune*.

Someday, perhaps, Gus will become a businessman and read about the stock market himself. After all, as Sue delights in telling her active young son, his mother got him in the mall at Marshall Field's.

What Is a Traditional Family?

When *Life* magazine published a special collector's edition on the American family, the editors described an image of families in the "good old days" before babies like Gus were rescued from abortions and before babies were born addicted to cocaine. This earlier type of family seems like a dream today. In the dream the mother doesn't freak out; she doesn't *go* out. She carries a plate of homemade cookies and some nice homilies for consumption. Dad knows best; he's so straight, so tame, so tall, so knowing. In the dream, the kids are only slightly more mischievous than the dog. The dinner table groans. The moon and stars twinkle overhead in the sweet-smelling night.[11]

The only problem with this warm picture of family life is that it probably never existed, at least for most people. The *Life* reporter concluded that there was no such thing as a normal family in the past, and there aren't any now. People who care deeply about families and are committed to strengthening family life sometimes urge us to return to the days of traditional families. As we read depressing statistics and encounter more and more reports about family decline, we look backward to the way we think families must have been in the past. Many among us long for a return of traditional family values and wish that we could reestablish traditional families in our homes and communities.

But what is a traditional family? It may be that some of us are caught in what has been called a nostalgia trap, wishing for the return of a type of family living that nobody ever had.[12] Even traditionalists probably would applaud Sue Rutz for raising Gus and her other adopted children in a nontraditional but stable home environment where the children live with Christian values that they might never have encountered otherwise.

To understand families, family problems, and ways to strengthen our own families, we need to look more closely at traditional families. We also need to be familiar with a few other terms that often pop up in books and articles. These words aren't always defined in the same ways, and like most family terms, their meaning may differ from culture to culture.

The nuclear family typically refers to a mother and her children and almost always includes the father. Usually the nuclear family is a group of people who are related by blood, kinship, and legal ties (like marriage or legal adoption) and who live or at one time lived in the same residence. The definition can be extended to include single-parent homes and homes in which grandparents live with and raise their grandchildren.

The *extended family* includes all the descendants (and their spouses) of a common great-grandparent. This means that your extended family includes aunts, uncles, cousins, and other relatives that you might not even know.

College textbooks sometimes talk about the *family of origin* (sometimes called the family of orientation), which is another term for the immediate family (parents along with brothers and sisters) into which you were born. The *family of procreation* is the family that you start. It includes your spouse and children and later includes your grandchildren, if you have any. None of these terms triggers so much debate, however, as the term *traditional family.*

Traditional families, as we have seen, are mentioned often by people who decry the decline of the family and sincerely want something better. The following definition, written by a sociology professor, is a little stuffy, but if you read it slowly, you will discover a good definition of what most people mean by a traditional family: "A family situated apart from both the larger kin group and the workplace; focused on the procreation of children; and consisting of legal, lifelong, sexually exclusive, heterosexual, monogamous marriage, based on affection and companionship in which there is a sharp division of labor, with the female as full-time housewife and the male as primary provider and ultimate authority."[13]

When families are undergoing so much change, they are tempted to wish they could return to the relative stability of the traditional family, when most people shared similar values and when people's roles in the family were clearly understood. Some Christian writers even suggest that the traditional family is the type of family that God intended, and they urge us to return to this fading way of relating.

But historians are unanimous in showing that the so-called traditional family existed for only a very short period of time, mostly in the late nineteenth and early twentieth century. Most families in the Bible or in history could not be described as traditional, and the word never applied to the majority of African American families, to recent immigrants, or to families in many parts of the world. The much-lauded traditional family was American, middle-class, white—a short-lived part of our history.

Before the industrial age, families were more like business ventures: Husbands and wives worked together on farms or in other enterprises, with children helping and learning the family trade. Parenting was done together, and the father rarely went off to work in the morning, leaving the mother at home to care for the kids. In times of war, when the men were gone, the women assumed extra responsibilities, but in normal times the couple worked together and stayed committed to each other and to the family, even if they weren't always happy.

This began to change with the coming of the industrial age. Men no longer worked at home. They went off every day to factories or to offices, and the women stayed home as homemakers and caretakers of the children.[14] Many wives found great fulfillment in these roles, even as they do today, but others were frustrated and welcomed the opportunity to work apart from the home, especially when World War II called for extra effort from everyone. Almost overnight, women's roles began to be liberalized. As the economy changed following the postwar economic and baby boom, many couples found that employment for both parents had nothing to do with vocational fulfillment; the husband and wife both needed to work if their families were to survive economically. Unlike the past, when both parents worked alongside each other within the family and inside the home, both parents began to work outside the home, most often at different jobs. Frequently the children were left with other people, and often the children had less parental guidance and more opportunity to get into trouble.

Today, most of us would like to see a return to more stability in the home and greater commitment to our families, but we recognize that the traditional families that we watch in old television shows or hear proclaimed in sermons are not likely to return. We also realize that those idealized traditional families that seemed to be glamorous and ever stable may have had more problems, frustrations, and weaknesses than we realize.

What Is a Biblical Family?

Before going further, however, we need a clear description of what we mean by families, a description that will last through the change that individuals and families are experiencing from all sides. The Bible is the best place to look for that description. As we have mentioned, families are not discussed much in the Scriptures. Even so, the biblical writers gave several guidelines that can help us define what we mean by a family.

The scriptural family involved a man and woman who were married to one another, committed to each other, and sexually faithful. Sometimes the couple was childless, but most often the husband and wife had young or grown children. Siblings and extended family members were assumed to be a part of the larger family (Gen. 46:27; Acts 7:14).

While the Bible says little about families with adopted children—Moses is an exception—it shows that believers are adopted by God as full members of his family (Rom. 8:14-17; 2 Cor. 6:18; Gal. 3:26; 4:4-7). Just as adoption makes us fully a part of God's family, it could be argued that legal adoption makes the adopted person fully a part of the adoptive family (Eph.1:5).

Unrelated people who live together may be as close as family members, but technically they are not family. In biblical times, slaves and servants were not family members, even if they lived in close proximity (John 8:35).

Husbands, wives, and children had specific family roles, and although the major responsibility rested with the male, husbands and wives were to be mutually submissive, and family members were all to be respected as equally valuable people (Eph. 5:21-24; Col. 3:18-21).[15]

Scripture gives no comment about working fathers or stay-at-home mothers, no definition of a traditional family, and no seeming interest in whether a nontraditional living arrangement like the one Naomi had with her two daughters-in-law is really a family. Sometimes the Bible uses the word *family* in ways that go far beyond the traditional family that is often discussed today. Believers, for example, are all members of the family of God, even though we are not related by kinship or blood ties (Gal. 6:10). We are part of God's family because we are adopted as sons and daughters (Eph. 1:5).

After looking at the various shapes and textures of the family, we can affirm that although many people worry about the family, it is still a great idea.[16] The family is a great idea because it was God's idea. Despite the changes that put all of us under pressure, many families grow together, even in the midst of the greatest adversity. The Jochims are an example.

J I L L

I first met Paul and Janell Jochim after a morning church service when they were serving coffee to church members. They were friendly, gracious people who gave no hint that the clearly handicapped girl on the chair nearby was their older daughter—a young woman whose never-ending needs have changed their family forever.

The Jochims were excited when their first child, Jill, was born two years after they had married. Jill was a model child, who had a pleasant disposition. When the Jochims noticed that Jill's development lagged, their doctors told them not to worry. They assured them she would catch up soon.

Janell and Paul saw the beginnings of some unusual behavior in Jill while they awaited the birth of their second daughter, but after baby Jami came home, Jill changed dramatically. Her twelve-word vocabulary had begun to shrink, and the model child began to throw terribly violent tantrums. One day she banged her head on the stone hearth of the fireplace but seemed to feel no pain. She moved incessantly, hitting, kicking, shaking the baby, and biting herself. Paul would go off to work every day knowing that his wife would be caring for a new baby and trying to protect herself and the baby from an increasingly disruptive two-year-old. But Jill's behavior went beyond the normal terrible twos; this was clearly not normal.

When Jami was three months old, the family took a vacation to visit relatives in Arizona. The trip was a disaster. Jill threw her food around the room, pitched gelatin all over the walls, and seemed to delight in throwing glasses filled with milk across the room. Spanking did no good. It soon became clear that Jill needed help.

When they returned home, the parents took their daughter to the first of many doctors, psychologists, and child-care experts. One doctor described Jill's condition as "minimal brain dysfunction," but nobody told her parents what that meant. Paul felt like a special target when people told him that Jill's problems were the result of jealousy over her new sister and frustration because she wasn't getting enough attention from her father. Paul's workload as a senior merchandising manager for JCPenney and his volunteer activities with the local Jaycees and Red Cross were blamed for Jill's self-abuse. The professionals told Paul that if he would spend more time with Jill, she would get better. Guilt was piled on guilt, and Jill's dad concluded that he was a bad father, whose neglect of his elder daughter was causing all the family problems. Some people even hinted that Paul and Janell were causing Jill's bruises and were only denying their violent behavior.

Life in those early days was very difficult. Paul and Janell were embarrassed to take Jill to church. They couldn't leave her with the other kids, and they suspected that other parents blamed them for their inability to control their two-year-old.

Since Jill seemed to be awake and moving about the house all night, the family physician prescribed a mild sedative, but this made Jill more active. She would sleep during the day but stay up all night laughing, giggling, and moving all over the house. The parents noticed that when she bit herself, banged her head, or fell, she never cried and never gave an indication that she felt much of anything.

In July 1979, almost three years after Jill was born, the family took her to a psychiatric clinic for a weeklong intensive evaluation. The week away turned into nine weeks, and the parents were allowed only one brief visit every week. Whenever they arrived, they were taken through two sets of locked doors and escorted to a small room where they could see Jill, but only under the watchful eye of a clinic escort.

Finally the doctors told Paul and Janell that they had completed the evaluation and that they could take Jill home. They announced their diagnosis: *mental retardation with autism.*

How does a young Christian family handle news like this? Janell and Paul cried all the way back home and kept asking how their beautiful daughter could "have that." Many friends and Jill's grandparents had been praying and waiting to hear the outcome of the evaluation, but when Paul and Janell reached for the phone to make their calls, they both sobbed uncontrollably. Paul remembers it as one of the worst days of his life. There was nobody who could understand, nobody who could offer support or give meaningful encouragement, no Christian who could answer why a loving God would allow this kind of tragedy to disrupt a family, maybe for the rest of their lives. "We didn't want to believe it," one of the parents said, "but we didn't know what else to believe."

Christians like the Jochims normally would find support in the church, but going to church was becoming increasingly difficult, almost not worth the effort. It took such a long time to get Jill ready, and when the family arrived, people would stare or show in not-so-subtle ways that they were uncomfortable in the presence of this strange child. Jill was too disruptive and too dangerous to be taken into the service, so the parents took turns sitting with her in an old broom closet while the other parent went to worship. In the place where they most expected to get support, they didn't find it.

One time the Jochims took Jill to the Mayo Clinic for an evaluation and were told that there was no hope for improvement. When the doctors recommended that Jill be put in an institution, both parents rejected the idea and took their daughter home. For a while they tried a special diet that was supposed to help autistic children, but Jill didn't get better, and her family only got busier trying to prepare special meals. For years the parents kept believing that something could be done. "We were willing to try anything or go anyplace," Janell said. "But as time went on, we began to accept that this is what life will be like, and we began to adjust."

By the time Jill reached age seven, she seemed to be settling down. She was less rambunctious and more lethargic. She was having increasing trouble walking and was having frequent seizures. Hoping to gain insight from other parents who had autistic children, Paul and Janell got involved in the Autism Society, where eventually Paul served on the board of directors. When their family picture appeared in the organization's newsletter, their family life took another turn.

Two women who saw the photograph wrote to the Jochims with startling news. Both women commented on how Jill held her hands: She clenched her hands together and cupped her fingers. They suggested that this gesture might indicate that Jill was suffering from Rett syndrome rather than autism. As Janell read the letters, she became so upset that she couldn't finish reading what the strangers had written.

Trying to keep an open mind, the Jochims learned as much as they could about Rett syndrome. They learned that in 1965, over a decade before Jill was born, an unknown Austrian physician named Andreas Rett noticed behavior like Jill's among his patients and wrote an article that appeared in a small-circulation German-language medical journal. Nobody paid much attention until 1983, when an article was published in a widely read English-language neurology journal. Several European physicians had reviewed thirty-five cases of girls like Jill, and Rett syndrome became known to the American medical community.

Jill's behavior didn't change any with this news, but the family had to adjust all over again. They were able to confirm that their daughter did indeed have Rett syndrome. They got involved with the Rett Syndrome Association, and in time Paul was invited to serve on the international board of directors. Knowing the tremendous impact Rett syndrome has on the family, the Jochims formed a parents' support group in the northern Illinois community where they had moved.[17]

Strangers began to call, and the Jochims found themselves encouraging other parents and serving as advocates for children's rights in local school districts. Schools with limited budgets don't want to spend money trying to educate children who will never learn very much when they could be spending the money on students whose futures are bright. Like parents of handicapped children everywhere, Paul and Janell Jochim understand the financial problems that their child puts on the school, but they only want their daughter to learn basic living skills. And they know about high costs—Jill's seizure medication costs almost one hundred dollars every month.

How does a Christian family cope with these intense stresses? As I listened to the Jochims tell their story, I was struck with their patience, perseverance, compassion, and willingness to submit their personal needs to the greater needs of their family. I suspect there are thousands of families like them, people who rarely complain but whose schedules, dreams, vacation plans, finances, and whole lives are controlled in part by a family member who needs perpetual care and who may never be able to express appreciation or say thanks. This, of course, puts strain on families, but Paul Jochim's attitude is probably typical: "Caring for Jill is like caring for a one-year-old baby who never grows older, so you have to decide whether you will get bitter or better."

Jill's parents decided that they would get better. They have become active in helping other parents of handicapped kids, especially parents of the estimated 1,600 girls who have Rett syndrome. It isn't easy living with someone who has a condition that has no known cause, no treatment except seizure control, and no immediate hope for a cure. As Christians, the Jochims believe that God must have some purpose for their difficulties, and they believe Romans 8:28. But in their case, they wonder if they will ever know in this life the good that God is working out for "those who love him, who have been called according to his purpose."

Now that they are living far from their relatives in Nebraska, the Jochims have no extended family to give them help. Paul, Janell, and Jami have pulled together and are stronger as a family because of Jill. They all have more patience, and they have learned to give to others in need.

"You don't win every day," Paul said, "but you don't give up.

You don't give up on your daughter, and you don't give up on yourself." Almost everything is a hassle, but when things are difficult, these parents keep going. They often need help from other people. They fight against the temptation to become bitter. As we talked in their home, I didn't sense any bitterness. As this family continues to deal with tremors that threaten to send their family into collapse, they have chosen to love their children and remain faithful to their responsibility to care for them, no matter what it takes. They have accepted the challenge and the changes, and they are learning to live with them. With God's help and the support of their friends, they make the best of a difficult family situation.

Jill's sister, Jami, has learned to cope as well. Paul and Janell were reminded of this when they read a story Jami had written in her fourth-grade class.

> One morning, I lay in bed. My family except Jill, my sister, were still sleeping in bed. I heard a knock outside my window. I got up out of bed and went to my window. And what did I see? A fairy godmother floating in midair. I nearly fell out of my skin!
>
> She said, "This is your lucky day. I grant you *one* wish."
>
> "You do? I wish my sister Jill would be able to talk again."
>
> And with that she said, "Bring me Jill." I did, but it was pretty hard to get her up. She was listening to her *Maranatha* tape, and she was yelling. I finally got her to my room, closed the door shut, and walked over to the fairy godmother. She waved her hand and sprinkled dust on Jill.
>
> Suddenly Jill could talk! I couldn't believe it.
>
> I told my mom, called my dad at work, and told all my friends and neighbors. When I lay in bed at night, I thought about how lucky I am to have a sister.

Now that Jami is a teenager, she continues to show compassion and care for her older sister. "I see some advantages to having a handicapped sister," Jami said when we talked together. "We don't fight because Jill can't talk. We get to park in handicapped parking because Jill can't walk very well. When we went to Disney World, we got in front of all the lines and got to go on the rides more than once."

But Jill's condition also requires Jami's patience. At Walt Disney World, for example, Jill could handle only the little kids' rides, and those weren't very exciting for her teenage sister. If the family wants to play a board game, like Monopoly, Jill doesn't throw the dice properly, and she may suddenly flip over the board. At times Jami "gets stuck baby-sitting" because only a few people are willing to care for a handicapped teenager. Sometimes Jami has felt frustrated because she gets disciplined and sent to her room, but that never happens to Jill, who wouldn't understand. When the family goes out, people often stare, although Jami has learned how to handle that: "I just stare right back."

Jami sees her sister as one of God's gifts that has taught the family to be patient and sensitive to other people. Jami, for example, volunteers to help as the gym teacher for a handicapped boy at school. Her friends aren't turned away because of Jill. They love her and talk to her, which surely helps Jami in the teenage days, when peer acceptance is important. "We could be worse off," the young high school student said cheerfully. "Jill's condition is hard for my parents. It puts them under stress, costs a lot, and takes a lot of time every day to dress Jill, feed her, and care for her most basic needs."

In talking to a newspaper reporter who wrote about their family, Paul Jochim summed up the family's feelings about Jill. "She'll never be a cheerleader; she'll never go to the prom or to a football game. But maybe, in a way, Jill has touched more lives by never saying a word than I ever will in my lifetime."

Some people would call the Jochims a family of survivors, people who have learned to rise above a difficult situation and turn their tragedy into triumph. They aren't well known. They don't want to be seen as heroes or super-Christians. But their day-after-day persistence, courage, and determination are examples of how families can and do rise above adversity and sometimes even surprise themselves. Despite the demanding needs of their daughter, the Jochims realize that they can't let Jill's problems dominate their lives, destroy their marriage, sink their careers, or squelch Jami's growth as a normal young woman. So the family members stay involved in their community and are active in their church. Jill's needs do dominate their lives, but the Jochims continue to live and serve faithfully and fully. Every day they rise above the affliction that rocked their family. They are examples of a family that can survive and grow beyond a family shock.

4

FAMILIES ON
THE FAULT LINE

WHILE browsing in a Canadian bookstore, I recently came across a two-inch-thick volume with an imposing title. One reviewer described *The War against the Family* as "an impassioned, eloquent and important book about the health of our society's very foundation—the family."[1] So I bought a copy and lugged it home. Backing his arguments with numerous statistics, taken from Canadian sources, the author described how government, economics, education, the radical feminist and homosexual movements, and even "the liberalism of the mainstream churches" have taken positions and developed policies that weaken the family. Illustrated with lots of charts and diagrams, the book shows how "the law has bent to the purposes of antifamily ideologies—to the detriment of freedom, the family, free enterprise, democracy, and the law itself."[2]

American writers have preached similar messages. *What Ever Happened to the American Dream?* Larry Burkett asked in a book with chapters titled "Blueprint for Disaster" and "Preparing for the Worst." William Bennett, described by the *Wall Street Journal* as "Washington's most interesting public figure," has written about *The De-Valuing of America* and argues that we are in a fight for our culture and our children. More depressing is a book titled *The Family under Siege,* written to document "what the new social engineers have in mind for you and your children." Even as I was writing the above words, the UPS delivery man came to my door with yet another hot-off-the-press book about how the media, personalized morality, "the idolized self," and mindless education are combining to destroy American families.[3]

It is difficult to read these books and stay optimistic. Their messages leave me feeling depressed, hopeless, paranoid, and tempted to put aside the books along with dozens of other forecasts of despair that have appeared in recent years. Many of us would agree with Michael Novak that the best defense against this onslaught is "the economically and politically independent family, protecting the space within which free and independent individuals may receive the necessary years of nurture."[4] But the prophets of doom, including many who are respected Christian leaders, argue that even the independent family is in danger of being swept aside. Most of these alarm-sounding writers present persuasive and carefully compiled statistics to support their pessimistic predictions. It isn't easy to ignore their views.

We live in scary times. We see family problems all around us, and we sometimes fear for our own marriages and children. We see families in which drugs, sex, and other things pull family members away from their faith. We know that even good marriages break up and that kids from Christian homes get pregnant or get into trouble with the law.

In many ways we live like families perched on a fault line in earthquake country. Sometimes we feel tremors, but we cling to the hope that our marriages will stay intact and that our kids will grow up relatively unscathed—as most do! We are grateful when our families avoid major shake-ups or manage to pull through the tremors that crumble so many homes. At the same time, we are nervous lest our marriages weaken or our children make foolish decisions that could change the course of their lives forever. Many of us live with the anxiety that the next rumble of family tension or seismic wave of discouragement could crack the foundation of our family life and cause our home to collapse without warning.

Pessimists, Optimists, and Realists

Many books and articles that roll off the presses increase our anxiety because they tell us about only the tremors. Books with titles or subtitles like *The Futility of Family Policy, Family Change and Decline in Modern Societies,* or *Unholy Matrimony: The Case for Abolishing Marriage* see the family as a flimsy structure that will topple with the next rumble of change or pressure.

Other writers see more hope for the stability of the family. Books like *Here to Stay: American Families in the Twentieth Century* and H. Norman Wright's *Family Is Still a Great Idea* suggest that the family structure is sound and able to withstand seismic movement. Other self-help books offer hope and advice for building better families.[5] Surveys by Christian researcher George Barna have led him to conclude that despite the changes in our society, most of us "continue to maintain the belief that when all else fails, the family will be there to pull us through."[6] (See list on next page.)

Regardless of our different perspectives, almost everybody agrees on at least three issues.[7] First, we agree that American families have changed drastically in the past two or three decades. More couples postpone marriage and then have fewer children. More mothers now work outside the home (over 65 percent of women with children aged three to five years are employed). The divorce rate may have slowed a little, but it still is too high. The number of single parents has increased, and we have seen a steady increase in the number of families without fathers, children without families, and families without homes.[8]

Second, it is widely agreed that the economy with all its shake-ups and instability has had a great impact on families. At a company luncheon on Secretary's Day, an insensitive and ill-informed employer recently suggested in passing that most married women work so they can have extra cash as spending money.

That's not true. Most often, when a husband and wife both work outside the home, they need two incomes to make ends meet. According to a California legislative report, if both spouses were not working, 35 percent more two-parent families would live below the poverty line than are there today.[9] Despite an increase in two-paycheck families, total family income (adjusted for inflation) has dropped 8.3 percent since 1973, and some expenses have gone up dramatically. In 1949, for example, medium-income workers spent 14 percent of their gross monthly incomes on mortgage payments. Thirty-five years later people at the same income level spend 44 percent on their mortgages. The proportion of children living in families with incomes below $10,000 has risen from one in ten in 1973 to one in six today.[10]

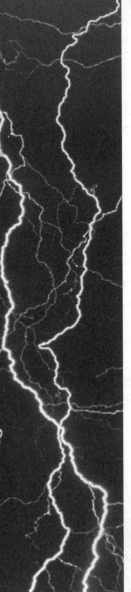

BARNA'S FINDINGS ABOUT THE FAMILY

1. Marriage is not dead. Nine out of ten Americans are married at some point in their lives.
2. Cohabitation (living together as husband and wife without getting married) is widely accepted. But when people get married, those who lived together before marriage have a substantially higher likelihood of getting divorced than do people who lived separately.
3. Most parents do not think that they have the greatest impact on their children. And they don't think television has the greatest impact either. Instead, they think the greatest influences come from their children's friends.
4. It is widely believed that about 10 percent of all adults are practicing homosexuals. The truth is that homosexuals represent only about one percent of the population, despite the fact that they are powerful, vocal, and influential in their impact on politicians, the media, and others.
5. Before they reach the age of eighteen, two out of three children born this year will live in a single-parent household.
6. Single-parent households are becoming more common in America. Most of these families live in or on the verge of poverty.
7. More than half of all mothers with children under six years of age are currently in the workforce.
8. Contrary to popular belief, most homemakers are even more satisfied with the quality of their lives than are women who have children and work outside the home.
9. Increasing numbers of adults in their twenties and thirties are choosing to return home to live with their parents.
10. When a woman has her first child, the chances are about fifty-fifty that she will not be married to the child's father.
11. Family values and lifestyles differ significantly between whites, blacks, and Hispanics.

Adapted from George Barna, *The Future of the American Family* (Chicago: Moody, 1993), 22–23.

JOB LOSS AND THE FAMILY

LESLIE PARROTT, ED.D.
Center for Relationship Development
Seattle Pacific University
Coauthor of *The Career Counselor*

The only certainty about losing a job is that it hurts; it is painful for the whole family. In fact, researchers have discovered surprising similarities in the nature and severity of struggles suffered by families of the terminally ill and families of a terminated employee. Each has financial difficulties, poor self-esteem, and negative emotions leading to depression. Both groups of families suffer similar crises.

The word *crisis* literally means "decisive moment." The word *career* in Latin is literally translated as "progress along a difficult road." A career crisis may thus be thought of as a *decisive moment along the difficult road toward progress.* And for families who have suffered unexpected job loss, the decisive moment can be just as devastating as being diagnosed with cancer.

Families who have been jolted by job loss need to avail themselves of old-fashioned support. When Job's friends heard about his troubles, they set out to comfort him. Scripture says, "They sat on the ground with him for seven days and seven nights. No one said a word to him, because they saw how great his suffering was" (Job 2:13). The family that has suffered a job loss feels a void. Suddenly missing, along with a job, are important pieces of the family's identity, cherished perceptions of who they are, a sense of purpose and meaning, and a large piece of their social support network. These losses must be mourned, and the family can find great reassurance in supportive community.

It is ironic, but those who suffer a job loss can have new hope. The apostle Paul often talked about the opportunity for hope in the face of tough times. When I counsel a person who has lost his or her job, I often think about what Paul said to the Thessalonians: "We continually remember before our God and Father your *work* produced by faith, your *labor* prompted by love, and your *endurance* inspired by *hope* in our Lord Jesus Christ" (1 Thess. 1:3, emphasis added). His words remind me that every family who suffers a job loss can be inspired by hope to endure. ✤

Fortune magazine concluded that economic change accounts for only "a modest fraction of earth-shattering family change."[11] But even affluent *Fortune* readers would agree that a lot of families are devastated by high rates of unemployment, sky-rocketing health-care costs, and the needs of older relatives who live longer than their ancestors and who often depend on their financially strapped adult children. A nationwide study by a private Washington, D.C., research organization concluded that American families are so preoccupied with earning enough money to keep themselves from falling behind financially that they are distracted from their abilities to raise children. The families with most financial troubles are the families least likely to attend PTA meetings, back-to-school nights, class plays, and high school football games.[12]

The third area of agreement concerns changes in the nation's demographics—statistics about the makeup of the population. As our nation approaches the twenty-first century, one third of its population will be nonwhite. The highest concentration of minority families will be Hispanics (their numbers are expected to increase by 187 percent between 1980 and 2030), followed by African Americans, Asian Americans, and Native Americans. We are becoming a multiracial, multicultural, and multilingual society. As a nation, we are changing color.

We are also changing age. Today there are 20 people over age sixty-five for every 100 adults under age sixty-five. By 2030, it has been estimated that there will be 40 people over age sixty-five for every 100 adults who are younger. And as this percentage of elderly people increases, the percentage of younger people will go down. If we don't have major wars, natural disasters, or disease, thirty-five years from now there will be more people over age sixty-five than people under eighteen. Consider what that will do to families. Who will pay for the health needs of all these older people, and how will kids respond when they have grandparents, great-grandparents, and living ancestors who are even older?

Statistics like these can be interesting and sometimes disturbing, but I'm never sure what to do with the numbers that appear in professional journals and on the pages of *USA Today.* Statistical reports of stress in the population and articles about the world in 2030 don't seem to have much relevance to my family today, or to yours. Perhaps when we know something about these family trends, we are more aware of the dangers and more motivated to keep our own homes from falling apart. More often, however, I suspect the statistics only increase our anxieties about what might put our families under stress.

What Puts a Family under Stress?

Stress is a part of life. Without the pressure, uncertainties, tension tremors, and occasional shocks that invade our families, life would be simpler and a lot less challenging. But life isn't like that, especially in these days when statistics show that all of us are shaken at times by change and unexpected jolts.

These family jolts and stresses are of three kinds: stresses that come from our society, personal stresses that invade our individual families, and stresses from our minds.

Stresses from Society

Everybody knows that families are influenced by what happens in societies. Think about it.

When a society encourages divorce and makes it easy for couples to separate, every member of the broken family is affected, especially the children.

When television dominates a society and a home, academic achievement in children tends to be lower, sensitivity to violence is dulled, and sexual immorality is taken for granted. High involvement with television and greater family stress go together—although we aren't sure which comes first.[13]

When economies are bad and people can't get jobs, whole families suffer. More frequent arguments, depression, anxiety, psychophysical distress, and less cohesion in the family all can result.[14]

When work, career building, and the materialism of a consumer-based economy all become highly valued in a culture, parents get involved in pursuing the American dream, and families too often get pushed aside.[15]

When teenage pregnancies are taken for granted, young families suffer. Teen pregnancies are common throughout the society, but pregnancy rates are especially high among poor and poorly educated mothers, many of whom are African American and subject to continual poverty and joblessness. About 40 percent of teenage pregnancies end in abortion, and of the teen mothers who give birth, most are unmarried. Ninety-three percent of these young mothers try to raise their children alone. Their kids grow up in families where there is little hope for improvement and where self-esteem is at rock bottom. These kids lack the love and influence of a father, are at greater risk of health problems, tend to do poorly in school, and have a higher-than-average likelihood of getting into trouble. Sadly, many of these young people repeat the cycle and become teenage parents themselves.[16]

What happens when a society seems powerless to stop this cycle, applauds the actions of people like Murphy Brown, and dismisses the value of fatherhood? According to a recent report, more than one quarter of U.S. children have little or no contact with their dads, and the social and emotional consequences can be devastating. For these kids, fatherlessness is not the problem; there are lots of fathers. The problem is a lack of father love and modeling in a society where—at least until recently—fathering has been viewed as relatively unimportant. As a result, thousands of kids grow up with what Robert McGee calls "father hunger."[17]

While several decades ago most people may have agreed about what was right or wrong and may have shared similar views on the family, that's less true today. How we view social influences and changes in the society depends a lot on our perceptions, beliefs, and backgrounds. When President Clinton came to the White House and quickly proposed a change on the issue of gays in the military, the nation sent up howls of protest—and approval. Mention the words *gay rights, abortion, right to choose, right to life, working mothers, home schooling, sex education, values clarification, prayer in school,* or *gun control*—all social issues that can impact families—and you immediately arouse sharply contrasting opinions.

Sometimes we feel helpless and overwhelmed by the social forces we are unable to influence or stop. The manager of a local bank recently wrote about this in a letter to his customers:

We tend to forget that the government we have today is vastly different from the government we had fifty, thirty, or even twenty years ago. The government now is larger, more bureaucratic, further removed from direct accountability, more entrenched in entitlements, less able to respond to the true needs of its citizens, and deeper in debt than at any other time in this country's history. And it's getting more so every day.

In his Gettysburg Address, President Lincoln spoke of the democratic ideals as a government of the people, by the people, for the people. Ours is still a government of the people—the ultimate power still comes from ordinary citizens in the form of elections. Ours is still, to a fair extent, a government for the people, though the power of special interest groups is a genuine threat to this popular notion.

Can we accurately say, however, that ours is a government by the people? Not really. Not anymore. Our voice is limited to periodic elections where we can try to vote the worst of the scoundrels out of office. On a day-to-day and month-to-month basis, we have practically no influence over how we are actually governed, how government programs are run, how much we are taxed or how the tax money is spent.[18]

How then, do families deal with stresses from society when we feel so helpless to stop their influence? We can, and must, pray. We can be involved with the political process and with our local public schools, even though our actions might be resisted.[19] We can provide alternative education through Christian schools or home schooling. We can strengthen the educational and youth programs of churches and parachurch organizations. And we can remember that early in life, a child's most basic values are learned at home—from the words and actions of parents. In all of this we can keep our personal stresses in perspective.

Stresses from Family Crises
It hit the family like a bolt of lightning, literally.

Research psychologist Merton Strommen was driving with his wife, Irene, to their mountain chalet a few miles from Buena

Vista, Colorado. Along with two of their five sons, two daughters-in-law, and six grandchildren, the Strommens had been hiking together before their two-car caravan headed for the vacation that everyone was anticipating. Other family members, including their son Dave, had promised to join them soon.

After the caravan stopped for ice cream at a local dairy, the grandchildren and their parents piled into one car and left for the chalet while Merton and Irene stopped at a store. When they reached their mountain retreat a half hour later, they knew something was terribly wrong.

"There was a message here when we came," their son Tim announced. "Dave has been hit by lightning. He was alive when the ambulance left for Buena Vista Clinic." Without hesitation, Merton wheeled his car around and headed down the winding five-mile road. His family followed, and all rushed into the clinic.

"You can't see him," the receptionist said gently but firmly. "You'll have to wait here." Whether that wait was for ten minutes or an hour, it seemed like an eternity before the family was ushered into an office where they met two doctors.

"We've worked on Dave for over an hour," said one of the doctors in a compassionate, weary voice. "We've done all that could be done. Your son died instantly. The lightning penetrated his mastoid and traveled to his heart, coming out directly below it. At no point during the time we worked on him were we able to establish a connection between his heart and brain. At 5:25 we pronounced Dave dead."

As Merton and Irene looked at Dave lying on the table, they saw no sign of pain or shock in his facial expression. His strong, athletic, twenty-five-year-old body, handsome face, and tanned skin were tinted purple from the shock of lightning—and frozen in death. The father stepped out of the room, and his grandchildren watched as he broke down in great, wrenching sobs.

The hours that followed were filled with tears, intense emotional pain, attempts to pray, and heartbreaking decisions. The family had to inform the other two brothers. Somebody needed to go to the local mortuary. A pastor whom they barely knew appeared at the door to bring comfort and support to a numb, hurting family. One of the daughters-in-law turned to the kids, who had been crying hysterically, and suggested that they create crayon drawings to show what they were feeling.

Soon Dave's closest friend arrived from the camp where he and Dave both had brought their church youth groups for fun, relaxation, and spiritual challenge. The friend described how the accident had happened. Dave had gone to see if it was safe for the camp's teenagers to go climbing after an earlier rain shower. While he was walking along a ledge, the lightning struck, hurling his shocked body onto the rocks in the ravine below.

The tremor of that August afternoon tragedy sent Dave's parents and family into terrible grief and a healing journey that is described in a moving and helpful book.[20] The Strommens are a healthy family, maybe like yours, who faced unexpected, heart-rending tragedy and learned to come through it.

All families have stresses that shake their worlds. A relative dies. A loved one gets old and feeble. Physical and sexual abuse occur behind closed doors, where the neighbors never see. A teenager gets arrested or pregnant. Somebody breaks into a house. There is a car accident. A handicapped child is born. Unexpected serious illness appears. The family has a financial crisis. A father or mother slides into alcohol addiction, and family members are so embarrassed that they try to keep this hidden from people outside the home. The list is almost endless.

Two researchers at Syracuse University recently selected a group of experts in the field of family therapy—men and women who were experienced family counselors, had written books or articles on the family, and in many cases had been involved in teaching family therapy. This highly qualified panel identified major weaknesses of family life in the United States. (See list on next page.)

Notice that many of the stresses really are crises that influence some families in a community and not others. Divorce, job insecurity, anxiety about finances, jobs that make people feel overworked, or family conflicts are examples. When children experience conflict in the home, their grades go down and behavior problems increase. We know that children get along best in stable two-parent homes, but when that isn't possible, evidence shows that children function better in a harmonious single-parent home than in a two-parent family entangled with conflict.[21]

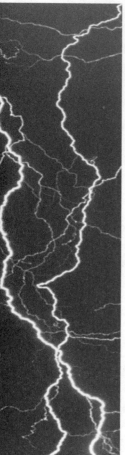

WEAKNESSES OF MODERN FAMILY LIFE

- Poverty, financial stress, anxiety about future financial security
- Mounting restrictions on access to health care and worry about lack of health insurance
- Work pressures, job insecurity, demanding employers who devalue the family, adults who feel overworked, inadequate financial, psychological, and day-care support for two-job or dual-career families
- Many people who try to cope with too little time, money, and support from others
- Parents who feel inadequate, often because they were parented poorly themselves and parent their children poorly and sometimes abusively
- Lack of support from extended family, community, or government
- Parents who are unavailable to their children because of work, divorce, drugs, mobility, or father absence
- Lack of sex education in the home, which leaves children to learn about sex through other sources that often are inaccurate and misleading
- Families and a society that focus on academic skills and physical fitness but do little to teach children and adults how to make relationships work
- High rates of substance abuse, emotional abuse, physical violence, sexual abuse, all with a lack of support for those who experience such abuse
- Widespread drug and alcohol abuse, often treated by programs that are supposed to be family oriented but are not

Adapted from Linda Stone Fish and Janet L. Osborn, "Therapists' Views of Family Life: A Delphi Study," *Family Relations* 41 (October 1992): 411.

As I looked at the experts' evaluations, I noticed one glaring omission. These people failed to realize that religious families tend to be more stable families. Their faith in God gives them reason to hope. When God is pushed to the fringes or out of families altogether, problems in the home are more likely to appear and persist.[22]

Several years ago, my mother began ruminating on how bad

things are in this world. "It's awful," she said more than once. "I don't know why anybody would want to bring a child into this world when there are so many problems."

At some time maybe you have heard or said similar words yourself. But after I had heard my mom express these sentiments several times, I reminded her of something that I have to keep reminding myself: God still is in control. He who resides in the lives of Christians is greater than the satanic forces in the world (1 John 4:4). I thought of this again recently when a friend described his church, where the pastor was very active politically. "In sermons we hear a lot about the president," my friend said thoughtfully, "but we don't hear much about Jesus." Regardless of our politics, we need to keep aware of Jesus.

Stresses from Our Minds

Everybody can see the earthquakelike shocks that *come from the outside*—from society or from family crises—but it is harder to see the stresses that *come from the inside*—from our minds. Deeply held beliefs, attitudes, and values may be hidden someplace in the recesses of our brains, but these can have a powerful impact on families and family members.

Sometimes, for example, family members have differing religious beliefs or attitudes about lifestyles. When these ideas clash, families experience serious disagreements and prolonged aftershocks in the home. Recently, I read about a Chicago judge whose mother was a poor immigrant with a limited grasp of the English language. She was surprised to learn that Jews in this country go to temple and not to synagogue, but when she heard that Abraham Lincoln had been shot in the temple, she assumed he was a great Jewish hero. In his honor, she named her son Abraham Lincoln Marovitz. You can imagine how this deeply orthodox mother responded when her son failed to find a Jewish wife but instead became romantically involved with a "tough minded Irish lass from the south side."

When a professional-journal article recently listed some weaknesses in modern family life, I was struck by how many of these reflected attitudes, values, and beliefs like the faith and mind-set of Mrs. Marovitz.[23] When a husband and wife have different religious views or if devout Christian parents have a teenager who claims to be an atheist, the family will feel the impact of the tension. When parents decide to live for themselves, without considering the needs of their children, everybody suffers, and the children often become more stressed than their self-centered parents.[24]

Because many parents don't believe in the need to spend prolonged time with their kids, a lot of socialization comes from baby-sitters, television, and other nonparental influences. That can lead to later family conflicts over values and attitudes. Since there is widespread confusion about what it means to be a good mother or good father, everybody feels the ambiguity, uncertainty, and subsequent stress, especially when original families break up and merge into stepfamilies. When fathers have the attitude that mothers should handle most of the child rearing, the kids lack father contact and are confused about male roles. The mothers, in turn, are overburdened, frustrated, and often justifiably angry. When people conclude that the government should solve their family problems, there can be increasing frustrations and feelings of helplessness if things don't get better. If parents resist disciplining or setting high standards for their children, the young people often have more freedom than they can handle.

On one of my trips overseas I had a long dinner discussion with a counselor who lives and works in an Eastern country. Unlike counselors in Europe and North America, where he had taken his training, my friend rarely works with individuals. "In my country the family is more important," he said. "If there is a problem, the whole family knows about it. They all work to give support or to solve the problem, and directly or indirectly they all are involved in the counseling."

In contrast to my colleague, many of us live in a culture where individualism is valued above almost everything else. We treasure independence, personal freedom, self-fulfillment, and individual rights. The "me-generation" mentality is not as common as it was at one time, however, and there seems to be a new interest in communities, small groups, and giving to others. Still, the

TALKING TO CHILDREN ABOUT DEATH

SANDRA PICKLESIMER ALDRICH, M.A.
Dean of Students, Focus on the Family Institute for Family Studies
Author of *Living through the Loss of Someone You Love*

Earl's mother died when he was ten, and he refused to attend the service. His grandmother, concerned about what people would think, insisted he "straighten up." A family friend wisely stepped in, offering to stay with Earl. All that afternoon the two of them walked through the village, the friend gently encouraging the child to talk.

In addition to listening, adults can do several other important things for grieving children:

1. *Tell children about the death right away.* As difficult as it is, telling children gives an explanation for the tears, visitors, and endless phone calls. It also confirms that the children are part of the family.
2. *Tell children the truth.* Many times a parent, thinking death is too stark for children, gives an unhealthy explanation such as "Grandma's gone on a long trip." That's not only a lie and a postponement of the inevitable, it may lead a child to resentment because Grandma didn't say good-bye.
3. *Share your faith with grieving children.* Remind children of comforting Scripture passages. Even preschoolers benefit from hearing that God helps us through painful situations. Verses such as Romans 8:35-39 promise that nothing, not even death, can separate us from God's love. First Thessalonians 4:13-18 emphasizes the hope we have in the Resurrection. The thought that we will see our loved ones again offers comfort.
4. *Allow children to attend the funeral.* Not only do children need to feel part of the family unit, but they also have many questions answered when they witness the funeral ceremony.
5. *Affirm children's feelings.* The most common adult reaction to children's expression of emotions other than sadness is "Don't feel like that!" Normal emotions may include anger, guilt, and even relief. Children don't create their feelings. Remember that feelings are not right or wrong; they just *are*.

Being able to verbalize pain is the first step toward resolving it. By helping grieving children deal with rampant emotions today, we have strengthened future adults.

value of individualism and autonomy goes deep in many of our minds.

This commitment to individualism can free us to build careers, pursue unique dreams, succeed economically, and find personal fulfillment in life. But individualism also can lead people to make decisions and take actions that seem good for themselves but may not be good for their families. Individualism, for example, has been linked to father absence, to the ease with which many people move toward divorce, to the failure of a separated parent (most often a man) to pay alimony or to see his children, and to the failure of grown children to visit or care for older parents. Sometimes the individualistic mentality is linked to the antifamily rhetoric of extreme feminists, the authoritarian male domination in some homes of extreme traditionalists, and the tendency of others to devalue and shun the family altogether.

It isn't easy to walk the narrow path that allows us to build both successful careers and successful families. Both take time and effort; sometimes both make demands that pull us in separate directions.

Even in a society where individualism is valued, however, many people do manage both to succeed in their jobs and to maintain healthy families. In the 1950s, family members were strongly committed to one another. Extended family members visited each other often, helped each other financially, and helped with child care or household tasks. They were committed to permanent marriages. Surprisingly, some research suggests that things have not changed a lot since then—even with our emphasis on individualism and commitment to careers.

In one survey, 55 percent of the people said they could call on a relative in the middle of the night if needed; two out of three believed they could borrow $200 from a relative for an emergency; 71 percent agreed that marriage is "a lifelong commitment that should not be ended except under extreme circumstances"; and 85 percent of surveyed married people indicated that they would select the same spouse if they had to do it all over again. Of special interest is a survey report that eight out of ten divorced and separated people still believe that marriage is a commitment for life.[25]

SHAME IN FAMILIES

SANDRA WILSON, PH.D.
Visiting Professor, Denver
Conservative Baptist Seminary
Visiting Professor, Trinity
Evangelical Divinity School
Author of *Shame-Free Parenting*

"I wish you had come for help sooner."

Pastors say this to couples with shipwrecked marriages. Physicians say it to patients about their alcohol-ravaged livers. And these or similar words are repeated daily in thousands of less dramatic scenarios in which long-hidden problems finally become too obvious to ignore.

These stories all reveal an unbiblical sense of shame that binds individuals and families into increasingly destructive patterns of living. This kind of shame comes from the lie that says human beings and their families ought to be perfect and free of problems. When people believe this lie, their obvious mistakes, unwise choices, and other acknowledged shortcomings leave them feeling disgustingly different and hopelessly isolated from the altogether flawless beings they think they're supposed to be. These shame-bound people and their families cope with these painful feelings by stonewalling reality. They build a thick wall of denial that lets them barricade the truth about personal weakness and family problems and hide all of this from themselves and others.

To be sure, this fantasy fortress of denial defends against feelings of shame and abandonment. But it does more. Shame-based denial blocks problem solving and healthy change. Getting help with a problem requires admitting that the problem exists. This is precisely what the shame-lie forbids.

Only truth about the pervasive effects of our sin and the perfect provision of God's grace can dissolve the superglue of shame that keeps individuals and families stuck in repeated patterns of hurtful living "to the third and fourth generation." God's divine democracy—There is none perfect, no not one—describes *every* person and family. Only as this *bad* news emerges from the shadow cast by shame, can the *good* news of God's redeeming, transforming grace shine its healing light into families stumbling in shame. ✺

Some people would challenge these conclusions and argue that the survey findings do not fit with the statistics about divorce, infidelity, spouse abuse, and child neglect. It has become acceptable for many people to say they agree with traditional family values, but what they say on a survey might be very different from what they do with their lives.

I agree, but change sends tremors through society. Many people realize that their houses and families are built on shaky ground, where there are few (if any) religious beliefs, clear standards of right and wrong, or solid family values. When they experience the groundswell of stress from society, from conflicts, and from uncertainties in their own minds, these people realize that their families must be built on firm, biblical, solid-rock underpinnings, or they will not withstand the inevitable shocks of living on the fault line of change and uncertainty.

How we deal with stress depends a lot on our perceptions. If we expect the worst in our families, our expectations can turn into a self-fulfilling prophecy: Often what happens is what we expect. Research has compared families that cope effectively with stress and those that do not. The families that manage it poorly assume that there is little hope and that they are helpless. Once they begin to think they are helpless, they start acting as if they are helpless. As a result, they slide deeper into discouragement and inactivity. How a family perceives crises has a powerful influence on how they cope and survive.[26]

But we have another choice. We can choose to see the stresses as an inevitable part of life and choose not to let them destroy us. We can determine, with the help of God and our family and friends, that our families will remain durable, resilient, and healthy even in the midst of stressful tremors. We can learn from the examples of other families who have withstood major crises and have come out of them stronger and full of faith. We do not need to live on the fault line in anxiety and fear. We can commit ourselves to understanding the stresses that can threaten our families and to undergirding our families with foundations that will last despite earthshaking change.

5

UNDERGIRDING THE FAMILY

MAYBE you have heard about the California college professor who was watching television and heard that "another random act of senseless violence" had occurred in his community. As he watched the newscast, the professor wondered what it would be like to have a community where people showed random acts of senseless *kindness*. The next day, he gave his students an usual assignment: to do something out of the ordinary to help somebody and then to write about the experience. The students responded with enthusiasm. One young man bought twenty blankets at the Salvation Army thrift store and gave them to homeless people under a bridge. Another waved a motorist into a nearby parking space and drove to the only other available space almost half a mile away.

Somebody in a local bank heard about the experiment and printed bumper stickers urging people to "commit a random act of senseless kindness." The stickers were sold for a dollar each, and the money was given to a local charity. The police department put the stickers on their cars. The idea was broadcast on radio stations, spread in schools, and encouraged from pulpits. Even in families, with their conflicts and ever present tensions, people started showing kindness.

The professor was amazed, and so were many others. It seemed that almost everybody in the community of 100,000 people wanted to get involved. For a time, at least, the people were applying a basic biblical principle: "Always try to be kind to each other and to everyone else" (1 Thess. 5:15).

And the kindness had an impact on the whole city.

All of us know, however, that newscasters, talk-show hosts, therapists, social commentators, and ordinary people don't normally spend time thinking about acts of kindness. More often, we focus on issues and events that are dramatic, shocking, or of tear-jerking "human interest." It is more absorbing and intriguing to hear about acts of violence, psychopathology, uncontrolled lust, government corruption, and families gone awry than to read about human strengths, resources, coping skills, and normal, healthy behavior.[1] Reporters and counselors, among others, are trained to look for pathology, and whenever we are looking for something bad or unjust, more often than not we find it.

Harvard psychiatrist Robert Coles once described the emphasis of his training. "I was not trained to think of the family as a means by which people pull together, learn from one another, gain mutual strength, and sometimes collectively fail, but still nevertheless persist," he told a group of family counselors. Instead, Coles's psychiatric training emphasized that people in families are individuals filled with "defenses working against impulses and struggling with a superego."[2]

We need to take a different approach. When buildings are erected in earthquake-prone areas, construction supervisors must adhere to special codes to ensure that the building will be capable of withstanding strong ground motions. If our families are going to survive the tremors and seismic waves of conflict and change, we must make sure that they are undergirded with firm foundations and structures that will withstand strong movement.

To start we might remind ourselves of this obvious fact: Almost nobody sets out to have a life filled with problems, difficulties, and turmoil—despite the fact that sinful human nature sets us on this course from birth. When problems appear, they indicate that something has gone wrong. Individuals and families who show symptoms of pathology and lack of control are demonstrating that their lives have been undermined by sinful thoughts and actions, a lack of skills, insensitivity to other people, wrong motives, misinformation, self-defeating behaviors, bad experiences, dysfunctional family patterns, or other influences that weaken the foundations of our homes and lives.

Instead of wringing our hands about these situations, we should explore how distressed families are undermined or poorly built so that we can learn how to help each other find the courage and capabilities to get our lives and families rebuilt on more solid foundations.[3]

Kevin is an example. A baby boomer, born in the early 1950s, Kevin recently went to his physician complaining about chest pains and other physical symptoms that the doctor blamed on stress. Kevin worked sixty to eighty hours every week for a company that was having financial difficulties and that laid off people consistently, without warning. In place of high morale and worker camaraderie, the employees had a spirit of intense competition. Like racehorses in the final stretch of a derby, employees were jockeying for position, trying to retain their places and keep from being eliminated.

Following the death of his father, Kevin had become "the man of the family" when he was only thirteen. In the years that followed, he learned to take his responsibilities seriously. He had risen quickly to become a competent business executive, and he wanted, in addition, to be a good family leader, a good husband, and a good church member. He often volunteered to help out in his congregation or community, and for a while he even took over as the church janitor. People liked Kevin. They described him as a "superperson" who was kind, gracious, and always ready to listen or chat.

With all of the demands and stresses, however, Kevin's efficiency plummeted. He didn't have the time to invest in his family as he (and they) wanted. Relationships became strained at home and at work. Some things got forgotten and didn't get done, or they were done halfheartedly and inefficiently.

Before long, Kevin began to feel like a failure. He got anxious, occasionally panicky, nervous, easily flustered, and depressed about what was happening. He started to withdraw from people and began to think that he was incompetent, that he couldn't manage his life, and that maybe he wasn't as skillful and as capable as he had thought. Perhaps you can identify with what Kevin was going through. I can.

At the suggestion of his doctor, Kevin went to see a Christian counselor. Together they looked at every piece of the young executive's overloaded life. It was clear that some things could not change; he worked in a stress-filled environment, for example, and competition was a part of his job. But Kevin began to see that he had allowed himself to be spread too thin. He acknowledged that he had been dropping the ball too often, and he realized that other people had reason to complain about the inefficiency. His withdrawal, apathy, distress about himself, feelings of failure, and physical symptoms were all evidences of his fatigue, his inability to say no, and his attempts to do too much.

Life for Kevin was not really falling apart, and his family was not destined to self-destruct—at least not at that point. But he needed to reevaluate his priorities, his lifestyle, and his driving ambitions. With the counselor's help, Kevin learned to set some limits, to manage his time more effectively, and to reestablish his priorities—including the investment that he wanted to put into his family. As he started to relax, his wife, children, and co-workers noticed. Kevin became less down on himself and more realistic about what he could and could not do. His family, his work environment, his inner sense of well-being, and his attitudes all began to change. Today he talks enthusiastically about the commitment he has made in his family. Everybody sees how his life has changed—for the better.

And he has no more chest pains.

Family Life Can Be Beautiful

In the midst of his stress, Kevin knew that his life and marriage were resting on a shaky foundation, and he took steps to rebuild. In contrast, a majority of people think their marriages and families are in pretty good shape, despite all the reports of family problems and the predictions that families are falling apart. For almost twenty years, the National Opinion Research Center has been asking husbands and wives to answer this question: "Taking all things together, how would you describe your marriage? Would you say that your marriage is very happy, pretty happy, or not too happy?" The answers have not varied much over the years. Sixty to 65 percent of the men and women surveyed have reported that their marriages are "very happy." An additional 30 to 35 percent have said their marriages are "pretty happy," and less than 5 percent have felt that their marriages are "not too happy."

The same surveys have asked people how much satisfaction they get from their families. Over the years, 42 percent have reported "a very great deal" of satisfaction, 33 percent checked "a great deal," 11 percent said "quite a bit," and 7 percent reported "a fair amount." The categories "some," "a little," and "none" were checked by a combined total of only 7 percent.[4]

Of course, these figures may be distorted because people who are really unhappy with their marriages tend to get divorced and then they don't get surveyed about their marriages. And it is probable—although I can't prove this—that if people are unhappy about their families, they aren't likely to have much interest in answering questions about marriage and family life. All things considered, however, survey figures suggest that millions of people get a great deal of satisfaction from their family lives, despite the challenges and crises that all families face, at least periodically.

TRAITS OF A HEALTHY FAMILY

Members of a healthy family
- Communicate and listen
- Affirm and support one another
- Teach respect for others
- Develop a sense of trust
- Have a sense of play and humor
- Share responsibility
- Have a sense of right and wrong
- Have a strong sense of family in which rituals and traditions abound
- Have a balance of interaction among members
- Have a shared religious core
- Respect the privacy of one another
- Value service to others
- Foster family table time and conversation
- Share leisure time
- Admit and seek help with problems

Adapted from Dolores Curran, *Traits of a Healthy Family* (Minneapolis: Winston Press, 1983).

Several researchers have looked at healthy families and tried to discover what makes them tick. This kind of information lets people like Kevin and the rest of us know how we can build families that are stable, fulfilling, and maybe even beautiful.

Writer and educator Dolores Curran surveyed five hundred people who work with families. Then she compiled a list of fifteen traits of a healthy family. (See previous page.)

Nick Stinnett and John DeFrain were more scientific in their approach. Their study of three thousand families uncovered six qualities of a strong family.

SIX QUALITIES OF A STRONG FAMILY

Strong families are characterized by

1. *Commitment.* Members of strong families are dedicated to promoting each other's welfare and happiness. They value the unity of the family and are committed to one another and to the family group.
2. *Appreciation.* They express a great deal of appreciation for each other.
3. *Communication.* They have good communication skills and spend a lot of time talking with each other.
4. *Time Together.* They spend considerable high-quality time with each other.
5. *Spiritual Commitment.* These families have a high degree of religious commitment and strong faith. Most belong to organized churches and have a religion that is a personal, practical, day-to-day experience rather than something theoretical.
6. *Coping Ability.* They have the ability to deal with crises, bad situations, and stress in a positive way that helps them to grow.

Nick Stinnett and John DeFrain, *Secrets of Strong Families* (Boston: Little, Brown, 1985).

Much different is the work of Paul Faulkner, who was asked by a vice president of Wal-Mart if he had any information about how people could get ahead in their work without losing their families. In attempting to answer the question, Faulkner discovered a disturbing quotation from Tom Peters, one of the nation's best-known experts in business success. Peters wrote a book that launched a powerful emphasis on excellence in business, but he didn't think that people could extend that excellence to their families.

> We are frequently asked if it is possible to have it all: a full and satisfying personal life *and* a full and satisfying and hardworking professional one. Our answer is *no*. . . . The price of excellence is time, energy, attention, and focus at the very same time that energy, attention, and focus could have gone toward enjoying your daughter's soccer game. We have found that the majority of those that are successful in business have given up family vacations, Little League games, birthday dinners, evenings, weekends, and lunch hours, gardening, reading, movies, and most other pastimes. We have a number of friends whose marriages even crumbled under the weight of a devotion to a dream.[5]

Paul Faulkner, who disagrees with Peters's conclusion, found thirty couples who were known to be successful in both their careers *and* their families. The group included several corporate executives, a football coach, an attorney, a surgeon, a cattleman, an architect, a university dean, and people in various other fields. Along with his wife, Gladys, Faulkner visited all thirty people over a period of four years, spent several days in each of their homes, and watched. "We felt none were trying to 'put on an act' for us," Faulkner wrote in his book.[6] They were living examples of people whose families and lifestyles challenged the depressing conclusions of Tom Peters. The Faulkners think there are hundreds, perhaps thousands of other families like the ones they observed. The eight messages that came from these families are summarized in the list on the next page.

Disagreement about the Family

Not all people agree on what a family should be like. When *Parade* magazine asked, "What kind of person do you want to marry?" eighteen-year-old Bart Stanley wrote that he wanted "an old-fashioned woman" who wouldn't dress in fancy business suits or go to work in the fast-paced business world. Instead, he wanted a wife who would stay home, clean the house, wash dishes and clothes, take the kids to baseball and ballet practice, "and prepare a home-cooked meal for the family when I get home from work."[7]

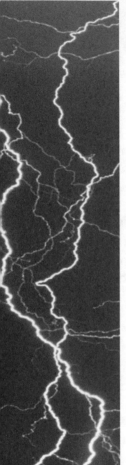

EIGHT MESSAGES FROM FAMILIES THAT HAVE CAREER SUCCESS AND FAMILY EXCELLENCE

1. Successful families "parent with a *purpose.*" The parents know what they want and aim precisely to get it with all diligence.
2. The families have clear, lasting *values.* They help family members answer questions, find meaning and purpose in life, and provide stability. Values include a strong religious faith and high esteem for family members.
3. The families show obvious, effervescent, overflowing *love.* This includes expressions of appreciation, encouragement, and forgiveness.
4. The families hold a *servant mentality.* They serve one another and frequently are involved in serving people in the community without boasting.
5. They have the gift of *laughter.* They laugh easily and they laugh a lot, but their humor is never caustic, embarrassing, or cutting.
6. They have *transparency.* These people are open, honest, and able to communicate easily. They have no family secrets.
7. They show *mutual support.* When the children are young, they sense a closeness. When they get older, they are given autonomy. As adults, the grown children remain connected to the family support system, but not so connected that they feel caught or entrapped.
8. They learn to *cope positively* when they face tragedy or failure. Almost all families encountered normal adolescent rebellion, but they were emboldened by adversity. They refused to be victims, and they emerged as victors.

Adapted from Paul Faulkner, *Achieving Success without Failing Your Family* (West Monroe, La.: Howard Publishing, 1994).

The teenager's letter provoked hundreds of protests, plus a letter from a young woman who explained that Bart had described "the kind of person I've always wanted to be—there for my family and not have a career." She added that there "shouldn't be any of this Mr. Mom stuff" and asked that her letter be forwarded to Bart.

CORPORATE LIFE AND THE FAMILY

Paul Faulkner, Ph.D.
Abilene Christian University
Condensed from *Achieving Success without Failing Your Family*

Can you advance in the corporate world *and* have a great family life? Not usually! Most highly successful people lose their families along the way. The long hours and relentless pressures take their toll on both the executive and his or her family. Tom Peters said it best: "We are frequently asked if it is possible to have it all: a full and satisfying personal life *and* a full and satisfying professional one. Our answer is *no.*"

But Peters' ominous prediction is not 100 percent correct. Some top corporate executives have strong and flourishing families. What is their secret?

These executives make a powerful commitment to Christian principles. One executive father told me, "We base our family on the *principles* found in the Bible and the *people* found in the church."

These executives are seen as models by their children. One daughter said, "You can't fool us, Mom. We saw the knee prints in the carpet beside your Bible." And they *saw* their fathers go without sleep, turn down corporate board positions, and in some cases, fix breakfast for everyone in the house—five days a week.

These executives teach their children how to give. One young executive said of his father (the president of a large corporation), "I want to be just like my dad. He gives away *40 percent* of everything he earns."

These executives leave their work—at work. The wife of a General Motors executive said, "My husband leaves all his work woes at the bridge on his way home." Another said about her husband, "When he is home, *he is home.*" These fathers were somehow able to make a major shift from work to home. They knew that the qualities it takes to be an effective executive (exacting, precise, analytical) were not necessarily the qualities needed to be a good dad (tender, compassionate, flexible). Good executive/fathers are aware of the differences and are able to make the shift from executive to father smoothly and easily.

These executives don't trust much in their financial successes. One president of a division of IBM said to me, "We don't have anything we can't live without."

These executives limit their outside activities. Recreational and social activities like golf and tennis are put on hold until their children leave home. The family is the focus. One executive wanted more exercise, but rather than join a health club, he arranged instruction in tennis for the whole family. Successful executive/dads make a point to "be there" for the children's school performances or sports events. It cost one executive a position on the board of one of the nation's largest retail corporations, but he chose his family and didn't give it a second thought.

These executives bring their families to work. One owner of a hundred-million-dollar grocery store took his son with him to the bank board meetings even when the president of the board discouraged it. The son is now on the bank board.

These executives have a remarkable ability to overcome difficulties and tragedies. In the midst of dealing with extreme poverty, illness, personal problems, or business reverses, these families kept this attitude: "It's not the losses that count, but how you deal with them. Our best work is done when we are working against the wind."

These executives don't take themselves too seriously. Humor is a constant companion in these successful corporate families. When asked about the importance of humor in their family, the wife of a successful corporation owner said, "On a scale of one to ten, humor is a fifteen!"

These executives believe wholeheartedly in the power of parenting. They know that parents do have the power to make a difference, and they trust in that power. They are proactive, not reactive. They value—they *treasure*—the influence they have in the lives of their children.

Most effective executives are like Michael Jordan, who is a one-of-a-kind basketball player but an ordinary baseball player. A successful executive who also has a close, loving, and dedicated family is about as rare as the successful two-event super athlete, but it can happen. And when it does you will see the qualities mentioned above.

Three years later the magazine reported that the two had "hit it off like you wouldn't believe," were planning to get married, and intended to raise "as many children as God sends us."[8]

How different were the conclusions of a *Time* magazine essay in which writer Barbara Ehrenreich proclaimed an idea that is "nearly unthinkable: that the family may not be the ideal and perfect living arrangement after all—that it can be a nest of pathology and a cradle of gruesome violence." She criticized the millions who "adhere to creeds that are militantly 'pro-family,'" argued that millions of others flock to therapy groups to heal the damage caused by family life, lauded the "long and honorable tradition of 'anti-family' thought," and quoted a British anthropologist who stated that "far from being the basis of the good society, the family, with its narrow privacy and tawdry secrets, is the source of all discontents."[9]

A columnist in our local paper was quick to respond. After criticizing Ehrenreich's outburst, the newspaper writer concluded that the family may be imperfect, but there is no plausible alternative.

> Over the last generation, we have tried relieving families of fathers, and the consequences have been grim for both mothers and children: more poverty, delinquency, insecurity, and general hardship. The main lesson of that experiment is that the traditional family is more vital and difficult to replace than we ever suspected.
>
> That's why there is such broad agreement that we need to shore it up some way or another. . . . The nuclear family is not the most universal institution for nothing. No society has found a better way to handle the crucial task of rearing children. This society has found a worse one.[10]

People today clearly have different ideas about what's best for the family. You may disagree with both Bart Stanley and Barbara Ehrenreich, but we all know about changes that appear to be rocking the family, and many of us worry about the fate of our own families.

Questions about the value of families are not new. Social historians tell us that for generations, people have viewed the family as the core of social stability, but there have always been some who have questioned its value. For decades people have feared that the family is about to collapse. These fears tend to increase in times like ours—periods of social stress and pressure.[11]

But there is hope. Even family therapists—the experts who work day after day with troubled marriages and conflict-ridden families—see the hope. Many of these counselors now realize that while many families are confused and troubled, others show remarkable resilience and flexibility. Despite family instability, antifamily legislation, or economic and social uncertainties, most people are committed to forming and being part of a stable family. According to one influential family counselor, we need to quit putting so much emphasis on what is wrong and instead focus on preventing problems, on more clearly defining what is healthy about families, and on finding ways to build this health into our individual families.[12]

As I was thinking about all this recently, I grabbed a pencil and began to jot down some "truths for our families." I can't document all of these conclusions with scientific evidence, but I'm willing to bet that most of them are valid and worth remembering. As you read the list on the next page, you may want to add a few truths for your family.

How Do We Build Healthy Families?
Several years ago, I had dinner at the top of a tall building in Tokyo. It wasn't until we were seated that I thought to ask about earthquakes.

"Japan is on a fault line," my host confirmed, but he described how the high-rise building had been constructed. "It's somewhat flexible," he said. "When we had an earthquake several years ago, the top of this building swayed several feet, back and forth, throwing dishes and people on the floor." He told me that most of the waitresses had quit their jobs following the quake (I could understand why), but he added that everybody really was safe because the building had been designed to withstand tremors like the one they had all experienced.

During the time that I worked on this book, I sat near a window from which I could watch workers constructing a new house. They dug the foundation, laid the footings, built the walls, put on the roof, and now are working inside to complete the building that soon will be home to a new family in our neighborhood. I don't know anything about the construction of houses, but I sense that the builders have erected a stable structure. Unlike Tokyo, the area in which I live almost never is shaken by earthquakes, but we get strong winds and occasional icy onslaughts in winter. The new house in our neighborhood is likely to stand firm and secure, like that high-rise building in Japan, because both have been build solidly to withstand the shocks of nature.

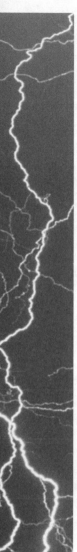

TRUTHS FOR OUR FAMILIES

1. Despite all the change and turmoil that disrupts family life, God is still aware of what is going on and is still in control.
2. If most people had to do it over, they would marry the same spouse they have now.
3. Even though divorce rates are high, most marriages stay intact.
4. While 3 percent of women living with men in America suffer at least one violent domestic incident during a given year, the good news is that 97 percent do not.
5. The majority of families are not seriously dysfunctional, most kids do not become "adult children of dysfunctional family backgrounds," and most of us are not in need of recovery.
6. No family is perfect and without problems and periodic crises.
7. All parents make mistakes, but most of their kids survive very well, even without therapy and twelve-step programs.
8. When families and marriages have problems, counselors can often help.
9. It is possible (but admittedly more difficult) to have good marriages, healthy families, and stable kids even when we live in bad environments or in a chaotic, immoral, God-rejecting society.
10. We can raise kids successfully even if we don't have all the answers.
11. We can raise kids successfully even if we haven't read parenting and marriage books and even if we aren't perfect.
12. Even good parents sometimes have rebellious kids.
13. Even bad parents sometimes have healthy, adjusted kids.
14. When things are not going well in your family, that does not mean that all is hopeless. Often "this too will pass."
15. We won't understand everything that happens to us.
16. God cares about each of our families.

Like the construction workers, we need to build families that will stand firm through storms and change. Dr. Froma Walsh is codirector of the University of Chicago's Center for Family Health, a former president of the American Family Therapy Academy, and a leading authority on how families function.

Drawing on many years of study and research, she has suggested several well-proven components of "healthy family functioning."[13] Her conclusions form the basis for the following guidelines for building healthy families.

1. Encourage Family Commitment

Healthy families consist of mutually supportive people who genuinely care for one another, feel a sense of being connected to each other, and are committed to their families. All of us who live in families will disagree with each other at times, and most will have conflicts. But the members of healthy families have the sense of all being a part of the same family.

A few days after I started writing this chapter, Julie and I celebrated our thirtieth wedding anniversary—and concluded that we should go for another thirty years. We don't have any secret formula for keeping together, but if I had to pick one word to describe our relationship, it would be *commitment.* Each of us made a commitment for life, and we're determined to have a good marriage, even when times are tough. Like most others who have been married for a while, we know what it means to commit to each other "for better or for worse, in sickness and in health," when we have no financial worries and when we have no money.

Someone has likened commitment to a postage stamp. Its usefulness consists in its ability to stick to one thing until it gets there. There is no proven formula for commitment. It involves making a decision—to stay with a marriage, to complete a task, to achieve a goal—and then persisting and acting on your decision.[14]

2. Show Respect Even When You Disagree

With candor, warmth, and a dash of humor, President Clinton's mother described how she reacted when her son Bill came home with a girlfriend named Hillary. "I confess that, for me, Hillary has been a growth experience," Virginia Kelley wrote in her autobiography. "I love her dearly now, and I believe she loves me. . . . But when we first laid eyes on each other, it was like the old immovable object running up against the irresistible force." The two women were very different. They had different backgrounds and contrasting values. But to their credit, they learned to respect each other's differences even though they didn't always agree.

Most families at one time or another have values clashes. When they were growing up, our kids knew our values, and they knew that we disapproved of some of their tastes, friends, and attitudes. One night I reached a point of despair when I watched one of my kids leave the house and wondered what would become of her. Our other daughter gave me the answer. "Dad, I know it's difficult for you," she said. "But my sister knows what she has been taught, and maybe she's going through a stage or exploring new things right now. Of course, she doesn't expect you to change your beliefs or values, but what she needs more than anything is to know that you still love her."

I never got better parenting advice.

Julie and I have great rapport with our daughters now, and I think it stems in part because we all love and respect one another, are willing to give each other autonomy and freedom to be ourselves, and try not to get uptight when our perspectives differ.

The same applies to marriage. According to Froma Walsh, in healthy families couples have "a relationship characterized by mutual respect, support, and equitable sharing of power and responsibilities." That can happen without anybody having to ignore or bypass the biblical teaching about roles in marriage.

3. Take Family Caregiving Seriously

I am part of an accountability group in which three men recently became fathers for the first time. After a few weeks of changing diapers and adjusting to the idea of being parents, they all reached the same conclusion: Taking care of kids is much more work than they ever had anticipated.

Every parent knows that caring for children is demanding, time-consuming, and sometimes difficult. But healthy families dedicate themselves seriously to nurturing, protecting, supporting, helping, and instructing children, teaching them values, helping them accept authority, and giving them increasing autonomy as they get older.

Unlike our ancestors, however, bringing up kids may not be the major caregiving task in most of our lives. Many of us will spend even more years taking care of older parents, sick spouses, and others who now live longer because of the benefits of modern medicine. Healthy families don't neglect vulnerable family members; we care for them with compassion and respect. Abundant research shows that people are physically and emotionally healthier when they have caring, committed, ongoing relationships with family members and friends, especially during times of stress.[15]

When we read so much about problem teenagers who are self-centered and uncaring, it is encouraging to read about fourteen-year-old Angela Morris. She was baby-sitting for her neighbors' children, who were ages two, three, nine, and ten, but the parents never returned home. Angela tried to care for the children. She skipped school for a few days and then called an emergency meeting of her friends. They gathered in a pizza shop and organized round-the-clock shifts to dress, feed, and supervise the children.

"If I had known all this beforehand, I wouldn't have taken the job," Angela said when the story became public. "But I really love those kids and didn't want them to split up in foster homes." The eighth grader and her friends finally told their secret when their money ran out after two weeks. Police, who began looking for the parents to charge them with child neglect, also praised the young baby-sitter and her friends. They were more serious about child care than the children's own parents had been.[16]

4. Provide Family Structure

I like to think of myself as an independent person who can come and go as I want. Maybe most of us think that way. But we're seeing that families and societies unravel when there is no structure and no rules.

An editorial writer expressed this beautifully when he or she wrote about "the coming apart of America":

> Sometimes societies come apart cataclysmically, as happened in Rwanda and the former Yugoslavia. Sometimes they come apart subtly, almost imperceptibly, by degrees, as seems to be happening now in the United States.

FOR THE CHILDREN—
THE GIFT OF ENCOURAGEMENT

DANIEL S. SWEENEY, M.F.C.C.
Center for Play Therapy
University of North Texas
Author *Play Therapy: Handbook
of Interventions with Children's
Problems*

Children are a reflection of what they experience, and they tend to internalize these experiences. Following a recent earthquake in California, a father walked into the kitchen carrying his three-year-old daughter. When the little girl saw dishes and cans strewn every-where, she quickly blurted out: "Daddy—me no do, me no do!" Children indeed internalize so much.

What a child sees or does is related directly to the child's self-concept and identity. Frustrated adults, in dealing with confusion in children or with their challenging behavior, often look for quick methods of control rather than to the child's deeper need for affirmation and encouragement. Instead of a controlling response, we can turn these situations into unique opportunities to give children the blessing of a positive self-image.

Encouragement can and should be given anytime a child attempts a task. Too often generic praise such as "Great picture!" is given when a child succeeds. This can lead to a child misinterpreting his or her value as a person. Whether the child fails or succeeds, encouragement can always be given for the effort. For example: "I can see you worked hard to use many colors in that picture."

Encouragement is not only a gift; it is God's command (1 Thess. 5:11). Knowing one's position in Christ is healing, and a self-image based on such knowledge is spiritually and emotionally healthy. For children to experience this reality, the adults in their lives must establish and pass on a heritage of blessing and encouragement (Deut. 6:7). Salvation itself is not dependent on performance but is freely given (Eph. 2:8).

Could it be that encouragement to a child's heart is akin to grace? Surely it is life-giving and healing. We owe our children nothing less.

The Census Bureau last week came forth with one more piece of worrisome evidence of the unraveling of American society at the most fundamental level. . . . According to the bureau, births to unmarried women increased more than 70 percent in the ten years between 1983 and 1993. By 1993, 6.3 million American children—27 percent—were living with a single, never married parent. That was as compared with 3.7 million children in such situations in 1983 and only 243,000 in 1963. . . .

Not all of the blame for all of America's social dysfunctions can be laid to the increase in single-parent families. But virtually everyone except diehard ideologues now recognizes that children who grow up in single-parent households, especially when the parent has never been married, are more likely to be troubled and to make trouble. And it doesn't take a majority of troubled or troubling children to make a neighborhood unlivable or a class unmanageable.

The focus, of course, falls on the single mother. But children are not immaculately conceived, and there are legions of absent fathers out there as well. When adults, men and women, take flight from responsibility, families fail to form, children suffer and society, slowly and by degrees, comes apart.[17]

Healthy families have stability because they are organized, with clear responsibilities and guidelines that are consistent and predictable. In America we value freedom, but freedom is not the complete absence of restraint. We gain freedom through commitment, discipline, and self-control. The pianist who plays with ease and dexterity can do this because he or she has spent hours in disciplined practice. In a similar way, healthy families have a sense of freedom because they have established some guidelines for living.

This is no plea for greater rigidity or for families to be run like tightly disciplined armies. But when roles are not clear, duties are not recognized, discipline is nonexistent, and structure is lacking, the family members live without stability or freedom and in the midst of confusion and uncertainty.

5. Be Flexible

Whenever I travel, especially overseas, I remind myself that "the name of the game is flexibility; if I can't be a flexible traveler, I should stay home." I have watched a lot of frustrated travelers in airports who don't share my attitude. Flexible people cope better.

Recently I was on an airplane traveling from the West Coast to Chicago. I was seated on the aisle in the middle section of a wide-body plane. At the other end of the row was a young mother with an eighteen-month-old daughter who screamed for most of the four-hour trip. I admit that I thought of moving to another seat. I had a briefcase full of work to do and was looking forward to some quiet time on the cross-country flight. Why, I wondered, was I sitting next to this incorrigible kid whose actions were impossible to ignore?

About an hour before we landed, I noticed that the mother was crying. "Please be quiet," she begged her daughter. "Please don't disturb all these people anymore."

I unbuckled my seat belt and slid across the empty seats toward the drama that was taking place at the other end of the row.

"I asked the doctor for some medicine to make her fall asleep, but it isn't working," the mother sobbed as she expressed her frustration. Surprisingly, the child had grown quiet, and the three of us talked while the plane landed. The mother and child were on the first leg of a journey to Germany, where the woman's husband was stationed in the army.

I reminded the woman that once we were swallowed up by the crowds in the airport, no one would give her any more dirty looks, and everyone would forget how her child had acted. A man, who to that point had been sitting quietly in the seat in front of the woman, turned around, told us that he also had a young child, and gave the woman a word of encouragement. I think she felt better when she walked into the airport. I know I felt better. My work hadn't been done, but I sensed that maybe I had helped this woman, in a small way, to be a little more relaxed as she prepared for the transatlantic part of her trip.

We've all known frustrated family members who can't handle stress or adjust when they have to change or master the transitions that come as kids grow up and everybody gets older. Healthy families are able to adapt, even when they encounter crises, conflicts, and unanticipated demands for change.

6. Make Good Communication a Priority

It probably isn't true that every family book in existence mentions the importance of communication, but most do. This is because bad communication creates incredible problems while good communication lets us deal effectively with a multitude of potentially troubling issues. Effective communication involves honesty without hostility—speaking the truth as we see it in a spirit of love, without put-downs or other conflict-arousing language. Healthy families express a willingness to understand and to let others know what we feel. Family members recognize that everyone should have the opportunity to be heard and to hear, and they determine to resolve dissension and deal with issues, even when they would prefer to bury antagonisms, deny the hurts, ignore the friction, or withdraw when things get tense.

This is difficult to do, especially when some family members want good communication but others don't. In healthy families, everybody learns to communicate openly and with mutual consideration.

7. Build Your Resources

Someone has suggested that successful family counseling rests as much on the resources of the family as on the expertise of the therapist. It can be a tough assignment for a counselor to turn unhealthy families into healthy ones when there is poverty, unemployment, isolation from others, little in the way of support, and not much interest in the help that comes from God.

I have several friends who have been in prison and who have told me about the difficulties of staying free after their release. Many have no money, no jobs, no good place to live, no family support, no faith, no job skills, no real ability to handle stress, and no friends, except the friends with whom they got into the trouble that led to their time behind bars. It isn't surprising that most of those who get released soon end up back in jail. Almost without exception, the people who stay out are those who have support, encouragement, financial help, and other resources to help them get back on their feet.

You don't have to be rich to have a good family, but the healthiest families have enough financial resources to meet their basic needs, have a supportive network of friends and relatives, and sense that they are part of a community—including a church community—where they find security, acceptance, and other "human resources."

8. *Know What You Believe*
In her academic language, Dr. Walsh writes that healthy families have a "shared belief system that enables mutual trust, problem mastery, connectedness with past and future generations, ethical values, and concern for the larger human community."[18] Much simpler is the old slogan that used to dot billboards and appear on bumper stickers: The family that prays together stays together.

It is true, of course, that some religious couples live in misery and conflict but stay together because they're afraid of God's displeasure or rejection from their church friends. Psychiatrist David Larson was aware of this possibility as he pored through dozens of research reports and articles. He concluded that the scientific findings were overwhelming and consistent: Religious commitment is positively associated with maintaining a marriage. The higher the commitment, the more satisfying is the marriage, the healthier are the people in the family, and the better is everyone's mental health.[19] Families are healthier when family members are religiously committed.

At Home in a Heartless World
An Australian friend of mine recently wrote about the state of the family in his country. He quoted Marx's faulty idea that the family was "antiquated" and destined to vanish along with capitalism. My friend described a seventeen-year-old who thought that his

home was not much different from a gas station or a garage—a place to refuel or park yourself at night. In contrast to this attitude, a poll found that 70 percent of Australians report that the family gives them their greatest satisfaction. Despite these different perspectives, my friend concluded that the family is one place where we can be "at home in a heartless world."[20]

That's not true of all families. Some homes are places shaken by violence and abuse, crumbling because of parental neglect and failure, undermined by conflict, or faced with ongoing groundswells of abuse, insensitivity, and marital infidelity. But families need not collapse. They can be built to withstand the shock waves that could undermine family stability. Even when family members experience trauma and tension, they can regroup, rebound, and rebuild marriages and families that are firm, balanced, and stable. Tony's family is an example.

TONY

Tony was a workaholic. He had all the characteristics. He left for work early in the morning and stayed late at night. He worked on Saturdays and usually pulled work from his briefcase after church on Sundays. At the office, he skipped coffee breaks with his co-workers, often "grabbed a sandwich" for lunch, and ate at his desk. His work was invigorating, sometimes even exciting, and often he would feel a surge of enthusiasm when he tackled the challenges in his fast-paced life.

Tony was on the way up in the corporate world. That was his goal, and everybody knew it. He was bright, articulate, eager, and hardworking. He was also determined to overcome any obstacles that might block the progress of his career. When annoying physical symptoms began to interfere with his work, he made an appointment to see a doctor to "get things taken care of right away."

At age thirty-three, Tony should have been in the best of health, but he was bothered by persisting pains in his neck and chest. Sometimes he felt light-headed, and his hands would get cold for no apparent reason. He had trouble sleeping and admitted that he struggled with waves of anxiety that pushed him to work harder and appeared to make his physical symptoms worse. At times he had trouble concentrating, and despite the vigorous lifestyle that everyone could see, he felt drained of energy and unable to enjoy much of life—sometimes not even his work.

At the physician's request, Tony took a number of medical tests, but the results all gave the same message: The physical symptoms did not have a biological cause. Tony's body was working fine, but the severe stresses connected with his hectic lifestyle were taking their toll and triggering the pains and illnesses. The doctor recommended that Tony see a counselor.

Away from his hyperactive work environment, seated in the relaxed atmosphere of the counselor's office, Tony talked about his life and family. He had been raised on a farm in Montana, one of six children who learned early about hard work, difficult circumstances, and financial stress. When his father died, Tony was only thirteen, but he became the family caretaker and felt responsible for the whole family. Living in a home in which emotions were not expressed, the young man kept his grief, insecurities, worries, and other feelings locked inside. When an older brother took advantage of him sexually, Tony felt angry, violated, and shocked, but he didn't tell anyone. When his mother married a "harsh and distant" stepfather who was far different from Tony's "loving and kind" natural father, the family held together, but the teenager felt that life in his home was continually disruptive, tense, and difficult.

By the time Tony reached adulthood, he had experienced many of the losses, childhood stresses, adolescent struggles, and family shocks that have sent others into lives of rebellion or substance abuse. Instead, Tony went to college, worked hard, got his degree, found a wife, and became the father of two children. "I love my family dearly," he told the counselor. "I want to provide for them financially so they won't experience the struggles I faced." But after eight years of marriage, Tony's workaholic lifestyle had left his family emotionally empty, struggling to survive in a home where they felt abandoned by the man of the house, who was off building a career.

With the counselor's help, Tony began to look carefully at each piece of his life. He admitted that his stimulating job was also very stressful. The company for which he worked was driven by competition. Workers competed so fiercely with one another that they felt like enemies, each pushing and driving to stay alive and on the track for promotion. Tony was not the only one who skipped lunch or worked ten- to sixteen-hour days, but he was so insecure and anxious to succeed that he had begun to mistrust all of his co-workers. He spent less and less time with them, so they in turn pulled away from him, didn't give him much support or encouragement, and began to think that he was some kind of hermit—self-centered, paranoid, and weird.

It is easy to imagine how all of this was affecting Tony's wife and children. They felt forsaken, neglected, and unimportant, despite Tony's insistence that he was working hard to provide for their security. His wife felt angry, unappreciated, and unloved. She had begun to have physical problems, was becoming careless in her appearance, and felt resentful because all the duties of parenting had fallen on her shoulders. Tony and his wife had no time for communication, real intimacy, and relaxation. Sex had become routine and rushed. Life in general was the same.

In the midst of all this, the family kept going to church, but their religious faith did little to alleviate the stress or make things better. Tony was active on several church committees, but he served out of a sense of obligation. He resented the demands of these responsibilities and felt that they were adding more stress to his life and pulling him away from his work and career.

Without thinking, Tony had developed a lifestyle that allowed his work to shape his religion, dominate his life, and create a home that was very much like the sad and difficult home in which he had been raised. The young farm boy—who had lived in a family filled with disruption, tension, and difficulties—had created a home like that for his own children.

The young man who had lost his loving and kind natural father and had endured the treatment of a harsh and distant stepfather, had become a sometimes harsh and distant father himself. The man whose own father had died at a young age was building a home where his own children felt that they too had lost a father, not to death but to the incessant demands of work.

Having grown up in a home in which emotions were not expressed outwardly, Tony created a similar home for his children. His behavior resulted in a home with lots of insecurities but not much love, a home in which feelings of anger, loneliness, and abandonment were squelched. Unless something was done to bring change, it seemed inevitable that someday the festering feelings would erupt like a volcano, spewing resentment and rocking the house that Tony was too busy to build on a firm foundation of father love and attention. But Tony's life changed. It was nothing dramatic; there were no life-threatening crises or spectacular encounters with God. The change was much slower and more routine.

With the help of his counselor and the support of his wife, Tony began to see his life in a different perspective. He recognized that his fast-paced lifestyle could be leading not to success and acclaim but to self-destruction and the loss of everything he was working so hard to attain. He realized that his physical symptoms probably were warning signs that more serious trouble was ahead if he didn't slow down. He was shocked to realize that he was creating for his children an environment that was as unhealthy and difficult as the home in which he had grown up. Tony's wife wanted him to enjoy and succeed in his work, but she was not looking for wealth. She wanted a less-pressured husband who cared about his family, showed that he loved and respected his wife, and once again felt the joy that had been drained away by the demands of his self-imposed work-dominated lifestyle.

One day, the counselor asked Tony what he would really like for his life. Even Tony was surprised at the diversified list that came to mind as he answered the question: less pressure from work, regular dates with his wife, a night or two every week with the family, more interaction with his colleagues at work, regular times alone with God, time for reading the Bible, fewer duties at his church, an exercise program, the development of new friendships, and the freedom to develop his gifts or abilities without always having to succeed and perform.

These became Tony's goals, and he worked to reach them with his characteristic dedication and enthusiasm, taking small but sometimes painful steps. He continued to work hard at his job, but he courageously reduced his pace of activity, cultivated new relationships, and became a key employee advocate within his company. He made time to be with his family and glowed with pleasure on the day when his wife told the counselor that she and her husband were a team again. Despite resistance from a few of the leaders, Tony resigned from some of his church responsibilities. He began to see God and the church in new ways and experienced a revival of interest in spiritual things. As his stress lessened, the physical symptoms faded and disappeared.

Does Tony's story sound too good to be true? His life and family are much better than they were, and things are going well. Never mind that they have struggles as every other family does. Never mind that Tony worries about reverting to his old work patterns and is fearful that he might once again ignore his family, forget the advice of his counselor, and get back on the workaholic treadmill. When he agreed to let his story be included in this book, Tony asked that we not use his real name and that we change a few minor details to protect the privacy of his family. But like everyone else in these pages, Tony is a real person with a story that is true.

Many of us know people like Tony, people whose backgrounds, insecurities, past decisions, and personalities have combined to produce addictive, potentially self-destructive lifestyles. Many of these people are active in their churches and communities but are addicted to work and success, controlled by their lusts and impulses, frustrated by their failures or tired marriages, caught in constant worries about finances, or struggling with insecurities that seem to kill all hope of family joy and stability.

Tony may look like an exception, a rare case of a man whose life and family turned around and began moving in positive directions. But there are others, maybe millions, who have made similar lifestyle changes—often with the help of sensitive counselors, supportive friends, and a loving God.

6

MARRIAGE AND THE FAMILY

I HAVE a lot of friends who are single; you probably do too. Most of these people will get married, but some are content to stay single. Many realize that marriage problems are common, that marriage seems to be getting less popular, and that many people approach marriage nervously.[1] Often these people look at marriage with understandable caution. They have heard the old cliché that it is better to be single and wish you were married than to be married and wish you were single. Thousands have seen their parents go through divorce, and they don't want to experience similar pain in their own lives.

It is a fact, however, that most adults get married and that people whose marriages end in divorce or the death of a spouse tend to get married again. Of course, God allows some to remain single, and the Bible never implies that to be unmarried is to be second class.[2] But God created human beings in such a way that for most of us it is not good to be alone. According to the Bible, marriage is honorable.[3] According to a large pile of scientific articles, marriage is also good for your health and emotional well-being.

A professor at the UCLA School of Medicine (or maybe one of his students) once read 130 scientific studies that examined the link between marital status and "personal well-being." The professor, Robert H. Coombs, had noticed that "the media glamorize the single status implying that the unmarried are unencumbered with the problems that beset their married counterparts."[4] How-

101

ever, his research overwhelmingly and consistently pointed to the conclusion that married people are happier and experience less stress and emotional difficulties than their unmarried peers.

For example, consider these scientifically demonstrated conclusions:

- Studies consistently find more alcoholism and problem drinking among the unmarried than among the married.
- Records extending back to the nineteenth century show that the highest suicide rates occur among the divorced, followed by the widowed and the never married. The lowest rates are among the married. The closer the interpersonal ties, it seems, the less likelihood of suicide.
- Research shows that married people live longer than the unmarried, go to doctors less often, and make less use of other health-care services. "Virtually every study of mortality and marital status shows the unmarried of both sexes have higher death rates, whether by accident, disease, or self-inflicted wounds."
- Overall, married people are healthiest. The divorced and separated have the highest rates of acute and chronic conditions that limit their social activities. When married people get sick, they recover faster and more completely than single people do.
- Schizophrenia and other forms of mental illness are more common among the unmarried, and studies of mental-hospital admissions show that the highest rates are consistently found among the divorced, followed by the widowed, single, and married (who have the lowest rates).
- When people are given self-report psychological tests that rate their happiness, married people consistently are happier and more content than those who are not married.

- Married people are better able to handle stress. One team of researchers looked at medical students, all of whom had been screened by psychological tests and personal interviews before entering medical school. At that time there were no differences between married and unmarried students. As the school pressures mounted, however, the unmarried students experienced greater stress. When compared to the married students, more of the unmarried withdrew from school or considered quitting, and the unmarried reported more anxiety. When they married, their sense of well-being improved significantly.

In reporting all of this information, Coombs pointed to some things that already may have occurred to you. These research findings are general conclusions and there are exceptions. Some unhappily married people, for example, live lives that are so difficult that they have the highest (instead of the lowest) levels of stress, anxiety, misery, physical illness, and emotional pathology.

Marriage also seems to benefit men and women a little differently. In general, men benefit more than women, probably because women more often find themselves in the caregiver's role, giving support and emotional encouragement to husbands who receive but do not always give back. Married women who join their husbands in the workforce also find themselves under more stress than men. It was a male who observed—correctly, I believe—that "after a day at work, the typical husband still expects her to do a lion's share of the household tasks and to provide other services. Thus, she finds herself with two jobs (employee and supportive spouse) while her husband has only one (employee)."[5] It isn't surprising that working wives often feel especially tired. I would hope that this is changing as men and women in two-career homes share more of the household chores.

Based on his findings about the benefits of marriage, Coombs sounded sad when he wrote that the "therapeutic benefits of marriage remain relatively unrecognized by most youths, the media, and some helping professionals who, preoccupied with accelerating divorce rates and variant family forms, question the value of marriage in contemporary society."[6] Instead, we need to be teaching "that it is in each person's own best interests to establish and maintain a durable relationship with an emotionally supportive spouse. A lack of this resource is a mental health deficit."[7]

None of these findings will surprise Christians. In the beginning, God said that for best results, a man and woman should marry and remain with each other faithfully, for life. Now we see more and more scientific backing to show what God knew all the time.

What Do We Need in Marriage?

Christian counselor Willard F. Harley, Jr., believes that the best way to keep a marriage happy and stable is for spouses to meet each other's needs. When any of the spouses' basic needs are not met, the couple feels a vacuum that begs to be filled. When needs aren't being met within the marriage, one or both of the spouses might sense a powerful temptation to fill that need with someone outside the marriage.[8]

Based on his research and over twenty years of counseling experience, Harley concluded that the basic needs of men are sexual fulfillment, recreational companionship, an attractive spouse, domestic support (such as a well-maintained, peaceful home), and admiration—in that order of importance. Women's basic needs are a little different: affection, conversation, honesty and openness, financial support (and a sense of security), and the husband's commitment to the family.

Since the counselor published this list, I suspect he has been criticized by people who disagree or who think all of this is sexist. But we need to keep the list in perspective. Consider, for example, the man's need for sexual fulfillment and the woman's need for affection. This doesn't mean that men don't want affection—to be held, talked to lovingly, and comforted—or that women don't like sex. Psychologist Kevin Leman writes, "When a man shows a woman the right kind of affection, it prepares her to enjoy tremendous sex. Many women can enjoy sex to a higher degree than men."[9]

MYTHS ABOUT AFFAIRS

Henry Virkler, Ph.D.
Professor of Psychology, Liberty University
Author of *Broken Promises: Understanding, Healing and Preventing Affairs in Christian Marriages*

Several myths about affairs sometimes make Christians more vulnerable than they need to be. One is the belief that *a strong personal faith in Christ inoculates a person against an affair.* While a strong personal faith in Christ may reduce to some degree the likelihood of an affair, the inoculation is far from 100 percent effective. There are probably several reasons why sincere, committed believers sometimes fall.

First, affairs happen in large part because we still are human beings. We don't cease to experience normal human emotions, needs, and desires simply because we are believers. If our emotional needs are not met in marriage, we will be attracted when someone outside our marriage begins to meet those needs.

Second, most affairs develop very gradually, usually over several months or even years. Because they develop so gradually, we may not be aware of the changes they are producing inside us.

Third, many inner dynamics that move a person toward an affair happen at an *unconscious* level. Thus they bypass our *consciously held* biblical values and commitments. Many Christians, by the time they consciously realize they are attracted to someone outside their marriage, experience the intensity of their feelings more strongly than the biblical convictions they once held so sincerely.

Fourth, never forget that we are in a spiritual battle. Satan is determined to destroy our happiness and testimony for Christ, and he will use any means at his disposal. He knows that one of the most devastating ways he can seriously damage our testimony, our happiness, and our family's happiness and security is to tempt us into an affair.

Thus, as believers we must always invest energy to keep our marriages strong and fulfilling and guard against relationships or temptation-producing environments that Satan could use to entrap us. It is good to remember the words of Ellen Williams: "If you are thinking to yourself, an affair could never happen to me, you are in trouble. To believe that we are immune leaves us wide open and unprotected." ⚓

Harley's list suggests that couples have better marriages when they seek to understand and meet each other's needs. If a marriage no longer meets both spouses' needs, couples tend to drift apart, sometimes living in the same home and sleeping in the same bed but isolated emotionally from one another.

According to Dennis Rainey, who directs an international program for strengthening family life, isolation is Satan's chief strategy for destroying marriage. Isolation results from the choices couples make. If we make the right choices and are sensitive to the needs of our spouses, then we experience love, warmth, security, intimacy, and a sense of oneness in marriage. If we make the wrong choices and ignore the needs of our spouses, then we "will know the quiet desperation of living together but never really touching one another deeply." Marriages like these may be intact and may appear to be stable, but isolation has drained them of their strength.[10]

What prevents a couple from meeting each other's needs so that their sense of oneness fades and they begin to feel isolated? For some people busyness and sheer exhaustion leave no time for intimate communication and time together. Others may be unwilling to share feelings and fears. Sometimes the couple would like to be close, but one or both of them are afraid, still carrying memories of painful childhood experiences in the families where they grew up. As a result, their lives go in different directions, and their marriages are never healthy.

What Makes a Healthy Marriage?
I have a friend who thinks that God likes to send surprises. Sometimes he leads us to places where we never intended to go, and he often uses the most unlikely people to accomplish his purposes.

The Promise Keepers movement is an example. It began in 1990, when a Colorado University football coach led a seminar of seventy-one men who committed themselves to God, to other men, to their families and churches, and to influencing the world. Nobody would have predicted that this gathering would explode into one of God's big surprises.

FIVE SECRETS OF A HAPPY MARRIAGE

1. Healthy couples have a clearly defined menu of expectations for their lives and their relationship.
2. Healthy couples understand and practice meaningful communication at five levels:
   a. The safest level of brief comments and clichés (such as "Have a good day!")
   b. The fact level of sharing information ("The radio says there will be rain tonight," or "The telephone bill is due tomorrow.")
   c. The opinion-sharing level ("I didn't like what you said yesterday.")
   d. The level of sharing and understanding feelings ("I'm scared that I'll fail" or "I'm really excited about the meeting next week.")
   e. The fifth and most intimate level of revealing our needs ("I'm so frustrated with my job and want so much to change" or "I'd really like to have sex tonight.")
3. Healthy couples are associated with a small, healthy support group to give friendship and accountability. In a healthy group each person feels the freedom, safety, love, and commitment to think out loud.
4. Healthy couples are aware of unhealthy or offensive behavior stemming from their heritage and backgrounds.
5. Healthy couples have a vibrant relationship with Jesus Christ. They have entered a relationship with him and depend on him as their primary source of abundant life.

Adapted from Gary Smalley, "Five Secrets of a Happy Marriage," *Seven Promises of a Promise Keeper* (Colorado Springs: Focus on the Family, 1994).

Three years later, more than fifty thousand men sat in a silent, pitch-black stadium and watched a single candle burn. Then it lit another. Each of those lit others, and soon the stadium was aglow with tiny flames, symbolizing the speed and impact that men can make as "promise keepers," whom God can use to bring light to the world. Even as these words are being written, men from all over America and the world are traveling to one of the Promise Keepers conferences that this year will bring tens of thousands of men to stadiums around the country. And the movement grows, calling men to commit themselves to integrity, sexual purity, racial reconciliation, and spiritual leadership. Promise keepers also pledge themselves to "building strong marriages and families through love, protection, and biblical values."

How can marriages like this be built? According to Gary Smalley, president of Today's Family, healthy couples demonstrate five qualities, which are summarized in the list on the previous page.

You won't be surprised to learn that these attributes are consistent with the conclusions of researchers who looked for the traits that characterize stable, enduring marriages. At the University of Colorado, for example, David L. Fenell designed a survey that was completed by 147 couples who had been married only once and whose marriages had lasted for more than twenty years. The surveyed husbands and wives were asked to choose characteristics that were most important to their marriages. These are listed below in their order of importance, based on the number of times each was mentioned.

THE TEN MOST IMPORTANT CHARACTERISTICS CONTRIBUTING TO LONG-TERM MARRIAGES

1. A lifelong commitment to your marriage
2. Loyalty and faithfulness to your spouse, especially when times are tough
3. Strong moral values that you both share
4. Respect for your spouse as your best friend
5. A commitment to sexual fidelity
6. The desire to be a good parent
7. Faith in God and a strong religious commitment that you want to give to your children
8. Wanting to please and support your spouse
9. Trying to be a good companion to your spouse
10. A willingness to forgive and to be forgiven

Adapted from David L. Fenell, "Characteristics of Long-Term First Marriages," *Journal of Mental Health Counseling* 15, no. 4 (October 1993): 446–60.

When Marriages Unravel

Brad was an imposing figure—six foot three, 240 pounds, a massive build, with a bushy beard and booming voice to match. Not quite forty years old, his presence seemed to fill the room when he rose to meet the counselor whom he reluctantly had agreed to see. Clad in cowboy boots, blue jeans, and open shirt,

Brad looked like a tough Harley-Davidson rider who could take on the world and overwhelm or intimidate any counselor who would dare to talk about any "huggy-feely-touchy" counseling issues.

When Brad entered the office and dropped his massive frame into the overstuffed chair, his bravado evaporated. Clearly he was hurting, and his powerful voice soon gave way to anguished sobbing as he poured out his story.

Brad was a biker, a loner of sorts. When he was younger, he had traveled around the country, working at odd jobs and never staying too long in any place. One day he dropped into a roadside cafe where he met the manager. Leanne was young, petite, pretty, blonde, and bored. She and Brad hit it off immediately. He appeared to be the strong, commanding type of masculine hero she had been looking for, someone who could meet her needs for fun and excitement. She, in turn, could give him companionship and sex. They decided to live together and take every opportunity to travel the country, looking for thrills and adventure. Eventually they even got married.

At first everything went well, but soon Leanne began to feel mistreated, taken for granted, and neither respected nor appreciated. Dependent, passive, easily intimidated, and in need of continual reassurance, she was overwhelmed by Brad's dominant personality. He was crass, self-centered, and too friendly with other women. She felt unloved, misunderstood, and increasingly depressed. "I got to the point where I hit rock bottom," she told her counselor later. "I couldn't move. I was paralyzed. I hated myself, hated my life, and was filled with anger and bitterness."

In the early years, Brad had used Leanne as his showcase: a beautiful, dainty little kitten whom he could parade before his friends and say, "That's *my wife.*" He didn't give much indication that he cared for her or was interested in her needs. Of course, she hated this indignity and verbal abuse. She wanted a partner; he wanted a playmate. She wanted respect and affection; he wanted someone who could be used to meet his needs at his bidding. No wonder Leanne resisted. She would have walked out if she had not been afraid of how Brad would react.

Eventually Leanne was able to get and hold a job where she got both a paycheck and opportunities to meet people who were gentle, understanding, and supportive. She and Brad shared a deep love for the little girl who had come into their lives, but clearly they were going in different directions. They hated their relationship, argued constantly, and began to withdraw from each other. Leanne changed her lifestyle, much to Brad's annoyance. She began hiking, got involved with various activities, and met new friends, including some who were male.

Brad began to see that he was in danger of losing his wife and daughter. His dainty spouse was emerging as the stronger person in their marriage. Big, tough, powerful Brad was turning into a whimpering puppy. He cried every day, was inefficient in his job, overflowed with anger and frustration, and wasn't sure how to make things better. In the midst of these changes he had become a Christian. He really wanted to turn his life around, but he didn't know what to do.

When Leanne decided to leave for a week, Brad and their little daughter went to stay with his mother. To everyone's surprise Leanne and Brad missed one another, but Leanne was afraid to work at building their marriage. She'd been hurt more than once, and even now she's afraid to trust. She thinks that Brad is manipulating her, using his newfound faith as a tool to claim that he has changed so he can get her back. She doubts that they could develop true intimacy or that he would ever respect her as a person of worth.

In the months since Brad first entered the office of his Christian counselor, he has changed. Even Leanne agrees. He is growing in his Christian life. He is trying to love, to give, to understand his wife and child. But Leanne is still afraid, and everybody who knows about their past relationship can understand why. "It's sad," their counselor said recently. "If only she could trust again and take the risk, the relationship would grow, and she would find exactly what she is looking for."

All of us know people who struggle with their marriages. They fell in love for all the wrong reasons, failed to recognize that marriage takes time and effort, and still are learning that a good husband-wife relationship demands unending quantities of the self-sacrificing commitment that theologians call unconditional love. Unlike most of the case histories that appear in books about marriage, Brad and Leanne haven't solved all of their problems. Maybe they never will. Like maybe millions of others, they are working at building a better relationship, but they haven't arrived.

Seattle researcher John Gottman believes that enduring marriages are the result of spouses' ability to handle conflict in their marriage. "In pursuit of the truth about what tears a marriage apart or binds it together, I have found that much of the conventional wisdom—even among marital therapists—is either misguided or dead wrong. . . . If there's one lesson I've learned in my years of research into marital relationships—having interviewed and studied more than 200 couples over 20 years—it is that a lasting marriage results from a couple's ability to resolve the conflicts that are inevitable in any relationship. . . . I believe we grow in our relationships by reconciling our differences. That's how we become more loving and truly experience the fruits of marriage."[11]

Gottman identified three problem-solving styles in healthy marriages. If we understand these, we can keep our own marriages more stable and help others have healthy marriages as well.

I still remember the first time a couple came to me for counseling and had a big argument in my office. We hadn't been together for ten minutes when they started yelling at each other, largely oblivious of me. I was sure they would come to blows and kill each other, sending my career as a counselor down the drain before it even got started. I was a young graduate student, training to become a psychologist, and I was idealistic enough to think that I could be effective in healing all the sick and broken marriages that couples would bring through my door. It didn't take many weeks for me to conclude that shouting was the only way that some couples could get each other's attention and communicate.

Problem-Solving Styles

All couples must learn how to handle their conflicts, and according to Gottman's research at the University of Washington, most of us adopt one of three broad styles for dealing with conflict.

The *validating style* describes couples who listen to each other and are determined to make communication a priority. Sometimes they squabble, and one or both may withdraw for a while. But they don't let differences fester for long, and they rarely shout. Usually they have "talks" or "conferences" to air their perspectives and work out their differences until they reach a mutually satisfying conclusion.

The *volatile style,* as you might guess, is a more passionate and noisy approach. This describes couples who seem to thrive on skirmishes. They shout, interrupt each other, and don't spend much time listening. They tend to be independent people who see each other as equals, who freely express their feelings—both positive and negative—and who "fight on a grand scale and have an even grander time making up." Many of these people respect one another and often have very stable, long-lasting marriages that they are quick to label as happy.

The *conflict-avoiding style* can be illustrated by a young couple who enjoyed each other's company and fought very rarely. When tension arose, they agreed that jogging in different places was more helpful than talking things out or arguing. Couples like this agree to disagree, rarely confronting their differences head-on. They also can have healthy marriages, even though most experts would say that they are pushing problems aside and not facing their tensions.

The Seattle researchers concluded that marital health did not depend on which conflict-management style was chosen. More important in predicting marital stability was the extent to which couples had positive interactions, like smiling at each other, touching, laughing, or giving compliments. In all three conflict-management styles, people in stable marriages exchanged five positive interactions for every one that was negative. In contrast, couples who were heading for divorce had far too few affirming and positive contacts and a lot more emphasis on the negative.

Marriages That Endure

What keeps couples together? Two researchers at the University of Tennessee interviewed couples who had been married for thirty years or longer, and several "key characteristics of enduring marriages" emerged. These include commitment, communication, intimacy, and religious faith.[12]

Commitment

Several years ago, the well-known president of a respected Christian college announced to the faculty and board of directors that he was resigning. At a time when other Christian leaders were quitting in shame, some because they had been unfaithful to their wives, this college president left with honor because of his faithfulness. His wife had Alzheimer's disease and needed him to be close and available. So he gave up his position of influence and prominence, convinced that he had a greater duty to be committed to his marriage.

What would you do in a similar situation? When God initiated marriage, he instructed couples to detach from their parents, be united with one another, and become "one flesh." He knew that some marriages would fall apart, but he let it be known that he hates divorce and had intended marriage to be a permanent commitment—like Christ's relationship with the church.[13]

Commitment is a willingness and determination to stick together, to make the relationship work. Committed people are loyal to one another. They build trust in each other by being honest and demonstrating consistent integrity. These committed marriage partners expect to stay together, work to resolve differences, survive the stresses that come to every marriage, and surmount the pressures that might tempt them to separate. One research study showed that marriages with a high level of commitment have fewer problems than others. Couples with a weak commitment or couples whose commitment becomes weak more often choose to leave when problems arise.[14] In working with problem-filled marriages, every counselor knows that success is more likely when the couple is dedicated to staying together, getting beyond their problems, and building a better relationship.

Communication

When couples go for marriage counseling, the most common complaint is poor communication.[15] When couples are getting along well, they often mention the strength of their communication. That won't surprise anybody, but research has shed more light on what makes marital communication bad and what makes it good.

Good communication more consistently occurs when there is mutual respect. It involves sharing feelings as well as thoughts, discussing problems together, and listening to each other's point of view while genuinely trying to understand. Good communicators don't try to manipulate or intimidate each other, don't ignore their differences, and don't use loaded phrases like "you always" or "you never." And good communicators who have good marriages are willing to forgive and be forgiven.

Negative messages—saying things that the other person won't want to hear—can be bad or good, depending on the couple. When a husband and wife have a good marriage, they learn from negative communications, and their relationship is strengthened as a result. But if a couple is having marital problems, the negative communications tend to make things worse, often starting arguments and leading to further discord.[16]

All of this is complicated further if one or both of the partners is depressed. Everybody has times of being down emotionally, so we are somewhat aware of how depression derails communication. Depressed people lack the energy or desire to communicate accurately, give the impression that they're uninterested in what a spouse or other person might be trying to say, focus attention on themselves, and tend to respond negatively to any criticism or unwelcome news.

Depression, of course, isn't the only obstacle to good communication. Sometimes gender is a culprit. Numerous investigators and counselors—and thousands of wives—have noted the tendency of many husbands to withdraw when problems need to be discussed. Women, it seems, are more willing to deal with problems head-on.

The longer Julie and I are married, the more we seem able to communicate with a gesture, facial expression, tone of voice, or

HELPING HURTING
MARRIAGES

EVERETT L. WORTHINGTON, JR., PH.D.
Professor of Psychology
Virginia Commonwealth University
Author of *Marriage Counseling* and
I Care about Marriage

Chances are that at some time a close friend will seek your help with a marital or family difficulty. Such problems are most frequently presented to pastors and professional therapists. Even before people consult a counselor about family trouble, though, they usually talk to a friend.

If you're consulted, you may feel swept into a swirling vortex of emotion and conflict. Your inadequacies may leave you gasping. Can you help?

Psychological research reveals important findings:

- Supportive, caring friends counsel as effectively as do professionals, except when the troubled people are experiencing severe problems.
- If you want to be a people helper, you'll probably have plenty of opportunity. Most pastors and other counselors are already overcommitted, so they'll increasingly enlist sensitive and motivated laypeople to help the needy.

You can help in three ways:

1. Promote good marriages and families through providing information, resources, or enrichment programs.
2. Prevent marital or family problems through educational programs and church-based groups.
3. Counsel troubled people one-on-one.

These facts point to a common theme. If we try to help each other be better disciples of Jesus Christ, we can bless each other and live out the pattern of discipleship that God has provided within the Bible.

Research shows that faith produces positive results in marriages and families. We trust in Jesus, not psychology, to provide health and healing for families. But psychological research has provided some useful ideas and mechanisms through which the Lord works. ◢◤

other nonverbal cue. This does not replace the importance of verbal communication, but our experience points to the fact that individuals and couples often develop different styles or ways of communicating. Sometimes the husband's way of communicating is different from his wife's communication style.

Probably you have heard of the couple who was having problems because the husband never said he loved his wife, and she felt he wasn't careful with their money. One day, after carefully saving some funds, he surprised his wife by purchasing the clothes dryer she had long wanted. He meant it as a way of saying "I love you." She perceived it as another example of the way he wasted their money. She wanted to hear the *words* "I love you." He tried to communicate the same message but with a gift. A counselor pointed out that they were trying to say "I love you" but in two different ways.

Swiss physician and counselor Paul Tournier, who wrote many books about relationships, had a great influence on me at one time in my career. One day we had a discussion about his marriage. "Nellie and I get along very well because we don't have any secrets," he said. The couple valued honesty, and when Nellie died a few days before their fiftieth anniversary, the old doctor told me that grief was easier because their marriage had no undiscussed or unresolved issues. The Tourniers had learned how to communicate.

Intimacy
Intimacy is hard to define. It can refer to sexual closeness, but in marriage it means a lot more. Intimacy is a connectedness that a couple feels, an ongoing ability to share interests, activities, hopes for the future, joys, values, feelings, pains, mutual trust, openness, and sexual affection. Intimacy implies that a couple feels togetherness. They are attuned to one another, pulling in the same direction, sharing similar values, willing to join as partners in working for goals they both consider to be worthwhile.

Intimate couples do not lose their unique characteristics and merge their personalities into one. Instead, they each maintain at least some interests and activities that are separate, and they appreciate what is unique about each other. They enjoy spending time together and most often are each other's best friend. At some time, all couples share periods of adversity and stress, but they go through these together and often conclude that they have grown closer as a result.

Intimacy in marriage is similar to what Larry Crabb has described as *oneness.*[17] Ideally, it is a relationship in which the husband and wife turn to Christ as two individual people who depend on *him* to meet their needs, including their needs for security and significance. As a couple, however, they turn to each other in mutual commitment to a partnership that allows them to develop their unique gifts but draws them together in a sense of oneness.

It has been said that a person's last thoughts usually express the passion of his or her life. When Jesus was praying a few hours before the Crucifixion, his overarching concern was not that his followers would be taken out of the world but that they would be protected from Satan and that they would experience oneness.[18]

Centuries earlier, when God created Adam and Eve, they were formed into a little community of two people who were not identical (one was male, the other was female) but who "became one flesh." Almost immediately, Satan came on the scene, sowing deception and causing rifts not only between the husband and wife but also between the couple and God. Throughout the Bible we see subsequent generations of human beings trying to come together and the forces of evil tearing them apart.

Then came Jesus Christ, God's Son, to bring a message of truth in contrast to the devil's lies, to shed his blood to pay for the sins of the world, and to reconcile human beings to God the Father. Jesus didn't force it, but he invited anyone to believe in him and to be reconciled to God forever.[19] He established the church as a body of believers, ideally bound together in a community of oneness. On the night before he died, Jesus prayed that future generations of believers would be one.[20] The church is to be an example of this oneness, and the relationship between a husband and wife is to be the most intimate model of Christ's relationship with his church.[21]

Religious Faith

All of this theology gets us to the importance of religious faith. In some marriages the husband and wife have such conflicting beliefs that religious differences become a source of conflict. More often, faith pulls a couple together, giving them strength and comfort (especially in times of need), a purpose for living, a reason to keep building the marriage, and the social, emotional, and spiritual support that comes from involvement in a body of believers. "Our faith keeps us close," one husband told an interviewer. "How would we ever have raised our kids and built a good marriage without a faith in Christ and a conviction that he is alive, compassionate, powerful, and in control?"

As Christians, we do not believe that we are alone in this big universe, struggling with all our might to keep our lives from falling apart. We are sons and daughters of God himself, people in whom the Holy Spirit lives. He wants the freedom to control and mold our lives. When we stop resisting this idea and give him control, we experience increasing love, joy, peace, patience, kindness, goodness, faithfulness, gentleness, and self-control.[22] These spiritual traits don't come immediately, like a bolt of lightning from the sky. But they grow and develop, like healthy emerging plants. As they mature, every one of these characteristics can make our lives more fulfilling and enable us to build better marriages.

Small Groups Can Strengthen Marriages

In addition to commitment, communication, intimacy, and religious faith, I would add one other ingredient for an enduring marriage: the involvement in small groups. At present, small groups are very popular. Every day, in North America alone, several million people meet with others in support groups, recovery groups, Bible-study groups, prayer groups, AA groups, accountability groups, writers groups, and a host of others. Experts differ about the ultimate effectiveness of this small group movement, but the people who meet together tend to be enthusiastic. Surely many would agree with Gary Smalley that marriages can be strengthened when couples are associated with a small, healthy support group.[23]

COUPLES MENTORING EACH OTHER

EDMUND CHAN, B.TH.
Pastor, Covenant Evangelical Free Church, Singapore

Mentoring. How often we apply it to our ministries and neglect it in our marriages. When a husband and wife commit to mutual mentoring, they not only enhance their personal growth, but they also strengthen their marriage. For those committed to such a pilgrimage, here are four principles for effective spouse-to-spouse mentoring.

1. *Establish a covenant for growth.* Early in our marriage, Ann and I established a mutual agreement to encourage each other to grow in the Lord. We want to be nourished and growing together. We started with a fresh dedication to the Lord. Then, we talked about some mutual goals in our common desire to establish a God-pleasing marriage.

2. *Cultivate trust.* Mentoring is not a technique; it is a relationship in which trust is foundational. The goal of mentoring is not to change one another but to help each other grow. Begin with mutual acceptance. Love each other unconditionally. Some couples may need to confess to each other and forgive each other for previous hurts. Build a mutual trust, desire the best for your spouse, then give permission for mutual accountability.

3. *Pray together.* The old adage is true: "Those who pray together stay together." Mutually agree not to allow prayer to be routine. Make it a time for honest soul-searching, sincere petition, and mutual ministry. Allow it to be a time to speak openly to the Lord about the wounds of our hearts, the cynicisms of our minds, the paralysis of our wills, and the overcrowding of our souls. Let the praying draw you closer to the Lord and thereby closer to each other.

4. *Make time.* Begin with a commitment to keeping the Sabbath principle. Allow one day in a week to rest, to affirm your faith, to appreciate your work, to assess your lives, and to adore your Master. Guard it as an important family time. Allow it to be a compass for the busyness of our lives, and let our spiritual disciplines overflow from that.

My parents were never in a support group, and their marriage lasted over fifty years. I can't imagine them meeting regularly with a group of three or four other couples to discuss their needs, pray for each other, talk about their problems, share their disappointments, and agree to be mutually accountable. But as I think about it, maybe their network of friends did for them what small groups do for couples today. In a generation or two past, when television was unknown and people were a lot less busy, they had time for sitting on the front porch on a summer night, chatting with friends or neighbors, discussing the affairs of the world, and giving each other the support, acceptance, and friendship that people in our society seek and often find in groups.

But without planning and a purpose for meeting, many people today wouldn't take the time to get together. That's true of me. I feel inner resistance every time Julie and I leave to go to our couples small-group meeting. I don't like to take the time, but almost always I come home refreshed and glad we went.

In these days when many churches are large and when congregations often have only one service each week, individuals and couples have a greater need to meet together in groups with other committed believers. It is there that we often find support, accountability, personal guidance, acceptance, a quiet time for prayer and Bible study, opportunity for reflection, safety, love, and help. Groups don't replace the importance of corporate worship in the larger congregation; groups supplement what the larger church is doing. However, groups aren't very helpful to people who don't take them seriously or who push them to a low order of importance. The best groups, including groups of couples, involve people who are willing to participate fully and who commit to meeting on a regular basis.

Making Marriage Work

They named their group Salt and Light, based on Matthew 5:13-16, and for three years I had the fun and challenge of being their teacher. Every week thirty-five or more young married couples gathered, eager for Bible study, for the chance to rub shoulders with other Christians, and for opportunities to discuss the challenges of their own lives.

This was not a typical cross section of society. We had several minority couples and three or four couples from overseas, but most were American and white. Almost all were career-conscious, college-graduate suburbanites committed to building marriages and families that would honor Christ and bring stability to the families they were in the process of building. Julie and I became their informal mentors, and like most teachers, we probably learned the most.

In spending time with these young couples, we learned again that it takes time and energy to build a solid marriage if it is to withstand the tremors of disappointment over infertility, the birth of a handicapped child, the death of an infant, or the distractions from insensitive in-laws. We watched as these couples struggled to balance their checkbooks, their careers, their spiritual lives, and the incessant demands of their young children. We concluded that excessive busyness was the biggest enemy of marriage, family life, and growth in maturity. These couples were committed to one another and committed to Christ, but many felt overwhelmed by the demands of their schedules, employers, church, and their own expectations. Their hyperactive lives tended to rob them of time for each other, and some privately admitted that they often felt too busy or tired for sex.

But most have survived and are growing. They are committed to their spouses and families and are determined to cope with the time commitments and pressures of busyness. They are willing to respect one another, accept personality differences, be flexible, and share their struggles. They want to live according to biblical teaching, to show mutual respect, and to love and remain faithful to their spouses. They accept some couples' decision to live out the traditional roles of homemaker mother and employed father, but they also approve if a couple reverses these roles (so that the father stays with the children and works out of the home while the mother goes off to her job) or if both determine to work on their careers and to share equally in child-rearing and homemaking duties. In brief, these people are committed and flexible. In these ways they are maturing in a changing world.

Like all of us, the couples in the Salt and Light class make mistakes and sometimes experience powerful family shocks and stresses. But most are good models for the children who will form their own families early in the next century. The couples we know are building marriages that will endure and experience fulfillment—even in a culture that is filled with confusion about sex and gender roles.

7

SEX, GENDER, AND
THE FAMILY

SOME issues are like hot potatoes; we don't like to touch them. They fire us up and sometimes burn us. We drop these issues because they are highly controversial and potentially explosive. They are issues like the sometimes passionate disagreements over women's roles, the discussion about whether there are innate differences between the sexes, extensive debates over abortion, the attitudes and activism of extreme feminists or gay protesters, and the fallout when a family member is involved in adultery, sexual abuse, or addiction to pornography.

All of these hot-potato issues relate to sex and to the fact that God made us male and female. Each of these issues has a profound impact on family life today.

Sex as God Intended—And What He Never Intended
Almost everybody knows the story of David and Bathsheba, how David's uncontrolled sexual fling destroyed Bathsheba's family and brought grief to both their lives. Less familiar is the passionate and tragic account of one of David's sons, a man named Amnon, whose violent rape of Tamar is told in 2 Samuel 13. Earlier in the Bible, we read about a group of sexually aroused men who pounded on Lot's door, demanding to have sex with some visitors who were staying overnight.[1]

Uncontrolled, self-centered sex is nothing new, and neither are the messages that come incessantly from all segments of our culture. Sexual fulfillment is the key to happiness, we are told.

Sex is purely recreational, a normal biological need that can be fulfilled in any way that is exciting and however we can get it—as long as it's "safe." Our culture often assumes that couples will sleep together before they get married, that single people will be sexually active, that most married people will not remain faithful, and that it would be unnatural to do otherwise.[2] Repeatedly we hear the message that abstinence is pretty much impossible, that marital sex is dull, tedious, and boring, but that sex outside of marriage is alluring, exotic, and exciting.

A college student recently described the attitudes of his campus friends, most of whom are agnostic or atheistic. They like to have intercourse because it gives them pleasure and fulfillment. Whereas a past generation of students searched for meaning and life purpose, many today look instead for ways to entertain themselves. Sex seems like a natural way to find enjoyment and diversion.

Throughout the culture there is evidence that most people still disapprove of extramarital sex, pornography, homosexuality, and even teenage intercourse. The rate of extramarital affairs has declined slightly, and men in particular are paying more attention to the emotional side of sex.[3] In a carefully controlled study that was hailed as the most sweeping survey of American sexual beliefs and practices, some of our earlier views about sex were challenged. Past surveys like the Kinsey report or the questionnaires sent to readers of *Playboy* and *Redbook* magazines questioned a narrow group of people who hardly represented the rest of the population and whose sexual practices were "weird and distorted." The more recent report found that monogamous couples have the most sex and are happiest with their sex lives, that homosexuality is much rarer than we have been led to expect, and that people who have been abused as children are more likely to have multiple partners and less likely to find sex fulfilling.[4]

Even if self-focused or deviant sex is less common than we might think, many people feel that the American attitude toward sex (anything except sex with children) still tends to be Just do it. Many value sexual experimentation and feel less guilty about sexual matters than might have been true of past generations.[5]

This sexual looseness is in dramatic contrast to sex as God intended. The culture's perspective deceives millions who eventually will discover that while sex can give moments of erotic ecstasy, sex apart from God's guidelines ultimately leads to emptiness, loneliness, brokenness, and rejection, often leaving a trail of disease and sometimes death.

It might have been easier for all of us if God had not made us male and female, but in his wisdom he created sex—including the sex organs and the nerve endings that let us feel intense physical pleasure. God declared that all of his creation was good, and that includes our sexuality. In the Garden, Adam and Eve were naked, and before their fall into sin, they had no reason for shame. The most obvious purpose of sex was procreation, which allows us to be fruitful and multiply. But sex also brings pleasure unmatched by any other experience. The Old Testament book Song of Songs describes the joys of sex in sometimes explicit detail and gives no indication that erotic sexuality is dirty or wrong.

Whenever the Bible talks positively about sex and sexual intercourse, however, it refers to married couples. Jesus spoke with approval about the permanence and "one flesh" nature of marriage. The apostle Paul wrote that marriage (not intercourse outside of marriage) is the desirable answer for the person who is struggling with sexual self-control. And when marriage occurs, the husband and wife are to give their bodies freely to each other and not hold back sexually.[6] This kind of sex is not a mere genital or biological act. It is an expression of the intimacy that God intended to characterize the permanent, all-embracing relationship of marriage.

Repeatedly the Bible warns against the enslaving influence of sexual behavior apart from marriage.[7] This is not because God wanted to spoil our fun and leave us standing in frustration, longing to be in bed with partners who don't care what he says. Of course, people can have sex without commitment, pregnancy, or disease. Many people "do it" and seem to get along just fine. But uncontrolled sex also leads to major social problems, including growing numbers of teenage pregnancies, the spread of AIDS and other sexually transmitted diseases, the increase of one-parent families, huge numbers of abortions, and both tension and breakdown within families. Educator Allan Bloom once wrote that sexual looseness teaches people about the erotic but somehow leaves them devoid of imagination, with few ideals, afraid of both isolation and detachment, and with no real ability to form lasting commitments.[8] Psalm 73 describes the tragic results of ignoring God's laws, and 1 Corinthians 6 suggests that the potential oneness that can come within marriage goes out the door when sexual immorality comes in.

Sex Gone Awry

Ronald Phipps was recently pictured in a newspaper article about kids who have kids. Seventeen years old and already the father of two children, Phipps told the newspaper that his sexual experiences had "started real early. Before I got taught about it, I was already doing it."[9]

Phipps has lots of company. While fewer teenagers are having babies now than teenagers did forty years ago, teen childbearing today is far more destabilizing and expensive, according to that newspaper series. The low-skill, high-wage jobs that a person could get to support a family have vanished—and so have many of the young fathers who count sexual experiences as a badge of masculinity but have no sense of responsibility or no employment to help support their children. Many of the more than 350,000 unmarried teenagers who become mothers every year are left to handle their babies without much help. More than half of these babies are fathered by males under the age of twenty. Even when these fathers want to take responsibility for their children, they have no parenting skills, no job skills that would lead to employment, and no mentors who could help them succeed.[10]

Teenage childbearing, most often apart from marriage, has become a cause and symptom of some of our greatest social ills: poverty, crime, welfare dependency, drug addiction, high dropout rates, and violence.[11] Sex among kids has spun out of control, and millions of people pay the consequences.

When President Bill Clinton visited Kramer Junior High School in Washington, D.C., a student asked a question that cut

HONESTY AND SEX EDUCATION

ESLY CARVALHO, M.A.
International Coordinator for
Eirene International
A Latin American Network of
Christian Counselors
Author *Mujer y Autoestima
(Women and Self-Esteem)*

"Mommy, can children get AIDS?"
I stopped cold in my tracks with
my daughter's question. I knew
bigger things lay ahead in this
conversation.

"Yes, honey, but only if their
mommy had it when they were
born. Why do you ask?"

"Well, the kids were talking
about it at school. Mommy, what
are homosexuals?"

I had guessed right. She went
on to ask even more questions:
"What are condoms?" (In Brazil,
where we live, they are called
"little shirts"—anyone can
imagine what that does to
children's minds.) "Where do you
put them? What if they fall off?"
She was only eight years old.

I was pleased and saddened
with this conversation. As a single
mother, I had struggled to create a
trusting relationship with my only
daughter. This conversation meant
I had succeeded so far: She came
to me with her hairy questions. I
felt sad, however, that children
had to know the starker facts of
life at a young age. Considering
that Brazil is the world's number-
two country in absolute numbers
of AIDS cases, reliable sex
information within a Christian
context had become, literally, a
matter of life and death.

Several principles had gone into
developing a trusting relationship
between my daughter and me.
These rules might be helpful for
others:

1. Always be honest. Tell the truth
   no matter how much you blush.
2. If your children have questions,
   give reliable, truthful, and
   appropriate information.
3. Rules are like promises: Try to
   have few of them, but keep
   them all.
4. Clarify boundaries and limits.
   Enforce what is off-limits.
5. Respect feelings: yours and
   theirs. We all have a right to our
   feelings, no matter how ludi-
   crous they may seem at the
   moment.
6. And when you blow it, confess
   it and ask for forgiveness.
   This helps keep all parents
   humble.

to the heart of our present debates about moral and social policy. "Since family life has been breaking down for the last thirty years," she asked, "what can my generation do to restore family values?"

The president hesitated and then gave this answer: "If you really want to rebuild the family, then people have to decide: I'm not going to have a baby until I'm married. I'm not going to bring a baby into the world I can't take care of. And I'm not going to turn around and walk away when I do it. I'm going to take responsibility for what I do. I wish there was some high-falutin' easy way to say it, but there isn't any way to turn this thing around except to turn it around."[12]

Mr. Clinton gave a good answer, even though he didn't mention the moral issue of abstaining from sexual intercourse before marriage.[13] He knows that teenage sex and births to unmarried young girls is not limited to poor inner-city kids. Within the past decade our society has seen a sharp increase in the number of educated, professional, Murphy Brown-type mothers who have sex without marriage, bear children, and raise them without spouses.[14] All around us we see evidences of sex gone awry, away from God's ideal and often with people taking little or no responsibility for their actions.

Sex without Responsibility

It probably attracted a lot of attention on the newsstands: the simple gold wedding band broken in two places, the solid black cover, the stark word *Infidelity,* and the interest-grabbing subtitle: "It may be in your genes." Inside the magazine, the *Time* editors devoted nine full pages to something known as evolutionary psychology. Its conclusion: "Lifelong monogamous devotion just isn't natural, and the modern environment makes it harder than ever."[15]

Most people already know that! We don't need a course in evolutionary psychology to know that living a moral life is a struggle that "consists largely of battling human nature." Keeping faithful to our spouses and restricting sexual intercourse to the privacy of marriage doesn't come naturally because human beings are not naturally inclined to be moral creatures.[16] The

Bible has been saying that for centuries. And most of us would agree with the *Time* writer's conclusion that "the first step to being moral is to realize how thoroughly we aren't."[17]

People who picked up the magazine hoping to find a biological reason for infidelity probably found what they wanted. But even the evolutionary psychologists agree that while sex without responsibility might seem natural, it tends, nevertheless, to destroy individuals, families, and especially young children. We all know of marriages and homes that have been torn apart by unfaithfulness. And we've seen what researchers now are able to demonstrate: parents who engage in "serial monogamy" (one marriage after another) more often abuse their kids—psychologically and physically—than parents who stay together.[18]

Someone has said that as long as there has been sexual desire, there has been infidelity. Affairs, adultery, infidelity, extramarital sex—all of these have been analyzed, explained away, often condemned, and sometimes encouraged by innumerable speakers and writers. Their conclusions may differ, but most people agree that infidelity can have many causes and that sexual affairs frequently bring a lot of hurt.

When asked the reasons why they were involved in adultery, a large group of people who had been involved in affairs replied that they were unfaithful because of their sexual frustration, curiosity, desire for revenge, boredom, need for acceptance and recognition, depression, urges for sex without intimacy, and escape. Affairs also come because some people are addicted to compulsive sex, to romance, or even to relationships. In a detailed description of how even Christians get hooked on sex, psychologist Grant Martin shows how some people get so caught up in adulterous behavior that they become like drug addicts—powerless to stop without help.

But even when adultery is addictive, sexual infidelity is a breaking of the emotional, spiritual, and physical bond between a couple. Dr. Martin writes, "Sexual unfaithfulness is a violation of God's commandments (Exodus 20:14; Matthew 5:27-28; 1 Corinthians 6:9). The consequences of concealed sin are an unprosperous life (Proverbs 28:13), separation from God (Isaiah 59:2), and spiritual death (Romans 5:12; 6:23).The risk of sexually transmitted disease, divorce, financial hardships, family separation, and emotional disturbances in children are additional potential results of marital affairs. Yet, in spite of these possibilities, perhaps fifty percent of the couples in our country engage in such activity."[19]

Most people who engage in sexual infidelity wish later that they hadn't made that choice.

Sex without Marriage

Woodstock '94 was a rain-soaked, twenty-fifth-anniversary reminder of the New York music festival that so dramatically defined the youth culture of the late sixties. Millions didn't buy into the countercultural values of the original Woodstock—hedonism, spontaneity, rebelliousness, "do your own thing" individualism—that spit in the face of middle-class beliefs of self-denial, orderliness, and respect for authority. But the self-centered morals and sexuality of that early baby-boom generation have permeated much of our culture. Sexual values and behaviors that are paraded so prominently in the media and accepted so readily by contemporary teenagers shock even modern parents who grew up thinking they were independent-minded liberals from the "Love Generation." Today, many teenagers sound a lot like their parents. They want sex without marriage, and they don't want parents or other adults to stifle their "lovemaking."

In the process of writing a book about adolescence, Patricia Hersch interviewed a lot of kids. She concluded that most children don't have many visible role models of adults who have committed, long-standing, intimate relationships. So it isn't surprising that for many adolescents, uncommitted sex is no big deal. "Kids today live in an environment where sex is an everyday thing between two people," one sixteen-year-old said. "They just think it is something to pass the time, or to have fun with, so let's do it."[20] What might have been hidden, taboo behavior in previous generations is now more open, more frequent, and more common even among younger kids. Many come home every day to empty houses where parents are gone, and couples have the time, opportunity, and sex-saturated media to show them, fairly explicitly, what they could do—and often end up doing.[21]

COHABITATION, THE CHRISTIAN, AND THE FAMILY

DAVID B. LARSON, M.D., AND SUSAN S. LARSON, M.A.T.
National Institute for Health Care Research

Want a sexually sizzling marriage that lasts? Then cultivate a Christian commitment and avoid the pitfall of living together before marriage.

Research studies show that women who regularly go to church and take their faith seriously are more satisfied with their marriages and sex lives than nonreligious women. Furthermore, studies show religiously committed women are more orgasmic—a stark contrast to the myth of the religious, frigid fuddy-duddies depicted by free-sex advocates.

Sex outside of marriage is hardly free, studies are showing. Although living together before marriage has become a culturally alluring concept, research documents that it has some serious side effects.

One study found that couples who cohabit—who live together without a marital commitment—abuse each other more severely and more often than either married couples or dating couples. Furthermore, cohabitation doubles the likelihood of later divorce if the couple does eventually marry.

Who might be more at risk for living together before marriage? Researchers found cohabitation rates are seven times higher among persons who seldom or never go to church compared to persons who frequently attend church. Parents' personal religious commitment and standards can also make an impact. If a mother frequently goes to church, her sons and daughters are only 50 percent as likely to have a live-in partner. By contrast, when mothers believe living together before marriage is acceptable, both sons and daughters are less likely to marry, and the chances of her daughter cohabitating with a boyfriend jumps 250 percent. Daughters whose mothers oppose cohabitation are much more likely to marry than to cohabit.

This research documents the fact that couples who attempt "trial marriages" can torpedo a potential lifelong marital commitment. No wonder Scripture gives clear mandates against premarital sex. A happier, sexually satisfying marriage is worth waiting for.

When teenagers get older, closer to the age of marriage, many of them live together as sexually active, unmarried adults in what has come to be known as *cohabitation*. Between 1970 and 1989, cohabitation jumped 740 percent; in the years between 1987 and 1989, it skyrocketed 1,892 percent among adults ages eighteen to twenty-five.[22]

It is worth noting that only 4 percent of the population over nineteen is living with someone of the opposite sex while not being married to that person. And most cohabitants think of living together as a prelude to marriage, a way to test out a potential spouse before tying the knot.[23]

The evidence suggests, however, that people who live together before marriage have an 80 percent greater likelihood of divorce when compared to people who did not cohabit before the wedding. A University of Wisconsin study found that married couples who cohabited have lower levels of overall marital satisfaction and lower commitments to marriage. People who lived together are less inclined to trust their spouses, more likely to have affairs, and often are convinced that they are not respected by their spouses after they do get married.[24]

Despite this, we have writers like the Harvard psychiatrist who recently proclaimed with confidence that "without the alternative of cohabitation, it is certain that divorce rates would be far higher than they are."[25] His tacit approval of sex between unmarried people ignores the growing evidence that sex without marriage, inside or apart from cohabitation, can have painful consequences that last long after the short-lived erotic thrills have faded.

Sex without Making Love
In popular jargon, sexual intercourse is called making love, but everybody knows that a lot of sex involves no love at all: compulsive masturbation, addiction to pornography, rape of any kind, sexual harassment, and forced sex within marriage. This abusive kind of sex hurts when it happens, and its effects extend into the future.

Consider again the issue of teen pregnancy. Two recent surveys, one in Illinois and the other in Washington state, found that more than half of the young mothers had been sexually abused when they were children. Most had been abused more than once, sometimes in violent ways, and often by men who should have been nurturing and protecting them: their fathers, grandfathers, brothers, cousins, or their mothers' male companions.[26] Because of sexual abuse, young women (and increasing numbers of young men) conclude that they are powerless to control their lives, their sexuality, and even their own bodies. In place of support and nurturing family relationships when they are growing into sexual maturity, these young people experience violence, fear, confusion, and attacks on their self-esteem. Is it surprising that the cycle of abuse and disrespect is repeated and passed on from one generation to the next?

When sex runs amok and deviates from the plans of God, everybody suffers and many are confused. Is there any way to help family members avoid the pain of uncontrolled sexuality?

We cannot avoid this question. We live in a culture where sex is flaunted on television screens, prominently displayed on the newsstands, freely discussed in schools, and experienced through a variety of forms, sometimes without much forethought or hesitation. Our public schools teach our children about the facts and the pleasures of sex in sex-education programs and media presentations, but the schools do not teach the moral dimensions of sexual behavior.

To counter these often perverted influences, we—parents and other believers—need to be models of self-control, abstinence, and purity. We must be willing to discuss sex honestly, admit its allure and dangers, and express the reasons for our sexual values. I agree with Stan and Brenna Jones when they argue that sex education—for our children but for adults as well—involves more than providing education.[27] Sex education involves teaching character formation through both our words and our actions. It assumes that what we do in response to the sexual forces that rumble into our lives largely will depend on who we are and on the kinds of people we are becoming.

Several years ago, long before it was popular to talk about values, a husband and wife wrote a book titled *Raising a Child Conservatively in a Sexually Permissive World.* The authors do not write from a Christian perspective, and some of their conclusions would be challenged by believers, but their goal is worthy—to guide parents and other sex educators in teaching children the "middle ground between an 'anything goes' lifestyle and equally unhealthy sexual censorship."[28] These writers argue that silence about sexuality teaches as much as openness does, but in a negative way. When we are honest, sensitive, respectful, and discrete in discussing sex, our children will develop greater sexual integrity and control. It is of interest, perhaps, that these authors don't conclude their book on sexuality with dire predictions about sexual collapse in the future. They pull together their conclusions in a chapter titled "The Family Is Alive and Getting Better." They see hope for the future of the family.[29]

What about Safe Sex?
Not long ago, a group of kids from our church went to a convention that included a True Love Waits rally on sexual abstinence. Sponsored by over twenty-five denominations, Protestant and Catholic, and by several teen-oriented youth organizations, the rally was one of many that have been held all across the country.

With permission from the local authorities, a group of convention participants fanned out over the lawn in front of the Washington Monument and inserted in the grass close to twenty thousand little sticks, each holding a card sent by a teenager who had signed his or her name to this statement: *Believing that True Love Waits, I make a commitment to God, myself, my family, those I date, my future mate, and my future children to be sexually pure until the day I enter a covenant marriage relationship.*

A report in the newspaper that comes to our house dismissed this as "part of the politics of the religious Right" and added, "The movement is downplayed by government policymakers and clinic counselors who say contraceptive devices are the best answer to the sharp rise in pregnancies."[30] The reporter might have added that, apart from abortion, there probably is no greater hot potato than whether or not kids should be encouraged to abstain from intercourse or go ahead with sex as long as they use condoms.

The safe-sex debate has rocked school boards across the country. Everybody wants to prevent teens from destroying

A SYMBOL OF PURITY

MARK McMINN, PH.D., LISA McMINN, M.A.

Mark, Professor of Psychology, Wheaton College

Lisa, Visiting Instructor of Sociology, Wheaton College

Mark is author of *Cognitive Therapy Techniques in Christian Counseling*

One of our family's favorite choruses is a prayer for purity:

Lord, make me clean like the new fallen snow.
Lord, make me clean like the mountain streams that flow.
Lord, make me new like the springtime green.
Lord, please make me clean.

How can we teach our children to make choices that reflect a desire to be clean and pure, faithfully obedient to God? One way is by using symbols. This chorus is full of refreshing symbols—snow, mountain streams, spring. Symbols remind us of the things we value most. We use another symbol in our family as a reminder of our desire for pure living.

When Danielle, our oldest child, turned thirteen, she symbolized her commitment to live a clean and pure life by accepting a ring from us. Two things about this event made it an important milestone for Danielle and our family (Sarah will get her ring this year, and Anna eagerly awaits the day when she will get hers).

First, after discussing the idea privately with Danielle, we discussed as a family what the ring symbolizes. It meant Danielle was committing herself to making wise choices about choosing friends and activities, to including us in the important decisions she makes, and to remaining sexually pure until marriage.

Second, we emphasized that Danielle was pledging faithfulness to God, not to us as parents. We are gradually giving her more control of her decisions, and at some point she will no longer be directly accountable to us. But she will always be accountable to God.

We call the ring a promise ring because it symbolizes her promises to God. We emphasized that faithfulness in leading a clean and pure life requires sexual purity, but it involves much more; it is a way of life that shows itself in every major decision and every relationship.

Someday our three children may replace their promise rings with wedding rings. We hope they will also see their wedding rings as a promise of faithfulness to God first and to their spouses second. In the meantime, we pray that they will have the strength to resist the temptations of evil that surround every adolescent and that they will be known for their faithfulness to God and others. 🔹

themselves—especially at a time when six thousand teenagers contract a sexually transmitted disease each day and when AIDS among people between fourteen and twenty-three years of age went up 72 percent in a recent two-year period.[31] At issue in the debate, however, is whether or not teenagers are able to control their hormones and even whether they should. It's a battle over core values.

Consider these facts:

- Three years ago the New York City Board of Education voted to distribute condoms in the city schools; a year later the same board reversed its earlier decision and ruled that abstinence should be the primary method of prevention taught in schools.
- Many programs encourage the use of condoms even though 4 percent of condoms break and 2 percent leak. Evidence indicates that pregnancies *increase* in schools where condoms are available. The rubber comprising latex condoms has intrinsic voids of 5 microns; the AIDS virus is only 0.1 micron.
- Evidence suggests that condoms fail to prevent pregnancies 15 to 20 percent of the time. "Would you use a parachute with a similar failure rate?" someone has asked.
- There is heated debate about whether or not birth-control-based sex education encourages or discourages sexual involvement. Planned Parenthood insists that such education does not lull people into a false sense of security that makes them more likely to have sex. Others, like the people who planned that rally in Washington, argue that the more you know about sex, the more you are tempted. An impressive body of research shows that education about contraceptives increases sexual activity.
- Some people suggest we should teach abstinence *and* safer sex methods, but critics argue that this sends a mixed message: "You shouldn't have sexual intercourse,

but since you probably will, here are some ways to protect yourself." Others argue that ignorance is never a good policy. They cite recent research showing that kids who learn the facts about sex and who have abstinence training are most likely to keep pure and free of pregnancies and sexually transmitted diseases.[32]

- Abstinence campaigns won't work with some kids, but they work well with many others. Sex Respect, an abstinence-only program, has an impressive and clearly researched track record to show that such teaching does cut teen pregnancies significantly.

A *Christianity Today* editorial suggested that sex education should focus less on reproductive "plumbing" and more on care and respect.[33] These two values should be reflected in our sexuality and in our response to the issue of gender as well.

Men and Women, Roles and Gender

It has taken half my adult life, but I've finally concluded that I wasn't the only kid in the world to be chosen last every time my schoolmates selected players for school teams. I've also learned that it is possible to be masculine without being athletic. I didn't know this when I was in school. Everybody assumed that guys were sports-minded; if you weren't a jock, people questioned whether you were a full-fledged male. This seems minor now, but it was a major issue for me when I was growing up, struggling with a poor self-concept, trying to decide who I was, and wondering what it really meant to be masculine.

Many of us still wonder. Apart from obvious physiology, is there anything that distinguishes males from females today? Do we have different innate characteristics? Should we have different roles in the home or in society? What about roles and responsibilities in the church? Has God given us different responsibilities and gifts based on gender?

Most of us have opinions about these issues, and often we disagree, even with our friends. I'm probably not the only one who feels cautious when I encounter books and articles on feminism or the modern men's movement, publications arguing for and against "biblical equality," and discussions about gender and male-female roles in the family. I wait to see where the writer or speaker will land on these issues, and I tend to dismiss those who seem too radical, especially if their conclusions differ from mine. Often that's how we handle hot potatoes.

Male and Female Roles in the Past

Stanley Graham, former president of the American Psychological Association, set some of this into historical perspective when he gave a talk titled "What Does a Man Want?"[34] Early in the century, male and female roles were clear, according to Graham. A man's home was his castle, and a woman's place was in the home. Young women grew up to become housekeepers, doing the laundry and raising the kids while the men got educations, went to work, and built their careers.

For many families this all changed when the depression hit in 1929. Almost one man in three was unemployed. Many men stayed at home with nothing to do while their wives struggled to hold everything together. The woman who maintained her role under great stress was a heroine, especially if she found a way to contribute financially to the family's well-being. The man without a job lost much of his identity.

Then came war. Millions of men went off with the military, and women took on new roles, managing their households and holding "war jobs," where they showed competence and stability that surprised many of their employers—and probably some of the women themselves. After World War II, large numbers of women gave up their jobs and turned to bringing up the first baby-boomer kids. But as the economy grew and technology accelerated, many women returned to the workplace. "By the mid-1950s," says Graham, "the stereotype of the typical American family composed of a breadwinner, a housekeeper, and two children began to break down as more young women sought advancement through education and more housekeepers entered the labor force."[35]

In the 1960s, the years that gave rise to the Woodstock generation, almost everybody talked about personal freedom. Contraceptive devices became more available, the risk of pregnancy was reduced, and both men and women became more "liberated" sexually. The women's movement grew rapidly, fueled in part by angry rhetoric and powerful leaders, but founded as well on the legitimate complaints of women who had been subjected to centuries of segregation and restricted access to opportunity.

In the workplace, many men were—and are—uncomfortable competing with women, especially with women who were capable and ambitious. Males began to experience the same frustration and role confusion that leaders in the women's movement had so clearly articulated. Then, less than a decade ago, an unlikely leader and poet named Robert Bly gave rise to the modern men's movement. Shortly thereafter Bill McCartney founded Promise Keepers, a movement of Christian "men of integrity," men dedicated to the seven promises listed below.

SEVEN PROMISES OF A PROMISE KEEPER

1. A man and his God: A Promise Keeper is committed to honoring Jesus Christ through worship, prayer, and obedience to God's Word in the power of the Holy Spirit.
2. A man and his mentors: A Promise Keeper is committed to pursuing vital relationships with a few other men, understanding that he needs brothers to help him keep his promises.
3. A man and his integrity: A Promise Keeper is committed to practicing spiritual, moral, ethical, and sexual purity.
4. A man and his family: A Promise Keeper is committed to building strong marriages and families through love, protection, and biblical values.
5. A man and his church: A Promise Keeper is committed to supporting the mission of the church by honoring and praying for his pastor and by actively giving his time and resources.
6. A man and his brothers: A Promise Keeper is committed to reaching beyond any racial and denominational barriers to demonstrate the power of biblical unity.
7. A man and his world: A Promise Keeper is committed to influencing his world, being obedient to the great commandment (Mark 12:30-31) and the great commission (Matt. 28:19-20).

Adapted from *Seven Promises of a Promise Keeper* (Colorado Springs: Focus on the Family, 1994).

Male and Female Roles Now

James Dobson argues that, historically, married men had two family responsibilities that exceeded all others in significance: to *protect* and *provide* for their children. "This is the contribution for which men were designed, physically and emotionally," he writes. "One of the greatest threats to the institution of the family today is the undermining of this role as protector and provider." If it is taken away, a man's commitment to his wife and children is jeopardized.[36]

Critics have responded that a man can protect and provide for his family without nurturing the family, cultivating loving relationships, or modeling Christlike behavior. And what happens if a man loses his job or his health and his wife becomes the provider and protector? What happens if a woman wants to work outside the home and become a major wage earner? Can a husband and wife share the provider, protector, and nurturing roles—like the Christian couple in which the wife works outside the home and the husband runs a business from his bedroom office while he keeps a watchful eye on the kids? How does a woman deal with hearing that she can have it all—a good marriage, children, a successful career, material possessions, and other personal achievements—and that children don't have to interfere with any of these pursuits? She reads this in books and hears it in sermons, but still she struggles with the relentless demands of motherhood, the never-ending needs, continual interruptions, and the uncertainty of how her children and maybe her marriage will turn out. Most women (and men) are beginning to see that they can't have it all and that they must make some tough decisions. At times the husband and the wife will have to forgo some personal satisfactions, at least temporarily, because of needs in the family.

Some Christian authors write impassioned books about the biblical basis for maintaining traditional roles. Other Christians, equally passionate and biblically astute, turn to the same passages of Scripture and argue for biblical equality. Oblivious to all of this, the kid who is chosen last in gym class still wonders if it is possible to be a real male even if he can't throw a ball and doesn't care anything about home runs and touchdowns.

Let's agree: There are no easy answers to the questions about gender. There *is* plenty of confusion, however, and concern about what one book called the "rocking of the roles" in marriage and society.[37] Committed believers have different opinions, and we probably will have to live with continuing disagreement and uncertainty.

Some things we know for sure. These are conclusions that most of us can accept.

- God has given us different gifts, abilities, opportunities, and responsibilities. Each person, before God and with the counsel of a few knowledgeable friends, should decide where he or she fits best and serves Christ most faithfully.
- In the Christian home, husbands and wives are to respect one another, love each other, engage in mutual cooperation and submission (Eph. 5:21). They are to ensure that their children are loved, nurtured, disciplined, respected, and prepared for responsible adulthood.
- Christians disagree on the roles of the male and female in the home—especially in terms of responsibilities—but there is no biblical justification for one person dominating, abusing, and/or ignoring another.
- Each couple should attempt to communicate with understanding and to arrive at a jointly agreed demarcation of roles and responsibilities, making sure that this demarcation shows mutual respect and is consistent with biblical teachings.

Before Julie and I got married, we talked a lot about these issues. We discussed what it did and did not mean for the husband to be the head of the home. We agreed that the husband's role was to be like Christ, who gave himself for the members of his eternal family, loves us, cares for us, and wants us to raise our children "in the training and instruction of the Lord" (Eph. 5:21–6:4).

141

"If I have a husband who tries to be like that," Julie said, "I'm not likely to worry about being dominated, squelched, or forced to submit." No husband is perfect, least of all me, but I have tried to respect my wife and kids (who are both daughters). I try never to put people down with my actions, comments, or insensitive joking, and they show the same respect for me and for one another. We make decisions together, work together as a team, and have settled on different responsibilities in the home. Still, we each try to help the other without falling into rigid kinds of roles—even though I'm not much of a cook and Julie doesn't enjoy taking out the garbage! For us, all of this works well, and we think it's consistent with the Scriptures. If you genuinely seek God's will and want to live in accordance with biblical teaching, the Holy Spirit—who knows about our personalities and abilities—might lead you into a model that is different from our family's.

Gifts, Roles, and Gender in the Home

Sex and gender issues affect us all. They have an impact on our families, even if we're oblivious to much of what is going on in the society where we live. To keep our values and families on track, we need to remember several key ideas.

Respect
Dictionaries define *respect* as holding another person in high esteem and regard, showing consideration and courtesy, having regard for the privacy of another person, and not interfering or intruding. Recently I accompanied a young ex-prisoner to see his parole officer for the first time. When we arrived at the parole office, I was surprised and favorably impressed when they addressed my friend as Mr. _____. The prison officials didn't talk down to him, and they treated him like a worthwhile human being. He was treated with respect at a time when he needed it most.

In contrast, ABC's *20/20* television news program interviewed a group of male university students who talked about their involvements with pornographic magazines and graphic sexual videos.[38] With great frankness, these young men described how

WHEN KIDS GO WRONG

LES PARROTT III, PH.D.
Center for Relationship
Development
Seattle Pacific University
Author of *Helping the Struggling
Adolescent*

Nailing down what is normal in adolescence can be like trying to nail gelatin to the wall. In general, the shift from normal to abnormal occurs when a teen's behavior begins to interfere with his or her ability to carry out daily routines or sustain relationships.

The following questions can help you decide whether your teenager is going through a harmless phase or is suffering from a serious problem.

- Is your teenager silent for long periods of time and often withdrawn socially, having few friends?
- Is your teenager considering dropping out of school or in danger of not completing high school? Is he or she failing classes?
- Is your teenager obsessed with exercise and diet? Does your teenager have an eating disorder?
- Does your teenager practice any form of self-mutilation in the form of teeth marks, cuts, or burns? What about homemade tattoos?
- Is your teenager involved in any kind of illegal activity? Has he or she been arrested or in trouble with the law?
- Does your teenager show an excessive fear of a particular family member, relative, or family friend? Is it possible that your adolescent could have been sexually abused and fears talking about it?
- Does your teenager have long periods of feeling worthless, helpless, guilty, or lethargic? Is there evidence of depression?
- Is your home life in chaos because of your teen? Is your well-being or performance at work suffering because of your teen's problems?
- Does your teenager show a strong interest in the occult, read about black magic, or get involved in antireligious activities?
- Does your teenager blow up with anger and get into fights a great deal? Has he or she been involved in vandalism or threatened someone's physical well-being?
- Are you concerned that your teenager may be sexually promiscuous? Is there a risk of venereal disease or pregnancy?
- Does your teenager report hearing voices that others do not hear, showing evidence of hallucinations or being out of touch with reality?
- Is your teenager having serious problems with sleep, such as

insomnia, repeatedly waking up at night, frequent nightmares, or sleeping too much?

- Does your teenager have morbid thoughts, talk about death a lot, or seem to be suicidal?

- Does your teenager spend time with a peer group that violates the rights of others? Do you have reason to suspect that he or she is involved in illegal activities or destructive acts?

- Does your teenager get drunk? Does he or she drive while drinking? Is your teenager experimenting with drugs that can kill?

- Does your teenager experience relatively brief periods of intense anxiety? What about panic attacks?

If you answered yes to any of the above questions, you have no doubt tried many things to help your struggling child. Perhaps you have talked with a friend who has gone through a similar experience. Maybe you have read a reputable book about the problem or consulted a teacher, guidance counselor, physician, or minister. These are all excellent resources, but when the problem becomes serious, it is time to call a professional psychotherapist. That decision can be scary. It's not easy to tell a stranger that all is not well in your home. But getting professional help for your teenager may be one of the most courageous and loving acts you can do as a parent. ✹

---

they learned to view all women as sex objects who are eager to have sex and who really don't mean it when they say no. This led some to date rape and caused interviewer Hugh Downs to conclude that pornography weakens men and degrades women. Without respect for their sex partners, the students had little control over their erotic impulses and little desire to stop their corrupting behavior.

When Jesus met a woman caught in the act of adultery, he didn't approve of the actions (John 8:3-11). He did not condone the lifestyle of the Samaritan who had had several husbands and was living with a man to whom she was not married (John 4). Despite the actions of these women, Jesus treated them both with respect and courtesy.

I want to respect my wife and daughters, so much so, that I'm not even tempted to take advantage of them in any way. I also want to respect my friends, my employees, my students, my neighbors, and even the strangers whom I meet in the grocery store. When we treat others with respect, as Jesus did, we are far less likely to slide into sexual harassment, gender squabbles, or abuse.

Sexual Control

Saying no to sex is not easy. We all know that. In a survey of one thousand adolescents in Atlanta, 82 percent most wanted help in saying no, according to an article in the *Wall Street Journal*. We need help because it's tough to stay pure on our own. Ask any of those kids whose pledge cards were stuck into the ground on the Washington Mall.

Saying no to sex is not easy. Ask any businessperson who travels and spends nights in motels, alone. Ask any married man or woman who chooses purity and faithfulness in a world where this is ridiculed or dismissed as an option. Ask any teenager who dates regularly.

When readers of *Discipleship Journal* were asked in what kinds of situations they would be most likely to face temptation, they responded with these situations:

"When I have not been spending much time with God".........81%
"When I have not had enough rest"..57%
"When life is difficult"..45%
"During times of change"..42%
"After a significant spiritual victory"...37%
"When life is going smoothly"...30%

What strategies were effective in helping these people deal with persistent temptation? They responded with a list of spiritual disciplines:

prayer...84%
avoiding tempting situations..67%
reading or studying the Bible..66%
being accountable to someone...52%
memorizing Scripture...33%
engaging in spiritual warfare...31%[39]

145

The following list gives some other suggestions.

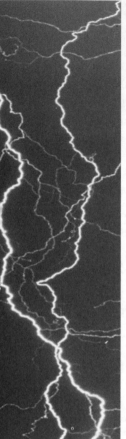

GUIDELINES FOR SELF-CONTROL

1. *Admit that you're vulnerable.*
2. *Think about the significant people in your life.* How does your thought life and any secret sexual (or other) behavior influence your relationships with your spouse, your children, other members of your family, and God? How does it affect your career and your image in the eyes of others?
3. *Make a decision to change.*
4. *Find a support base.* This may mean an individual or a group with whom you can be honest who holds you accountable, and who regularly prays with and for you.
5. *Stay away from temptation.* Steer clear of people, places, entertainment, reading materials, television programs, or anything else that is likely to tempt you. Plan ahead so you are not caught in situations where you are vulnerable and inclined to compromise.
6. *Expect resistance.* Some resistance might come from friends or work associates who present tempting alternatives. Much comes from the devil himself. Remember he can be resisted in the name of Jesus Christ (James 4:7).
7. *Keep communication open with God.* Ask him to keep you from yielding to temptation. Make prayer, Bible reading, and worship a regular practice.
8. *If you yield to temptation, ask for forgiveness, trust God to help you to change, stop berating yourself, recognize that God forgives, then move on.*
9. *Find a counselor.* When self-control problems persist, a good counselor can help you change.

Adapted in part from Len LeSourd, "Escape the Sexual Trap," *New Man* 1, no. 1 (July/August 1994): 46–48, 51–52.

Sexual purity is possible. Ask A. C. Green. He plays basketball, but he's not just any basketball player. Two-time NBA champion with the Los Angeles Lakers and former all-star, he plays alongside Phoenix Suns teammate Charles Barkley, who proclaimed in a Nike commercial that he was not a role model. Green took a different stance. Appearing on network television, he said, in effect, "I *am* a role model," telling young people: "Look at me. If I can stay sexually pure [something he has done for nine years in the NBA], then you can too."[40] It isn't surprising that Green has made headlines around the country, standing up for sexual abstinence before marriage.

A. C. Green models some basic and very relevant theology that has practical applications to issues about sex, repentance, forgiveness, and gender:

- God created us, made us male and female, and said that was good. He loves and respects each person, even though he doesn't like our sin.
- He knows about harassment, adultery, sexual discrimination, and the temptations that come from our society and from our own minds.
- His Holy Spirit is the divine Helper and Comforter who enables us to maintain self-control. We don't have to struggle alone.
- He has put us into communities and churches where we can find accountability, encouragement, support, and forgiveness. When we yield to temptation, he freely forgives those who confess, genuinely repent, and determine to go their way and sin no more.

J A N

It had been a busy Christmas in Jan's house, as usual. Guests from Scotland, Japan, New Zealand, and Mexico had joined her family and had shared happy laughter and plenty of food. The house seemed quiet after they all left.

Jan was the last to go. She hugged her mom and dad, and prepared to get into her car and drive halfway across the country in time for second-semester classes at a Christian college. "I left you a note," she said before leaving. "Please don't open it until tonight."

Later that evening Jan's parents read the letter together. It was carefully worded and clearly had taken a long time to write. Trying to use words that would soften the hurt, Jan told her parents that she was pregnant, that she was going back to school to clear out her dormitory room, and that she wanted to come back home to have the baby. Her parents, who had tried to raise their kids with strong Christian values, hugged each other, stood alone in the empty kitchen, and cried.

When Jan was asked to tell her story, she agreed. Here is what she wrote.

Jan's Story
I certainly am not an author and have never been asked to publish my thoughts about my experience. When I was asked to write this chapter, however, I felt that maybe I could help

someone who may at some time in life be in a similar situation, with an unexpected pregnancy. I would like to share with you some of the struggles that I went through as well as the lessons that I learned and victories that I won. These few pages don't give enough space to share everything. Maybe someday I will write my own book.

As usual, I went home for Christmas break after completing my third semester at college, but that Christmas break would be different from any other. I had missed a menstrual period and was almost certain that I was pregnant. Still, it came as a shock when I read the positive pregnancy-test results in the JCPenney ladies room while I was Christmas shopping with my mom. I kept saying that there was no way that this could happen to me. Reality, however, showed differently.

Ashamed to face my Christian parents, who had raised me to know right from wrong, I wrote them a letter and headed back to school, uncertain of what was to happen in the following days. Breaking the news to them was one of the hardest steps.

The next hardest thing was the reaction that I received from the man who was the birth father. I should have known his reaction would be negative, considering the rocky nature of our one-year relationship. Still, I was not prepared for his cool reception and complete lack of interest in the whole situation. I had expected more from him. My plans had been to stay in my college town and have the baby there, but when I realized that I wouldn't be getting any support from him, I knew that I had to leave.

I thought of going home, but I didn't for several reasons. First, I didn't want to embarrass my parents and was afraid of ruining my dad's Christian ministry. I also knew that it would be hard on them to see their little girl pregnant, and I feared that they would somehow blame themselves for my mistake. After thinking about options, I decided to call friends in California. Immediately they encouraged me to come. Two days later, I flew west and remained there until I gave birth to the baby.

I had many decisions to make. I am pro-life, so even in my stressful situation, abortion was not an option for me. I had seen the effect abortion had had on a few of my friends, and I knew that whatever choice I made about what to do with my baby and whatever painful consequences I would have to endure, I would choose them over the guilt and pain caused by abortion. I knew that even though I had made a major mistake by getting pregnant, this child was not a mistake, and I needed to make some important decisions about his or her future.

The first week in California, I met with Susan, a crisis pregnancy counselor from Bethany Christian Services in Bellflower. We sat in a restaurant and began to discuss my options. Was I ready to be a mother? Did I want to finish school? Could I do both? What about a father for the baby? Would he be around? Could I give to my baby the things that I wanted him or her to have? Would the baby be lacking if he or she stayed with me? Was I emotionally and spiritually strong enough at this time to instill in my child the proper morals and values that meant so much to me as I was growing up? What about finances, day care, diapers, and food? Could I provide all of this?

Then we discussed adoption. How would this choice affect my life? How would it affect my baby's life? In the long run, would it be a wiser decision for both of us? Susan also shared with me that one of the latest changes in adoption policy was a semiopen adoption, which her agency provided. I could choose a family for my baby and even would have the option of interviewing that family. Then, after the adoption was final, I could have partial contact with the family. Through the agency, we would be able to share letters and photos for as long as we decided. Out of my options, this was the choice that sounded best for both me and my baby. After a few months of consideration and prayer, I began the process with the agency.

But I had more decisions to make. After living at a friend's apartment for more than a month, I felt that I needed to be closer to Susan and the adoption agency, so I moved an hour away into a "shepherding home" that Bethany provided for me. My room and board were free, but I got a job to keep busy for the next several months and to have extra money for myself. Although the accommodations were less than perfect, I had prayed that God would give me an affordable place to stay, and he provided even better.

The next step was to get financial aid from the state. I could not afford all of the medical bills that were to follow in the next few months. My family helped as much as they could, but I had gotten into this predicament, and I didn't feel that it was their responsibility to get me out. A friend offered to take me to the welfare offices, and that was an experience in itself. It was humbling to stand in those lines. I wasn't prepared to beg the state for money. After being raised in a financially stable home, it was awkward to find myself in this environment, but I had no choice. The process took a lot of time and energy. It also took from me a lot of the self-respect that I had previously received from other people and experiences. Since then, I have found myself more sympathetic toward the people who will stand in those lines for the rest of their lives. I am also grateful that I will not be one of them.

I found it hard to find a doctor who would treat me under my financial circumstances. After my first encounter with one of them, I realized that it would be hard to find a competent doctor that I could trust to treat me as well as he would treat the women who paid to receive his services. Again, the Lord provided for me. Susan spoke with an obstetrician in her church. It was not his policy to accept medicaid clients, but he made an exception for me. From then on, I felt confident that I was receiving the proper care, and I got more than I ever expected.

Living so far away from my close friends in southern California was difficult, especially at such a stressful time of my life when I needed their support. With the money that I made waitressing, I was able to travel to see them every weekend. During each week, however, I spent my time working, writing letters, and shopping. Most of my afternoons and evenings were spent reading the Bible, listening to my Christian music, and talking with God. It was a very lonely time for me, but during that time, I was able to get to know God better. I learned about his immeasurable love for me and his mercy and forgiveness. Although I learned so much, I have never been able to understand it.

In the last few months of my pregnancy, I was getting anxious to start looking at family profiles and to begin making some decisions. Only three profiles were available to me because the baby is biracial. I had been praying for the perfect family for my baby, and when I saw the first profile, I knew I had found the right family. After I read the information about the family, their Christian background, their interests, and why they wanted to adopt a baby, I had no doubt that God had heard my prayers and had handpicked them especially for my baby. I never looked at the second and third profiles, and I have never doubted my decision.

My mother had flown out to spend the last five weeks of my pregnancy with me. She realized how difficult this time was for me and how much I needed her. I was eager to get back for the fall semester at school, which started a week after my due date. My doctor agreed that if I was ready to deliver but had not started labor, he would induce labor so that I could return to classes on time.

My mom and I got to the hospital early in the morning as instructed, and Susan came a few hours later. I had chosen my mom to be my labor coach, but I also wanted Susan to be there. Amazingly enough, I started going into labor the night before but was induced to speed up the process. It surely did, because twelve hours later, I gave birth to a healthy, nine-pound baby boy.

I had decided that I wanted to spend as much time as possible with him before I left the hospital and was thankful to have two full days. Those hours in the hospital seemed very unreal to me, and I felt as if I was in a dream. I felt deep emotions as I held my son during that short time. I felt completely drained, not only because I had just given birth, but also because I was trying to make sense of my own feelings and console friends who had come to give me comfort.

One evening, after everyone had left the hospital room, a nurse came to visit me. I will never forget that visit. I often wonder if she was an angel sent from God to give me the encouragement that I needed. I had never seen her before and never again saw her after her short visit. She shared with me the story of her unwed pregnancy, the difficulties that she encountered, and the struggles that she faced. Her story was so very similar to mine. However, after strongly considering adoption, she kept her baby. She shared that her life had never again been the same. She loved her baby and would never give him away, but she often wondered if her life as well as her baby's life would have been better if she had chosen adoption. She validated my uneasy feelings and praised me for the decision that I had made. I was grateful to her and thankful that she came in to see me that night.

The morning on which I had to give up my baby came before I was ready. Susan had prepared me as much as she could, but it wasn't enough. I asked to spend some time with my baby, but I was told that he was getting blood work done. After the tears welled up in my eyes, I explained to the nurse what was about to happen. Understanding my strong feelings, she went to see what she could do for me. As I sat back down on my bed, waiting for my baby, I opened my Bible to spend some time with God. I opened directly to the Psalms, where I had received most of my comfort during my pregnancy, and began reading what was in front of me. The verse was Psalm 118:24: "This is the day the Lord has made; let us rejoice and be glad in it."

I knew that God had chosen that verse especially for me so that when the time came, I would be confident that I had made the right choice and that God's hand was right there with me during this difficult task that was ahead. Immediately after closing my Bible, the nurse returned with my baby.

Susan and the director of the adoption agency arrived in the middle of the morning with the adoption and relinquishment papers. I really felt emotionally numb during most of my hospital stay, but as I began to sign these papers, the reality of the whole situation hit me with incredible force.

I was giving away my baby, the baby that had grown inside of me for the previous nine months. Words cannot express how difficult this was, but I sensed a peace from the Lord. It was a peace that I needed desperately, a peace that I never will understand.

The remaining time in the hospital flew by fast. My baby's new family arrived, and we spent time exchanging gifts and taking pictures. Then they were gone.

God carried me through the rest of that day and the days that followed. As my mom and I flew home, I reflected on my months in California. I was so grateful for my friends who were so committed to me during this time. Melissa painted my toenails every weekend when I could no longer reach my feet. She didn't do it because she had to; she did it because she loved me and wanted to make me feel good. She also spent many nights sleeping on the floor, allowing me to sleep on her waterbed. Brad spent numerous hours with me when I first arrived in California. We had special talks with each other, sharing our own personal life experiences that had taught us so much. During that time, he gave me the encouragement that I needed as I was about to face difficult days ahead.

I was also grateful for Julie, the fiancée of one of my close friends from home, who allowed me to stay at her apartment the first few months that I was in California. She never asked for money and made me feel welcome from the day that I moved in. And then there were Jeff and Jodi, who gave me unconditional love and support throughout my whole pregnancy. I often wonder if these people realize the impact they had on my life and continue to have on me when I reflect on those difficult months. I will never forget all the support that they gave to me, expecting absolutely nothing in return. It was an overwhelming experience.

Although my pregnancy was devastating to my parents, I never felt shunned or unloved because of the mistake that I had made. My father was more concerned about my life and helping me through a difficult time than he was about his reputation or the reactions of his friends and colleagues toward him. I strongly believe that God never plans bad circumstances for his children but allows them in order to teach us lessons that can change our lives. As a result of my pregnancy, I was able to take the time to work through some problems that I had with my dad and start over with him. I was also able to spend some time with my mom and grow closer to her. I learned a lot about her patience, forgiveness, love for me, and her love for Christ. And through it all, I felt the support and acceptance of my sister.

This has been a difficult experience for me, but I know that it was necessary. Over three years have passed since my son was born, and I continue to struggle with issues related to those events. However, because of the values that I was taught from my family and because of Christ's love, which was evident in their lives as I was growing up, those struggles have been easier to deal with. Because of their love for me and the strong family support that they gave to me, I have been able to take my experience and make an impact on the lives of others.

Postscript

Jan has moved to a different state, where she continues with her education and is preparing for a career in social work. Periodically, she gets pictures of her son. When he was two years old, the adoptive family agreed without any evident hesitation to let Jan and her sister visit, to see the little boy whom she would never know, and then to back out of his life until he is an adult.

Jan prepared a scrapbook for him at about the time he was born so he will know the circumstances surrounding his birth. She continues to have contact by letter with the adoptive family and is amazed at their love for their son and their understanding support of a birth mother who did what she knew was right.

Jan's story is a message of hope—to young people, their parents, and other family members who face the consequences of sin and wonder if life is ruined beyond repair.[41] If Jan had not become pregnant, her life would have been different and probably better. But she and her family have discovered and demonstrated that there *is* life on the other side of emotional, physical, and spiritual pain. Even though lifelong scars may remain, God forgives and heals.

Throughout the pages of this book you will find other stories, but none of them touches me more than this one. I admire Jan and her courage more than words can ever tell. I admire her dedication to Christ and her willingness to make herself vulnerable by telling this family story so honestly. I admire her mother, who stayed with Jan during the last weeks of her pregnancy, was there when the baby was born, and cried with Jan as she handed her precious baby son to the loving care of another family.

You'll understand why I have these feelings when you learn that I am Jan Collins's dad.

8

PARENTING AND THE FAMILY

A YOUNG seminary student recently told me about a parenting class he was taking. When the professor asked the students why they were taking the course, one couple replied that they wanted information so they could "do parenting seminars" following graduation. They had no children of their own and didn't intend to have any. They felt that kids would disrupt their parenting theories and interfere with their intended ministry of helping other parents raise their children! This attitude amazed me. We can counsel alcoholics or sexually addicted people without having these problems ourselves, but can people without children have credibility and effectiveness in running parenting seminars? I suspect that most parents—the ones who would come to the seminars—would say *no*.

The seminars might succeed, however, because so many parents are looking for answers. They know that growing up is tough, especially today, and despite all the reports of neglected and abused kids, probably most mothers and fathers want to do a good job in raising their families. Parents look for help wherever they can get it, sometimes never asking if the advice givers know what they're talking about or whether they have raised kids themselves.

I watched some of this frenzied search for information in a young father-to-be who attended our church. When his wife got pregnant, my friend raided my bookshelves, scoured the local library, consumed parenting magazines, and visited bookstores in search of parenting books. He read them enthusiastically, let us know that he intended to be the best father possible, and then became disillusioned and confused when the books said different things.

Now that he's a father of two young children, my friend knows that books and seminars and parenting tapes can't give all the answers. He agrees that his flurry of reading was an effort to calm his fears and control his anxiety about fatherhood. He is devoted to his children and wants to spend time with them, but he knows that parenting can be scary, both for the parents and for the kids.

Parenting Can Be Scary

"Once, they were the envy of the world, an exuberant army cruising on their fat-tired Schwinns [around] the curving streets of ten thousand subdivisions, sending a chorus of gleeful yelps that brought—in predictable succession—Christmas, birthdays and summer vacation." That is how a *Newsweek* writer described American kids of a few decades ago. "Unless you were black and people spat on you when you tried to go to school, or mentally handicapped and shut away in a misery-drenched state home, . . . life was pretty good and expected to get better."[1]

Not anymore! Kids live in a world of violent crime and hostile strangers. They face dangerous sexual enticements and warnings about kidnappers, stalkers, and even family friends, relatives, and priests. The average child watches 8,000 televised murders and 100,000 acts of violence before finishing elementary school. Many parents look the other way and perhaps try to convince themselves that kids are "little adults," competent to handle what they see on television or hear from their friends. Some adults get so caught up in the perception of competence that they teach four- and five-year-olds about AIDS or child abuse and provide anatomically correct toys that simulate pregnancy or the dismemberment that comes when we don't buckle up.[2] Day after day, kids sit mesmerized in front of television screens, watching endless children's programs and horror movies about child abusers and Draculas. They hear about dangers in their own neighborhoods and are scared to leave

PARENTING KIDS

WM. LEE CARTER, ED.D.
Child Psychiatry Associates,
Waco, Texas
Author of *Family Cycles* and
The Angry Teenager

It's impossible to summarize how to parent kids, right? After all, children are complex creatures and cannot be managed by just a few simple guidelines, right?

Wrong! Sure, parenting is the world's toughest job, but by following three key guidelines, parents can successfully manage most parenting dilemmas. The guidelines may sound simple, but they require practice. Follow them regularly, and watch your family relationships grow.

1. *Learn to think as your child thinks.* That is no simple task. Because we as parents are more experienced and wiser than children, we think differently. Too often we try to force *our* thoughts on our children. We reason, plead, or give sermons. The child's typical reaction is "My parents don't understand me." Children who feel misunderstood tend to act out their emotions, hoping that someone will accurately interpret their charades. Listen to your children. Let them know you understand.

2. *Keep your emotions balanced.* Your children watch every move you make. When children see that your emotions are out of bounds, they feel powerful and in control. When you are emotionally balanced, *you* are in control of the home atmosphere and will not be manipulated nearly as easily by your children. You will also be a good role model.

3. *Be consistent in discipline.* Predictability means security to your child. When you promise to give a specific reward or punishment, do exactly what you promised. Your children will learn that their worlds have boundaries. They will know what to expect from you and what you expect of them.

---

home. Sometimes their parents won't let them go out, even in "safe" areas. Nobody can blame parents for wanting to protect their children, but no one has counted the psychological impact of kids growing up scared in a perpetual state of hypervigilance.

Dangers outside the Home

Children, and the parents who raise them, have to cope with influences from outside the home and others that come from within. We all know the dangers from the outside: violence, sexual seductions, poverty, changing social standards, abandonment of clear religious training, a lack of heroes and role models, movies that glamorize infidelity and vulgarity, music groups that parade lewdly and spew violent lyrics, and the profusion of conflicting values coming from peers, teachers, sports heroes, television stars, pastors, and parents. You need not read very much to learn how schools, courts, governments, and sometimes churches too often undermine the roles and influence of parents.

Then there are the media, especially television. Despite the defensive denials from leaders in the industry, much of television glamorizes irresponsible sex, stimulates violence, proclaims the virtues of materialism and hedonism, encourages mindlessness, and discourages clear thinking or sound judgment.

Is a conclusion like that too damning? I agree with the researchers who concluded that television can have a negative or a positive influence on the family, depending on how families control their viewing.[3] Certainly television has influenced the society for good and has brought pleasure, information, and a broader worldview to millions of people. Accumulating research shows, however, that television can and does do incredible harm to people and their families.[4] The sentence that ended the previous paragraph is not an overstatement.

On the day of graduation from high school, the average young American will have spent 11,000 hours in the classroom and 22,000 hours in front of the television screen, much of that time watching violence in cartoons and movies. According to a five-volume report from the National Institutes of Mental Health, evidence suggests that this television viewing stimulates aggressive behavior in children and young people. Apparently the influence lasts for a long time. One longitudinal study found a strong relationship between what kids watched at age eight and their tendency to be aggressive at age nineteen and at age thirty—when they are launching their own families and relating to their kids.

Whole books have been written about the risks children face from our society, but the conclusion already is clear: Our families are impacted by cultural influences, especially television.[5] Parents need to monitor what young people watch and should view programs with their children so that they can talk about the difficult issues that arise. Parents must model good viewing practices, keep the television turned off except when they are watching a specific program, and monitor what comes into their homes and minds via cable. Parents should be ready to push the off button whenever programming is not in good taste. Some parents try to solve the problem and remove the temptation by not having a television set in the house. Others question whether that prevents children from learning the discretion that they will need to monitor their television viewing in the future.

Harm within the Home

Scary influences that interfere with good parenting are not all on a television screen or out in the community. In addition to the domestic conflict, sexual mistreatment, verbal-emotional abuse, and other forms of violence that occur within many families, other more subtle dangers come into the home.

The first of these is the influence of *employment*. When both parents rush off to work in the mornings and latchkey kids come home to empty houses in the afternoons, the unsupervised children often feel alone or scared, and many of their parents feel guilty. When the parents return from busy days at work, they are tired and often pressured by the need to run errands, do household chores, and get ready for the next day. Kids who need love, attention, and time often get lost in the shuffle, and the time that parents do spend with their children tends to be more rushed and distracted.[6] This can have adverse effects on the well-being and the emotional and intellectual development of the kids.

A Cornell University survey found that two-thirds of all mothers who are employed full-time would like to work fewer hours so they could stay home with their families. Before we call for a return of households with one homemaker and one wage earner, however, we need to recognize that many families need two incomes to pay the bills. Higher taxes, increased costs for

163

housing and health care, and the stagnation of real wages have put growing pressure on families with children. While some couples, driven by materialism and workaholism, pursue success and turn their kids over to baby-sitters, we must be cautious about condemning all working parents when we don't understand their motives or circumstances. And we need to be sensitive to hardworking parents like single moms and dads, who have genuine concern about their latchkey children but have no alternative to the long hours of work away from home.

One interesting study by two Michigan researchers compared the grades of three groups of high school students, some of whom had mothers working when the teens were in preschool and in grade school. The lowest high school grades were in students whose mothers had worked full-time or overtime when their kids were younger. The highest grades came to adolescents who grew up in homes where mothers were employed part-time. These were also the teens who most often talked about attending professional and graduate schools. The kids with mothers who worked full-time in the home had high school grades in between the others.[7] We can't draw too many conclusions from one research report, but maybe it isn't all bad if both parents do work, as long as one or both work only part-time and are home, available, and dedicated to the children.

Closely connected to employment is the issue of *time*. In my circle of friends, everybody I know is busy. Too many of us, parents included, seem to be rushing around all the time, uptight, pressured, unreflective, tense, and always behind schedule. We complain about the lack of time and the demands on our time, and we think we have less time now than we did in the past. Parents in the United States today spend less time with their children than do parents in any other country in the world, according to a Harvard researcher, and modern parents devote roughly 40 percent less time to child-rearing activities than they did a generation ago. A survey sponsored by a Massachusetts insurance company found that Americans blamed "parents having less time to spend with their families" as the single most important reason for the family's decline in our society. The reason for this reduction in time, according to the people surveyed, is the increased number of hours that parents with children devote to paid employment.[8]

The facts are different. In the middle of the last century, the typical workweek was seventy hours. By the 1940s it had dropped closer to forty hours, and it hasn't changed since. With laborsaving devices, Americans on the average now have more free time—defined as time apart from work, family obligations, or personal needs like cooking, cleaning, and sleeping—than they did twenty-five years ago. Why, then, do we feel more rushed and unable to spend time with our kids? Certainly more of our time is consumed by television, but pollsters have found that we also "believe a lot more things are vital now." So we put more pressure on ourselves to do more things.[9] We complain that time is flying by. But the time isn't flying; we are. And the kids get neglected and so caught up in our frenetic lifestyles that they become just like their parents.

Assets, Deficits, and Raising Children

Have you ever noticed that the Bible gives relatively little direct instruction about how mothers and fathers are to parent their kids? Much of the New Testament teaching about this can be summed up in less than twenty words: "Fathers, do not exasperate your children; instead, bring them up in the training and instruction of the Lord" (Eph. 6:4). How do we put this into practice?

Every year, thousands of middle school and high school students in school districts all across the United States take a survey designed by the Search Institute in Minneapolis. The results are helpful to local teachers and school administrators, and when the data is pooled in the Institute computers, some interesting and helpful information emerges.[10]

When researchers compare surveys of kids who break the law, have problems at school, or get involved with drugs with similar kids who do not get into trouble, we see interesting differences. The basis of these differences is seen in assets and deficits the two sets of kids have.

Assets are positive influences and characteristics, which can be either external or internal. External assets come mainly from outside the young person in the form of support from parents and others. Internal assets are commitments, values, and competencies that are built within so that kids can thrive competently and responsibly on their own. Some of these assets are summarized in the following list. In general, the more assets that a young person has, the less likely he or she will be to get into trouble. Parents are the main contributors of assets in a child's life.

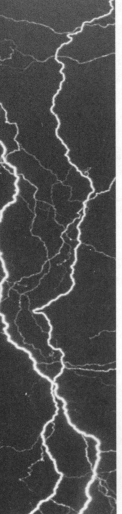

ASSETS THAT HELP KIDS GROW UP

External Assets (outside of the young person)

SUPPORT ASSETS

- Family support: families give love and encouragement
- Parent support: kids view parents as people available to give advice and support
- Parent communication: kids have frequent, in-depth conversations with parent(s)
- Other adult resources: nonparent adults are available to give support, advice, and conversations
- Parent involvement in schooling: parents want to help their kids do well in school
- Positive school climate: schools give a caring, encouraging environment

CONTROL ASSETS

- Parents set standards for appropriate conduct
- Parents discipline when a rule is violated
- Parents monitor where the kids are going and who they will be with
- Kids are home four or more nights per week
- Kids' best friends model responsible behavior

TIME-USE ASSETS

Kids spend one hour or more per week in:

- music practice or training
- extracurricular school activities
- organizations or clubs outside of school
- church or synagogue programs or services

Internal Assets (built inside of the young person)

EDUCATIONAL-COMMITMENT ASSETS

- Students are motivated to do well in school
- Students spend six hours or more on homework per week
- Students aspire to post–high school education (college or trade school)
- Students have above-average school performance

VALUES ASSETS
- Values helping people and often is involved in helping others
- Is concerned about reducing world hunger
- Cares about people's feelings
- Is committed to sexual restraint and postponing sexual activity

SOCIAL-COMPETENCE ASSETS
- Assertiveness skills: has the ability to stand up for personal principles
- Decision-making skills: makes positive decisions
- Friendship-making skills: makes and keeps quality friends
- Planning skills: plans and carries out events and projects
- High self-esteem
- A positive, optimistic view of one's personal future

Adapted from Peter L. Benson, *The Troubled Journey: A Portrait of 6th–12th Grade Youth* (Minneapolis: Search Institute, 1993).

Deficits are influences and characteristics that interfere with healthy development, cut a person off from assets, and lead to risky, harmful, and self-destructive behaviors like addiction, depression, suicide attempts, vandalism, school absenteeism, and reckless driving. The Search Institute has listed ten major deficits.

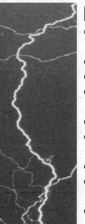

DEFICITS THAT HINDER KIDS' GROWTH

- Being at home for two or more hours per day without an adult present
- Watching television for three or more hours per day
- Frequently attending parties where peers drink
- Putting a lot of importance on hedonistic, self-serving values
- Feeling under stress or pressure most or all of the time
- Experiencing at least one incident of physical abuse from an adult
- Having had at least one incident of sexual abuse
- Having a parent who has a serious problem with alcohol or drugs
- Feeling a consistent lack of care, support, and understanding
- Having close friends who use drugs and/or have trouble at school

Kids who grow up healthy and most resistant to the dangers in society are the kids who have the fewest deficits and the most assets. To help kids survive their difficult journeys to adulthood, parents, community leaders, educators, and churches need to work together to decrease the deficits and increase the assets. Put in different words, parents should strive to give their kids support, controls, structured activities, a commitment to education, positive values, and skills that enable them to have social competence.

Where is God in all of this? Within recent years, many religious communities have been written off as out of touch or irrelevant to today's teens, but the church is very relevant, according to one Search Institute report. Some neighborhoods and communities stimulate a lot of assets in their young people. In these "healthiest communities," 70 percent of youth are involved in church at least once a month.[11] The church and parachurch youth organizations play a significant role in building assets—good character—in young people.

Competent to Parent

William O. Douglas, a former justice of the United States Supreme Court and a man who knew some of the most capable and influential people in society, once made this statement: "Few people I have known are competent to be parents. . . . The child who survives being brought up by its parents and emerges as an integrated person is an accident."[12]

I disagree! Even though parenting is not easy and few mothers and fathers feel competent to parent, the Creator chose to place helpless human beings in the hands of inexperienced and often immature young men and women. Surely he doesn't expect all of us to be such failures in parenting that only a few of our kids turn out okay, and then only by accident.

Parenting Myths and Values

Some time ago, I read some myths about parenting. I have added a few of my own and included these in the list on the following pages. These folk beliefs about parenting aren't all wrong, but they aren't all right either. Sadly, they bog down many parents and lead them to conclude that if their kids reach adulthood as integrated people, it will be only by accident. It is more accurate to say that our kids reach healthy adulthood by the grace of God and the committed efforts of parents who take their child rearing seriously.

To be effective in our child rearing, we need to resist some values and mental attitudes that often sidetrack parents. I know a young couple who sometimes baby-sit two preschoolers in an affluent home where the father appears to be consumed with his career and the mother, who works part-time, wants full-time child care so she can be free to read, go to luncheons, and enjoy life as she pleases.

My friends give an interesting description of the kids in that home, especially the four-year-old. "He's always scared and clingy. He has every toy imaginable, but he prefers to watch television and videos. He seems selfish, lacking in creativity, and not much interested in playing, even when other kids are around." When my friends have taken this child to the zoo or to playgrounds, he seems bored and not inclined to get excited about anything.

Will his busy and somewhat neglectful parents expect his teachers to make him creative and excited about learning? Will they blame somebody else if this little boy fails in school or gets into trouble as a teenager? Apparently these parents treat their children as adjuncts to their busy lives. They enjoy their kids, when it's convenient to do so, but they leave them with baby-sitters when other, more important things demand attention. They are parents who believe they can bring up kids and carry on with business as usual.

Hands-on Parenting
Julie and I are involved with a church where the congregation is young and where new babies appear frequently. One expectant couple recently described their summer activities—traveling, boating, sightseeing, and doing other things that won't be possible once they become parents. They joked about their "last fling," aware that life for them will change forever once they become parents.

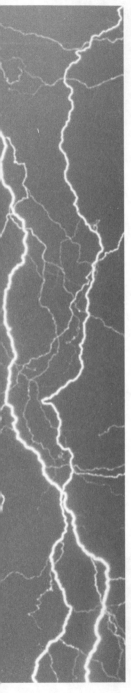

HALF-TRUTHS AND MYTHS ABOUT PARENTING

1. *Child rearing is fun.* It can be fun, but more often it is hard work, especially when your children know only three values: Gimmie! Lemmie! and Iwanna!

2. *Children are sweet and cute.* They are, sometimes, especially when they are young (and asleep). Parents often become disenchanted after children arrive because their "bundles of joy" so often are dirty, smelly, messy, noisy, and demanding.

3. *Children turn out well if they have good (Christian) parents.* Good families do tend to have good kids, but that is not always the case. Parents have the earliest and greatest impact on their children, but as the children get older, peer influence is stronger. Sometimes young people make it through childhood but overthrow parental values when they are adults. When children, including grown children, don't turn out well, parents aren't always the major culprits. Look at Isaiah 1:2. God was the perfect parent, but even his kids rebelled.

4. *Children improve marriage.* Research results do not support this idea. More often the opposite is true: Children put pressure on marriages. If a marriage is shaky, a child can intensify the problems.

5. *Personality doesn't count.* On the contrary, children and their parents sometimes have different temperaments. Some parents are impatient, quickly angered, or pushovers who are easily manipulated. Some kids are hyperactive, lethargic, or rebellious from the start. Each parent and each child is in some ways unique.

6. *Love is at the core of child rearing.* Love is crucial, and love covers a multitude of parental goofs. But children also need discipline, structure, standards, and stability.

7. *The only child is likely to be a problem child.* Not necessarily. One study found that only children are not lonely and spoiled; more often they are brighter, less spoiled, and able to get along with their peers better than children who have brothers and sisters.

8. *Childless couples are frustrated and unhappy.* For many couples this is true, especially if infertility prevents them from having the children they want. In contrast, many couples choose to remain childless. In one study of marital satisfaction, the highest scores were from couples who had chosen not to have children.

9. *Single-parent families are unhealthy.* The evidence is overwhelming: It is best for children to be raised in

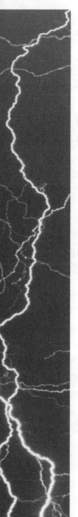

families that have both a mother and a father. Young people raised in one-parent families do have more problems later in life. But another conclusion is true: Millions of children are successfully raised by parents who are alone. Sometimes the home is more stable and healthy with one parent than when two are present and always in conflict.

10. *Children won't get into trouble if they are told the facts of life.* This has been called the sex-education myth. Sex education is valuable, especially when it comes from parents and with biblical values. But sexual behavior often is nonrational, influenced by hormones and passion, stimulated by people or circumstances, and only partly subject to intellectual control.

11. *Parenting is harder today than it was in the past.* That may be true, although we can't be sure what parenting was like in the past. Unlike our grandparents, parents today have hundreds of advice-giving books and articles that sometimes confuse more than they help, have fewer clear standards, must compete with the impact of television, have no clear parenting roles or models, often raise kids away from extended family members who could be helpful, and live in a culture where the schools, government, and media often undermine parents instead of supporting them in their role.

12. *Parenting ends when the last child leaves home.* Dream on! Most parents do not grieve too long over the empty nest; they miss the kids but enjoy the freedom from responsibility. Then, at least in America, increasing numbers of grown children come back home, where it's cheaper to live. They are known as "boomerang kids," children who come back after college, military service, or a divorce. Even if they don't come back, most grown children want parental support and advice, especially when they face crises or have families of their own.

Adapted from E. E. LeMasters and J. DeFrain, *Parents in Contemporary America* (Belmont, Calif.: Wadsworth, 1989).

These people don't plan to stop their careers, put their lives on hold, or let their future children control their lives. But they are going into parenthood with the right idea: Parents cannot expect to carry on as usual, treating parenthood as an expensive hobby or viewing their children like the advertising agency that pictured a baby on a leash under the bold words "A Child Is the

Ultimate Pet." Children are not pets or accessories to life; they are God-given treasures who take enormous amounts of time, energy, and attention. They take away our rest (especially at the beginning), cost a lot of money, interfere with our schedules, disrupt our plans, and at times bring pain and disappointment. I don't criticize those couples who, for various reasons, decide to remain childless. For some that is a valid choice, even though others may resist parenthood because of their own selfishness. For Julie and me, life has been deeply enriched because we have been parents.

Healthy Parenting

Mr. Henry Goebel was a seventh-grade science teacher who taught for over forty years. He worked with literally thousands of children and their parents, many of whom would seek his advice about child rearing.

"Mr. Goebel, we don't know what to do with our son," anxious parents would say to the wise old educator.

"Wait a year," he would respond, without much further comment. Within twelve months most of the problems would be gone (or be replaced by new ones), and 90 percent of the parents wouldn't be back. Only the still-concerned 10 percent would come for further guidance.

"Mr. Goebel, we've waited a year, and we still don't know what to do with our kid."

"Wait another!" Henry Goebel would say with quiet determination.[13]

Mr. Goebel's homespun advice may be a little simplistic, but he's got a point. When most child-rearing crises arise, parents can be sure that "this too will pass" if they wait a while. Sometimes, however, parents need to make decisions and take action. A laissez-faire approach to child rearing is not always best.

Neither is an approach that involves a frantic scramble for techniques that will work. When Julie and I faced difficult times in bringing up our kids, we didn't rush to psychology texts or self-help books for answers. More often we went to our knees and asked God for wisdom, and we went to our friends whose kids were a little older than ours and asked for their perspective. Often they already had been through what we were going through, and they had helpful, practical suggestions.

In her book *What Good Parents Have in Common,* Janis Long Harris explores characteristics that mark successful parents. After interviewing fifty well-balanced, productive Christian leaders, Harris reports what these men and women see as their parents' contributions to their success as adults. Her findings are good guidelines for other parents.

WHAT GOOD PARENTS HAVE IN COMMON: THIRTEEN GUIDELINES FOR SUCCESS

GOOD PARENTS . . .

1. encourage their children and build their self-esteem
2. communicate their love
3. create a positive home atmosphere (that includes laughter)
4. nurture spiritual values
5. show consistent, balanced discipline
6. make their children proud of them
7. create community—extended family, neighborhood, and church
8. give children the feeling that they are safe and emotionally secure
9. model a good marriage
10. take time to spend time with their children
11. teach financial values and skills
12. give children responsibility
13. are passionate about teaching values and integrity

Adapted from Janis Long Harris, *What Good Parents Have in Common* (Grand Rapids: Zondervan, 1994).

Of course, Harris isn't the only one to write a recent book about parenting. While I have been writing this chapter, the table at my side has been holding a stack of over twenty parenting books, most written by Christian authors and all filled with useful techniques for raising children and teenagers.[14] Parenting is a skill that we have to learn, and it is probable that each of these techniques has been helpful to some parents.

We must be cautious, however, lest we conclude that good techniques are all that matter. If techniques were all-important, we could pass our kids on to teachers, youth leaders, and other surrogate parents and expect that they would do the most effective child rearing. Too many parents take this route and wonder why their kids grow up messed up.

The answer involves love, attention, and showing children that they are valuable. Recently the people in a church on Chicago's south side got concerned about the large numbers of kids who were going home to empty houses after school. So the church started an after-school program that involved activities, sports, and tutoring. Before long the local school principal began getting reports about the improved behavior and better grades of the kids who were in this church-related program. So the school board applied for a government grant and set up a program of its own. It failed! The kids didn't want to go to the school program. Instead, they wanted to go to the church, where they were showered with affection, learned standards of right and wrong, and heard about Jesus. Even in dealing with kids for a few hours after school, techniques are important, but they aren't enough. They need to be applied with love, hugs, and a warm human touch, especially from moms and dads.

Great Dads and Incredible Moms

If you walk into almost any bookstore today, you'll find books about mothering and a lot of books about fathering. A woman in Oregon has written a whole book to show that moms can be incredible. A Kansas psychiatrist has written a book about the art of mothering. A California psychologist has written one book about daughters and their fathers and another book subtitled "Helping Fathers Relate to Sons and Sons Relate to Fathers." A counselor and father of two sons has a book telling dads "how to teach your son about sex and manhood." Two people in Colorado wrote about a strategy by which faithful parents can "pass the baton of faith" on to faithful kids. And two writers from the National Center for Fathering write about ways in which wives can help their husbands be better fathers. Added to this are the books that describe the "father hunger" that develops when children grow up without the love of a father and what they can do about it when they reach adulthood.[15]

BUILDING HEALTHIER PARENT-CHILD RELATIONSHIPS

JOSH MCDOWELL, M.DIV.
President, Josh McDowell Ministry
Author of *Right from Wrong*

A young Jewish man named Daniel made an uncanny commitment. He "resolved not to defile himself with the royal food and wine" (Dan. 1:8). Daniel stuck to his guns. He upheld the values taught to him at an early age. His convictions went deeper than the pressure of his circumstances. He knew the difference between right and wrong.

How do we raise Daniels in our homes?

In an age when sexual promiscuity is as rampant in the church as in secular society, we parents must develop good relationships with our children. It is there that we can positively and effectively teach our convictions and values, in particular about God's design for sex.

Looking at the seemingly insurmountable odds against your teenager, it would be easy to clamp down with rules. But *rules without relationships lead to rebellion.* Rules alone won't work.

Let me share four building blocks—I call them the four A's—that may help develop closer, healthier parent-child relationships. Applying these relational building blocks will go a long way toward establishing open, intimate relationships with your kids.

1. *Provide Acceptance.* Communicate love so that your kids know that you love them no matter what. This gives your kids *security.*
2. *Give Appreciation.* Add significance to your acceptance. Become a "good-finder." Look for attitudes and behavior that you can sincerely praise, compliment, and encourage. This gives your kids a sense of *significance.*
3. *Be Available.* Spend quality *and* quantity time with your children. Love really is spelled T-I-M-E. This gives your kids a sense of *importance.*
4. *Show Affection.* Hug your children. Shower them with kisses. And always tell them that you love them. This gives your kids a sense of *lovableness.* ✜

Maybe we have too many books like these, but at least some of them are sorely needed. Too often publications, articles, television programs, and movies have attacked both parents, creating the impression that mothering and fathering are second-best activities. Some extreme feminists have argued that demanding and immature children don't deserve the serious attention and energy of liberated and sophisticated women. Full-time moms sometimes are viewed as mindless, overweight women who have no sex appeal and little to contribute to society. Fathers often are seen as hardworking career builders whose other activities are reason for leaving most of the child rearing to women.

More recently, these harmful and grossly inaccurate pictures of parents have been changing. Mothers and fathers are both viewing their roles with greater respect, and many see new importance in their roles as attentive parents. Perhaps some of these healthy and long-overdue attitude changes have come from popular media articles that document the long-term effects of absent or neglectful parents. And the changes have come to many homes because of the faithful teaching of church leaders who have never doubted the importance and impact of both mothers and fathers.[16]

Parents and Children Growing Together

Kyle's mom and dad learned the hard way. Kyle had always been active and hard to handle, but as he got older, he became "unmanageable," "impossible to control," "a little hellion." The house was always in a state of disruption, and the family rarely sat down to eat together. Kyle constantly made demands, interrupted whatever routines were left, and defied both parents. He was getting involved with the wrong type of kids at school and had learned how to embarrass his family in shopping malls, at school, and in the church where the parents were actively involved. When the parents came to the office of a Christian counselor, they were in desperate need of help. Their son, who in many ways was out of control, nevertheless had taken over control of his family. These parents had a big problem; Kyle didn't think there was any problem at all.

SELF-ESTEEM AND THE FAMILY

LARRY DAY, PH.D.
Behavioral Healthcare Northwest
Author of *By Design and in God's Image*

In 1966, I completed a fifteen-month hitchhiking trip around the world. I lived with families in Europe, the Middle East, and the South Pacific. Returning home, I needed a worldview that would give meaning and worth to my life (self-esteem) and to all human life (human-esteem), as well as giving me a perspective on the value and importance of the family in a modern world. These are a few of my perspectives on how self-esteem relates to the Christian life and to our families.

1. *God is there, and he is good.* Life is here by design and finds its ultimate meaning and purpose in the person and presence of God.
2. *A secure sense of self-esteem is directly linked to the truth of our being made in the image of God.* The worth of every human being rests on this one great truth. God values and loves what he has created because we are made in his likeness. He loves us for who we are, not for what we do. An appreciation of this truth leads a person to a sense of worship. "I praise you because I am fearfully and wonderfully made" (Ps. 139:14).
3. *The Cross became the greatest symbol ever of the worth God placed on our lives.* I am convinced that one reason Jesus was willing to give his life for our salvation is that he saw our worth. He loves us because we are wonderfully made in his image. Many of us have trusted Jesus for our salvation; few of us have trusted Jesus with our worth.
4. *The family unit is stronger psychologically and spiritually when each person has a healthy appreciation of his or her own worth.* The degree to which we can appreciate our personal worth is the degree to which we can genuinely see the worth in others.
5. *The family was designed by God to fulfill the divine purpose of promoting the growth and development of God's image in each person (Matt. 19:4-5).* The family is the social and spiritual structure for helping people become fully human, fully alive, and fully Christian.

Christians can be at the front of the parade telling the world about the love of God and the worth he gives each of us as bearers of his image. We can hold high the banner that reaffirms the importance of the family in a modern world.

Several factors could account for unmanageable behavior like Kyle's: parents who are too lax or too controlling, mothers and fathers who lack good parenting skills, kids who are calling for attention, or perhaps something biological in the child. Within recent years, research has shown that some people have a brain chemical imbalance that makes it difficult and sometimes impossible for them to sit still or concentrate, even when they try. Sometimes called attention deficit hyperactivity disorder (ADHD or ADD), this condition is seen most often in children, but it can persist for many people into adulthood. Kyle's counselor checked this out, and the boy was put on medication that replaces the missing brain chemical.[17] That helped to calm him down and increase his attention span.

But the counselor also helped the parents see that they were encouraging Kyle's disruptive behavior. If he acted up in public or when one of his parents was on the phone, they would give him what he wanted so they could stop his outbursts. That's what psychologists call reinforcing negative behavior. The counselor taught the parents to resist this kind of manipulation, and he urged them to each spend twenty minutes a day in "special-time activities" with their son.

That was not easy. Kyle said he wasn't interested, and the parents claimed that they didn't have twenty minutes a day to give. Then, when they agreed to the program, neither of them knew what to say for twenty minutes. But they learned to listen, to show genuine interest in their son, and to reinforce the positive things he did. Slowly, communication improved and Kyle's behavior started changing. The parents learned that parenting, like marriage building, needs a high level of investment.

"Kyle's family was great to work with," his counselor said later. "It was good to see a family in chaos coming back together, to see the power a family can have when they work on their relationships."

Some Parents Hurt

Kyle should be happy because his family is mending. Kyle's parents have reason to be happy too. They may not know it, but families in their neighborhood face ongoing pain and disruption. Some kids don't turn out as their parents expected, and the

THE NEED FOR GODLY MOTHERING

GRACE H. KETTERMAN, M.D.
Child Psychiatrist, Former Medical
Director, Crittenton Center
Author of *Parenting the Difficult Child*

On a shelf in my office stands a bronze figure, full of memories. A mother, hair swept into a bun, long skirt blowing, holds her child on her hip while feeding a flock of hens. The child's gaze is fastened on the busy chickens she can almost hear clucking. It was a Mother's Day gift from my children. Symbolically, it is a poignant picture from my past.

Mothering has been derogated by women in this and recent decades. Competing with men has become a cause. The glamour and materialism of a career have deceptively outglittered the often drab and even drudgery-laden tasks of bearing and nurturing the lives of children. Feminism has shifted priorities and values so that it is now-centered. The total health of future generations has been relegated to forces outside the home and to persons who lack the commitment of a mother's imprinting love.

Perhaps the most urgent need of our era is the restoration of the high value of godly mothering. Crime, narcissism, and calloused insensitivity—all of such grave concern—cannot be cured by law or taxes. But they can be prevented by the wisdom of loving training and discipline. The motivation of wanting to please a committed mother can enable a child to forego instant, selfish gratification and help him or her learn self-discipline, compassion, honesty, and other values.

Those of us who cherish biblical values must teach and practice them consistently. Those of us who are mothers must see that responsibility as a high privilege. We must reclaim our role as the shapers and supporters of the next generation of leaders and parents. May we rise to the challenge.

---

parents are disappointed, confused, angry, and on edge. Their frustration spills out in sharp comments directed to each other. Parents in your neighborhood and mine have been rejected by their kids or have lost their kids to incurable diseases, mental disorder, or to the seductive influence of mind-twisting drugs. I know a father who hurts because his son has made a mess of his life and sits in a tiny prison cell. I know a Christian mother who prays for her son and believes that God will somehow intervene, despite the young man's consistent drinking and violent behavior when he gets drunk. We all know parents like these.

My hunch is that few hurting parents will read these words. A book on family life is not the kind of thing they want to read or can handle emotionally. They are people who need others to pray for them, to be interested in them, to accept them when they feel so defeated. These parents need to be encouraged to talk about their feelings of guilt. They probably feel guilt, even if they had nothing to do with the waywardness of their children. These parents also should know that they aren't alone, that hurting parents probably are more numerous than we may think. Someday many of them will have a new appreciation for the wonderful story of the Prodigal Son. That self-centered kid wandered far away from home and threw off all the values he had been taught. But he came back.[18]

Wayward children don't all come back, of course. Some destroy themselves. Some have parents who go to their graves grieving. The only thing we know for sure is that God understands and is still in control. I would hope that hurting and disappointed parents know, as well, that people like you and me are standing by and willing to care.

All Parents Get Older

At a conference not long ago, I saw an old friend who talked about the time when I was his Sunday school teacher. He was an undergraduate student at Purdue and had attended the class I taught at a tiny church that met in a small house across from the campus. I was a graduate student at the time, probably at least seven or eight years older than Judd. Today he has a head of beautiful white hair and is writing a book about the joys of being a grandfather. I told him that anybody who had been a student of mine obviously is too young to be a grandfather.

That's wrong. What's right is that parents get older and get to be grandparents and great-grandparents. This can be a joyful and

MAKING ROOM FOR DAD IN THE PARENTING TEAM

JUDD SWIHART, PH.D., AND NANCY
SWIHART, M.A.
Judd, International Family Center
Nancy, Manhattan Christian College
Nancy is coauthor of *Beside Every
Great Dad*

A massive old oxen yoke hangs in our barn, serving as a reminder of the teamwork that once was required for survival. We like to think that parents are yoked together in the bonds of parenting. Yet, too often the job of parenting is done chiefly by the mother. Children thus lose the benefit of the combined feminine and masculine input that gives balance and structure to their perceptions of themselves and their world.

When fathers are not involved, children are more likely to drop out of school, score lower academically, abuse drugs and alcohol, and engage in delinquent behavior.

Research shows that dads want to be involved with their children, but they feel hindered by obstacles. These include a scarcity of time, money, and energy; personal character flaws such as anger or impatience; a lack of good parenting skills; competition of outside forces for the attention and affection of the children; and lack of support from the man's wife.

Wives can do much to encourage their husbands in the parenting task: Pray for the obstacles their husbands face, give them space to interact with the children in a masculine way, and give them positive feedback.

Research shows that most husbands say their wives are their greatest asset in fathering. A wise wife and a loving mother will gladly make room for Dad in the parenting team. 🔅

---

fulfilling period of life—maybe even the best time of life—when the children are grown and the pace of living sometimes is slower. We all know, however, that this doesn't always happen. Parents can feel pain when their married children get divorced or have trouble with their own kids. Sometimes grown children and their parents face constant conflict. When you are older and your descendants are scattered in different parts of the country, you can feel lonely and have strong desires for closer family ties.

As we get older, our health begins to fail, and the kids who once needed their parents now find that the roles are reversed. The shift was dramatic in my life. On the day my dad had a heart attack, both parents turned to me. Overnight I became the family leader, even when my parents were both still alive. I learned what it was like to have my parents needing me more than I needed them. Now that they have died, I look back on those difficult times and have no regrets.

No Regrets

Perhaps that is what all parents hope for. We know we all make mistakes, but few things are more rewarding than receiving affirmation from your kids after they have grown up. Julie and I feel this way about our two daughters. Both had struggles at different times, but we all came through them and are stronger as a result.

Advice columnist Ann Landers must get a lot of mail from people who complain about their parents and blame their families, but letters like the following show that families can work very effectively and that parents can and do succeed.

Dear Ann Landers:

Can you stand one more letter from a daughter who blames her parents for everything?

I blame my parents for a happy childhood. They were always there when I needed them. They never missed one of my basketball games and always knew what to say when we lost.

I also blame them for my college education. They worked hard to support me and pay my way. I blame my parents for my sense of honesty and fairness. Dad never brought home from work as much as a pencil that belonged to the company.

It's my parents' fault that I'm open-minded and compas-

ENCOURAGING REVELATIONS FOR BATTLE-FATIGUED PARENTS

BUDDY SCOTT
Founder, Parenting within Reason
support groups for parents
Author of *Relief for Hurting Parents*

"A dark cloud has settled over our home and won't go away. From time to time, a tornado drops out and traumatizes us. Our family is under threat, our faith is being tested, our friends don't know how to respond, and we are feeling exhausted. What do we do?"

This cry for help came from a battle-fatigued couple whose teenaged daughter had begun to deceive, manipulate, hide things, sneak out, skip school, insult family values, and negatively influence siblings.

These parents felt lonely, but they were not alone. Losing kids to wrong-crowd influences is epidemic. Thousands of hurting parents are living under dark clouds and asking, "What do we do?"

Here are four revelations that pierce the dark clouds with rays of hope and provide a new and improved spiritual foundation on which to begin applying practical concepts and principles:

1. *Stop thinking you are abandoned.* Jesus Christ loves, understands, and supports hurting parents. Who was the hero of the story about the Prodigal Son? The hurting father. Be reaffirmed by this revelation.

2. *Realize that you and God have more in common now.* God lost Adam and Eve. Now you know how he feels, and he knows how you feel. The two of you are bonding in deeper companionship. Be comforted by this revelation.

3. *Stop blaming God for not answering your prayers.* You pray astray if you ask God to change your child by force. Christ knocks, but he doesn't barge in. Salvation is knocking; responding is up to your child. Be reassured by this revelation.

4. *Understand that the best witness has the best advantage.* React, therefore, in harmony with Christ by limiting yourself to *healing* attitudes and reactions rather than returning rejection for rejection. This will weight the struggle for the life of your child in your favor. Then give it time. Be empowered with trust and endurance by this revelation. △▲

sionate. They always accepted my weird friends and my off-beat opinions.

If I behave unselfishly, I blame my parents. They were always willing to help us take care of our pets, and they loaned us their car when we needed wheels. I also blame them for my ability to do a good job—they encouraged us to work hard and do our best.

Finally, I blame my parents for molding my siblings and me into people who know how to love. Every day of our lives, my parents set a fine example.

I hope that as a parent, I'll be as caring, patient, and wise as my mom and dad were to us.[19]

9

SINGLE PEOPLE
AND THE FAMILY

A MESSAGE on my fax machine told the sad story. Ben, one of the people whom I had invited to write an article to insert in this book, wanted to share some information about his own family.[1] "With great sorrow and not by my choice, I am seeing the end of my marriage," the message began. His wife had moved to her own apartment and had left Ben to raise their children. "The seriousness of the abuse she experienced as a kid has finally taken its toll," Ben wrote. "I was never able to find a way into her heart. She could not trust me."

The handwritten message went on to ask if I still wanted a short article for this book or if I would prefer to reconsider and turn to somebody else. My response was immediate: I thanked Ben for his honesty and concern about the book, but I told him I was more concerned about him. In urging him to participate, I wrote, "While most of the people who will contribute articles for this book have good families and intact marriages, I doubt that anybody has a perfect marriage or family. If we limited the contributors to people whose lives and families had never known disappointment and failure, we would eliminate everybody from writing—including me."

Ben decided to write the article. (It appears in this book, along with his real name.) But he chose to write about a topic other than his perspective as a recently separated husband who still hopes that his marriage will be saved. In the meantime, he is in the ranks of single parents.

Sue is also a single parent. As a young woman, she learned that her body never would be able to bear children. What she didn't know then was that she would never get married but that she would become the mother of an active family. Earlier we met one of her children, a gutsy little guy named Gus.

Several years before Gus was born, Sue adopted Candi, who came from an unstable, dysfunctional family. By the time Candi was two years old, her birth parents were wanted for murder. Everybody concluded that Candi was mentally handicapped, too slow to benefit from education, and not likely to have a very good future. But Sue took her, nurtured her, and loved her. Raising Candi has not been easy for this single mom, but one thing is certain: Candi is not mentally retarded. Her good grades in high school and her potential for continuing with her education are daily proof.

Gus and Candi's young sister isn't mentally handicapped either, but she has a different impairment: Caroline was born a cocaine baby with no feelings in her extremities. She came into the home when Sue got an unexpected call asking if she would be willing to take one more child. For a number of reasons, Sue had to make the decision and get to the courthouse with $600 in less than an hour. Sue's dad helped her get the car seat and a diaper bag before she jumped into a cab and dashed to the place where she would get another child.

Like Ben and Sue, Randy also lives alone. He is single, thirty-seven years old, and never married. Randy has many friends, a deep commitment to Christ, and an active involvement in his church. Randy wonders why he has not found a wife. He isn't gay, weird, ugly, a social misfit, or tied to his mother's apron strings. He was engaged twice and voluntarily went for counseling to deal with the disappointments when those relationships ended. Someday Randy probably will get married, but for now he lives by himself in a small apartment.

Ben, Sue, and Randy. All three are dedicated Christians. All three are single. Where do people like these fit into a book about the family?

Beyond the Nuclear Family

My three friends aren't part of nuclear families, in which a

186

husband and wife live together with children to whom they are related by blood, kinship, or legal adoption. But my friends are very much a part of two other families—their church families and their extended families.

The Church as a Family

The Bible uses several pictures to describe the church. Believers, for example, are called the people of God or the body of Christ. But we don't see members of the local church specifically described as a family (although this is implied in 1 John 3:1). Despite this, we all have the same Father, and we know that all believers are adopted into God's family (John 1:12-13; Gal. 4:4-7; Eph. 1:5).[2] In Ephesians 5, the clearest and longest discussion of marriage in the New Testament, the husband-wife relationship is compared to the ways in which Christ relates to the church. In many ways, therefore, the church is like a family.

William Barclay, a well-known Scottish Bible scholar, has described how Ephesians 5 was radical at the time it was written. In Greece, "home and family life were near to being extinct, and fidelity was completely nonexistent," according to Barclay.[3] In the Roman Empire things were worse. But Paul, the divinely inspired writer of Ephesians, had a different message. He called for women to be treated with dignity. He taught that "Christian marriage is the most precious relationship in life, whose only parallel is the relationship between Christ and the Church."[4] Little wonder that this idea has been described as a beacon of radiant purity, piercing the darkness of an immoral world.[5]

Since my three single friends are not living with marriage partners, they may find little help in knowing that the relationship of Christ and his church is a picture of the relationship between a husband and his wife. But like everyone else, my single friends can understand adoption. They know that they have been adopted into God's family, and depending on where they attend church, they can feel acceptance, encouragement, love, and close bonds with others in their congregations.

I was reminded of this at church recently when Julie and I met an old friend who told us sadly that he and his wife had separated after more than twenty-five years together. "I don't know how I would make it without this church," my friend said. "In many ways they have become a substitute family for me." Other believers feel the same way, especially when they live far from their childhood families, when their families have broken up, or when the death of a close family member has left them feeling alone and swallowed up by grief.

When I was single, living away from home and away from my parents and other relatives, I tended to think that I was on my own—a man without a family. Apart from one lonely Christmas overseas, surrounded by people who didn't speak my language, I wasn't bothered by being without a family nearby. I went to church and found my closest friends in the congregation, but I never thought of these people as being "family." I was young, my life was busy, and it was refreshing to be on my own. Families didn't much concern me.

I wonder if my thinking would have changed if I had continued living alone—like many people today. Maybe I would have given more thought to the fact that almost everybody has an extended family. They may be scattered geographically or live miles away, but our grandparents, parents, brothers, sisters, aunts, uncles, cousins, in-laws, and other more distant relatives still form our families. They help to give us our identities, and they need to be considered more often when we talk about family issues.

Extended Families

Someone has suggested that no family, and certainly no nuclear family, can provide for all the needs of its members. At a conference several years ago, Australian psychologist John Court said, "The nuclear family is not the kind of family which will survive until 2000, nor indeed would I want to fight for it. It is the extended family which has a long history of stability and the backing of Christian teaching."[6]

Maybe you won't agree with this conclusion, but we all recognize that the extended family has faded in its impact and importance during the past few decades, at least in America. As a nation we are a mobile people, often living great distances from the communities where we were raised. We are strong believers in individualism, busy with our careers and activities, and inclined to give little thought to the families in which we grew up—at least until a crisis or a death pulls us back. Sometimes we are glad to be away from the extended-family squabbles and gossip or the obligation to go to family gatherings. Most of us who have settled away from our extended families tend to get along fairly well, interacting with other couples and nuclear families who also are away from their families of origin.

But extended families give us roots, values, identities, acceptance, and family names. Wherever we travel or wherever we settle, we can find family ties that keep us from being isolated and alone. Even when we have no stable nuclear families of our own, the extended family is usually there to show us acceptance in spite of our faults and failures.

Sometimes we see this emphasis on extended families when we read the Bible, where genealogies and family histories were important. It could be argued that the Scriptures tie extended and nuclear families together and show how these relate to our membership in the family of God's people. Another Australian writer, Rowland Croucher, has summarized this concisely:

> The Bible is full of wisdom about family living. The creation ordinance is foundational (Genesis 2:24), but the Fall distorted family relationships (Genesis 3:16). Humans are made in the image of God—and we become more like God as we grow into loving, truthful, responsible people. Marriage and family are signs of God's love for his people. The Mosaic law was family-centered—e.g., the prohibition of adultery and the command to honor parents. When God became one of us in Jesus Christ, he was born into a family and raised and cared for in a family (Luke 2:51-52). Jesus' followers, the apostles, affirm a stable family life within the family of the church (Ephesians 5:22–6:4); we are to care for members of our family (1 Timothy 5:8). Some who forbid

marriage or encourage extramarital sexual relations are strongly rebuked (1 Corinthians 7:2; 1 Timothy 4:3). Earth is the place where God wants us to bear the family likeness of his Son (Romans 8:28f), and heaven will be a grand family reunion, where we shall belong to a spiritual, eternal family rather than a biological family (Matthew 22:30).[7]

Until we have that grand reunion, however, we live on earth in families that often are broken, imperfect, scattered, and sometimes shaken by a variety of family shocks.

Single Parenting

All of us are born as the result of a partnership between a couple whose sexual union has caused them to become a mother and a father. Ideally, the resulting children survive until the time of birth and grow up in homes where two biological parents act as partners in carrying out their parental duties. Everybody knows, however, that this ideal is becoming less and less common.

The numbers differ, depending on which survey you read, but census figures indicate that about 25 percent of American families are headed by one parent; in about 87 percent of the cases this is a woman. Estimates suggest that between 50 and 70 percent of children will experience the death, divorce, or separation of parents before the children reach the age of eighteen. This means that most kids will spend a portion of their growing-up years in a single-parent family.[8]

Fantasies and Facts about Single Parents

Katha Pollitt, associate editor of *The Nation,* sounds like a friend of Murphy Brown when she gives her views of single motherhood. "Marriage no longer serves women very well," Pollitt wrote in the *New York Times.* "If single women can have sex, their own homes, the respect of friends and interesting work, they don't need to tell themselves that any marriage is better than none. Why not have a child on one's own? Children are a joy, many men are not. . . . To take care of a child makes sense. . . . To take care of a husband after working all day makes much less sense, but most men seem to expect it."[9] Pollitt calls marriage an outworn institution, lauds single motherhood, and criticizes people who corral women into marriage "by making appeals to morality and self-sacrifice."

Diatribes like this are common in the media, and although there is ample evidence that some single-parent families get along well, we have seen that most of the evidence strongly points the other way. We know that kids from single-parent homes have more problems—like academic and learning difficulties, emotional distress, behavioral problems, and poor relationships with peers.

We also know that adults who grew up in single-parent families have less success in school, lower earnings, less likelihood of building stable marriages, more financial difficulties, and lower occupational prestige when they grow up—even when researchers take into account other important issues like the person's race, past family experiences, and other background factors.[10]

Less common are reports about the struggles of the single parents themselves. Single-parent families differ greatly, but many single parents, especially working mothers, feel overloaded, unable to find time for their personal needs, and often tired because they have gone without sleep or leisure so they could be available to meet the needs of their children. Many of these parents feel lonely, and some are keenly aware of their lack of a partner as they live in a society dominated by couples. Because single parents often shoulder the entire financial responsibility for their families, many single parents perpetually worry about money and paying the bills.[11] Facts like these tend to be forgotten by people who fantasize about how good it is to go solo in raising children.

Single Parents Aren't All the Same
Many people assume that single-parent families are all troubled and dysfunctional. That is not true. It also is not true that all single-parent families are alike. To use an extreme example, the family headed by a poor, unemployed, inner-city single mother is different from the family headed by an affluent single parent who is employed and able to afford day care for the children. Children

from both families may have problems; children from both may turn out fine.

To assume that all single parents or their children are the same overlooks the impact of issues like family circumstances (for example, whether the single parent is widowed, divorced, abandoned, or a never-married person who chose to adopt), parenting capability, income level, employment status of the parent, and degree of support from a former spouse or from the extended or church family. One study compared low-income, African American single-parent families living in Philadelphia. The families were not all the same. Some were dysfunctional, but the families that got along fine had clear boundaries and responsibilities for everybody in the home and closeness to friends and extended family members who could and readily did give support.[12]

Single Parenting Is Tough

Several years ago Julie and I got a Christmas card and a photograph from one of my former students who never married but who wanted to be a parent. The photograph showed the smiling adoptive mother sitting next to her two daughters, who appeared to be from India. My former student is a single mother by choice. The same is true of the priest who legally adopted two unwanted little boys as his sons.

More often, however, people don't choose to be single parents. They raise children alone because the other parent has died or has deserted, divorced, or separated from the spouse. Some people are forced to raise the children alone because their partners are in jail, away on military duty, or so busy with a career that the spouse at home is, in most every way, a single parent.

What problems do these parents face? One team of researchers from Oregon conducted in-depth interviews with sixty women and eleven men who were single parents, mostly white and middle-class.[13] The same issues surfaced repeatedly and were similar to the issues that other researchers have seen in poorer, nonwhite single parents. Each of these problem issues can make parenting more difficult and contribute to the disadvantages experienced by children from single-parent homes.

1. *Money.* The most common problems were money and financial worries. This was a problem for almost 80 percent of the sixty interviewed single mothers, but for less than 20 percent of the fathers. Plenty of evidence indicates that single mothers, especially those who have been divorced, usually experience dramatic drops in income. The departed spouse often fails to pay child support and the single parent is left with both a reduced income and the heavy expenses of raising children.
2. *Overload.* Many single parents work outside the home, some in demanding jobs that take time and energy. Over half the women and almost half the men who were interviewed mentioned the difficulty of juggling work and family responsibilities, trying to fit school and work schedules into family routines, and managing a household with no other adult to share the workload and decisions. After interviewing numerous divorced mothers, the writers of one book about parenting concluded that "being the head of a household is, for most women [and probably for most men], an eighteen hours a day, seven days a week, and 365 days a year job. It would seem that only the most capable, and the most fortunate, can perform all of the roles effectively."[14] Maybe it should surprise us that some parents and kids from single-parent families do as well as they do.
3. *Social Lives.* Most single parents have been married and most get remarried. That means that most are involved in dating, an experience that for some can be very stressful. Even those who remain single want to have social interaction with their friends, but this is difficult to fit into their schedules. Sometimes single parents feel like misfits, especially when they are involved with social gatherings attended mainly by couples.

4. *Roles.* Most single parents face conflicts and confusion about their roles. How does a woman, for example, be both mother and father to her children after her marriage breaks up, and what happens if she marries a new husband who has also been playing both mother and father roles? How do they blend their families and still keep peace with the kids?

5. *Former Spouses.* Divorced single parents face the added problem of dealing with a former spouse. They may face conflict, mistrust, manipulation, and other problems that make life more difficult for the single parent. In addition, the divorced single parents may feel rejected by people, including some Christians, who criticize unmarried parents for being unmarried parents.

In an insightful and practical book, Christian psychologist David R. Miller notes some of the questions that single parents face when they find themselves in the single-parenting role. The questions, which appear in the list on the next page, are good topics for friends or counselors to discuss with single parents.

Miller suggests other issues that may appear and cause additional dilemmas for single parents. For example, after a divorce or the death of a spouse, a child sometimes slips into the role of the departed spouse, becoming the single parent's confidant or defender, or taking over adultlike roles such as parenting other children or doing extra household duties. Usually this isn't good for either the children or the single parent. In addition, some single parents lose perspective and become burdened by their parenting responsibilities. Others are overwhelmed by guilt, feelings of incompetence, or overdependence on their family of origin. A few newly single parents resume dating and begin acting like adolescents—at the same time that their children are trying to act more like adults.

But these are exceptions. They shouldn't blind us to the fact that many single parents rise above their stresses and live very productive lives.

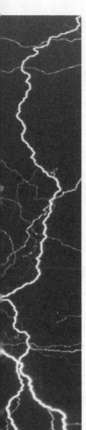

QUESTIONS SINGLE PARENTS FACE

1. *How do I parent alone?* This can be stressful and anxiety producing, complicated by concerns about discipline, finding employment, and developing relationships.
2. *Is it okay and normal to feel as lonely as I feel?* And how long will this last?
3. *How do I cope with all the demands?*
4. *How will I manage financially?* Single parents who go to many church-based counselors find advice that is long on principles (remember to tithe, don't go into debt) but short on how to manage on a day-to-day basis.
5. *Is there life after divorce?* More than anything else this is an expression of worry about the future.
6. *What will my family become?* Parents worry about the adjustment of their children, how being raised by a single parent will impact their futures, how the family will relate to extended family members, etc.
7. *Am I a strong enough Christian to trust God to meet my needs?* Often single parents feel that their faith is being tested by the pressures, and many wonder if they will fall short.
8. *Will I ever again be accepted as a full member of my church?* Or will I always carry the label of being different?
9. *What resources are available to me?* Who or what can help me with my finances, finding employment, developing friendships to combat my loneliness, or giving me help with the burdens?

Adapted from David R. Miller, *Counseling Families after Divorce: Wholeness for the Broken Family* (Dallas: Word, 1994), 212-214.

Single Parenting to the Tenth Degree

While single-parent families are never ideal, some of them are headed by remarkable people, mainly women. Most of these women never wanted to be single parents, but they manage to bring up their children successfully despite financial hardships.

Grethel Beyah is such a woman.

For seventeen years, Beyah survived in an abusive marriage. The family moved repeatedly, usually after they were evicted when they had no money to pay the rent. One cold Chicago winter, Beyah was trying to help her husband load their furniture from the street into a truck. "I just went to the back and started crying," she said, "and the tears were freezing to my face it was so cold out."[15]

The couple went for counseling, but that didn't help. They eventually called it quits and got a divorce. The young mother was left with nine children, several of whom were too young to go to school. "God gave me insight to do things I didn't know how to do," Beyah reflected recently. Her divorce forced her to be both mother and father for her family. "I knew I was left with the responsibility of raising my children to be productive people, and I just had to pull from whatever was inside of me. I wanted to give them a foundation that could take them all the way. My philosophy was 'If I die today, where would my children be?' So I tried to prepare them to be self-sustaining."[16]

Beyah got a job working for Sears, but one person's salary didn't go far in clothing and feeding ten people. "We were hungry," she said. "We were not clothed too well. We didn't have anything much to go on except each other." Still, the busy mother tried to contain her kids. "I figured once the streets got hold of them, I would lose them," she reasoned, so she kept them busy in free dance, music, and gymnastic classes offered through the park district.[17] She limited their exposure to television, supervised what they watched, and often discussed with them what they had seen. One by one the children grew into young adulthood. All were high school honor students; three were valedictorians. Seven of the nine earned university degrees, and two are college seniors.

When it became clear that all nine children would earn bachelor's degrees (two have gone on to graduate programs), Grethel Beyah decided to go for the tenth degree—one for herself. When she got it last winter, after maintaining a B average and completing all the requirements for a degree in computer science from DeVry Institute of Technology, all of her kids were there. "I sacrificed for my children and got all of them through school and out on their own," she said. "Now it is my turn." The graduation speaker mentioned Beyah's commitment to excellence, and one of her children described her as a woman of integrity, perseverance, and caring.[18]

Despite their best efforts, not all single parents are able to succeed as Grethel Beyah has. Children from some homes stray into harmful paths despite the best parenting. But others are like fifty-four-year-old Beyah, who walked across the stage to get her diploma. Section by section the audience rose to applaud, and a few cheered. The applause grew louder and lingered. If I had been there, I would have applauded, and I bet you would have too.

Single-Parent Families Can Be Healthy

In an earlier chapter, we considered the work of the Search Institute in Minneapolis. Those same researchers recently studied children who are being raised in single-parent families. "If you could wave a magic wand, we would guarantee that every child had two responsible, caring, and committed parents," the researchers wrote in a report of their work. "But given that this won't happen, our challenge is to discover ways to maximize the number of strong, two-parent families while also supporting all families—including single-parent families—in their efforts to raise healthy children."[19]

When the researchers compared young people from families headed by one parent with those from two-parent families, they found that kids from two-parent homes had more of the assets, or building blocks, that promote health and help young people thrive. But many single-parent homes nevertheless are able to provide the assets that enable children to thrive and survive the growing up years. The list on the next page looks at the assets possessed by young people from single-parent families.

This study led the researchers to conclude that statements about two-parent families being good and single-parent families always being bad overstate the case. "True, two-parent families have the edge. Being a single parent is tough work, and it is not optimal for children. But with special effort—with the support of individuals, communities, and institutions around them—single-parent families can be supportive, healthy families in which young people will thrive."[20]

Strengthening Single Parents

Single parents can take heart: For most single parents, things get easier as time passes. Some research found that about 25 percent of the single parents surveyed said that single parenting got harder over time; most of these parents were having difficulty managing adolescents. Roughly 10 percent reported that things stayed the same, but 65 percent said that single parenting got easier. Often these parents got into a routine, became less anxious and more confident, and reported that they had grown in five key areas of family strength.[21]

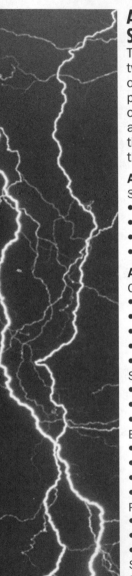

ASSETS OF YOUNG PEOPLE WHO THRIVE IN SINGLE-PARENT FAMILIES

This chart looks at young people (in grades six through twelve) from single-parent families and compares two groups of students: those who thrive versus those who experience problems. "Thrivers" are those who are involved in none or only one of twenty at-risk behaviors (such as frequent alcohol use, illicit drug use, sexual activity, depression, theft, vandalism, or school absenteeism); "non-thrivers" are those who are involved in five or more of these behaviors.

Assets	Thrivers	Non-thrivers
SUPPORT		
• Family is supportive	64%	34%
• Parent is a social resource	59%	34%
• Parent is involved in schooling	29%	18%
• School climate is positive	37%	18%

Assets	Thrivers	Non-thrivers
CONTROL		
• Parents discipline	60%	41%
• Parents monitor children	79%	64%
• Parents have standards	85%	47%
• Young people spend time at home	73%	54%
• Kids have positive peer influences	37%	16%
STRUCTURED-TIME USE		
• Involved in music	26%	15%
• Involved in extracurricular activities	58%	44%
• Involved in church or synagogue	57%	31%
EDUCATIONAL COMMITMENT		
• Motivated to achieve in school	82%	53%
• Wants further education	31%	15%
• School performance is good	49%	27%
• Homework gets done	31%	15%
POSITIVE VALUES		
• Values helping people	60%	41%
• Concerned about world hunger	53%	34%
• Values sexual restraint	52%	7%
SOCIAL COMPETENCIES		
• Has planning skills	62%	49%
• Has good self-esteem	53%	32%

Adapted from *Search Institute Source* newsletter (June 1993).

1. *Parenting skills,* the first of the five, include learning to set limits, being patient and supportive of children, helping children cope with their problems, and fostering independence. Parenting seminars or church-related parent-training programs can help single people acquire these skills. Mentoring programs in which experienced single parents assist the less experienced are also effective. Small groups of single parents can share parenting concerns, give mutual encouragement, and provide opportunities for acquiring new parenting skills.

   The researchers who make these suggestions never mention the word, but the essence of good parenting is *love.* The best parents are able to love their children, just as Christ loves us unconditionally, with guidelines for effective and healthy living.

2. *Family management* includes learning to be well organized and dependable. This involves managing the checkbook, cooking nutritious meals, and coordinating home schedules with school, community, and church programs. Some people do this well and seem to be naturally organized. Most others learn by trial and error, often with the help of relatives, older parents, and counselors. Evidence suggests that for single parents who are divorced, co-parenting works best for the children and sometimes helps everybody to manage better. This works best if the separated parents can put aside their hurts or hostilities and work together for the good of their children without shuttling the kids back and forth so that they always feel uprooted and have no sense of where they belong.

3. *Good communication* in families involves building a sense of honesty and trust, listening carefully, conveying ideas clearly, and not sending confusing or double messages in which a parent says one thing and does another.

4. *Personal growth* consists of feeling that things are moving along well and that the family can succeed, despite
   the persisting insecurities that most parents feel. This
   is a positive, cautiously optimistic attitude that says, for
   example, "With God's help and the support of my
   friends, I think we'll make it, and my kids will be okay."
5. *Financial strength* doesn't depend only on the size of
   one's income. More important is the parent's sense that
   he or she can provide for the family. For example, one
   mother said, "I found that I could take care of myself
   and my daughter without relying on someone else. I
   didn't go to my parents for financial assistance or
   anyone else, and I felt good that when I had a minor
   crisis, I was able to work it through and take care of it
   myself."[22]

How the Church Can Help

Church families can also work with single people, including
single parents, to develop creative ways to build relationships,
meet needs, challenge thinking, and stimulate both spiritual
growth and accountability. When Julie and I joined with some
others to start a new church two or three years ago, we didn't
have the resources or expertise to develop a singles ministry.
Single people and married couples were both integral parts of the
new church, serving on the committees, planning for the future,
participating together in small groups. We didn't divide people
into a "married couples class" or a "singles class."

As the church has grown, however, the single people have
realized that they have some special needs, unique interests, and
time flexibility that others don't have. So they often go off for lunch
as a group after church, have some of their own social activities,
and sometimes have meetings to discuss the needs of single
people. They have tried to avoid cliques, and they welcome a few
married couples—those without children seem to fit best—who
enjoy their company. While most of the single people are in their
thirties and forties, the group includes two older women who like

SINGLE PEOPLE AND THE FAMILY

MIRIAM J. STARK, PH.D.
Chair, Department of Pastoral
Counseling and Psychology
Trinity Evangelical Divinity School

A door slams. A voice calls, "Hi, Mom. I'm home." Not unusual, except that the owner of the voice is thirty-four, not a teenager. Today many single adults are living at home with parents and extended family. Even for those with separate residences, family connections often remain strong. Living single in a relational world is not easy. Families can be a tremendous source of support or a major hindrance.

In our society marriage is a rite of passage marking a new developmental stage of independence and adulthood (Gen. 2:24). Single people often struggle to find a way to make that transition. Parents may resist their twenty-four-year-old daughter moving out on her own even though they would encourage her to marry. Perhaps families need to develop new rites of passage. Family involvement in moving and a formal open house, for example, may deepen family bonds as the single adult begins life away from home.

Family attitudes toward singleness need to be evaluated honestly. Underlying fears ("What's wrong with you?") can warp family relationships and self-esteem. That "it is good for a man [or woman] not to marry" is hard for many families to accept (1 Cor. 7:1). Family pressure may foster hasty, disastrous relationships. Hidden messages ("You can't make good decisions on your own") can strangle independence and produce helplessness, ultimately a family burden. Open discussion can prevent hidden bitterness and resentment.

Acceptance and understanding are crucial for both the single adult and the family. God made us relational beings, and he "sets the lonely in families" (Gen. 2:18; Ps. 68:6). Now we must make those families places of mutual support and nurture throughout a lifetime. ✺

to join with them and who feel accepted as part of the family, even if they sit on the sidelines while others are more active.

This group works to avoid being isolated from the rest of the congregation. They participate fully in all-church activities, never schedule any activity that would conflict with other church functions, worship as part of the congregation (not choosing to cluster and sit together as a group), and try to serve in various capacities, including teaching the kids and taking turns in the nursery. Many recognize that they have more available time than couples with children, so the single people are available to give extra help when others are involved with nuclear-family activities.

What has happened in our church might not fit in yours. Every congregation is different, except for this: In the body of Christ we are all equals, regardless of our family status (Gal. 3:28). Single people might not experience the same family shocks that married couples encounter, but we all need support, mutual encouragement, and opportunities to serve in God's family. We must never get so enthusiastic about family values and family strengths that we forget the people who are like Jesus in at least one important way—they're single.

SCOTT

W hen Scott Thelander agreed to help with an outreach
program to kids in gangs, he never dreamed where
his involvement would lead.[23]

Scott, a single man, graduated from seminary and moved to
California to enroll in a doctoral program that would train him
to be a professional counselor. Like most students, he had a
part-time job along with his full-time studies at the university.
Already stretched to the limit, Scott was hesitant when a friend
asked him to help out with a program intended to reach
Hispanic gang members through youth activities, once-a-week
outings, and Bible studies. Somewhat reluctantly, Scott agreed
to get involved, but he made it clear that he could help only for
the summer. Shortly after he started and without warning, the
youth program ended because it ran out of money. All of the
paid staff members were transferred to other places, and Scott
was left with the kids.

Most of the kids drifted away, but several young Mexican
immigrants wanted to keep in touch with Scott. They took
him to meet their families, who lived in an Orange County
working-class community. In the months that followed, Scott
got to know the Martinez family very well.

How could a *guero* from Indiana relate to an immigrant
family from Mexico?[24] Scott wisely decided that the most important thing he could do to build a relationship was to observe

the Martinez family and learn about Mexican-American families. He said very little at the beginning, even when the kids talked about behaviors that Scott knew could be harmful. As a counselor-in-training, he suspected that the kids probably would test this tall white man to see how he would react to their bad language and tough attitudes. They respected the fact that he was religious (even though he was not Catholic), but they must have wondered if Scott would be intimidated, condemning, arrogant, or impatient once he got to know them better.

Instead, the guero kept coming back to their sometimes dangerous neighborhood. He suspended judgment when they talked, listened attentively, and tried to understand, even though he was saddened by some of their values, activities, and plans. Scott learned about their stereotypes of police as bad guys intent on wiping out good gang members. As the relationship developed, Scott gently pointed out some things that would give them a more realistic perspective of policemen, all of whom are people with feelings and most of whom have families, just like the gang members' families.

Scott wisely decided that his role as a Christian in this situation was to accept the kids where they were and not to be aggressively evangelistic. He maintained his Christian commitment and shared the gospel when it was natural. He prayed that God would love the kids through him. Scott sensed that sharing his faith in a crosscultural setting meant being sensitive to the culture, respecting the community values, and building trust.

Scott knew that he was earning their trust when they suggested that he dress like them. He declined, but he did grow a goatee for the summer. The gang members were too young to follow suit, but they clearly were delighted with Scott's willingness to get involved with them. They began to give him their trust. They also gave him some streetwise instructions about areas to avoid at night, brought him into their homes, let the neighbors know that he was a friend, and began to realize that the man from Indiana could be a friend to a family from Mexico. This was a new learning experience for everyone.

How easy it is for any of us to look at people who come from different backgrounds or whose experiences differ from ours and lump them all together. We hear about ghetto families, Native American families, blue-collar families, Asian families, preachers' families, Hollywood families, families in the South— or in the North and forget that each of these families is composed of people like us.

Scott quickly learned that the Martinez family and their neighbors are much like any family: They have good times together, disagreements, trouble managing their kids, family politics, and financial stresses. But Scott also noticed some important differences in this Mexican immigrant community. Here the extended family is very important; the relatives spend lots of time together and stick together, especially when things are difficult.

The Martinez family suffered a family shock when their son Alex joined a gang. Alex was a bright kid, but he was bored with school, had poor grades, and was unable to sit still long enough to concentrate. When he started having behavior problems, he dropped out of school altogether. That's when he joined the gang, which helped him feel accepted, more powerful, and significant.

Alex Martinez, Sr., the young man's dad, has been employed in a steady but low-paying job for twenty years. He wants his children to do well and succeed better than he has, so he and his wife were upset when Alex joined the gang. One of their nephews had been shot and had almost died because of his gang activities, so the Martinez parents were worried about their son.

In the gang Alex joined, new members were initiated by being "jumped in," or beat up, by older boys. Sometimes the recruits would get drunk first so that the beating wouldn't be so painful. These new members, often no older than thirteen, became the most zealous. They dressed like the rest of the gang. They participated in gang activities such as stealing from cars, painting graffiti on buildings, or doing drive-by shootings.

The gang that Alex joined was more interested in camaraderie and mischief than in violence, but the members liked the excitement and rebellious nature of the group. Girls sometimes had their own gangs, but most hung around the male gangs, where they shared in the thrills. That was how Alex met girls and learned to be involved sexually.

As the gang members get older, some of them want to settle down and become more conventional, but they don't know how. They often find only one way to withdraw from the gang, and Alex took that route. He got a girl pregnant.

When Alex's parents discovered that his girlfriend was pregnant, they were angry and shocked. They were also a little relieved. Probably they knew that gang members who become fathers don't have to be active members, attend all the meetings, or be heavily involved.

Scott watched how this family dealt with their family crises. He noticed that no one talked about abortion or marriage. "We value children and life," Mrs. Martinez said, but the family also indicated that they expected their son, still in his teens, to get a job and act like an adult. The sad part is that Alex didn't know how to do this. His whole life had been spent living for the present, never thinking about the consequences of his actions, and rarely concerning himself about the future.

The parents knew what to do about the pregnancy, however. They met with the girl's parents, discussed the situation, and agreed that the girl should move in to the Martinez home, where the couple shared a room and a bed together until they moved recently to another state. To this point there has never been talk of a wedding, but after the baby was born, they took her to be baptized in the Catholic church.

Scott was invited to be the baby's *padrino,* or godfather. In this invitation the family offered Scott an official, long-term place in their family, a high honor that was not given lightly. Knowing that to refuse to be the godfather would have been a grave insult, Scott wanted to accept the invitation, but he is not Catholic. Drawing on what he had learned when he worked alongside missionaries in Bolivia, Scott explained that he would be honored to be the godfather as long as no one would have to lie about his religious affiliation and as long as he could play a part in the spiritual development of the child. The family respected Scott's feelings and readily agreed with this request. They applied their own "don't ask, don't tell" policy. They went to a large parish where the priests perform many baptisms and don't ask about the religious affiliation of the godparents.

When Alex couldn't find a job, some relatives in Arizona suggested that Alex, the girl, and their baby move to their state, where employment possibilities were a little brighter. After Alex left, his father concluded that Scott probably wouldn't visit the Martinez home anymore. But Scott has continued to visit these warmhearted people, who have become his friends.

What has this immigrant family taught this single man about families?

First, families are alike in many ways. All families are made up of people: mothers and fathers, brothers and sisters, aunts and uncles, kids and grandkids. In many ways we are alike. All families have trials and triumphs. All families face problems that are complex and not easily solved.

Second, while families are similar in some ways, all families are different in significant ways. Each family lives with different rules, expectations, and values. Each does things in ways that outsiders might not understand. For instance, when Scott had lived with his own family in Indiana, he had learned that everybody pitched in to help around the house. When Scott spent time with the Martinez family, it was natural for him to carry some plates to the sink after dinner. He learned quickly that most Mexican men don't do this. He became aware of the male-female role differences that he had not seen in the families of his other friends. Scott noticed other differences in how the Martinez family responded when Alex could not find a job. No one thought it unusual that relatives from another state became involved and offered help. Giving emotional support, practical help, and resources were expected parts of the role of the extended family.

Scott learned not only from the way the immigrant family operated but also from the operating procedures in the gang that Alex joined. Gangs exist for a variety of purposes, and they have different rules. For Alex, the gang appeared to be an adolescent group that was not intent on murder or turf wars like some of the gangs in other urban communities. Gangs like the one Alex joined thrive in places where there is poverty, substandard housing, poor-paying jobs (or no jobs), low levels of education, and tension between parents and their adolescent children.[25] The gang gives kids identity, recognition, status, acceptance, and power. It also gives structure and consistent ways of doing things. This, in turn, gives a feeling of security to a lot of kids who don't have it otherwise.

Alex's gang differed from the Asian street gangs that were studied by two social scientists. The Asian gangs were not concerned about territory, gang names, or clothing and tattoos that might draw attention to their members. Instead, the goal was getting money. These gangs, like many that are not Asian, were tied to adult criminals who directed the gang activities.[26]

All gangs influence families. That certainly was true of the Martinez family. As I listened to Scott tell his story, I could see that he had helped Alex adjust to adulthood in the United States. The young man became less dependent on the gang when he had a mentor who showed him respect and acceptance. His family, in turn, was grateful. Alex's dad once told his family that his stereotypes about white people and how they act began to break down when Scott came into their lives.

This story of Scott and the Martinez family reminds us that families come in all shapes and sizes. We all can—and must—learn from each other. We all can grow from becoming involved with families that are different from our own.

Our family has had the experience of living for a while in a community where we didn't understand the language and where we were foreigners. We learned a lot about family life from observing the families around us. Several years ago, one of my daughters dated a Mexican who lived and worked in the United States even though he was here illegally. I don't know if I once harbored prejudices or misconceptions about immigrant people who live in our community, but my discussions with Juan changed my views permanently. Without intending to do this, my daughter's friend gave me a new and lasting appreciation for his countrymen, many of whom are hard workers who strive to raise their families in a new land where they often struggle with language and feel like foreigners.

Your family may never live overseas, but many of you live in culturally and ethnically diverse neighborhoods, towns, or cities. As you encounter people of various cultures, many of whom may be refugees or immigrants, be open to learning from them and be open to helping them adjust.

Families everywhere experience shocks that threaten to topple them, but with the help of family members, the extended family, the community, and the church, they can remain strong. The following chapters will explore several family crises that can send additional shock waves through families.

PART TWO

FAMILIES IN THE MIDST OF CRISES

10

DIVORCE AND THE FAMILY

"I HATE divorce."

That's a clear message, especially when you realize it comes straight from God's mouth.

When the Bible uses the word *hate,* it most often refers to people who hate one another, hate God, or hate believers who follow God. Very rarely does the Bible indicate what God hates, and never is the object of God's hatred stated more bluntly than this: God hates divorce.[1]

He's not alone. Hundreds of thousands of former husbands and wives hate divorce, and so do scared kids whose parents have separated, grown-up children who still bear the scars of family breakups, grandparents who smiled proudly at the weddings of their offspring then watched with agony as those once-happy marriages disintegrated in anger, distrust, and sometimes hatred.

Divorce Takes Its Toll

Melinda Blau experienced the upheaval of divorce firsthand. For nine months after she and her husband, Mark, decided to separate, they lived in chaos. Blau says of her situation:

> We lived together in daily confrontation, sharing our apartment, car, summer house, and children. When he finally moved out, our nastiness only escalated. We were in the thick of a legal battle, hiring experts to protect us and

marshaling friends to support us. One of Mark's buddies, whose loft apartment overlooked mine, had a telescope pointed to my bedroom window. I made sure several of my friends were ready to testify in court to Mark's insensitivity and cruelty. We were frightened, angry and guilty, and eager to point fingers.

Mark and I never meant to hurt our children. Yet, in the wake of our separation, 11-year-old Jennifer, anguished by divided loyalties, developed into a precocious caretaker, fiercely protective of everyone, especially her younger brother. Eight-year-old Jeremy began lying and having problems at school. He looked depressed. One day, when I saw him leaning dangerously over a banister, I called out to him, "Watch out! You might fall."

"I don't care," he answered. He meant it. . . .

By the time we all piled into the cramped office in downtown Manhattan for our first family therapy appointment, we already were swirling in a maelstrom of divorce madness. Mark and I went at it, rehashing old arguments, not hearing anything but our own anger. The kids looked on, frozen, trapped in our rage. "Jeremy and I sat there in the same chair, our arms linked, like a wall," Jennifer, now 24, recalls. . . .

Our legal divorce was finalized in 1983, but achieving an emotional separation proved far more elusive. We had joint custody and every intention of cooperating as co-parents— except we didn't know how. And our children, now living part-time with each of us, stumbled between our houses on a path littered with our marital debris.[2]

After plenty of mistakes and several negative experiences with incompetent therapists, Melinda Blau and her former husband learned to live apart, and their kids are adjusting to young adulthood. I don't know if any of them has an interest in God, but looking back over the past fifteen years, they probably can understand why their Creator hates divorce.

Divorce in the Past Few Decades

Our society's perspective about divorce has changed during the past few decades. In the 1950s, people believed that parents should stay in unhappy marriages for the sake of the children. If a couple did decide to divorce, the law assumed that they had some valid reason. Often this led to expensive and emotionally painful courtroom maneuvering and litigation.

During the 1960s, things began to change. Spurred in part by feminism and a widespread belief in self-determination, people began to reject the idea that divorce was pathological, destructive, or harmful to the kids. Marriage came to be seen as a partnership of autonomous individuals who could dissolve their relationship whenever they wished. No-fault divorce, allowing couples to end their marriages if they had reached a state of "irretrievable breakdown," made marriage a union that is easier to begin and terminate than most business partnerships and other legal contracts. Not surprisingly, all of this led to a rise in the divorce rate. By 1975, for the first time in our history, more marriages were ended by divorce than by death. Today, at least one-fourth of Americans who marry eventually become divorced.[3] Now we are seeing the fallout.

Even secular therapists have come to change their minds about divorce. When family therapist William Doherty first started teaching at the University of Minnesota in the mid-1970s, he viewed divorce as a mere inconvenience—an experience that causes a year or so of stress for adults and children until everybody bounces back and recovers. That's not the way it usually works. Based on his counseling and research, Professor Doherty has entirely reversed his earlier position. Now he tells clients and students that he is "biased toward marriage" and convinced that "all things being equal, children need and deserve to grow up in a family with two parents who love them and love each other." Boston family therapist David Treadway agrees. He calls divorce a lose-lose proposition.[4]

Well-known family life writer Frank Pittman never pretends to be neutral with the couples who come to him for counseling. Divorce lawyers and others brush aside all the research on the harmful effects of divorce and try to make us "believe that children are little adults masquerading as infants, trying to trap their parents into feeling guilty," according to Pittman. "They will not be convinced by anything. And yet we see it every day in our offices, that the most significant event of a person's life is the parental divorce."[5]

Why Do People Get Divorced?

If divorce is this harmful, why do so many marriages break up? Almost every answer you might give probably has been an issue in somebody's divorce. Many people have insecurities, personality traits, poor social skills, or past experiences that leave them longing for relationships. As a result, they make unwise choices and get into bad marriages. When these marriages end, the same needs, problems, and ways of behaving carry into other marriages. I remember counseling a woman who had been in three marriages, all to alcoholics. She hadn't driven them to drink. Instead, something seemed to attract her to these kinds of men and blind her to the potential problems until it was too late.

More often, marriages break up because of conflicts over things like career pressures, family violence and abuse, extramarital affairs, immaturity, differences in religion, lifestyle conflicts, or substance abuse by one or both spouses. When a carefully selected group of 437 divorced or divorcing men and women were asked the reasons for their separations, they talked about a lack of closeness, emotional emptiness, differences in values, frequent disagreements, and communication failures. The list on the next page shows the most frequently given reasons from both husbands and wives.

The types and numbers of disagreements are important, but even more significant may be *how couples handle their conflicts*. Many have a "conflict-confronting, conflict-avoiding" pattern where one spouse, usually the wife, confronts the other with areas of concern, disagreements, and complaints. Often these complaints are expressed with strong emotions that get progressively stronger when the confronted spouse, often the husband, withdraws, ignores what he is hearing, or responds with defensiveness, resentment, and anger. Do you get the picture? One spouse gripes and the other withdraws, then reacts.

REASONS FOR DIVORCE

Ten Most Common Reasons	Males	Females	Total
1. Growing apart, losing a sense of closeness	79%	78%	79%
2. Not feeling loved and appreciated by spouse	60%	73%	67%**
3. Sexual intimacy problems	65%	64%	64%
4. Serious differences in values or lifestyle	57%	63%	60%
5. Spouse unwilling or unable to meet partner's needs	48%	64%	56%**
6. Frequently felt put down or belittled by their spouse	37%	59%	49%**
7. Emotional problems of spouse	44%	52%	48%
8. Conflict about spending and handling money	44%	50%	47%
9. Severe and intense conflict and frequent fighting	35%	44%	40%
10. Conflicts about roles (e.g., division of labor)	33%	47%	40%**

** Denotes statistically significant male-female difference on item.

From Lynn Gigy and Joan B. Kelly, "Reasons for Divorce: Perspectives of Divorcing Men and Women," *Journal of Divorce & Remarriage* 18 (1992): 169–87.

A different way to deal with conflict, one that also leads frequently to divorce, has both the husband and wife keeping silent and rarely arguing, but they are at odds over almost everything. Each of them has different expectations and perceptions about family life, marriage, child rearing, and religion. Often these couples have few shared interests, activities, friends, or reasons to stay together.

In both situations, children see their parents at odds with each other, inconsistent in discipline, disagreeing about child rearing, and so focused on their own struggles that they fail to give adequate attention to the kids. This conflict can have an adverse effect on young people and on their self-esteem, even if their parents stay together.[6] Many children who later suffer following a divorce probably had the seeds of insecurity and inner tension planted long before their parents' divorce was final.[7]

What Does Divorce Do to the Family?

Families shaken by divorce often feel unsettled, angry, confused, and unhappy. Household routines get disrupted, roles and relationships change, incomes tend to go down, and the older children, especially daughters, often take on extra responsibilities at home, including care of younger siblings. The adults sometimes experience new levels of sexual impulsiveness.

In time, things settle down, sometimes after a move and the initial acceptance of one's new lifestyle and marital status. Divorce-recovery groups and support from family, friends, and church members can help the process, but recovery is harder and slower when divorcing people face criticism and rejection. Most divorced people eventually feel a new sense of stability and sometimes contentment, but the scars of divorce remain.

In a culture promoting the idea that each person deserves to be in a fulfilling relationship, it is easy for some people to conclude that leaving a difficult marriage is a good way to avoid problems. People who make this decision will look for others who agree. Most often these other people are found outside the church and therefore offer no accountability, no awareness of biblical teachings about the sanctity of marriage, and no awareness that divorce involves sin that needs to be confronted, confessed, and followed by changed behavior.

Sadly, however, many divorced and divorcing people want the support and biblical accountability that the church can provide, but the church turns the other way and responds with cold and insensitive scorn. This adds to the pain of people going through divorce. Most divorced people maintain their religious beliefs through it all, but many leave their churches because of the rejection, lack of understanding, and minisermons about the permanence of marriage and the sin of divorce. Some congregations abandon divorcing people at a time when they feel the greatest need for support, friendship, and forgiveness to offset the loneliness and guilt. Sometimes these insensitive church members and their leaders forget that the God who hates divorce still loves the people who suffer the effects of divorce.

I am glad to say that many compassionate, caring churches and Christian leaders are accepting the challenge of minister-

TRUST, LOVE, AND FORGIVENESS

Patrick Springle, M.A.
President, Baxter Press
Adapted from *Trusting: Knowing Who and How to Trust Again*

A friend of mine, Susanne, was deeply hurt by her husband. When the children became teenagers and wanted more freedom, he couldn't stand his loss of control over their lives. He criticized virtually every word they said and everything they did. Susanne often tried to mediate, but her efforts only made him more furious. He exploded at her just as he exploded at the kids. Slowly she gave up and walled herself off in her own bitterness.

One Sunday she heard the pastor talk about forgiveness, but she blurted out to me privately, "I can't forgive him! I just can't!" Then she gave her reasoning: "If I *forgave* him, I'd have to *trust* him. And I don't ever want to let him get close to me again!"

"But the Lord doesn't ask you to *trust* him," I told her, "just to *forgive* him."

Susanne looked puzzled. We talked at length about how foolish it would be to trust someone who isn't trustworthy. Those who don't earn our trust shouldn't receive it. I told her, "I hope he will begin to change as you work through the hurt and anger together, but he may not. As much as he changes, as much as he proves to be trustworthy, you can wisely trust him. Not more, and not less."

The Scripture commands us to love others, even those who have wounded us, and to forgive the offenders (Rom. 12:17-21; Col. 3:13; 1 John 4:11). But we are never commanded to trust people. Scripture often commands us to seek wisdom, but trusting untrustworthy people isn't love; it's foolishness (Prov. 1:7; 10:14; James 1:5-8; 3:13-18). 🔹

---

ing to divorced people and their families. Many churches offer divorce-recovery programs that help people feel support, deal with their anger and hurt, forgive the former spouse, and receive forgiveness from God and others. In many other ways these churches help divorced people through the transition into a new place as a formerly married person or a single parent. Some churches call this their "rebuilders ministry."

They are helping shaken families rebuild after the shock and trauma of divorce.

We must remember that divorced people and their families are not all the same. Some couples divorce and are able to communicate well enough that they don't abandon their kids, tear them apart emotionally, force them into adult responsibilities, or leave them to swim alone in a sea of adult problems and worries. Some kids and single parents are much better when they get free of the abrasive and abusive confines of a problem marriage. Women take longer than men to adjust to divorce—in part, no doubt, because women most often assume the care of the children and experience a greater income drop when compared to their former husbands. With time most people readjust and move on with their lives. Sometimes stepfamilies are formed—Brady Bunch style—and everybody seems to get along fine.

Some adults and children seem to thrive and emerge as competent, apparently happy people, especially if the divorce freed them from conflict-filled, dysfunctional, and "personally limiting family relationships."[8] But overall—when compared to intact, low-conflict, stable families where there is no divorce—the following disturbing facts hold true:

- Children from divorced and remarried families show more problems with schoolwork, poor social relations, tendencies toward depression and anxiety. They also act out behavior such as aggression, resistance to authority, noncompliance, delinquency, and substance abuse. Children of divorce are less adept at playing with schoolmates, are more inclined to feel lonely and rejected, have a more negative outlook on life, and lack identification with role models.[9] In one survey of divorced adults, 61 percent said the family breakup had a negative effect on their children; only 7 percent said the divorce had been good for their kids.[10]
- When compared with children whose families remained intact, schoolkids from divorced homes showed sharp drops in school grades (and grade-point average) in the

five years following the divorce. For many of these young people, especially boys, the grade decline and increase in behavioral problems started before the divorce, suggesting that tension between parents had a bad impact on the children even before the separation occurred.[11]

- According to data from a national sample of over seventeen thousand children under age eighteen, young people living with single mothers or with mothers and stepfathers were more likely than kids who lived with both biological parents to have repeated a grade of school, been expelled, or had emotional or behavioral problems.[12]

- Children from two-biological-parent families show better adjustment than other kids. There is more communication in their homes, more cooperation, more time spent in family activities, less arguing, and more consistent parenting.[13]

- Many of the differences between intact biological families and single-parent or stepfamilies were related to family socioeconomic status and other issues. Taking into account "variables of hardship" such as poverty, Canadian research found negligible differences in academic performance or childhood psychiatric disorders between children from single-parent and intact families. The families that got along better often had higher incomes with parents who had better education and better occupations. Divorce often leads to financial instability and sometimes to parental depression. These, in turn, can account for some of the resulting family problems.[14]

- Following the divorce of their parents, children of all ages experience fear, anger, depression, and guilt that tend to modify within eighteen months, depending in part on the stability of their lives after the marriage breakup. When young adults grow up and become adult children of divorce (ACOD), they are less likely than people from intact families to describe themselves as being "very happy." The ACOD people are more likely to report poor physical health and are more inclined to be bothered by crying spells, insomnia, worry, feelings of worthlessness, and despair. Divorce remains a central issue in their lives, regardless of how well adjusted they may seem. According to one study, more than half of the people who came from divorced families entered adulthood as "worried, underachieving, selfdeprecating, and sometimes angry young men and women."[15]

- If we discount the impact of socioeconomic differences and compare young adults whose parents divorced with young adults from intact families, the people from divorced families had poorer relationships with their parents (especially with their fathers), higher school-dropout rates, and more personal problems. Many more of the young adults from disrupted families had sought psychological help. This was true even when the children of divorce were raised in blended families.[16]

- Grandparents suffer too. When adult children divorce, their parents are forced to make difficult adjustments, especially when grandchildren are involved. While the crisis of divorce can give grandparents new opportunities to give care, support, and advice, they must be careful not to become over involved. Grief, anger, depression, disappointment, and loss can all come to grandparents. Sometimes they are cut off from seeing their grandchildren because of distance, family tension, or custody arrangements that bar contact, especially if a daughter-in-law or son-in-law has the children. Often grandparents are called to baby-sit, become substitute parents who raise the children, and provide increased emotional and financial support at a time when their own emotional, financial, and physical resources may be limited.[17]

LONG-TERM EFFECTS OF EMOTIONAL OR LEGAL DIVORCE

JIM CONWAY, PH.D., AND
SALLY CONWAY, M.S.
Codirectors, Midlife Dimensions
Adapted from *Adult Children of Legal or Emotional Divorce*

Phil, a young man from a divorced family, smiles and talks pleasantly to people. He is involved with the singles group, appears to be very successful, and is completing his Ph.D. Yet inside he carries a pathetic amount of negative baggage because of his parents' divorce.

Phil has been unable to develop intimacy. He learned that people are not to be trusted and that he cannot have confidence in his own feelings. He has dated many women one or two times but never has been able to go deeper in a relationship. He does not trust them or his emotions. He said sadly, "It's best to stay away from people."

Phil's eyes dart around the room, betraying the typical insecurity and low self-esteem so common with adult children of divorce. "I don't think I will ever marry," he has said. "I'm sure my marriage would end in divorce."

Sadly, his statement probably is accurate. If he did get married, even to a very stable woman, their marriage would probably fall apart. Researchers have found that, compared to children from intact homes, adult children of divorce tend to experience an increased level of depression, anger, hostility, sadness, sorrow, and anxiety regarding future relationships. They have difficulty in dealing with memories. They are more vulnerable to stress and have more feelings of emptiness, uncontrollable rage, worry, isolation, and bitterness. They have a sense of being overwhelmed and a reduced level of self-esteem. It is hard for them to trust and build lasting relationships.

Marvin, age fifty-two, sums up the feelings of many adults whose parents divorced. He is still very angry at his parents. He says, "It hurts because my mom insists that divorce doesn't hurt the children. It hurts that she speaks in nasty ways against my dad. True, he never was warm, but he still is my dad—a part of me."

Marvin was six years old when his parents divorced. His life is like a series of earthquakes with loss after loss or, to use his words, "a chain reaction." "I do not remember Mom and Dad as married. I can see them together only when I see their old photographs. I still reach out to Dad as if my arm were extended, but he is always distant."

Many adults like Phil and Marvin

walk around looking like great successes yet feeling very empty inside. They fool most of the people around them, and often they fool themselves. If you have friends like Phil and Marvin, you can help in several ways:

1. Encourage children, teens, and adults to express their feelings about their parents' marital conflict, separation, or divorce.
2. Recognize the painful connection between childhood baggage from their parents' legal or emotional divorce and the likelihood of marital stress for these adult children as they marry.
3. Provide nonjudgmental groups for children and teens as well as for adults who are in marital stress to work through problems stemming from their parents' legal or emotional divorce.

Rich, a man in his midforties, wrote, "Divorce not only damages the couple involved but even more the children. In my opinion, divorce is almost *worse than murder.* At least with murder you kill the victim quickly. With divorce, everyone suffers lifelong damaging effects to the emotions and self-esteem at the deepest level. This is like a slow death from which recovery— if it happens at all—is slow and painful. Only God can undo the damage to my self-image, my feelings of incompetence, my limited social skills, and my inability to trust others." ◢◣

Sociologist David Popenoe, who has devoted much of his career to the study of families in the United States and Scandinavia, has made this powerful assertion: "Social science research is almost never conclusive. There are always methodological difficulties and stones left unturned. Yet in three decades of work as a social scientist, I know of few other bodies of data in which the weight of evidence is so decisively on one side of the issue: on the whole, for children, two-parent families are preferable to single-parent and stepfamilies."[18]

What Do We Do about Divorce?

Near the beginning of this book I promised to steer away from the gloom-and-doom thinking that characterizes so much that is written about the family. If you have read the previous few paragraphs, however, you will agree that it's easy to be pessimistic when we consider the fallout from divorce.

But Christians still have hope. Despite the failure of many marriages and the problems that follow, all is not lost. We need not wallow in despair because we believe in a compassionate, wise, and powerful God. Of course, he doesn't always prevent people from divorcing. Christian marriages break up too, sometimes even after sincere people have prayed that this wouldn't happen.

When asked about the place of religion in marriage, researcher David Larson answered enthusiastically. "The data are quite striking," he said. "Religiously committed people not only have much lower rates of divorce, but their level of satisfaction and enjoyment of marriage is quite high."[19] And while some church members reject or show a sinful disdain for divorced people, God's love and compassion are unfailing. They give comfort and hope, even to those whose marriages and families have fallen apart.

When we consider the prevalence of divorce in our culture, most married people probably fit into at least one of the following categories, none of which is hopeless.

Some Couples Stay Married

To get married and to stay married is God's ideal; it is what most of us want and hope for in marriage. This is best for the husband and wife, best for their children, and best for their parents.

Is it possible to divorce-proof a marriage so that a couple stays together and maintains a good relationship? Probably not, but some things can decrease the likelihood of a division.

Some Couples Reconcile

In working with children of divorce, one writer noticed that almost all of them clung to the fantasy that their separated parents would get back together. Sometimes that happens, although the percentages are small, especially if the separation has been followed by a divorce. In the National Survey of Families and Households, a team of researchers tried to discover what kinds of people try to reconcile after a period of separation. They focused on race, age, and education and found none of these made much difference, although poor people and the poorly educated are more likely than others to try reconciliation. Perhaps these people feel that they have little control over their lives. They know their lives won't change much if they go through with divorce, so they separate—sometimes for long periods—and save the expenses of divorce.[20]

Are Christians more likely to reconcile following a separation? I can't support this with research data, but we know that most people act in accordance with their beliefs and values. Christians who value the sanctity and permanence of marriage are more likely to "try one more time" than are people who have a lesser commitment to keeping marriages together.

TAKE THESE STEPS TO PREVENT DIVORCE

- *Make a commitment to stay together and to be faithful.* When Julie and I got married, we made such a commitment, and we've been together for thirty good years. We're vulnerable like everybody else, but we've learned that when you determine to stay together and be faithful to each other, you are less likely to drift into thinking, "Maybe separation or unfaithfulness would be better than what we've got now." Thoughts like that often pave the way for follow-up action.
- *Pray and worship.* This is not a simplistic suggestion. Families that pray together do stay together—that's more than a slogan. Consistent involvement in a caring, Christ-honoring local church gives a couple support, friendships, accountability (especially in groups), and continual awareness of who God is and what he is like. Summarizing the results of a Gallup survey, psychologist David Myers concluded, "Those who pray together also more often say they respect their spouses, discuss their marriages together, and rate their spouses as skilled lovers. Likewise, those who worship regularly together are more often happily married than those who don't."[21]
- *Communicate, even when you don't feel like it—especially when you don't feel like it.* Communication involves taking the time to listen, even when taking time is not convenient. Think about Proverbs 18:2: "A fool finds no pleasure in understanding but delights in airing his [or her] own opinions." Communication is concerned with understanding and with expressing your feelings, perceptions, and frustrations honestly and without making accusations. Your goal is to have a win-win solution to every problem, not a

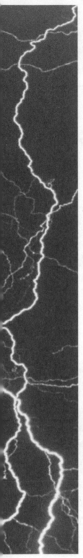

battle where each spouse tries to defeat and rise in victory over the other.

- *Practice forgiveness.* Good marriage has been described as a union of two "awfully good forgivers." The Bible instructs us to forgive one another, even though this is not always easy (Eph. 4:32). Writers Jack and Carole Mayhall once described a marriage that ended in divorce because the couple had
  1. an inability to forgive little things
  2. a tendency to hold grudges
  3. an undisciplined thought life
  4. a refusal to say "I'm sorry"
  5. an insensitivity to the spouse's feelings
  6. a refusal to try seeing situations from the other's point of view
  7. an inflexible spirit[22]
- *Help one another and bear each other's burdens (Gal. 6:2).* Marriage is a partnership, and good partners help each other. Christians differ in their views about the roles for each spouse. Whatever you think, be ready to lend a helping hand when your spouse needs it, even if that normally isn't your job!
- *Take time away.* We all need time to get away from the pressures of life. Sometimes couples need rest and rejuvenating time together, away from the kids. They may need short periods of time away from each other. When I was a teacher, dealing with students all day, I sometimes needed twenty minutes by myself when I got home before jumping into the family activities. Julie needed those minibreaks too.
- *Fight the tendency to drift apart.* Couples often drift apart without anybody noticing. We get busy with our individual activities and forget to keep our spouses involved. When our kids were small, Julie never had time to read, so I would follow her around the house and read a book aloud to her so she could think and talk about things above the two-year-old level.

Some Couples Adjust to Divorce

It would be tempting to conclude that divorce *always* leads to continued misery and increased personal problems or that single-parent homes and stepfamilies are always bad. That isn't true! Single parents and parents of blended families know that adjustments will be difficult. Blended families, for example, can face power struggles, conflicting loyalties, mistrust, unrealistic expectations, and resistance. Success is better when couples have a strong relationship, are open to counseling to help them adjust, have support from friends or relatives, and are not being undermined by outsiders, including people in the church.

PROBLEMS RATED BY FIRST-MARRYING AND REMARRYING COUPLES JUST BEFORE MARRIAGE AND FOUR YEARS LATER

First-Marrying Couples

BEFORE MARRIAGE	FOUR YEARS LATER
1. Money	1. Money
2. Relatives (in-laws)	2. Communication
3. Jealousy	3. Sex
4. Communication	4. Relatives (in-laws)

Remarrying Couples

BEFORE MARRIAGE	FOUR YEARS LATER
1. Money	1. Communication
2. Recreation (job, child care, visitation)	2. Sex
3. Relatives (children and ex-spouses)	3. Recreation
4. Communication	4. Money

From S. Stanley, "Trying Marriage Again," *Center for Marital and Family Studies Report* (spring 1988): 2.

Evidence suggests that blended families will get along much better when stepparents and stepchildren have good relationships. Building these kinds of relationships takes time, determination, and understanding. Some experts suggest that stepparents can reduce jealousy, misunderstanding, and favoritism by sharing family histories. Often these family members need to help one another grieve over losses and try to reduce competition, especially competition for parental affection. At the beginning of all this, increasing family flexibility may be more important than building cohesion.[23] Families also need to recognize that God is able to help and encourage blended families, just as he helps intact families.

As the material in the list indicates, problems for couples in their first marriage are not greatly different from the problems for couples who remarry. Even so, building a second marriage or going it alone as a single parent is not easy.[24] But it can be done.

Some Couples Struggle to Adjust

Whether or not divorced people remarry, they often struggle with problems that their nondivorced friends don't face. If you have friends or family members who are trying to put their families together after divorce, you can do several things to help.

For the person who is single again, try to be available to listen. Pray for your single-again friends, give them periodic hugs (sometimes people long for physical contact), surprise them with a note of encouragement or a few flowers. Provide a meal—at your house, theirs, or a restaurant. Offer to help with child care. Let them know you are available to help with cleaning, moving, or other "muscle tasks." Try to get your church involved, or get your friends involved with the church.[25]

These newly divorced people may experience guilt, shame, and a deflated self-esteem. Those who are Christians may struggle with theological questions about divorce. Is divorce okay in the eyes of a God who created marriage as a lifetime relationship? Is remarriage acceptable for the committed believer? Respected and scholarly theologians don't always agree in their answers to these questions, but the questions need to be discussed—with prayer and Bible study—so that the divorced person can reach some conclusions and move on with life.[26]

For the children of divorce, let them know that they are special and accepted. Try to help them feel a sense of security. Depending on your relationship, you may be able to spend time with them, cultivating a mentoring relationship. But take special care not to show any behavior that could be interpreted as inappropriate or abusive. Many of these kids have been hurt by adults, so they need love and the freedom to trust. Be a consistent encourager to the custodial parent and try to get the kids (and the parent) involved with a church that is sensitive to the children of divorce.

For the noncustodial parent, remember that these parents often hurt too. Most want to stay involved with their children, sometimes as co-parents. Evidence suggests that many children appreciate active involvement by both parents.[27]

Noncustodial parents, especially fathers, often feel excluded from the family after divorce. More than half gradually lose contact with their children, and a recent survey found that most of these parents experience depression, constant worry, and a yearning for their kids. Surprisingly, perhaps, fathers who were most involved with their children before the divorce are the most likely to become disengaged and to shut out their children after divorce. These fathers may be trying to protect themselves by withdrawing, but they desperately want contact.

Noncustodial parents, fathers or mothers, need opportunities to talk to sympathetic and nonjudgmental listeners, to deal with their faltering self-esteem and sense of loss, and to find ways to continue a satisfying and unthreatened relationship with their children. That's good for all the family.[28]

For adult children of divorce, those people who have grown up wounded and then have become parents themselves, remember that many of them carry attitudes and fears from their backgrounds. Some, for example, are overprotective of their children in an effort to make them feel secure; some are reluctant to accept the spouse as a full partner in parenting. In some families, the parent who came from a broken home becomes distant from his or her own family because there have been no models showing them how to be good parents and spouses. One father, for example, didn't have any holiday traditions at home when he was growing up, so he would withdraw to watch more and more television as Christmas got closer. Many parents from divorced homes live in fear of failing as their parents did.

That often happens, but not always. Parents who grew up in divorced families can relate to healthy families in the church or neighborhood, who in turn can be examples and mentors. Adult children of divorce can talk about their frustrations and anger, learn to manage stress and conflict, strive to gain self-confidence, and talk to their divorced parents to find out what really happened. Says one counselor, "Understanding your parents is an important step toward letting go of the pain of the past and moving, with greater confidence, toward the future."[29]

Are We Stuck with Divorce?

When I was a seminary professor, it was interesting to observe my students' attitudes toward divorce. All were committed young

THE CHRISTIAN FAMILY
AFTER DIVORCE

DAVID R. MILLER, PH.D.
Liberty University
Author of *Counseling Families after Divorce*

Ginny turned her face away from me and began to weep softly. She was totally unprepared to face her recent divorce.

"I can't do it. I'm not strong enough to raise my girls by myself, and I don't care if I ever see Bob again. Ever! He said that he left me because he needed his space, but I know he left because he couldn't take the responsibility of being a husband and father. I don't know how I could have been so wrong about him."

Ginny is only twenty-seven years old and is experiencing pain, sorrow, and confusion beyond her years. People like Ginny are in our churches and are asking pastors and counselors for help. What can we do?

What Ginny Needs

1. *Social support.* Recently divorced people, especially parents, need help in entering a social world as single persons, not with an emphasis on dating necessarily, but on fellowship to reduce loneliness, the breeding ground for sin.
2. *Spiritual affirmation.* Yes, Ginny can be divorced *and* be a good Christian woman and mother. "Two to make a marriage but one to make a divorce" must be accepted by church-based helpers who can share Bible teachings on living the Christian life as a divorced person.
3. *Financial advice.* Divorced people tend to be financially stressed and worried, often more by the feeling of not knowing what to do than by actually doing the wrong thing.

What Ginny's Children Need

1. *Reassurance.* Children of divorce feel responsible. Help them understand that the divorce was not their fault.
2. *Parent strength.* Ginny's children need to see a mother strong enough to care for them alone, a mother who is able to convince her daughters that she can rear them on her own. Ginny must model God's power for her daughters.
3. *Information.* Most divorced parents fail to tell their children what they need to know about the future. Children need to be protected from parental sin, but they need to know what is planned for *their* future.
4. *Ministry.* The church family must accept Ginny's children and understand that they will have a tough time for a year or two.

men and women who were students of the Bible, dedicated to obeying and serving Christ, but they viewed divorce in different ways. Some were vehemently opposed to divorce under any circumstances. They could state their position clearly and give an articulate theological defense of their views. Others, equally committed and able to defend their convictions, were much more understanding and tolerant of people whose marriages ended in divorce. For a long while I wondered why my students differed in this way.

In time it became clear. The attitudes of the students largely depended on whether or not they had met divorce face-to-face. Students who had never talked to a divorced or divorcing person were much more rigidly opposed to divorce than those who had relatives, friends, or fellow believers whose marriages had collapsed. These students were not building their theologies on their experiences; they were all committed to obeying the Scriptures. But they differed in their levels of understanding and compassion. The more accepting students agreed that God hates divorce and that they wanted to live and counsel in accordance with biblical principles, but they showed a care, compassion, and sensitivity that their less-experienced classmates lacked.

I'm probably not the only one who goes to weddings these days and wonders, even as the bride and groom stand at the altar, if their marriage will survive. In the past, we didn't think that way because most couples who made a lifelong commitment intended to stay together, and they did. Now that divorce is easier and more acceptable, even Christian couples separate with less hesitation than couples might have shown in the past.

We need to show sensitivity to their struggles without forsaking biblical teachings on the permanence of marriage. We need to give guidance, help, counsel, and sometimes confrontation even while we show a willingness to understand and to love. We need to encourage couples in behaviors that will avoid or prevent divorce, even though our society might urge them to abandon their marriages and move on. We need to encourage separated couples toward reconciliation, knowing that this can be possible despite the gloomy predictions of some people in our culture. We need to agree that despite the shocks and stresses that mar-

ARE WE STUCK WITH DIVORCE?

JOHN TRENT, PH.D.
President, Encouraging Words
Author of *Life Mapping* and
co-author of *The Blessing*

I don't remember the night my father called home to tell my mother he wasn't coming back. I didn't notice her tears or see her wondering what a displaced homemaker did. After all, this was long before any "displaced homemaker" programs existed.

The year was 1952 when my mother became suddenly single. She had three young boys under age three to raise. No job. No degree. No relatives or large bank accounts to draw on.

I didn't hear her cry herself to sleep that night. But as the days and years unfolded, I came to understand a crucial decision she had made soon after my dad left: With God's help, she would make for us boys a home filled with love and encouragement, a home in which we would learn about commitment, even though we would live in the wake of a broken commitment.

Traveling around the country, I have spoken with hundreds of single parents. Many worry that despite their best efforts, the dissolution of their marriage will undermine their children's commitment to their own marriages. Yet that doesn't have to be the case.

For example, my older brother, Joe, has been married for twenty-five years; my twin brother, Jeff, has been married for twenty years; and Cindy and I have been married for nearly seventeen years. What did my mother do to help teach commitment to her children?

1. *She spent her time building up her children, not tearing down their father.* As I was to learn in later years, my mother could have taken shot after shot at my father: Not only was he unfaithful to his marriage vow, but he never made a child-support payment. Yet my mother was wise enough to know that dishonoring him wouldn't build anything positive in our lives. She wasn't untruthful or a Pollyanna. Yet she felt her time was better spent encouraging us boys rather than filling our hearts with anger toward our father.

2. *She used our situation as an opportunity to teach responsibility.* From my earliest memories, our family was a team. And that meant that as a teammate, everyone had responsibilities around the house. Early on, it was just cleaning off the dishes. But later we were assigned specific tasks that taught responsibility and helped spread out the household load.

3. *She never missed the opportunity to tell us about God's unswerving commitment to us and about how we could be men of commitment as well.* It never seemed incongruent to me that while my mother's marriage had ended in divorce, mine could be solid. Fully a thousand times, I remember my mother telling us of God's unfailing love and encouraging us to be men of our word, men who followed through on their commitments.

I learned to be a Promise Keeper long before the men's movement began, in large part due to a wise single-parent mother who stressed encouragement, responsibility, and commitment.

Are we stuck with divorce? In an imperfect world, the short answer is yes. But that doesn't mean we can't make major dents in divorce by drawing on God's strength to teach our children to stay strong and committed—for a lifetime.

---

riages face today, it is possible—with the help of God—to keep families standing firm and secure.

One of the best ways to avoid divorce is to encourage unmarried people to move into marriage cautiously and to avoid relationships that are potentially catastrophic. Lynn almost made that mistake.

L Y N N

Several years ago, our elder daughter, Lynn, spent four years as a university student in Scotland. Lynn got her degree in history but has always been a literary person who appreciates words and things that are well written.

Shortly before Julie and I were due to leave on a speaking trip overseas, Lynn dropped us a note and mentioned, almost in passing, that she had become engaged to a young man from England. They were planning to be married within a few months but would not have a church wedding because Vincent was not a Christian.[30] Indeed, he opposed the church, claimed to be communistic in his thinking, and appeared to be developing a drinking problem—although he denied this.

How were we to respond to our daughter's decision? From my perspective she was heading for a marriage that was certain to be miserable and destructive—a marriage that was very likely to fail and end in divorce.

Julie and I had never met Vincent, and since we were on different sides of the Atlantic, it seemed unlikely that we would meet anytime soon. We sensed Lynn knew the dangers of the action she was about to take, but I felt I needed to communicate with her. I decided to write a long letter that she could mull over. At the time I had no intention of sharing it with anybody except her. Now, four years later, she has given her permission for me to share it with you. Here is what I wrote.

I wish I could respond to your letter in the same chatty style that you used, but as you surely know, our hearts have been very heavy during this past week and there have been a lot of tears. Your mother and I know you are an adult, and you certainly are intelligent enough to make wise decisions, but we wonder if you really have considered the implications of the step that you are about to take.

I have struggled, trying to decide how to respond. I didn't want to lay a guilt trip on you (that never works and I don't want to be manipulative). Still, this may be the most important letter that I will ever write to you. As you know, next to your decision to accept Christ, the choice of a marriage partner is the most significant and life-altering decision that you will ever make. I suppose Mom and Jan will take a different approach when they write, but will it surprise you if I try to tell a story?

THERE once was an old sheep (actually he was middle-aged) whose ancestors had long ago departed from the green hills of Great Britain and had come to a new land. The sheep and his ewe (she was a web-footed ewe because she came from the land of Oregon) settled in the middle of their land where they gave birth to two precious ewe-lambs. The father sheep wasn't perfect (no sheep are), but he and his mate tried to raise their lambs as best they could. Sometimes they made mistakes, and sometimes the father sheep got so busy working in his pasture that he neglected to watch his lambs closely.

The father sheep wanted to guide his lambs and give them direction in the way that they should go, but he also wanted to give them freedom to romp around the pastures. Some of the other father sheep had put high fences around their lambs, resulting in tension and rebellion. But this father's lambs never showed much rebellion—although they sometimes moved away from the place where the other sheep worshiped their Creator.

One day, the father sheep and his mate watched as one of the lambs left the fold. It was hard to see her go, but the parents were proud of her courage in going to another pasture (in pursuit of a sheep skin), and they determined to help her on the journey. She moved across a large body of water and lived among other sheep that baa-ed with a strange accent. These other sheep apparently knew or cared little about the Creator that the father sheep worshiped.

Sometime later, the father sheep saw his precious lamb on a high cliff, about to jump into a valley called marriage. It was a valley that could be filled with flowers and the finest of music and majestic poetry. But the lamb was not planning to jump in that direction. She was about to leap into a different part of the valley, into an abyss that must have looked beautiful from where she stood on the ledge, but the father could see the rocks and pain and conflict and loneliness in the rugged valley below.

When the father sheep saw the danger, he was concerned for his lamb's safety. He cried out to her, "Don't jump!" His voice got louder, "For God's sake, don't do it!"

At first he had considered not shouting. He wasn't sure that his voice would be heard across the water, and he knew that his lamb was wise enough to think before she leapt. But he knew that all sheep have unclear thinking when they are in love.

The father sheep wondered if he would alienate his little lamb and make her angry if he expressed himself so openly. That, he concluded, was a risk he would have to take. Who would not call out a warning to a creature in grave danger, especially when he loved the creature so much? The father sheep knew the Creator loved the lamb even more and would be sad about the leap. The Creator has told us not to be unequally yoked with lambs who do not worship the Creator. He warned us for our protection, because he wants us to experience ultimate joy.

As the father sheep strained his eyes through the mist (in the air and in his eyes), he noticed that his lamb was busy reading books—studying for exams that would help to influence her future. She seemed unconcerned, or perhaps unaware, of the dangerous plunge that she was soon to take.

So the father sheep lay down on the grass in his pasture and began to wonder why his lamb was even on the cliff.

Had the black sheep—the one who is the father of lies and the enemy of the Creator—so twisted the thinking of the lamb that she had become insensitive to the Creator's tugs? True, she had not been in close contact with the Creator or his followers and had chosen, instead, to surround herself with those who are in bondage to the black sheep. Had she become too involved with the lambs in the black sheep's fold? Surely the lamb on the cliff knew that the Creator always forgives, freely. Surely she knew that no sheep, absolutely no sheep, is too far away to come back. Even the Lamb of God once told a story about going out to rescue and to welcome back a sheep that had lost its way.

The lamb on the cliff certainly knew that one wrong action or unwise decision can never be corrected by another wrong behavior or faulty decision. It is far better to back out—at least for a while—than to go ahead with a life-altering choice made perhaps because of guilt, sympathy, or because friends have been told and arrangements have been made. The ewe-lamb knew the father sheep has a friend who backed out of a big wedding two days before the ceremony—and lived to be grateful that he had made the courageous decision. The lamb also knew another sheep who had not backed out and had lived instead with years of intense pain and misery.

Maybe the lamb felt trapped on the cliff, afraid to back away lest the other sheep become critical. But didn't she know that the Creator always gives courage to enable us to do what we know in our hearts is right? And didn't she know that there were other sheep, even in her pasture, who knew the Creator and who would give her the help and the guidance that she might need?

Perhaps the lamb felt that the marriage leap would be the only way to stay on the other side of the water. The provisions were not always plentiful for foreign sheep in that distant land. But surely she knew that the Creator would provide in the future as he had in the past—in part, no doubt, through giving his provisions to the father sheep.

The father sheep wondered if the lamb had considered that she was entering a new family—a family in which she would live for the rest of her life. It would be a family with values, attitudes, and ways of thinking that would determine, in large measure, how she would live from the leap-time on and raise her young lambs. Her new family would influence whether she would be treated with respect and honor, whether she could freely worship and serve her Creator, whether she would experience arguments in place of sincere mutual attempts to work out differences, whether she would be shown kindness and dignity. Would the new family provide for her physical, financial, medical, and spiritual needs? Was the new family the best that she would want for her life and her future lambs? Surely she knew what the father sheep had said so often: The best predictor of future behavior is past behavior. What she had known about her potential mate's behavior in the past, she would know in the future.

The father sheep's heart ached as he thought about the countless times he had prayed that she would find a mate who honored the Creator and would treat his ewe-wife like a princess.

The father sheep thought about his own life—how he had seen all his friends get married and wondered if the Creator could provide someone for him. One day a friend said to the father sheep (who at that time was a bachelor sheep), "You can trust the Creator to lead you to someone beyond your wildest imagination." And that is what the Creator did.

As the father sheep lay in the grass, he wondered what he should do. His lamb had the freedom to make her own choices, so the father sheep and his mate decided that nothing would be gained by rushing across the water and up to the cliff in an attempted rescue operation. That would only anger the lamb—and rightly so.

But the father sheep could do three things. First, he could pray to the Creator and ask others to pray too. He and the mother sheep did not spread the news all over the pasture, but they asked a small group of other sheep to pray fervently that the lamb's eyes would be opened, that she would not be deceived by the black sheep, and that the Creator would give her the courage and the wisdom to make the right decision. In a distant pasture, perhaps the most fervent prayers were coming from the lamb's grandmother ewe, from the only grandparent that was left.

Second, the father decided to write a letter telling the lamb about his true feelings, assuring her of his love (even if she leaps off the cliff), and asking if it would help if she could come to the home pasture for a period of time after her exams—and before she made her leap. The father sheep would find the money for the journey. Maybe she would prefer to make that delayed trip to Ireland to visit for a week with her Christian friend there. The father sheep knew that time away often helps sheep get things into perspective.

Third, the father sheep could tell his lamb that he still was committed to helping with her education. The leap would not be the only way, and certainly it would not be the best way, to find a shelter and make ends meet. Of course, if the lamb decided to leap, the primary responsibility for her future would rest in the hands of her new family.

The father sheep made no evaluation of the partner the lamb had chosen. The two had never met, and the father sheep could rely only on what he had read in the lamb's letters. But still, the father sheep was deeply saddened because his lamb was about to enter a lifelong relationship with a sheep who did not know and worship the Creator.

As the father sheep thought further, he had only two requests: that the lamb would listen to two tapes made by a shepherd at the place where they worshiped and that she would at least take half an hour to talk honestly about this leap with the Creator.

As the father sheep thought about these things, he noticed that it was getting dark. Soon May would be gone. The father sheep and his ewe were about to embark on a long journey to a distant pasture, to talk with people about the Creator—who is known to many as the Lamb of God. Whenever the father sheep goes on these journeys, he notices that the black sheep creates distress and difficulties. Was all this part of the black sheep's doing? Perhaps. But the mother and father sheep decided to go on serving the Creator and trusting that the Creator, who is sovereign over all the world's pastures and far more powerful than the black sheep, would intervene in the life of the lamb on the ledge.

So the father sheep watched the darkness fall. Again he committed his lamb to the Creator's tender care and asked that she would be kept in his special love while the days passed. And the father and mother sheep walked slowly out of the field where they lived and went for a while to the oriental pastures of Korea.

And the father sheep sent much love to his ewe-lamb on the cliff.

The letter arrived in Scotland after Julie and I had left for Korea. One day in a big church in Seoul, I told the people about Lynn's engagement, and as is the custom in that country, everybody in the room prayed out loud at the same time, asking God to protect Lynn from a bad marriage.

Their prayers were answered—not immediately but a year later. The couple agreed to delay the wedding, and a few months later Vincent came from Britain to spend Christmas with Lynn's family. We welcomed him warmly and wanted him to feel accepted. He even agreed to go to church with us because, he said, it would be an "interesting cultural experience." He appeared touched by the messages. When he left, I felt an ache in my heart for a young man so much in need of love, family stability, and a walk with Christ—but a man whose mind and life seemed to be so closed to the Good News.

Before Lynn and Vincent left, Lynn told us privately that she knew the marriage would not be good and that they had delayed it indefinitely. But she did not want to reject Vincent because he had felt rejected all his life. We agreed to pray that God would find a different way to take care of the relationship and prevent the marriage.

And that's what he did!

11

FAMILIES IN THE MIDST
OF GRIEF AND LOSS

IT happened while this book was being written. It rocked the community, shocked the nation, and plunged a young father into intense grief. Psychiatrists, police officers, and talk-show amateurs all shook their heads in disbelief, unable to comprehend or explain the senseless actions of a twenty-three-year-old mother named Susan Smith.

Separated from her husband, Smith was dating another man who "didn't want any kids around." So one night Smith drove to a secluded place, parked her car on a slope, then let it roll gently into a lake; her two sons—Michael, age three, and Alex, fourteen months—were strapped into the backseat. Smith told police that her children had been abducted, made a tearful plea on television for their return, and experienced an outpouring of love and support from people all over the country as authorities initiated a nationwide search for the two little boys. A few days later, Smith confessed to the crime that still leaves people in her community outraged, trying to understand and wondering why she did it.

Newspapers, television, and movies frequently remind us that other people's families aren't like ours. I can't imagine what must have gone through Susan Smith's mind when she watched her car slide into the waters of that lake. But neither can I imagine what it must be like to be part of a homeless family, an immigrant family, a family that lives with a terminally ill relative, or one that struggles because a relative is in prison or because no family members can find a job. Most of us don't try to understand. It takes enough energy to handle our own needs and occasional family shocks without getting distracted or involved with the lives of "different" families, who seem so unlike our own.

Regardless of circumstances, class, education, race, country of origin, place of residence, or past experiences, all families are composed of people who have feelings, frustrations, worries, griefs, and hope for the future of their children. We can hear in the news about gang members, illegal immigrants, people with AIDS, drug users, welfare abusers, or even the rich and famous, but if you are like me, you forget that these broad categories include people like us, created and loved by God, dealing with family pressures, and often concerned about their kids.

A team of Chicago reporters recently spent a year examining and writing about urban families, many of whom live in poverty and danger and face a daily whirlpool of stresses and difficulties. At the end of the series, a few days before Christmas, the reporters turned away from the broken homes and reported on "families that defy the odds." In the midst of threatening circumstances and painful losses, there were families who showed that "discipline, encouragement and love are the not-so-secret ingredients to success."[1] As I read about these families, I realized that many of them are headed and held together by people who are genuine heroes.[2]

Heroes, according to one definition, are admirable people who see a giant or dragon before them but go into battle determined to win. The hero participates in life courageously and acts decently, without personal rancor or revenge.[3] Every community and almost every church has families that act like heroes. They face giant challenges and react with realistic determination, courage, and hope, and with a willingness to form partnerships with others who can help them win over major difficulties. We cannot and should not expect all families to act like heroes, but at some time, all families face the challenges and crises of family illness, aging, and death.

Loss of Health
What do we do when somebody in the family gets sick? If the illness is minor, the sick person takes it easy for a few days, family

members adjust to the temporary change in schedule, and soon everything is back to normal. For an estimated 14 percent of the population, however, activities are limited permanently by a chronic medical condition. This increases to 25 percent of people between ages forty-six and sixty-five and 45 percent for those who are older than sixty-five. "Serious illness not only takes over the patient's life, it also greedily expands to consume the energy and resources of the patient's family," according to the authors of a major report on illness and the family.[4] Illness can be like a terrorist who appears at the doorstep, barges inside the house, and demands everything the family possesses in terms of time, energy, stability, well-being, and money.

Discussions about coping with cancer or managing disability sometimes overlook the fact that illnesses are never static. Often the disabled family member's condition keeps changing, and that calls for changes in everybody else as well. If the illness is a long-term one, like the condition of Jill Jochim, the type of care needed will change as the ill person and the caregivers grow older. "Each phase of an illness poses its own psychological demands and developmental tasks that require significantly different strengths, attitudes, or changes from a family," writes one specialist on illness and families.[5] Often an illness starts with a crisis, moves to a chronic phase that may last for years, and eventually results in death and the family's grieving and transition into living without the relative who has died. During this time of caregiving, families still must deal with the challenges of making a living, paying the bills, taking care of the children, and handling the periodic crises that invade all of our lives.

Despite these difficulties, however, most of the caregivers I have known are not resentful. They may get very tired, worn down by the constant demands, and frustrated because their freedom is severely restricted. At times they may feel guilty for wanting some relief from the caregiver duties, but they also are glad to care for loved ones who cannot care fully for themselves.

It is difficult for family members to be heroes when their lives are disrupted like this. Many struggle to find time for rest, for hope, and for a balance between the demands of the person with a chronic illness and the other family needs. Many know that the attitudes of family members can help patients get better or worse, but this can put more pressure on caregivers. Families of the chronically ill need encouragement, practical help, and guidance in planning and making decisions. They need the realization that they have not been forgotten. The church has no equal in giving this assistance and helping families be heroes in the face of continual illness.

Families and Aging

For the first seventeen or eighteen years of my life, my grandfather lived in our house. It wasn't a big place, but Nan—I never did learn why we called him by that name—seemed to fit in pretty well. Because he had already retired from his work at the steel company, he was free to take me places when I was a boy. He always came with us on family outings and was present whenever we had guests. I think my parents resented this at times; they rarely had opportunity to be alone with their kids without my grandfather being nearby. When there were conflicts, he always gave the same response. "You'll be old someday too!"

When he died at age eighty-one, I missed him, but I went on with my studies at the university, not realizing that he had influenced me in more ways than I recognized at the time. Indirectly because of him, I wrote my master's thesis and my doctoral dissertation on the problems of the elderly, and I have had an interest in the problems and challenges of aging for all of my life. And like my grandfather, I'll be old someday too.

My lifelong interest in the elderly has left my shelves filled with books and journals about aging and my head filled with facts about the increasing numbers of older people in the world. We can all expect to live longer than people did in my grandfather's generation. With age, however, come retirement and health problems, financial stresses, high medical costs, disability, the need for affordable and accessible housing, and sometimes conflict with the younger generations. Increasingly we hear reports of elder abuse, most often the action of grown children who mistreat their parents.

Older people and their adult children have special family challenges. Somebody has estimated that the average woman in

HONORING PARENTS

DENNIS RAINEY, M.A.
Executive Director, FamilyLife
Campus Crusade for Christ
Author of *The Tribute*

Recently, *Tonight Show* host Jay Leno devoted five minutes to a monologue on a surprising subject. His father had died the week before, and Leno paid tribute to the man who had meant so much to him.

"If I'm ever arrested for anything," he closed, "and they put me on trial, and my lawyer tries to blame my parents for what I did, don't believe him. *I was raised right!*"

Perhaps Leno's comments were so surprising because we live in a culture that seems to attack parents rather than honor them. Even in the Christian community, little is said about the fifth of the Ten Commandments: "Honor your father and your mother, so that you may live long in the land the Lord your God is giving you."

And yet this command may be one of the most profound in Scripture, especially to adult children. I've come to see that there is much more to honoring your parents than most realize. Indeed, I believe that penetrating and mysterious benefits are tied to fulfilling this command.

A surprising number of people feel they have not handled their relationships with their parents well. Many adult children feel they've never "grown up" in their parents' eyes. And others feel unable to honor parents who continue to hurt, ignore, or manipulate them.

But in case after case I've seen that when adults choose to honor their parents, something happens. They've called it one of the most meaningful faith steps in their spiritual journey, and they've seen healing in their relationships.

Honoring your father and your mother is the forgotten commandment today, even among pastors and counselors, but it may be a key step to restoring relationships with our parents and growing toward spiritual maturity.

---

the United States will spend more years caring for an elderly relative than she will spend caring for her young children. Without warning and often when they are at the height of their busy careers, some people become family caregivers who are called on to provide for older relatives, helping them deal with crises, an illness, or the sudden disability of a spouse.[6] The problem is complicated for the estimated 25 percent of elderly Americans who have no adult relative living closer than 100 to 200 miles.[7]

This happened to me. I was asked by a magazine to write an article about the challenges of the sandwich generation—those middle-aged people who are sandwiched between older relatives and their own teenage children. I wrote the article, sent it to the publisher, and forgot about it until my father had a sudden illness that demanded my time, attention, and extensive travel because my parents lived 600 miles away. Overnight I was the family leader, the one to give my parents encouragement and direction when they needed it most. When the magazine with my article appeared, I read it from a different perspective, with the eyes of one who had become a sandwich-generation caregiver instead of somebody who had merely read some articles and written about it.

Families and Death

Few people get very far into life without encountering death. Grieving families face a crisis that demands change, readjustment, time to feel and express sorrow, and the long and difficult process of picking up life and going on—without the person who has died.

A few days before my father died, he asked if I thought he would be forgotten. I assured him that he would always be remembered by the family he was leaving behind, but we agreed that memories fade as the years pass. Now, several years after his death, I don't think about him every day as I used to, and I don't even think about him every week.

Maybe that's the way it should be as we let go of past relationships and move on with our lives. Still, we miss something in our modern society, where family members are scattered and we rarely hear or pass on stories about the experiences of our parents and grandparents. These stories can enrich our lives, strengthen family ties, and give us a sense of being rooted in our family histories.

I've got a few photographs that help me remember my parents and a lot of memories that tie me to my roots. My mother and

WHEN AIDS HITS HOME

STEPHEN ARTERBURN, M.ED.
Cofounder, Minirth Meier New Life Clinics
Author of *Winning at Work without Losing at Love*

Lying in a San Antonio hospital bed in 1988, my brother, Jerry, announced to my parents that he had become their worst nightmare. As a homosexual, he had contracted AIDS and knew that he would die. At that time fears of transmission through casual contact with a person with AIDS were rampant. The newspapers reported about houses that had been burned down in order to chase away men and women who had AIDS. Many preachers claimed that AIDS was God's judgment and punishment for all homosexuals.

My parents not only learned the news in the context of these troubled times, but they also lived in Texas, where being a deacon in a Southern Baptist church and having a homosexual son would cause people to question their faith, their integrity, as well as their ability to be effective parents or leaders. Faced with these realities, my parents had to decide whether to reject my brother and send him away or to do what Jesus would have done. They chose the way of the Lord.

The night my brother told my parents about his homosexuality and AIDS, they without hesitation moved from their shock to the side of my brother's bed, where they hugged him and invited him to come home with them. They pledged their undying love and assistance to him, and my brother accepted their offering of love.

When the church heard the news, the leaders of the church, rather than recoiling in disgust, came to our home, prayed with Jerry, laid their hands on him, and prayed for his peace and healing. Every day someone from the church came to bring food and a hug. The church members told my parents that the church would pay any expense not covered by insurance. And it did.

All of this outpouring of love brought my brother back to a commitment to Jesus. In his final days he spent hours studying Scripture, singing praises, and praying. Jerry died in my parents' home on June 13, 1988.

The message of Jerry's life and death is simple: When AIDS hits home, do what Jesus would do. Love even when it is uncomfortable to love. Reach out to those who are hurting, even if they don't want to be loved. Jesus told us that when we have loved "the least of these," we have loved him. When AIDS hits home, just do it.

father were married in the depression days of the 1930s, and they learned the value of handling their money carefully. At the end of their lives, they didn't have many material things, but they were rich in other ways and had saved carefully for the future. Although my family didn't have a lot, we weren't poor either. As a child I was spared the anxiety of having to face the loss of our financial security.

Loss of Financial Security

How does a family cope when the money runs out? Alvin Sims probably knew. When he died recently, the obituary indicated that he had spent his adult life working with poor urban kids and their families. His friends described him as fun-loving, jovial, very sensitive, and able to manage people. He was godfather to more than fifty young people, helping them obtain financial aid to continue their educations. On cold winter nights, he often would be active in the midnight basketball league that he had helped develop to get kids off the street and pointed into programs that would help them complete their educations and find jobs.

A few blocks from where Sims lived and worked, Lue Ella Edwards got permission to turn a broom-closet storage room in her inner-city apartment building into a tiny, after-school retreat center where young neighborhood girls could come to do art projects and get help with their schoolwork. Edwards brightened the cinder-block walls with colorful depictions of Tweety Bird and Sylvester the Cat, and every day after school she showers her young visitors with love and guidance.

One Sunday at a church gathering, Edwards had a "chance" meeting with an Ameritech executive from the suburbs. As the two women talked, Edwards described her concern for the girls in her neighborhood, and her new suburban friend, Patricia Yauch, agreed to help. She started by collecting $600 from her co-workers for books, blocks, and games for the center. The girls told their friends, and mothers soon began appearing with their children, asking Edwards, "Please help our daughters. Help keep them from joining girl gangs and becoming pregnant."

As Edwards and Yauch got to know each other, they agreed that the girls from the club should visit the Ameritech headquarters outside the city. As the girls took other trips, they began to see a new world with possibilities they had never imagined. Nobody, however, could have anticipated what happened next.

Edwards and seven of her club members were invited to Washington, D.C., where one of them appeared on national television. They had breakfast with some senators, toured the city, and had lunch seated at tables on the White House lawn. They all met the president and his wife and stayed in a fancy hotel where, according to one of the girls, "They got a big TV, a 'mote control, a big ole bed and a shower." None of the girls had been on a plane before; most had never even been to the airport. All returned to their mostly fractured families with new dreams and hopes for the future.

Somebody has said that most change doesn't take place from the top down; it comes from the bottom up. Working from the bottom up, Alvin Sims and Lue Ella Edwards have made a difference in the lives of many families. So have Patricia Yauch and her co-workers from Ameritech.

Social scientists and people in the media have helped to focus our attention on poor families, many of whom live in crowded city neighborhoods and some of whom are homeless. These families have appeared throughout the pages of this book, and we'll see more before we get to the end. Some are families with problem kids who have grown up feeling unloved, neglected, and sometimes abused by their irresponsible parents. Others are single-parent families, struggling alone or with the help of extended family members, working to make ends meet and trying keep the kids out of trouble.

Others may be like the working-class Rivera family, who live in an urban neighborhood. "We keep saying that family matters, that with a stable family and two caring parents children will grow up to a satisfactory adulthood," sociologist Lillian Rubin wrote in describing the Riveras. "I've rarely met a family that's more constant or more concerned than the Riveras. Or one where both parents are so involved with their children."[8] The mother was a full-time homemaker, stay-at-home mom until their youngest child was twelve; the father has been with the same company for twenty-five years, working his way up to be supervisor of the shipping department. This has been a warm, respectful, and caring family.

Even so, something went wrong.

"We tried to give the kids everything they needed," the father said with a sense of bewilderment in his voice. "Sure, we're not rich, and there's a lot of things we couldn't give them. Be we were always here for them; we listened; we talked. What happened? First my daughter gets pregnant and has to get married and forget college; now my son [age nineteen] is becoming a bum," idling his time away hanging around on a street corner.[9]

Everybody would applaud the love and caring that is seen in families like the Riveras. Regardless of economic circumstances, families get along better when there is love, care, and sensitivity. But often this isn't enough. Apparently we need something more than a stable family setting, Rubin suggests. "Growing up in a world where opportunities are available makes a difference. As does being able to afford to take advantage of an opportunity when it comes by. Getting an education that broadens horizons and prepares a child for a productive adulthood makes a difference. As does being able to find work that nourishes self-respect and pays a living wage. Living in a world that doesn't judge you by the color of your skin makes a difference. As does feeling the respect of the people around you."[10]

The neighborhoods in which we live, the opportunities available to us, the people we know, the political and economic status of the times and countries in which we live all can have an impact on how our families cope. Families are not independent islands, safely separated from the chaos, change, and perils of the nearby mainland culture. Families are a part of the surrounding culture. As the culture changes or disintegrates, often families change and sometimes fall apart as well.

How do poor, working-class, minority, and other families survive, especially when they face repeated disappointment? They turn to their extended families or friends. A few seek help from counselors or social-service agencies, while many try to navigate the red tape of assistance-giving government bureaucracies. Most of the families trudge on by themselves. Few families have the money or inclination to be part of family enrichment semi-nars, so many find support, solace, practical help, positive adult models, and spiritual refreshment in their churches.

Lillian Rubin doesn't even mention religion in the index of her book on working-class families, but faith in God and involvement in a church or synagogue can do much to strengthen and sustain ordinary people who have faced "the disappearing jobs, declining incomes, massive immigration, contested gender relations, and racial tensions [that] have invaded the lives of working-class Americans, eroding their incomes, their families, their dreams."[11] People who live near big cities know about church-sponsored soup kitchens, homeless shelters, after-school educa-tion programs, camp experiences, and sports leagues that help strengthen families who live in depressed neighborhoods and who struggle financially. These people know that nothing beats the caring, Christ-centered church as a place of refuge and a launching pad for healthier families.

Jesus had a great compassion for the poor in his society, and he spent time with the misfits and the spiritually empty, affluent people as well. If Jesus walked the earth today, probably he would be concerned about these families who struggle, many with disappointment and little hope.

As we ponder the needs of disadvantaged families, we might forget needy families at the other end of the socioeconomic scale. These are families who live in big homes with manicured lawns in the better parts of town. Many of these people "have it all" in terms of money, opportunities, and career success, but they learn that prosperity, possessions, power, and prestige can't buy stability and happy homes. Parental neglect and abuse, sub-stance misuse, or rebellious teenage behavior may abound, but unless it erupts into something sensational and criminal, the family problems are hidden behind smiles on the cocktail circuit or tucked from public view behind walls of affluence. These people can afford to consult expensive private therapists who aren't inclined to write books or journal articles. As a result, professional publications focus on poorer families, and we often forget that rich and successful people can and do have family problems too.

Sometimes the problems and pressures in families have nothing to do with one's race, place of residence, or income. Consider the Johansons.

Infertility and Adoption

Ken Johanson didn't look much like a businessman who sits all week behind a desk in the corporate offices of McDonald's. When I first saw him, he was standing in front of an audience of about four thousand people—including a host of kids—talking enthusiastically to a puppet. When Johanson and his wife, Debbie, met me later, I quickly learned about their love for kids and their long involvement in children's ministries. I got the impression that Ken's job—making customers of McDonald's restaurants happy—might have been a nod to Ronald McDonald, the famous clown whose enthusiasm and love of kids is a lot like the Johansons'.

On their first date, Debbie mentioned that she would never be able to bear children. "I gave Ken every opportunity to back out," she said, "but we got married six months later and went on with our lives." Five years into their marriage, the Johansons began to think about adoption. Knowing nothing about the process, it didn't seem unusual when their family doctor called to say he had a baby available. A lawyer friend prepared the necessary papers, and without even meeting the biological mother, the new parents brought Mollie into their lives.

Several years later, when Mollie was almost seven years old, they were having lunch—in McDonald's, of course—and met some friends who were foster parents for a six-month-old boy. The baby, Alex, was a cocaine baby who had so many potential problems that nobody wanted him.

That afternoon Ken called Alex's caseworker to say they would be happy to adopt Alex and would be glad to pick him up that very day. For the first time the Johansons ran into bureaucratic red tape. The caseworker had so many children under her jurisdiction that she didn't even know who Alex was, but the interest of these potential adoptive parents led the state agency to look closer. The agency discovered that Alex wasn't as problem prone as they had thought, and soon a doctor adopted him.

Thus started the long process of getting a sibling for Mollie. The state agency investigated the Johansons thoroughly, visited their home more than once, checked their credit rating, took fingerprints, and required numerous interviews in which they asked every question imaginable. After nine months, the Johansons were told that they had been approved as adoptive parents but that they might have a long wait until a child was available.

The Johansons were told about a sixteen-year-old mother who wanted her baby, Anna, to have an adoptive family in which she would have an older sister. As a result, Anna became a Johanson when she was twelve days old.

Suddenly life changed. Mollie was quiet and well-behaved; Anna was spirited and filled with energy. The family was able to rule out attention deficit disorder in their young daughter and soon realized that they would be raising two very different children, including one dynamo who never sat still.

A few years later, when the Johansons began thinking about another child, the adoption agency said that no family could adopt more than two newborn children. The Johansons wanted another baby and were willing to consider biracial, handicapped, or older kids. The agency held firm to its policy and indicated, furthermore, that Ken and Debbie were too old to be adoptive parents because their combined ages had passed eighty—just barely.

So how does a family find a third child to adopt? The Johansons told everybody they knew about their wish to adopt, and they began what would be an emotional roller coaster as their hopes would rise and plummet with each new possibility. Once, the Johansons had been promised a child, but the birth mother backed out the night before the baby was to be released to Ken and Debbie's care. As the months passed, they refused to let themselves hope, even when one pregnant young woman described herself as the surrogate mother for the waiting family. Throughout the woman's pregnancy, they called often for long conversations filled with questions and concerns.

Twenty minutes after the baby was born, the mother called and told the Johansons that their new son was ready. They named him Anders, Swedish for Andrew. When I met Anders, he was seven months old, rolling around the floor, making his first attempts to crawl, and filling the room with his smiles and apparent enthusiasm for life.

Anders hasn't started on Big Macs yet, but he will. And some day maybe he'll even get to meet Ronald McDonald.

Growing Up Adopted

When the Johansons' kids grow up, how will they feel about being adopted? Probably pretty good—according to research on adoptive families. A recent one-million-dollar research project that studied 881 adopted adolescents and their families is the largest and most complete study of adoption ever done in the United States.[12] Among other conclusions, the findings show that adopted young people

- are as deeply attached to their parents as are their nonadopted siblings, even when the adopted children are of a different race than the parents
- have *better* mental-health scores and *fewer* psychological symptoms than a comparison sample of public school adolescents
- have self-concepts (measured by tests of self-esteem) that are as high or higher than their nonadopted peers

Several factors explain the reported strength of adoptive families, including the fact that these parents very much want children and, unlike biological parents, have had to pass strict screening requirements. Even in the best adoptive families, some children have problems; when this happens, there is a tendency to blame the adoption. But most adoptive parents are competent in raising healthy children, and they are glad that they adopted.

Their adopted children are glad too, although most of them would like to have some future contact with their biological parents. Research on this is inconclusive, but in general it appears that such contacts can be good because they answer questions adopted children have and help them feel a greater sense of

A WORLD FULL OF FAMILIES

DEVLIN DONALDSON, M.A.
Director of Development,
Compassion International
Author of *How to Be a Boss without Being Bossy*

Like so many other people, my wife and I sponsored a child through Compassion International. Katiuska Lopez is a young girl who lives in Guayaquil, Ecuador. We have prayed for her, visited her, and met her family.

Katiuska is one of four children from three fathers. Her stepfather was a drug addict who came to faith several years after I met him. Her mother's name was Narcissa, but when she became a Christian, she changed her name to Magdalena, a profound statement about her self-image.

Having chosen to wait some time before having children, my wife and I were flustered by the repeated questions from Magdalena about why we didn't have children. Children were the only treasure in her culture. Our decision to wait was baffling.

While I was in Guayaquil on later visits, I saw the Lopez home change from a bamboo hut, barely hanging above a tidal pool/open sewer, to a cement-block home on ground that had been filled in over the water. The Lopez family has persisted against all odds, deeply concerned about survival, faith, their children, and love.

As I reflect on my visits, I know I have learned from this family. Stranded at a lower rung on Maslow's famous hierarchy of needs (which ranges from needs for food, shelter, and safety to needs for love, esteem, and self-actualization), the Lopez family has no time to ask what they should do with leisure time. Self-actualization to them means staying alive to see tomorrow. They never ask about the effect of fads on their lives; they are consumed with getting by. The best education isn't the issue for their children; *any* education is the issue. God to them isn't about changing the fabric of their society; knowing him is about changing the very fabric of *their own* lives. Hope is far more important than activism in their expression of faith. Whether or not their society embraces Jesus, the Lopez family does. He is their only hope.

Compared to the Lopez family, I am affluent. In this affluence I am challenged to remember that my family's survival is not based on fads, education, or money. It is based on Christ alone. If I am distracted by wealth and leisure, I have disrespected those who struggle to survive.

As followers of Christ, we are compelled to look beyond our own families and find what we can give to others. For it is only in losing ourselves that we find life in all its fullness.

self-identity. When adoptive parents are willing to speak openly about adoption without dwelling on it, the children handle their adoptive status with little difficulty.

Our society, unfortunately, still believes several myths about adoption. But mounting evidence suggests that every one of these myths is false.

MYTHS ABOUT ADOPTION

- Women who work outside the home will not make good adoptive mothers
- Children from one religious background cannot be raised properly by adoptive parents from another religious faith
- Older parents are not good adoptive parents
- Single parents cannot raise adoptive children properly
- Parents should not be permitted to adopt children from another race
- Divorced people should not be allowed to adopt children
- Older children will not benefit from adoption

Adapted from E. E. LeMasters and J. DeFrain, *Parents in Contemporary America* (Belmont, Calif.: Wadsworth, 1989), 227.

The last myth suggests that adopting older children will end in failure. Evidence indicates that older children can be adopted successfully, although the process of adjustment might be more difficult for both parents and children. "We cannot overstate the power of early placement," wrote the researchers in the adoption study. "It is likely a key ingredient in the successful attachment of child to parent (and vice versa). And such attachment, which is strong among the vast majority of families in this study, is an important precursor to positive identity and psychological health, both of which are commonplace among the adolescents in this study."[13]

Foster Families

I wonder how Charles Dickens would respond if he were alive today and discovered that his story of Oliver Twist had been turned into a popular musical? The story of Oliver was noted for its sensational descriptions of London's criminal world in the 1830s and for its attack on England's mistreatment of the poor.

Oliver was a poor orphan boy who knew what it was like to live in an orphanage.

Today, we don't have many orphanages. Instead, when children are orphaned or when they have to be removed from abusive or neglectful families, they are sent to foster homes. Foster parents are supposed to provide stability and express instant love, but they are not supposed to get too attached to the child because they may have to give up the child at any time. Parents are paid, minimally, to keep the children, some of whom are shunted from one foster home to the next and get progressively harder to handle with every move. Often these children feel insecure, hesitant to trust anybody, and convinced that they have to maintain control if they are to survive. As a result they become expert charmers, con artists, or manipulators of foster families and social workers.[14]

Foster parents have difficulties of their own. The state sets limits on how much they can discipline a foster child. They have to deal with a bureaucracy that often demands paperwork and other hassles. They live with the uncertainty that a foster child may be taken without warning, and many foster parents are faced with the challenge of accepting a stranger-child from a dysfunctional family in which there was distrust and abuse. Almost overnight, the foster parents are faced with the duty of integrating that young person into the environment of a relatively happy home.[15] Sometimes everybody suffers as a result.

But not always. Foster parenting can be a positive experience, and although these placements officially are temporary, often the foster children stay.

Homelessness

Can you imagine what it would be like if you didn't have a place to live, if you had to sleep in your car or curl up at night on a sidewalk—with no place to wash, no toilet, and no money for food? What would it be like if you had a family but didn't have housing?

If we haven't been there, we probably can't begin to understand the special challenge of living as a homeless person. Nobody can predict the numbers of people who will be homeless on any given night, but the estimates range between 300,000 and 500,000 or higher in the United States alone. There is no typical homeless person, although there is a higher percentage of minorities (especially African Americans) than in the general population, more veterans, a disproportionately large number of substance abusers (including alcoholics), and increasing numbers of families (especially single mothers) with children. Perhaps 20 to 35 percent of the homeless have a serious mental illness, many of the homeless have marginal job skills, and almost all are poor.[16]

While it is true that some homeless people are aggressive and manipulative panhandlers, others are too ashamed to ask for work or money, and they remain in poverty because they don't know how to escape. It is wrong to assume that all, or even most, homeless or very poor families are lazy, unwilling to work, and content to live off welfare payments. True, some are poor and homeless because of their substance addiction, personal laziness, or wasteful self-indulgence, but other families and individuals face poverty and homelessness because of a physical or mental handicap, an inability to find work, a lack of knowledge or skills, or the results of personal catastrophe like bankruptcy.

Regardless of the reasons for poverty, Jesus nevertheless instructed his followers to give to the needy (Luke 14:12-14). Later New Testament writers listed caring for the poor as a test of whether our faith is really genuine (James 1:27; 2:14-16; 1 John 3:16-19). I agree with the former pastor who wrote that "any system—whether secular or religious—that feeds the able-bodied lazy is a counterproductive system. It does them and the rest of society a disservice," but by "all means we must care for those whose circumstances and disabilities leave them poor."[17] To start, we can give time, give goods (like clothing), give money to those who work with the homeless, and seek to give them skills and guidance. None of this is intended to make us feel guilty or to manipulate anybody into rushing to volunteer at a homeless shelter—even though most of these islands of hope could use more help. Homeless families are among those who have special challenges that make it difficult to cope and to maintain a normal family life.

HELPING A FRIEND THROUGH GRIEF

SANDRA PICKLESIMER ALDRICH, M.A.
Dean of Students, Focus on the
Family Institute for Family Studies
Author of *Living through the Loss
of Someone You Love*

The call comes just after dinner. Your friend chokes back sobs as she tells you that she's at the hospital; her beloved husband has just died of a massive heart attack.

You stammer a few quick questions: Is anyone with her? Will she be all right until you can get there?

The next few days are a blur of funeral arrangements, housing out-of-town guests, and preparing army-sized casseroles. Then, suddenly, the funeral is over, and only you are left to help your friend through the dismal days ahead. Here are a few things to remember:

1. *Grief is a process.* Your friend may never get *over* her sorrow, but she can get *through* it as you walk with her. You may know from experience that brighter days are ahead, but you can't rush another person into them.

2. *Encourage your friend to talk.* Those of us who have experienced great loss may be tempted to tell how we survived, all under the well-meant guise of encouragement. But this time it is *her* grief, and she needs to walk through it.

3. *Anger is a normal response to pain.* Notice that I'm not saying anger is *desirable,* just normal. God can handle our emotions. He knows our hearts and sees the anger anyway, so why shouldn't we talk to him about it?

4. *Avoid pious comforting.* Too often we feel as if we've accomplished our Christian duty if we show up, quote Romans 8:28, and go on with our lives. Let me stress I *do* believe that verse: "And we know that in all things God works for the good of those who love him, who have been called according to his purpose." But people who grieve need to quote it to themselves, not hear it from someone else.

5. *Offer practical help.* Often well-meaning friends tell the grieving person, "Call me if you need anything." But how much better it is to offer a specific way we want to help.

6. *Keep praying for your friend.* ◢◣

Grieving over Family Loss

Family counselor Norman Wright often asks a thought-provoking question to the people in his counseling room: "What is the loss that you've never fully grieved over?" He reports that roughly 80 percent of his clients are able to think of an answer. Nobody likes to lose or to be a loser, so we don't talk about our losses; often we don't even think about them. As a result, we tend to bury the emotions that always accompany loss, and we carry these as baggage, sometimes through our whole lives.

Wright has described the loss of his retarded twenty-year-old son, who died unexpectedly on an operating table, sending shock waves of grief into the home of his Christian family. The Wright family knew the importance of admitting and talking about their grief, then learning to move ahead "with an empty place in life . . . changing the emotional attachment and investment in whatever was lost to something new that can give satisfaction and fulfillment." They recognized that it usually takes about two years to mourn the loss of a loved one. The family knew, as well, that a part of recovery is to "take the freed-up emotional energy that used to be invested in your loved one or whatever was lost, and reinvest it in other relationships, activities, objects, roles, and hopes that can give emotional satisfaction back to you."[18]

Losses come in all shapes and sizes. Most losses send individuals and families into a period of shock. We can understand the shock and grief of families that lose a loved one in death, lose their possessions in a fire or earthquake, or lose their hopes and financial security when a job is terminated or a career collapses. But losses shake families in other ways as well. We don't have space to consider the unique needs, challenges, and adjustments of families with a physically or mentally handicapped child, families of prisoners, military families, families who have a delinquent or incorrigible family member, the families of alcoholics, people who live with a workaholic family member, people who have a family member who has a dangerous job, rural families with their unique stresses, families that live in fear of neighborhood crime, families of the mentally ill, families in the midst of crises, or families that are dominated by memories of a past traumatic stress.

The list could continue, but the conclusion is clear: They all have losses that put them under stress—sometimes under stress that goes on without relief. They are families that need other people and other families who care, who can give support and encouragement, who can offer practical help, and who can keep grieving families aware of the God who understands, comforts, and brings hope.

12

ABUSIVE AND DYSFUNCTIONAL FAMILIES

MAYBE you saw it on the news or read about it in the newspaper. The president of the United States mentioned it in a speech, and people all over the country shook their heads in disbelief.

Robert Sandifer lived his whole life in a poor inner-city neighborhood of Chicago, far away from the high-rise apartments, shoppers on Michigan Avenue, and tourist attractions that bring people to Chicago from all over the world. Robert's world, bounded by a few blocks, was overrun by violence and gangs. A child-abuse expert from Rhode Island, reflecting on Robert's environment and life in the city, called him "a poster boy for everything that's wrong with society and families and the systems that are supposed to protect vulnerable people."[1]

Robert's mother started having children when she was fifteen. A caseworker's report described her as unstable and not inclined to take responsibility for her actions or her children. She bore four of these children from Robert's father, who lived with the family for a time and then drifted away, later to be arrested and sent to prison on drug and weapons charges. Scars on Robert's body suggested that he had been whipped with an electrical cord and burned with cigarette butts.

Born into this dysfunctional, irresponsible, and abusive family, Robert grew up without encouragement or support. "He is lonely and feels poorly about himself," a caseworker wrote after meeting with the diminutive child when he was ten. "He has a sense of failure that has infiltrated almost every aspect of his inner self.

Since he is so bound up in trying to manage negative feelings of inadequacy on the inside and the pressure his environment is exerting from the outside, Robert is emotionally flooded." The caseworker added that his way of dealing with these inner and outer pressures was to "back away from demanding situations and act out impulsively and unpredictably. He is caught up in a never-ending cycle of emotional overload and acting out. His anger is so great that his perception of the world is grossly distorted and inaccurate."[2]

When the state took Robert and his siblings from their unfit mother, he was placed in a temporary juvenile facility, but he ran away and eventually was sent to live with his grandmother. She tried to control him but seemed oblivious to his problems and denied that he had ever been harmed.

Perhaps it was inevitable that the boy would get involved with gangs while he was still very young. He became a member of the Almighty Black Disciple Nation, where the discipline helped him find structure and the emphasis on "love, life and loyalty" maybe gave him some hope. A gang's strict rules and lofty proclamations can fill the emotional void in children who like danger and crave love. That described Robert—whom everybody called Yummy. He was a dedicated gang member, but he made a big mistake.

One summer night he was involved in a shooting that left his fourteen-year-old neighbor dead and another boy with a spinal injury. The police knew that Robert was behind the trigger; witnesses had seen him do it. Newspaper and television reporters disclosed that authorities were looking for a sixth-grade boy who already had had a string of arrests, who had been a felon at age nine, and who had become a murder suspect at age eleven.

Early one morning, the police found their "man." He was lying lifeless in a pool of blood on a pedestrian walkway where gang-related graffiti defaced a nearby brick wall. Within hours the suspected murderers had been found: two brothers, ages fourteen and sixteen, members of Robert's own gang. They had killed Robert to keep him quiet. Gang leaders had ordered the shooting, afraid that Robert might talk and focus too much police and media attention on the activities of the Almighty Black Disciple Nation. The next day, the *Chicago Tribune* carried a sobering headline: "Robert: Executed at 11."

A few days later, Yummy's picture was on the front page of the same newspaper. His eighty-six-pound body was lying in a casket surrounded by white and yellow mums. The neighborhood parents took their kids to view the body so they could see the end result of a life controlled by violence and gangs. Robert looked peaceful, far from the guns that had dominated and ended his life. At his side was a teddy bear.

Newspaper editorials can pack a punch. Commenting on Robert's death, one editorial writer summarized the problems that many families—especially poor urban families—face.

> There will be no justice in this case until the leaders of the street gang who organized this horror are held accountable.
>
> But even if they all rot in jail, it won't stop the killing of children. That will take a social consensus, both within the communities directly stricken by this outrageous violence and in the community at large.
>
> It will take an assault on all the symptoms, such as teenage childbearing, single-parent families, drug abuse, and the ready availability of guns. It will take continued reforms of the juvenile courts and child-welfare services. It will take an overhaul of urban schools so that they don't lose more students than they graduate, and they graduate students who are, indeed, prepared for life and work.
>
> But above all else, it will take jobs.
>
> Nothing shapes the character of an individual, a family, a community as much as the way they get their living. What distinguishes underclass individuals, families, and communities is that they get their livings in distorted fashion: through welfare or the underground economy of drug-running, prostitution, or other illegal activities.
>
> Welfare demands nothing from its recipients in the way of effort or discipline. Lacking the structure, discipline, and order that work imposes, their lives become unstructured,

undisciplined, and disordered. They essentially become superfluous, tucked away from the society at large, recognized, sadly, only when they resort to violence.[3]

Unrecognized and largely forgotten is the impact of these violent acts on the families and communities that are left. When *Fortune,* the business magazine, published a series of articles on children in crisis, one article pictured a nine-year-old Californian named Moises Contreras, who was playing with two handguns while his mother looked on, smiling broadly and apparently with approval. The photo caption mentioned that the boy's brother was a gang member and that the guns are "two of many in their home."[4]

Guns like these are being used most often by kids to kill kids. In statistics that set the United States apart from all other westernized nations, death by violence—especially gun violence—has become the leading cause of death among adolescents. The numbers are especially grim among urban African American males, but the gangs and the violence clearly are spreading. Guns are easy to get and increasingly are being used to maim, murder, threaten, and terrorize. They leave a landscape littered with people who grieve and fear.

A Virginia psychologist recently interviewed sixty mothers, each of whom had had a son or daughter who had been murdered. Each woman handled the situation differently. Some mothers talked to medical doctors or ministers. Other mothers changed their place of residence. A few purchased handguns, and still others installed new locks to increase their sense of security. Many of the mothers tried to be strong for the sake of the other family members, but when they were asked about the killings, they often would "break down and cry and say that this is the first time they've been able to talk about the murder." It is not surprising that most were fearful, angry, and weighted down by the trauma that had torn apart their lives.[5]

As most people are aware, the violence is not limited to urban gang warfare. The National Committee for the Prevention of Child Abuse estimates that about 4 percent of American children (2.7 million) suffer from violence, abuse, or neglect. They are victimized on the streets, but the abuse also goes on at school and in the home. Many of these children have no safe havens. They are molested and beaten, sometimes by parents, relatives, close family friends, or baby-sitters. A Colorado psychiatrist suggests that "we have created a culture in which millions of young people have an unbelievable amount of rage in their hearts, a feeling we assured them of by giving them such horrible infancies and childhoods."[6]

These horrible experiences can be divided into four overlapping categories: neglect, physical or sexual abuse, substance abuse, and verbal abuse. All four are seen in families at all socioeconomic levels, in every type of community, and among people of every race, class, age group, and sexual orientation. There is evidence that all four occur in Christian homes as well as in the homes of non-Christians.[7]

Neglect: When Family Members Are
Emotionally or Physically Absent
The director of county social services in one western community recently described some of the young people under his care.

> Kids today have no role models. They have no connection to anything. . . . We have lots and lots of kids out on the street by age 10 and 12. No one cares about them. . . .There are many kids aged 5 and 6—just little children—who are on their own. They are forced to get themselves ready for school in the morning, and then they come home after school to an empty house until late at night—midnight in many cases. Often, there's no food in the home for them. And we find their parents sitting in a bar; no concern at all for what these little children are doing.
>
> We see it more and more. Every month. And the kids have given up. Since infancy, there's been no love, no support. We have kids in treatment now who didn't get their diaper changed for two days when they were infants. And if they cried because of the pain of diaper rash, their mother or father came in and slapped them. But most damaging, they just left them alone. They didn't love them.[8]

Some of these neglectful parents are alcoholics or they have never learned to be responsible. Many are lonely and seek friendships. Often they are weighed down by a variety of stresses, and frequently they are depressed—too depressed to care for their kids.[9]

These reports might imply that most neglectful parents are like the self-centered Chicago couple who left their two small children alone over Christmas and went away on a vacation in the South. But many parents genuinely care for their children. However, even the children of these parents often feel neglected and abandoned because their fathers and mothers are too busy with their work, lifestyle, community involvement, or church activities. These parents don't leave their kids with unchanged diapers or take off on vacations while the children are home alone. They are parents who want to provide for their children, to find the most competent baby-sitters, and to be good role models. Most would be surprised to learn that their children feel neglected.

Physical and Sexual Abuse: When Family Members Are Cruel

Within recent years, thousands of popular and professional articles have alerted us to the prevalence of abuse in the home.[10] Abuse claims a variety of victims: children, adolescents, spouses (mostly wives but also many husbands), older people, family members with handicaps, and others. Sometimes the abuse is violent, involving fists and weapons. At times it is sexual with erotically aroused relatives or family friends penetrating the privacy and the lives of their unwilling victims. Frequently the abuse is verbal, characterized by criticism, condemnation, intimidation, or demeaning humiliation.

Long before football star O. J. Simpson was arrested following the murder of his wife, he was known to the police in the community where he lived. His wife had called for help eight times before the 1989 night when police arrived at Simpson's door to investigate a report that he had blackened his wife's eye, split her lip, and choked her. The football legend told the officers, "This is a family matter. Why do you want to make a big deal of it?" Those words, says columnist Anna Quindlen, speak for thousands of other batterers "who think it is unworthy of public notice that

FAMILY VIOLENCE

GRANT L. MARTIN, PH.D.
CRISTA Counseling Service
Author of *Counseling for Family Violence and Abuse*

A scream of fright, muffled cries, bruises and broken bones, emotional scars that last a lifetime. These are the results of violence. But these cries for help do not come from victims of terrorist attacks, armed robberies, or muggings. These are the cries of victims of family violence, which includes abuse of children, spouses, and the elderly.

Child Sexual Abuse

Approximately 250,000 new cases of sexual abuse are thought to occur every year. Perhaps one out of every three girls and one out of six boys are reported to have been abused by the time they are eighteen. In spite of the amount of public information about the subject, child sexual abuse continues to be an epidemic. Such abuse is a profoundly disruptive, disorienting, and destructive experience. The long-term aftermath can last a lifetime.

Spouse Abuse

A spouse killing a spouse accounts for 15 to 20 percent of all murders committed in the United States. One study estimated 3.5 million women and 250,000 men are battered each year by a spouse or intimate partner. As many as 28 percent of all couples will engage in some form of physical abuse during their marriage.

Abuse of the Elderly

A congressional committee on aging estimated that about 4 percent of the nation's elderly may be victims of some sort of abuse. This would amount to about 1.1 million older Americans who would be victims of abuse every year.

Within both the church and secular community, these figures should compel us to do everything possible to stop this tidal wave of violence. Tears are meant to be signs of sorrow, grief, temporary pain, and joy, not a constant companion of those who face chronic mistreatment.

they assault the women they live with, bully them with words, silence them with looks, finally shut them up with their fists."[11]

Is all of this overly dramatic? Journalists are not stimulated by the regularity of normal domestic life, in part because the people who read newspapers or watch television expect something exciting and newsworthy. That is why we hear so often about families with grievous interpersonal problems and so seldom about the more numerous cases of people who live together in reasonable harmony. That is why we hear frequent reports about spectacularly broken and abusive homes, unconventional living arrangements, or the family problems of British royalty, but we don't hear much about the stable and nonabusive homes where the majority of mothers, fathers, and children live.[12]

What, then, do we know with certainty?

- Family violence is neither new nor uniquely American. It has existed throughout history and in many countries, sometimes leading to unspeakable cruelties and no rights for the victims.[13] Even though violence is prevalent, however, it isn't right.
- There is no single cause of family abuse and violence. The influence of violence displayed on television has been widely reported and documented, but this is only one issue.[14] Others suggest that violence increases when there is continual or traumatic stress on family members who lack the skills to cope. Some abuse may be encouraged by cultural acceptance of violence— including the media's tendency to glamorize violent behaviors. In some cases, the abuser is mentally ill or controlled by alcohol or drugs. Other abuse may stem from the personality characteristics of perpetrators who lack self-control and are self-centered, impatient, or hypersensitive. People with poor self-concepts are more likely than others to abuse, and so are people who themselves were abused as children.
- While family abuse takes many forms, including abuse of the elderly, the most prevalent are child abuse and

FAMILY ABUSE THAT NOBODY SEES

MARK R. LAASER, PH.D.
Birchwood Center
Author of *The Secret Sin: Healing the Wounds of Sexual Addiction*

Rob is the successful senior pastor of a growing church. All indications point to a dynamic ministry. He is charming, preaches wonderful sermons, and is an effective administrator. Most members of the church look to him, his wife, and family as models of the Christian home.

Beneath this exterior success, however, is a very lonely man. Rob's marriage is distant. He works too hard and long, and has no real, intimate friends. On one occasion he had an affair with a member of his church. He is guilty and shameful and doesn't know with whom he can talk.

Rob comes from an abusive family. Although he is responsible for his sinful behaviors, he is influenced by the legacy of sins passed down from one generation to another. Rob's parents did to him, for the most part unconsciously, what was done to them and what he, in turn, might do to his kids.

A family can perpetuate two major forms of abuse. The first type occurs when the safety of our minds, bodies, or spirits is invaded. Yelling, screaming, hitting, fighting, put-downs, sexual molesting, and judgmental preaching are a few of the ways that people can be invaded. Rob has been led to believe that he is really a terrible person because some of these things have happened to him. He is left trying to prove his worth to himself and others, even to God. None of his accomplishments brings him anything more than temporary relief.

The second type of abuse occurs when people don't get the love and nurture they need emotionally, physically, and spiritually. This is a matter of abandonment. Some families simply don't ever talk about feelings; others never affirm each other; and many never touch. Even the most active church-going families may never talk about spiritual matters at home. Such abandonment leaves a hole in a person's mind and spirit. This type of abuse is intangible but powerful. Even though he is successful, Rob feels unlovable and concludes that no one is taking care of his needs. From an early age, Rob learned to take care of others and not himself. While this makes him a great pastor, he is terrible at self-care. He hasn't had the modeling to be honest about his feelings. He thinks, *If you really knew me, you'd hate me.* Rob projects his wounds of abandonment onto his wife, family, and church members and is secretly very angry. This leaves him estranged from all those around him.

Invasive abuse and abandonment leave us developmentally impaired, often like adolescents in our behaviors. Those may cause us to search for substitutes for the love and approval that we crave and lack. Sex, money, work, status, role, power, food, superficial relationships, nicotine, and alcohol are a few of the ways people seek to deal with their loneliness. Many of them will not find healing until they can come to terms with their families. Jesus invited us to become like little children in our faith. Sharing our childhood wounds with a skilled Christian counselor, grieving the wounds and letting them go, maturing, and forgiving our families are essential parts of that process. Only then can we be really childlike in our trust of our Father God, our Brother Christ, and the entire family of the church. 🞂

---

wife abuse. In the United States roughly 2.7 million cases of child abuse—mostly physical and sexual—are reported annually. About 40 percent of these have been substantiated. The number of substantiated cases has increased, but this may reflect more skillful methods for detecting abuse rather than an increase of abuse. The same is true of spouse abuse, which occurs in couples at all levels of society. Regardless of the causes and statistics, violence toward children and women (along with less frequent violence toward husbands) is a major social concern in our society.[15]

- Family members, especially children, who witness abuse are dramatically affected. They are more likely than others to abuse drugs and alcohol, run away from home, engage in delinquent behavior, or engage in immoral or assaultive sexual behavior. One Oregon study found that 68 percent of delinquent youth in treatment centers had witnessed their mothers' abuse (some had murdered their mothers' batterers) or been abused themselves.[16]
- When faced with violence, family members can flee, fight, or cower in fear. For some, such as children and

ABUSERS IN
THE FAMILY

DANIEL R. HENDERSON, PH.D.
Staff Psychologist, Pine Rest
Christian Mental Health Services
Author of "Breaking the
Stranglehold: Treating Sex
Offenders"

"The Lord is slow to anger, and abounding in steadfast love, forgiving iniquity and transgression, but by no means clearing the guilty, visiting the iniquity of the parents upon the children to the third and the fourth generation" (Num. 14:18, NRSV).

The generational consequences of parental sin are made abundantly clear in abuse. Jim was a teen who entered our adolescent sex-offender program after sexually abusing a young male cousin. As I worked with Jim and his family, we unraveled a tangled web of incest involving sons and daughters, parents, aunts, uncles, and grandparents. In at least two instances, children were born of the incest. Jim's offense had been, in part, retaliation against the victim's father, who had sexually fondled Jim's sisters. Most disturbing was that this family had come to view incest as a normal part of family life!

Jim paid a price for his own healing: He separated from his destructive family environment. His parents refused to face their role in the legacy of abuse. Research with sex offenders shows that up to 75 percent of offenders were themselves sexually abused. Eighty to ninety percent experienced some other form of abuse as children.

It is distressing to counsel adults whose wounds of abuse are not yet healed and who are now caught in a cycle of abuse with their own children. Sadly, the church has its share of people wounded by abuse. How tragic to corrupt, through exploitation and abuse, the parental relationship intended to model our "Abba" relationship with the heavenly Father. Perhaps in part, Jesus had abuse in mind when he said, "If any of you put a stumbling block before one of these little ones who believe in me, it would be better for you if a great millstone were hung around your neck and you were thrown into the sea" (Mark 9:42, NRSV). ◢◣

the elderly, escape is not possible, and the victims cannot defend themselves against their abusers. Others, like spouses, might have the freedom to flee or the strength to fight back, but they fear the social implications of making the abuse public, the embarrassment, or the struggle of trying to get along financially if the family breaks up. As a result, abuse continues, often unreported and undetected, sometimes in the homes of political, community, or religious leaders whose violent behaviors are never suspected outside of the home.

• Strange as it may seem, it is possible to both abuse and love. Violence and intimacy often go together in the same families.[17] Therapists have often noted that couples frequently have very passionate sex in the wake of their guilt and reconciliation after a violent argument. Clearly, abuse is a complex subject, difficult to understand and harder to stop.

Substance Abuse: When Family Members Misuse Alcohol and Drugs

The thirteen-year-old daughter of an alcoholic drew a poster with these words: "He gets booze; We get nothing, like bikes." The word *booze* was surrounded by the drawing of a bottle. The word *nothing* was in the biggest letters, and there was a small drawing of a bicycle at the bottom of the page.

People who work with or who have lived in alcoholic families know that these homes are often marked by poor communication, lack of trust, denial, physical and emotional neglect, and physical-emotional-sexual abuse.

Within the past two decades, increasing attention has been given to the mental, emotional, physical, and relational problems that come to adult children of alcoholics—sometimes known as ACOAs. These people reach adulthood carrying a major burden of pain and personal problems that have their roots in dysfunctional alcoholic homes. Often ACOAs need help if they are to forsake the impact of their past experiences and go on to build fulfilling lives and healthy families.[18]

FAMILIES IN THERAPY

FRANK MINIRTH, M.D.
Minirth Meier New Life Clinics
Author of *The Power of Memories: How to Use Them to Improve Your Health and Well-Being*

"I am a teenage werewolf. Semisane by day and longing to howl at the moon at night—in hopes somebody will listen! My parents are two-headed monsters, and my brothers and sisters are halved. Nothing is really mine; it's all 'theirs' or 'ours.' Nothing is the same as it used to be, and I resent having to deal with it. I just want to be left alone."

Tommy is an adolescent in the throes of adjusting to his new blended-family lifestyle. As if adolescence isn't tough enough, he has to adjust to having two moms, two dads, new siblings, and many confusing expectations. So he finds himself and his family in therapy.

They are not alone. Families have undergone tremendous change in today's modern world. Over sixty million Americans are involved in stepfamily relationships, impacting one out of every three children. The divorce rate for first marriages is 40 percent, 60 percent for second marriages, and 80 percent for third marriages.

But this is only one among a myriad of changes facing today's families. Families are alive, constantly changing and adjusting, always seeking a new center of balance. Change is inevitable, and families can either become victims of these changes or choose to challenge them, survive, and grow. Some families draw closer together and gain strength from one another, while others become fragmented and disintegrate.

Too often, family members just keep silent about their feelings, letting bitterness grow. Secretly blaming each other results in confusion and misunderstanding. The longer this goes on, the more magnified the problems become.

So many families have no idea how to identify and express their feelings. Family therapy has two major goals: helping the family resolve current conflicts and helping them develop better communication skills to resolve future conflicts. Learning to work through conflicts appropriately can deepen and broaden a relationship. It can promote better understanding and create a closeness that did not exist before. Rather than letting the family ship capsize, why not grab the oar of family therapy and begin rowing to shore? 🐦

Verbal Abuse: When Family Members Attack with Words
"Sticks and stones may break my bones, but words will never hurt me." Most of us know very well that this old saying is not true. Words can hurt, especially if they demean, intend to cut, and focus on the victim's weaknesses.

Most family members do not suffer from physical abuse, but in many families some members are systematically diminished by another. This is what counselors call emotional abuse. It may involve belittling ("You're fat," "You're stupid"), deliberate humiliation ("I'm ashamed to have you as my son"), nagging ("When are you going to clean up your room, pick up your clothes, do your homework, take out the garbage?"), or unfavorable comparisons ("You'll never be as smart and successful as your brother"). This kind of verbal barrage wears down the victim—sometimes a spouse, more often a child. If most of the abuse is directed at one person, other members of the household soon join the abuser and become verbally abusive too.[19] Eventually, the receiver of these verbal comments begins to believe them and comes to the point where he or she feels unworthy as a person but worthy of the abuse. "When your self-concept has been shredded, when you have been deeply injured and made to feel that the injury was all your fault, when you look for approval to those who cannot or will not provide it—you play the role assigned to you by your abusers," writes Andrew Vachss, a novelist and crusader for emotionally abused children and adults.[20]

Because verbal-emotional abuse leaves no visible scars, it tends to be overlooked. Change comes only when the victims begin to realize that the abuse was not deserved and that we are all valuable people, created by God, worthy of respect and love.

Where Is the Hope?
Is family violence as common as all of the professional articles and media reports would have us believe? Is it worse? Are the statistics inflated or understated?

Questions like these are important for social-service agencies, government policymakers, demographers, and others who try to help the families in abuse-dominated homes. If the abuse is in your family, however, or if a relative or friend is trapped in a miserable home situation, the statistics don't matter much. You know from personal experience what the researchers discover scientifically, that conflict in the home can lead to lower self-esteem in the family members, make it harder for kids to get good grades, lead to distrust, and sometimes bring on psychological problems. When the family is in conflict, family members feel pent-up anger, the kids often get into trouble, and everybody finds it harder to get along with people outside the home.[21]

While I was reflecting on these issues, I talked with an old friend whose thirty-eight-year-old marriage seemed to be falling apart. Our conversation took place in church while the worshipers drifted out after the service. We were among the last to leave. My friend's face revealed his hurt, and his eyes easily filled with tears. I doubt that his kids were brought up in a physically or verbally abusive home, but apparently there was little genuine warmth. My friend admitted, however, that he had tried to hurt his wife in a moment of anger, shortly before they separated, and during recent weeks he has reflected a lot on his track record as a husband and father. Counseling hasn't helped, and my friend wonders if his marriage will ever be restored.

We have chatted several times in recent weeks, and most of the conversation has focused on his pain. That's not surprising. When we are hurting physically or emotionally, it is hard to think about anything else. But my friend has come to see life from an entirely new perspective. While his marriage is dying, his Christian commitment seems to have sprung alive. God is no longer a faraway appendage to my friend's life. Instead, God has become a very present help in this time of trouble. The church is no longer a place to go on Sunday; the church has become a body of caring brothers and sisters who encourage, pray for, listen to, and make themselves available to a family man who needs help, love, acceptance, direction, and forgiveness. My friend finds strength in worship and involvement with compassionate members of the body of believers.

"What would you say to readers of a book about the family?" I asked at one point. His reply was simple and to the point.

"Just tell them this," he said. "It isn't possible to survive unless you depend on God. There are too many pressures on the family." Then he added a postscript. "Tell them that I would never survive without the church."

People of all political persuasions know that something must be done to stop the out-of-wedlock births, the fathers who abandon their responsibilities, the kids who kill kids, and the homes where abuse and violence is an everyday occurrence. Jesse Jackson argues that people need jobs and urban renewal, "not moral lessons on how to live." However, a newspaper columnist disagrees: "Jobs and urban renewal are important, but every day more Americans sense that the social and moral fabric of the country is disintegrating and needs to be restored. More than that, they sense that individuals, taking personal responsibility, must make the difference."[22]

Ideally, taking personal responsibility starts in the home. In the family, children acquire the values that they will bring into adult society. The family is where children learn how to get along with other human beings, how to distinguish right from wrong, and how to build trust, mutual respect, and tolerance. As families are, so is society, wrote William M. Thayer. "If well-ordered, well-instructed, and well-governed, they are the springs from which go forth the streams of national greatness and prosperity—of civil order and public happiness." Parents should be aware, then, that the upbringing they give their children is not strictly a private matter. It is a preparation for citizenship and the improvement of society. In short, "happy families make a happy land."[23]

But the prevalence of abuse shows that something different often happens. When families are not happy, when violent parents stimulate violence in their children, or when greedy parents breed greed in their children, everybody suffers. This gives a challenge to decent and concerned people in the community, especially to people in the church. If children are not learning moral values in their homes, they will have to learn someplace else. Often that means learning in churches that use recreational programs, Sunday school classes, and creative community-outreach projects to teach and stimulate the values that often are not taught in the home.

For some people, learning these values is exceptionally diffi-

PUBLIC FAMILIES AND PRIVATE FAMILY SECRETS

DIANE LANGBERG, PH.D.
Psychologist
Author of *Counsel for Pastors' Wives*

Both statistics and the news seem to indicate an alarming deterioration of the American family. Abandonment, sexual abuse, violence, adultery, and many other problems appear to have swallowed up the structure we call family.

Many within the Christian community have responded with a strong defense of the family. Churches and organizations look for ways to decry what is happening and to support existing families. The family is a God-ordained structure, so we are right to run to its defense. We must, however, ensure that we defend the family in the proper way. We do not want to be in the place of supporting a structure without regard for the dynamics within that structure.

Sadly, many families, including those in the Christian community, are only externally intact structures. When the cover is removed, we find rage, hate, abuse, and destruction. Such a structure is far removed from what God ordained. We do not want to preserve the privacy of families in a way that feeds the secrecy of incest. We do not want to protect the authority of parents in a way that serves as a breeding ground for violence and abuse.

The nation of Israel is an example of a God-ordained structure gone wrong. Jeremiah says, "An appalling and horrible thing has happened in the land: the prophets prophesy falsely, and the priests rule as the prophets direct" (Jer. 5:30-31, NRSV). In other words, those in leadership were maintaining the nation's structure, but they did it through lies and human authority. Jerusalem was destroyed because of violence, oppression, and abuse. The nation did not walk in a way that honored the God who had ordained its existence.

Our defense of the family needs to be much broader than a protection of the structure itself. Yes, we need to protect the structure, for it is God's design. However, our voices need to speak out just as forcefully against the hidden and ongoing abuse in many homes. May the structure we rise to defend be one that is a demonstration of who God is in the midst of his people. May our most private lives manifest his love and justice so that the world may know that he is God! 🔹

cult because they are trapped in what have come to be known as dysfunctional families—a catch phrase for modern families that don't work very well.

Dysfunctional Families

All families are dysfunctional; they are not what God intended. Because we are fallen people, we have fallen, dysfunctional families. Every family can learn, grow, and improve to become more like the families God intends them to be.

Books and articles about dysfunctional families most often are concerned with homes that are *severely dysfunctional,* characterized by physical violence, abuse, threat, and misery. More common are *moderately dysfunctional* families. Physical abuse in these families may be rare or nonexistent, but emotional tension, verbal put-downs, disrespect, or a marginal ability to cope may all be present. The families may not be falling apart, but few would say that the people in the household are happy, fulfilled, and getting along well together. Some of these homes are pressured by ongoing stress, such as financial difficulties, the incessant demands of a disabled child or terminally ill adult, the anguish of a mentally ill family member, or someone's excessive drinking. Other families have problems because they have never learned basic skills of money management, stress management, ways to get and hold a job, or interpersonal relations. These families limp along, surviving but not thriving. Sometimes they are willing to learn from good mentors like Scott, who has helped the Martinez family, from community- and church-related stress-management and skill-development programs, and from family-enrichment seminars. Too often, however, the problems go on from generation to generation because the families get locked into a cycle of family dysfunction and take it for granted that things probably will not get any better.

The Dysfunctional Cycle

Dysfunctional families show several characteristics that allow them to survive but that prevent them from changing.[24] These include

- *Rigidity.* As the family gets more abusive and unpredict-
  able, everybody becomes more rigid, unwilling to
  change, inflexible in their viewpoints and behaviors.
- *Silence.* In dysfunctional homes, nobody talks about
  what is happening in the family.
- *Denial.* Nobody admits that there are problems because
  that would rock the status quo and call for some kind of
  action. By denying the problems, nobody takes responsibility to do anything that might bring improvement,
  nobody does anything to change, and nobody admits
  that anything needs to be done.
- *Isolation.* As we have seen, no family is an island, but
  the dysfunctional family tries to cut itself off from
  healthier communities and relationships.
- *Roles.* Family members tend to take on specific, rigid
  roles. Often, for example, one person will be the
  dependent family member. In alcoholic families this is
  the drinker, who depends on others and fails to take
  care of the family members. The person who takes the
  role of the *enabler* works to hide the family problems,
  protect the dependent family member(s), and try to
  hold the family together. One of the children often takes
  the *hero* role, doing everything right, acting like a little
  adult, trying to help the enabler. Sometimes there is a
  scapegoat, who displays delinquent, defiant, or
  underachieving behavior and who, often unconsciously,
  draws attention away from the dependent person's
  irresponsibility because everybody is concerned about
  the scapegoat's apparent problems. The *forgotten child*
  gets lost in the shuffle, and the *mascot,* if there is one, is
  seen as being cute and immature. As they grow up,
  dependent people and enablers stay in their roles;
  heroes develop a compulsive need to control others and
  save the world; scapegoats remain irresponsible and
  impulsive; forgotten children stay socially isolated and
  sometimes are misfits; and mascots remain immature

and dependent. The grown children often marry people from other dysfunctional families, take their roles into the new marriages, and eventually create their own dysfunctional families.

Adults who were raised in dysfunctional families live from crisis to crisis and don't look too closely at themselves. In this way they can avoid having to change. Often they lock on to rigid ways of behaving and refuse to budge even if they are headed for disaster. They have difficulty with intimate relationships and often slip into compulsive behaviors such as drinking, eating too much, fanatic dieting, workaholism, or perpetual bickering.

Illustrating the Cycle

Some of this dysfunctional cycle was seen in the family of a fourteen-year-old boy who was arrested for vandalism and referred for counseling. The parents felt he was depressed and reported that he talked at times about suicide. When he met with the counselor, the boy—we'll call him Don—was very distraught. He cried, talked about how terrible things were at home, and expressed a lot of anger toward his father.

Don's father had grown up in a home where there were many demands but not much love. If a child "stepped out of line," he or she was disciplined, sometimes harshly. The father's parents always had told their kids what they were doing wrong but never mentioned or affirmed the kids for what they did right. When he had a child of his own, this father used the same rigid methods that had been used on him. Don claimed that his dad was physically and verbally abusive; the father claimed that he was trying to mold his son into an upright, solid, admirable young man. But the young man felt browbeaten and never able to please, so he looked for affirmation elsewhere—among the friends with whom he was getting into trouble. They drank together and took drugs. They often complained about their fathers, who, they concluded, didn't love them.

Don's mother, clearly an enabler, tried to protect the father's reputation and keep rapport with the son while she rescued him from his problems. But the father and son were going in opposite

MENTAL ILLNESS AND THE FAMILY

PAUL MEIER, M.D.
Minirth Meier New Life Clinics
Author of *Don't Let Jerks Get the Best of You*

"My sister's mental illness created confusion and tension in our household. We wrestled with crisis intervention and endless questions—financial, medical, practical, spiritual, and even legal. We rationalized thoughts and actions and struggled with disbelief and coping. We were frightened, angry, frustrated, overwhelmed, and vulnerable. We blamed each other: We all felt guilty for something. We knew some tough decisions would have to be made before this situation would tear our whole family apart. We just didn't know what to do with her. I hear stories like this every day from clients.

One in four families in America is affected by mental illness, making it our nation's number one health problem. And yet when our family members are unstable, mental illness is the last thing most families want to consider because of the stigma involved. We would rather attribute our family member's moods and behavior to a bad attitude, laziness, or "just a phase." Mental illness is a medical illness, not a personal weakness. Today, many chemical imbalances can be corrected through medications, and many new techniques in psychotherapy make the outlook for the future bright.

Mental illness in the family is handled in stages:

- recognizing the symptoms
- grieving, accompanied by shame and/or blame
- seeking professional treatment
- accepting and acknowledging the limits of treatment and recovery and focusing on a positive future for the whole family

As families move through these stages, it's important to

- discuss the situation openly and assess the situation realistically
- set necessary limits
- be compassionate, patient, understanding, and supportive
- learn what you can about the mental illness and treatments
- recognize signs of relapse and agree on a treatment plan in advance
- don't allow family relationships to deteriorate
- get respite from caregiving responsibilities
- join a family support group

Put aside the embarrassment or sense of shame you may feel. With timely intervention and professional treatment, you and your family will face a brighter tomorrow! ⚞

directions, and she felt that she was fighting a losing battle. Like her husband, the mother worked long hours. Their latchkey son was showered with material things, but he didn't get much parental attention because there wasn't much time.

In counseling sessions the family settled into their roles, rigidly refusing to admit the real problems and unwilling to budge. But the counselor sensed a real love for one another. It took a while, but eventually the father owned up to his harsh ways, the son admitted that he didn't want to be getting into trouble and that he really wanted to get close to his dad, and the mother began to let go of her enabling-rescuing behavior. As they learned to communicate, the family grew healthier, took small steps toward change, and got along much better. They even began to recognize that their faith could be a unifying force. With prayer and the guidance of a counselor, this family was able to break free of the verbal abuse and the dysfunctional behaviors that had kept them apart.

Breaking the Cycle and Recovering

The popular recovery movement that stimulated so many books and articles during the 1980s has faded and today is not as influential as it once was. Nevertheless, many families and family members still need help in breaking away from the lingering effects of harmful backgrounds and the ongoing impact of destructive cycles that continue to bring havoc to their lives. Counselors today use a variety of intervention programs that teach people skills, including communication and parenting skills. These social programs are especially powerful when the help is accompanied by genuine Christian love and sensitivity. Individual counseling can be helpful to many people, but most family-life experts agree that therapy works best when the whole family is involved.

Some family counselors follow a three-part approach to break the dysfunction cycle.[25] First, they help the family move toward *emotional expression,* helping them admit and express their stuffed-down feelings of anger, shame, grief, and hurt, without letting this become an exercise of stirring up vengeance that leaves everybody feeling more frustrated.

RECOVERY AND THE FAMILY

DALE S. RYAN, PH.D.
C.E.O., Christian Recovery
International
Coauthor of *Life Recovery Guide*
Bible study series

If alcohol were the problem in an alcoholic family, then getting rid of the alcohol would be the solution. If the abuser were the problem in an abusive family, then getting rid of the abuser would solve the problem. But merely taking away the drug of choice or getting rid of the "problem person" rarely works. Such interventions often leave a family system unchanged—just as dysfunctional as before the problem was "solved." Addiction and abuse are systemic dysfunctions. No family member remains unaffected. Everyone becomes part of the problem.

Recovery, therefore, must also be a systemic process. It will impact every family member. This does not mean, of course, that when one family member begins a recovery journey, everyone in the family will welcome the changes that recovery brings. On the contrary, the most common response in a dysfunctional family to someone getting help for themselves is "Well, I knew all along that there was a problem, and it's a relief to know I was right. There was a problem, and it was you!" Recovering addicts and alcoholics often find that family members feel uncomfortable when difficult emotions, once medicated away, now become a part of the family. Some people in recovery experience hostility when they start telling the truth in family systems that have been committed to silence for generations.

The family system can be tough territory in which to recover. That is why recovery requires us to invest in alternative experiences of "family." Part of the benefit of support groups and therapeutic relationships is that they provide new and healthier experiences of family dynamics. Self-destructive patterns that may have been practiced for decades and passed down for generations can't be broken without finding relatively safe "families" in which to practice new ways of being.

The good news is that just as one person's destructive behavior affects everyone in a family, one person getting healthier also has the potential for positively impacting each person in a family system. Vicious intergenerational cycles of dysfunction can be broken! The future does not have to be like the past. ♣

Second, counselors involve the family in *cognitive restructuring*. This means helping people understand how the problems started in the first place, enabling them to see what family members are doing to keep the problems going, and teaching them how thinking and behavior can change. As part of this thinking process, family members need to develop a healthier, more realistic concept of God, learning how a more intimate relationship with the Creator can help each of us to see ourselves as God sees us. In turn, we often come to realize that God's view of the people he created often differs from the views we have about ourselves or the views we heard from our parents.

Third, counselors lead the family in *behavioral change,* teaching them new skills, helping them learn discipline, getting them out of destructive relationships, or ridding themselves of addictions. If the addictions involve substance abuse or eating disorders, medical help must be part of the treatment. And whatever the problem, families need to learn that healing is better when the family members are involved in a supportive, worshiping body of believers.

Counselors can take many approaches to therapy, and families can find many ways to get help with their abusive and dysfunctional problems. Many different political, theological, and psychological theories about how families can be helped will work with at least some families. At times, though, we need to stand back and realize that God works in remarkable and sometimes surprising ways to help families, usually it seems, through the help-giving actions of available people, including counselors. No people have seen this more clearly than those in the family of Adrián Hernández.

A D R I Á N

The outdoor cafe at the Hotel Condado Beach isn't far, in miles, from the poverty-entrenched barrios of San Juan. But the setting where Adrián Hernández and I sipped coffee must have seemed light-years away from the Puerto Rican ghetto where he spent his childhood. Seated at a round table under a big umbrella that shielded us from the morning sun, we felt the refreshing breezes that had skipped across the bright blue ocean waters nearby. Tourists joined local residents making their way along the sun-drenched street not far from our table, but my attention was riveted on the story that unfolded during our two hours together.

Adrián began by reaching into his pocket to retrieve two items, a business card and a well-worn photograph. The card identified my friend as the associate director of Misión Alpha y Omega, a rehabilitation center for drug addicts in a place named Trujillo Alto. The executive director, a gracious and friendly man named Carlos Rodriguez, had joined us under the big umbrella, and I noticed that both their cards carried the same message: *Tú no tienes problemas, tú eres el problema* (You don't have problems; you are the problem). Adrián's photograph was a picture of his family—two sons, a younger daughter, and a lovely wife—standing at a table surrounded by flowers. The significance of that card and family picture unfolded as Adrián described his life.

"For seventeen years, I was a mainliner, somebody who took drugs through the veins," he began. Born in 1955, Adrián was the youngest of eight children—six boys and two girls—who were joined two years after his birth by an infant female cousin who grew up as a member of the family. All of them were poor, very poor. Adrián's mother labored from morning to night trying to care for the family, and, for a while, his father had a regular job at a beachfront hotel.

From the start the young boy knew the love of his mother but felt no affection from his father. "Maybe he loved me, but he never showed it," Adrián said. "He came from a harsh family and tried to be a tough guy, even at home. If I did something wrong, my father kicked me or hit me in the face."

At one time Adrián's father worked in construction, but soon he started prolonged visits to the countryside to see his family. Sometimes he would be gone for months at a time, apparently in the company of a female friend. Once in a while he would reappear, only to have bitter arguments with his wife and then to disappear again to the country.

Adrián's mother was a Christian who tried desperately to provide for her needy family and to protect them from their abusive and insensitive father. The older boys were of no help. By the time Adrián started school, all except one of his brothers was addicted: one to alcohol and three to hard drugs—mainliners.

Adrián explained that everybody smoked pot or shot dope at school. The older kids introduced the younger to the habit. Rare were the lonely holdouts, like Adrián's sole brother—fourth in the family—who resisted the temptations and peer pressure. He never touched anything and today has a good job and a stable family. Nobody can figure out why he was able to steer clear of the drug trap. Adrián wasn't as successful.

As a boy Adrián felt empty, lonely, rejected, insecure, scared, and shy. He had problems getting along with the other kids, didn't respect his teachers, and rarely responded to discipline. All of his friends were doing drugs, and Adrián found security in their group. When he was high, he felt accepted, important, secure, and confident enough to talk to girls. As he grew older, he tried alcohol, downers, marijuana, LSD, speed, and other substances—supplied not only by his friends but also by his own brothers. While Adrián was still in his teens, he decided that he would stick with heroin and cocaine.

At a time when other young Puerto Ricans were heading off to college, Adrián was working at odd jobs in San Juan and living with a girlfriend whom he had met in one of the disco clubs. Drugs helped overcome his shyness with women and enabled him to have more prolonged and less inhibited sexual experiences. It wasn't long before Adrián's girlfriend got pregnant. The two young people decided to get married and move to New Jersey, where they could leave their problems behind and start over.

In those days, Adrián hadn't seen the words that someday would appear on his business card: "You don't have problems; you are the problem." His in-laws helped him find a good job, and the young family moved into an apartment owned by his wife's cousin. But Adrián's insecurities and addictions accompanied him north, and he soon discovered that one of his wife's relatives was a drug dealer. Adrián became his "drug-checker-outer," who would try different substances to check out their strength before they got to the streets. Like the cupbearers of the ancient kings, the young Puerto Rican never knew what was going into his body and lived with the realization that any of the doses could be fatal. Even so, he was able to work, to sell drugs, and to steal—often taking money from his wife. Nobody knows why he never got caught and thrown into jail.

After seven years, Adrián's wife had had enough. She left with their three children and went back to San Juan. The experience shocked her husband into finding a drug-rehabilitation program, but it didn't help. When he called his wife and pleaded for another chance, she agreed to take him back. Soon he was home in Puerto Rico, on the island where he grew up, determined to start afresh. But one month later he was back on drugs, and his long-suffering wife decided to call it quits. She kicked him out and filed for divorce.

This began the worst period in Adrián's life. He went to live together with his four brothers in a drug-infested apartment.

He stole and broke into cars, but somehow he avoided arrest.
And he tried another drug program, then another—six
altogether. One of these let the participants continue to smoke
and take drugs in moderation. Moderation didn't work for
Adrián. In two programs he was expected to go to the streets
and beg for money that was lining the pockets of people who
claimed that they wanted to rehabilitate addicts. Five times he
took part in programs that used methadone, which Adrián saw
as another drug to which he could become addicted.

In the meantime, Adrián missed his family and began to lose
his brothers. The oldest died of complications from AIDS,
which developed from his drug use. The second brother
committed suicide at age thirty-three, unable to get free of the
alcoholism that had drowned out his life and future. The third
oldest brother, a Vietnam veteran, seemed hopelessly
addicted—and remains that way today. Another brother, the
one closest in age to Adrián, also died of AIDS.

Was he moving to a similar fate? Adrián must have wondered. He was depressed and tired. "You have to be tired to
change," he said. "I had hit bottom."

So Adrián tried another attempt at recovery, probably
without much hope or enthusiasm. But God knew what he
needed. In 1989, in his middle thirties, Adrián entered the
Misión Alpha y Omega program, which he now helps direct.
He came empty, and they filled him with love. He came
uneducated, and they offered to help him finish school. He
came without discipline, and they gave him structure that he
accepted because it was so steeped in loving kindness. He
came without the love of his earthly father, and they showed
him a heavenly Father, who loves without condition. Adrián
came without any models of male strength or stability, and he
found strong, compassionate, tender men who pointed him to
Jesus, the ultimate model. One day Adrián yielded his broken
life to Christ. He became a Christian, and for the first time, he
sensed that there was hope.

Guided and encouraged by his program leaders, Adrián
stopped the drug use and experienced the freshness of a clean,
healthy body. As his treatment progressed, he gained the

self-confidence that he had never known. He started studying and was encouraged to enroll in college and take the first insecure steps toward a degree. Nobody knew then that eventually he would graduate magna cum laude with a bachelor's degree—a major in computer science and a minor in administration.

But in those early days of Adrián's recovery, something vitally important was missing. He wanted the love and security of a family. Not just any family! He wanted his wife, Gloria, and their children, who were growing up as he had, in the care of a capable and caring mother but without the love of a father.

With fear and hesitation, Adrián contacted his wife, who agreed, cautiously, that he could visit the children. From the start she could see that her former husband appeared to be different. He no longer was taking drugs. He had stopped smoking and using bad language. He had a steady job and was studying for a degree. It was clear that he finally had grown up. He talked about God, not enough to turn her off, but enough for her to get interested. During his visits with the children, Gloria would stand behind the curtains and peek through the window to see if this apparent change really was genuine.

She had every reason to be skeptical. Was he being honest? Was he using religion to pretend he had changed? Was he sincere in his suggestion that they see a Christian counselor? Would it really be wise for Gloria and the children to accompany this man to church? "I didn't have to say too much." Adrián smiled as he recalled those visits. "She could see the change." In time, Adrián's wife also became a Christian.

It took longer for Gloria to warm up to Adrián's suggestion that they should remarry. But one day in 1992, almost fifteen years after their disastrous first marriage, Gloria and Adrián entered the Barbara Ann Rossler Church in San Juan and were remarried, with their children at their side. The pastor, a congenial and visionary man named Mario Rivera Mendez, had founded the church years before and encouraged the congregation to launch the rehabilitation program that saved Adrián's life and reunited his family. The photograph that I had seen when we first met was a picture of the remarried couple at their wedding reception with their children, Arián, Damián, and Emily.

The children in that family now know the kind of father that Adrián had longed to have when he was a child. Adrián helps his children with their homework, plays basketball with the boys, showers them with love, and lets them know of his love for their mother. Gloria still is learning to trust her husband, and he, in turn, understands and is sensitive to her concerns. When we talked about this story, we agreed that none of these words would appear in print unless all five of the family members approved.

There's a postscript to this story. Adrián's parents now live together, away from the public housing, in a little house not far from San Juan. His mother is happy. In these later years of her difficult life, his mother experiences the happiness that had eluded her for so long. "I can see it in her face," Adrián said. Sometimes they talk about it and pray together.

His father is happy too. When each of Adrián's brothers died, Adrián accused his father of killing the boys and ruining the family because he had treated them harshly and abandoned them repeatedly. "For years, I hated him from the bottom of my heart," Adrián said. But one night a strange thing happened. It was back when Adrián was in the treatment center, after he had become a Christian but before he remarried.

Adrián was praying near the end of the day and sensed that God wanted him to ask his father for forgiveness. Why, Adrián wondered, would he ask forgiveness from the man who had so wronged his life? Shouldn't the father be asking forgiveness from the son? The more Adrián prayed, however, the more he sensed that he had to do the most incredible thing that he could imagine—go to his father and ask to be forgiven.

The next morning Adrián fasted, and later he boarded a bus bound for his parents' cottage. After dinner he sat with his mother, sister, and father and asked for their forgiveness, starting with his mother and building the courage to express to his father what he had to say.

"I didn't know what to ask forgiveness for," Adrián told me, "but as soon as I opened my mouth, God brought some things to mind. My father forgave me, and then, to my surprise, he asked me to forgive him for his failures and past experiences. Almost immediately I felt that a burden had been lifted. For the first time in my life I sensed a genuine freedom."

Today, Adrián has a growing relationship with his parents, his siblings, and their families. In his own home in San Juan he is maturing as a husband and father who has a new appreciation for the meaning of family life. And he's involved in helping others rebuild their lives and reestablish family ties.

He understands the addicted people at Misión Alpha y Omega. He was there himself. He started as a dishwasher, then became a cook, barber, staff member, and now a partner with the director. "Helping people is a pleasure," Adrián said as he and Carlos left for their car. "At last, I am doing something important, something significant."

Adrián's life and family have been restored because of the grace of God. "If it had not been for the Lord," Adrián concluded, "I'd be where I really should be—in jail or dead!"

13

FAMILIES ON THE BATTLEFIELD: RADICAL FEMINISM, GAY RIGHTS, AND ABORTION

THE frail, aging nun walked slowly to the microphone and began to speak. Mother Teresa had been invited to address a large crowd of religious and community leaders gathered in Washington for the annual Presidential Prayer Breakfast. Seated at the head table were the president and vice president of the United States with their wives and other prominent dignitaries.

The speaker was not intimidated by her prestigious audience. "I feel that the greatest destroyer of peace today is abortion," she said, "because it is war against the child, the direct killing of the innocent child, murder by the mother herself. By abortion the mother does not learn to love but kills even her own child to solve her problems and, by abortion, the father is told that he does not have to take any responsibility at all for the child he has brought into the world. That father is likely to put other women into the same trouble. So abortion leads to more abortion." With gentleness and great conviction, the speaker focused on her politically minded audience: "Any country that accepts abortion is not teaching its people to love but to use violence to get what they want. This is why the greatest destroyer of love and peace is abortion."

At that moment the audience leaped to its feet and interrupted the speech with thunderous and prolonged applause. It must have been an awkward moment for the country's top political leaders, who remained seated, staring at the linen tablecloth, their hands motionless.

When the speaker finished her talk and President Clinton rose to give a response, he made a significant and soul-searching statement: "How can you argue with a life so well lived?"[1]

The way we live is a reflection of our moral values. These values have been changing in recent years. The changes, in turn, have contributed both to the family shock that is undermining many homes and to the recent resurgence of debates about values.[2]

At the Washington breakfast, Mother Teresa and President Clinton showed that they had differing opinions about abortion—an issue that has continued to divide entire nations, especially ours. While pro-life advocates fight for the rights of unborn children, the pro-choice defenders contend for the rights of women to control their own bodies. People in the more radical segment of the feminist movement are in the thick of the battle, and sometimes they have support from powerful gay-lesbian groups, who also fight to express and advocate their homosexual lifestyles. Antigay forces push their agendas too.

We find moderates and extremists in almost all camps of this civil war. Television cameras duly record the frequent skirmishes, in which we hear lots of shouting but not much listening. The camps organize marches in the streets, expensive advertising campaigns, variations of political maneuvering, and appeals for media attention. At least in America, no issues arouse more controversy, create more division, or lead to more bitter fights than the issues of radical feminism, gay rights, and abortion.

Few people are neutral. These issues are anchored in our clashing values systems and already are having a profound impact on our individual families.

Feminism and the Rights of Women

Katherine Kersten is a lawyer, writer, and insightful observer of the feminist movement. When she was asked to speak on National Public Radio about the role of women, Kersten described her numerous conversations with women from many backgrounds and walks of life.

A lot of these women fear for their children and their futures, she stated. But their major concerns aren't about their daughters' careers—even though women in the marketplace still face greater obstacles to success than men do. "Something more profound" troubles these women, Kersten wrote in describing her radio discussion. They are troubled by the environment in which our children are growing up and by the moral, cultural, and social deficit they are going to inherit. "What we need," she said, are "more decent people, of a kind only strong families and dedicated parents can produce. We need people of character— self-controlled people who know right from wrong and are committed to the common good. The women I know want their daughters to become such people."[3]

In the early days of feminism, between the 1840s and 1940s, feminist leaders fought for equal rights and equal opportunities for women. Their courageous activities opened the voting booths, courthouses, political offices, university classrooms, and boardrooms to women. Many who follow in their stead continue to press for the respect and equality that women deserve, including equal pay for equal work. Most women probably share these traditional feminist goals, but why do two-thirds of American women refuse to call themselves feminists? And why do almost four women in ten believe the women's movement has made their lives harder rather than easier?[4]

After reading through the seminal books of the modern feminist movement, Kersten noticed that something changed in the mid-1950s. Women stopped thinking of themselves as strong, wise, resilient, capable, and resourceful people. Instead, many began to think of themselves as oppressed, vulnerable, bewildered, and suffering victims who could find understanding and acceptance only in the company of a "sisterhood" of like-minded victims. Betty Friedan described her generation as empty, marked by "nonexistence" and "nothingness." Gloria Steinem talked of becoming "a whole, independent human being" who would be truly free, truly visible, truly real.

Radical feminists believe, in part, that emptiness in women is caused by social institutions—including the church and the family—that are created by men who want to keep power for themselves by alienating and squelching women.

In recent years, some women have described feminism as

their religion: a me-centered faith in which women who claim to be empty nevertheless look into themselves to find "authentic identity" and "the goddess within." At a much-publicized conference, sponsored in part by the Minnesota Councils of Churches and funded by several mainline denominations, the 2,200 female participants were urged to "re-imagine all that has been passed on to us through two thousand years of Christian faith" so that each woman could find "her own truth." The conference attendees were told that the deity of this RE-Imagining process is Sophia, "the suppressed part of the biblical tradition, and clearly the female face of the human psyche."[5] This is not far removed from Gloria Steinem's hope that by the year 2000 "we will, I hope, raise our children to believe in human potential, not God."[6]

This radical form of feminism has little room for families. The founder of the National Organization for Women (NOW) once described family life as "a comfortable concentration camp" for women who needed liberation. More recently, a writer for the *Los Angeles Times* argued that "traditional family values is a right-wing euphemism for 'a white family where Daddy's the boss.'" The article quoted the associate director of Wellesley College's Center for Research on Women; the director believes "the fact that children are raised in families means there's no equality. . . . In order to raise children with equality, we must take them away from families and raise them."[7] A *Declaration of Feminism* stated that "the end of the institution of marriage is a necessary condition for the liberation of women. Therefore it is important for us to encourage women to leave their husbands."[8]

Planned Parenthood, currently "one of the most powerful and certainly the best funded anti-family organization in America today," was founded by a radical feminist and advocate of unrestrained sexual freedom. Underlying Planned Parenthood programs is a contempt for parents, especially for parents who want to deny their children the pleasures of physical intimacy.[9]

Christian Feminism and the Family
A great way to make a point in an argument is to portray your opponents as extremists and then to attack the straw men (or straw women) that you have created. Read some of the media

GENDER ISSUES
ARE INTERNATIONAL

ESLY CARVALHO, M.A.
International Coordinator of Eirene
International
A Latin American Network of
Christian Counselors
Author *Mujer y Autoestima
(Women and Self-Esteem)*

The young woman standing in front of me didn't wear the *pollera,* the skirt typical of the Aymara indigenous women in this part of Bolivia. I wondered what had brought her to my office.

She had dropped by; that is the custom here. I was beginning to comprehend what people meant when they said that things were done in the "ever-present time." Since the present is always the present, there is no need to call ahead and make an appointment. I had quickly learned that it is very rude in this culture to turn someone away unless it is a dire emergency. To say that one didn't have time to see them immediately was perceived as a rejection of their person—not good for the reputation of a Christian organization such as the one with which I worked.

The woman stumbled through her story and warmed up as she saw that I was genuinely interested in what she was sharing. "You know, *doutora,* I came to see if you could train me to do things or if I could participate in one of your workshops. As you know [I didn't, of course], women in our church here can do nothing more than sweep the church, arrange the flowers, and prepare the food for special occasions."

She went on to unfold a heart-breaking story. She was married and had small children. Both she and her husband had studied and gotten a basic Bible degree. When he applied for a scholarship to further his theological training, they requested the granting organization to offer them a little more money so that she could study as well. Tears filled her eyes as she recounted how her local church wouldn't give her the necessary letter of recommendation because she was "the mother of small children and had no business getting more education."

My heart broke as I listened and realized how far so many women still have to come, even in a Christian context. And I was humbled to think of so many freedoms and rights women possess in our culture, not always realizing that others do not have the same access to the privileges that we routinely take for granted. ✤

bashing of evangelical Christians, and you will wonder where these "dangerous-narrow-minded-right-wing-fundamentalist bigots" are hiding. When an extremist killed an abortion doctor in Florida, this violent sin was condemned—and rightly so—by people on both sides of the abortion issue. But one group of feminist leaders called a news conference and condemned the entire pro-life, pro-family way of thinking as being in league with the man who pulled the trigger. How easy it is to paint gaudy portraits of your opponents as narrow-minded, angry, loud-mouthed extremists.

If I am not careful, I can do the same thing. Have the previous paragraphs painted an unfair picture of the radical feminist agenda and implied that all feminists are antifamily, antimale, into RE-Imagining, or proclaimers of free sex?

Nothing could be further from the truth. Whether or not they call themselves feminists (most do not), millions of women are dedicated to values that are far different from those of the radical feminist leaders. These more moderate women aren't all the same, of course, but they are glad for the greater sense of equality that women have attained, and they are committed to building greater opportunities for future generations. These moderates reject the caricature that a woman's place is solely in the home, waiting on her husband and forced to squelch her gifts, abilities, interests, and calling so she can stick around the house and do her husband's bidding. But these women—their numbers include many Christians—value motherhood, support strong family ties, applaud both those who work in the marketplace and those who work at home, believe in the sanctity of marriage, and are committed to sexual purity and faithfulness. They recognize that the women's movement, despite its more recent antifamily and other destructive extremes, nevertheless has helped to improve the lot of women, bring healthy balance to many marriages, and provide a brighter future for many kids.

Perhaps the radical feminists should be pitied more than attacked or ridiculed. They talk about their emptiness but fail to see that looking within their empty selves won't give their lives fullness and meaning. They challenge Christianity—one speaker drew cheers and applause when she proclaimed gleefully, "We have done nothing in the name of the Father, and the Son, and the Holy Spirit"—casting aside the only source of true peace and fulfillment, a relationship with Jesus Christ. They glorify rage, failing to see that anger begets more anger and often leads to depression. They focus on themselves and don't realize that no person who is preoccupied with self is happy. Many have a victim mentality and seem unaware that when people think and talk like victims, they begin to act like victims and others are encouraged to treat them like victims.

Far different is the thinking of Christian feminists and other believers who value women as individuals of worth, created and empowered by God. These people seek to be dedicated, godly women who want to live lives as wholly devoted followers of Jesus Christ, who recognize that single and married women are of equal worth in the eyes of God, who (among the married) encourage and are encouraged by their husbands, and who seek to nurture and discipline their children in ways approved by God. Some of these women may be involved in careers, living lives of professional achievement, but most view motherhood with equal dignity. Almost all reject the idea that women have a "right" to abortion. They are committed to the authority of Scripture, even though they have honest differences in the ways they view some biblical passages, especially those that deal with men and women. And they are faithful to their churches, even though many are distressed and sometimes angry at the teaching in some congregations in which women are relegated to subservient status and held there by oft-cited Bible verses that may not give as clear-cut guidelines about the roles of women as some Christian leaders proclaim.[10]

In its extreme forms, feminism seeks to destroy families. In its more balanced, biblically sensitive forms, feminism brings honor to the Creator and strengthens families. These are the women that Kersten talked about on that radio program; they are women of character, self-controlled women who know right from wrong, and women committed to the common good.[11]

Gay-Lesbian Pride and the Rights of Homosexuals

When I was a professor, I gave a lecture about homosexuality in one of my counseling courses and was approached later by a student who wanted to talk. Marty, a strong Christian, told me about his ongoing struggles with homosexuality. We talked about the insensitivity of some students who had used derogatory terms about homosexuals during our classroom discussion. Almost in passing, without expecting any response, I suggested that the attitudes of those students probably would change if they could hear firsthand about Marty's temptations and struggles to stay celibate and free from sexual involvement with other men.

A few days later, Marty called to say that he would be willing to share his story with the class. I could hardly believe how the students reacted. Their cynicism and insensitivity melted when they saw a brother, a fellow student, who was deeply committed to obeying the Scriptures and who wanted to honor God, but whose sexual orientation was causing ongoing anguish. Marty wasn't pushing for gay rights, proclaiming gay pride, or interested in fighting gay-bashers. He wasn't trying to reinterpret scriptural teaching about homosexuality, to argue that sexual union, or "marriages," between committed homosexuals really are okay, or to suggest that his homosexuality was rooted in his genes and beyond his responsibility for control.

Marty was struggling—like several of his classmates who talked with him later about their own struggles. He was, and as far as I know still is, committed to sexual purity, to monogamous marriage, to the family, and to serving Christ. But he struggled with temptations that, in the past, had led him into several sexual involvements with other males. And he felt wounded whenever he heard prominent Christians launching verbal attacks against homosexuals and promoting anti-homosexual hysteria in their fund-raising efforts. He was disturbed by those who lumped people like him with the radical minority of gays and lesbians who flaunt obscene gestures and lewd behavior in gay-pride parades and demonstrations. Marty never wanted to be a part of that.

Gay Rights and the Family

Marty's experiences in a seminary remind us that homosexuality is an emotional issue within the Christian community and without. When emotions run high, we can miss facts like these:

- A homosexual *orientation* (having an attraction to people of the same sex) is not the same as homosexual *behavior*. Like heterosexuals, people who are homosexual have a choice. They can give in to their temptations to engage in immoral sexual behavior, or they can remain sexually pure. Marty had a homosexual orientation; he was committed to avoiding homosexual behavior.

- The Bible says homosexual behavior is wrong. Many Christians would agree, however, that homosexual temptations (like other temptations, including those that Jesus faced) are not wrong in themselves, unless we dwell on these and engage in sexual fantasy and lustful desires. That, like overt immoral heterosexual and homosexual behavior, is sin.

- People who advocate special treatment for gays and lesbians are not all alike. Of course, there are extremes, like the lust-filled people who lack self-control and congregate at gay gathering places. But gay activist Larry Kramer once decried the "awful image" of some fellow homosexuals. They are "loudmouths, . . . men in leather jackets, fat women with greasy, slicked-back ducktail hairdos," he wrote. They are not part of a world "connected to mine."[12] Very often, however, the extremists are ridiculed—sometimes by Christians—and thought to be typical of all gays. We Christians face similar ridicule when one of our leaders has been involved in immoral behavior or when fellow believers do something foolish or immoral. We get annoyed when our critics link all Christians together. Christians aren't all alike. Gays aren't all alike either.

305

Very often, gays and lesbians carry the marks of respectability, dress like everybody else, and keep their sexual thoughts and preferences to themselves. Those who are champions of homosexuality plan their actions carefully and work within governments, corporations, educational institutions, and churches to promote their agenda. Sometimes they name the name of Christ and become like Mel White, who once was active and well known in evangelical circles, but who now is openly homosexual and described by *Christianity Today* magazine as "Gay, Proud, and Sadly Mistaken."[13]

• Despite valiant attempts to prove otherwise, there is no clear, replicable, convincing scientific evidence to support the notion that homosexuality is genetically inborn or chemically caused. The previous sentence is almost certain to be challenged as might this statement from a professor of psychiatry at the University of Toronto: "I have never come across anyone with 'innate homosexuality.' That notion has been a long-proclaimed gay-activist political position, intended to promote the acceptance of homosexuality as a healthy, fully equal, alternative expression of human sexuality. It has zero scientific foundation, though its promoters latch on to even the flimsiest shreds of atrocious research in their attempts to justify the notion."[14]

In my role as editor of a counseling magazine, I asked two scholars, Stanton Jones and Mark Yarhouse, to review the scientific research on homosexuality. Their review leaves little support for a clear biological basis of homosexuality.[15]

• Homosexuality is much less prevalent than the 10-percent figure cited by Kinsey. In their research review, Jones and Yarhouse wrote, "When the prevalence rates for male and female homosexuality are combined, homosexuality almost certainly characterizes less than 2 percent of the population."[16]

- There is heated debate about whether homosexuals should be encouraged to change their orientation and/or behavior, and there is controversy about whether change is even possible. Many professional counselors agree with the American Psychiatric Association that homosexuality is no more than a lifestyle preference. Some states are proposing legislation that would revoke the license to practice of any professional who would help homosexual people change—even if they came requesting this help.

  Numerous men and women report that they have changed from their homosexuality, but others report that "cure" has been impossible for them, despite heroic struggles. Success rates range from 33 to 60 percent, but there is little scientific evidence to show the effectiveness (or ineffectiveness) of Christian programs.[17]

- Leaders in the homosexual liberation movement have a strong antifamily agenda. Their "nonnegotiable demands" are listed on the following page.

How Do We Respond?

Where does all of this information leave us? It is true that some Christian leaders have been uninformed, insensitive, and inaccurate in their gay-bashing portrayals of all homosexuals as "perverts" or "weirdos." But bigotry is not limited to Christians. Homosexuals show similar insensitivity and ignorance when they use terms like "right-wing bigots" or "intolerant busybodies" to describe believers who resist the antifamily gay agenda.

We who are Christians, concerned about our families, need to show understanding and love for homosexual people, including those who struggle in silence, people like Marty who struggle openly, those who live quietly as lesbian or gay couples and "gay parents," and those who are militant activists. We must demonstrate compassion to homosexuals who suffer from AIDS, and we must show love, even to people who have no desire to change their homosexual lifestyles.

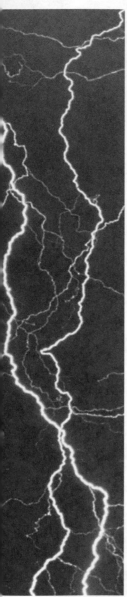

ONE GAY-ACTIVIST FAMILY AGENDA

ACT UP is an acronym for the AIDS Coalition to Unleash Power. This group used the pages of *The Advocate,* the nation's most prestigious homosexual magazine, to list the following *nonnegotiable demands:*

- Henceforth, homosexuality will be spoken of in your churches and synagogues as an honorable estate.
- You can either let us marry people of the same sex, or better yet abolish marriage altogether. . . .
- You will also instruct your young people in homosexual as well as heterosexual behavior, and you will go out of your way to make certain that homosexual youths are allowed to date, attend religious functions together, openly display affection, and enjoy each other's sexuality without embarrassment or guilt.
- If any of the older people in your midst object, you will deal with them sternly, making certain they renounce their ugly and ignorant homophobia or suffer public humiliation.
- You will also make certain that all of the prestige and resources of your institutions are brought to bear on the community, so that laws are passed forbidding discrimination against homosexuals and heavy punishments are assessed.
- Finally, we will in all likelihood want to expunge a number of passages from your Scriptures and rewrite others, eliminating preferential treatment of marriage and using words that will allow for homosexual interpretations of passages describing biblical lovers.
- If all these things do not come to pass quickly, we will subject Orthodox Jews and Christians to the most sustained hatred and vilification in recent memory. We have captured the liberal establishment and the press. We have already beaten you on a number of battlefields. And we have the spirit of the age on our side. You have neither the faith nor the strength to fight us, so you might as well surrender now.

From George Grant, *The Family under Siege: What the New Social Engineers Have in Mind for You and Your Children* (Minneapolis: Bethany House, 1994), 157.

But compassion and love do not mean that we must tolerate behavior that Scripture calls sin, passively do nothing to refute the antifamily agendas of radical gays, or make no efforts to protect our children from the demands of a powerful and highly vocal gay minority. Even if we accept the debatable assumption that some people are born with homosexual tendencies, we don't assume that such persons are free from responsibility to control their impulses or that they have a right to impose their beliefs on kids in public schools. And we don't agree that homosexuals should be viewed as a persecuted minority who should get special social privileges. What would ever happen if it could be proven that heterosexual aggression was inborn or that sexual abuse of children was built into our genes? Would that allow spouse abusers or child molesters to yield to their impulses, be absolved from responsibility for what they might do, be permitted to teach their views to young children, or be given special social status? The question is not as far-fetched as it might seem.

Surely it is true that gay people have been misunderstood and condemned unfairly. Some have even been murdered, like the young homosexual sailor who was beaten to death by a shipmate who didn't like "fags and queers." Gays and lesbians have every right to be protected from such abuse, to engage in useful employment, and to be a part of our society. As part of that society, they—like the rest of us—have responsibilities to control their sexual urges and self-centered behaviors. But that does not give them the right to push the antifamily gay agenda onto the more than 95 percent of our society who are not gay and who, according to several surveys, disapprove of homosexuality.

"In the context of America's muddled infatuation with tolerance, which demands we accept homosexual behavior as normative, we draw the line," Charles Colson has written. Then he makes a thought-provoking observation: "History shows that widespread homosexuality manifests itself in the advanced stages of a society's decline. In the Scriptures, spiritually rebellious nations flaunted their homosexual practices; many, like Sodom and Gomorrah, were consequently destroyed. . . . The further homosexual behavior is normalized, the more clearly those with eyes to see will recognize that our destruction is upon us."[18]

Even my friend Marty would agree.

Abortion and the Rights of the Unborn

Less than three years ago I went to the wedding of a couple whom I know fairly well. He came from a Catholic background but later became an evangelical Protestant, and they were married in the Baptist church where they met. They are committed believers who came to their marriage bed with the belief that birth control is wrong for Christians. If God doesn't want them to have children, they reasoned, they won't have any. If he blesses them with kids, they'll take as many as he sends.

I respect their beliefs. Many Christians agree with their position, including some of the better known among history's theologians. But others take the opposite view. They approve of and use contraceptive devices without giving the issue much thought.

Most people agree that couples are responsible for the care of children, and most would agree that too many children can be harmful to both kids and parents. That couple whose wedding I attended now have three children. They are healthy, active, demanding, and about all their parents can handle financially and emotionally. Should these parents now start using birth control? Should they refrain from sexual behavior at times in the month when pregnancy is more likely? These are difficult questions that have relevance to families and that sometimes become sexual hot potatoes.[19]

More explosive, however, are disagreements over what happens if an unwanted pregnancy occurs. This brings us to the volatile issue of abortion. At least in the United States, probably no other topic is more hotly debated and more divisive.

It is unfair to oversimplify a complex controversy, but even so, the core issues can be stated in a few words.

The *pro-life* position, which is held by many Christians, including Mother Teresa, rests on the belief that human life begins at the time of conception. Any intentional termination of human life after conception is murder—an unconscionable violation of a fundamental moral precept, the sanctity of human life. Abortion is murder, and people who perform abortions are murderers. When a pregnancy is terminated, the rights of the unborn infant are terminated. Most who hold this view would also reject procedures that cause the woman to get rid of any sperm-fertilized egg.

The *pro-choice* position believes that a woman has absolute control over her own body, including the times when she is pregnant. Any outside efforts to invade her body or to prohibit what she does with any part of her body—including what she does with a fetus or a sperm-fertilized egg—are a violation of the mother's rights. Attempts to restrict abortion are viewed as a serious assault on personal freedom and individual rights.

At its core, then, the debate is over human rights: the rights of the fetus versus the rights of the mother. Closely related is the debate over the time when human life begins; does it start at the time of conception or later? If it starts later, when does a fetus become a human? We can see these values in the ways people respond to what is aborted. The pro-life advocates believe that a human life is aborted; pro-choice people are more likely to say that "tissue" is removed.

In addition to these key issues of debate, other topics add to the controversy. People in both camps tend to lump their opponents together and paint them as being all the same and all ugly. For example, pro-life antiabortionists complain when media people like Ted Koppel and Phil Donahue host activist Paul Hill (the man who was convicted of killing two people at a Pensacola abortion clinic), call him an antiabortion leader (even though his radical views have long been condemned by most pro-life leaders), let him express his questionable interpretations of the Bible on national television, and imply that he represents the pro-life movement. "Only a few fanatic anti-abortionists pursue violence in the name of a cause," wrote Betsy Powell, president of the California Pro-Life Council. "Hill, who appointed himself the judge, jury and executioner, wounds the credibility of the pro-life movement and smears millions of peaceful, compassionate women and men."[20]

Pro-life advocates are guilty of similar injustice when they imply that the pro-choice position is characterized by "selfish, radical feminist women who abort their babies because bearing a child would be inconvenient and who pressure innocent young women into having abortions without informing them of the risks involved or the alternatives to abortion." We see extreme positions on both sides of the abortion debate, but we also see on both sides reasonable and compassionate people who differ in their strongly held views. And probably many more people don't know where they stand on the issue.

The controversy is made more complex because it is tied to theology, politics, and science. In terms of *theology,* for example, I believe that God creates life at the moment of conception and that only he has the right to terminate life. Since I accept the Bible as God's Word, I try to base my conclusions on biblical teaching. Like most evangelicals, I cannot condone abortion as a form of birth control. Had I been at that Washington prayer breakfast, I would have risen to applaud Mother Teresa's talk. If it is true that Bill Clinton believes human life starts closer to birth, then we have some understanding of why he remained seated in disagreement with the Catholic nun.

Wherever you stand in terms of *politics,* you need only look at the debates about Supreme Court nominees to see some of the political implications of abortion. The problem is made even more complex by pro-life arguments that easy access to abortion encourages sexual irresponsibility and a breakdown of family values. In contrast are pro-choice arguments that restrictions of abortion would mean the births of more babies to mothers who are unwilling or unable to provide child care for their unwanted children.

In terms of *science,* we see endless debates about the effects of abortion and postabortion syndrome.[21] As you can imagine, pro-life and pro-choice people differ in the evidence they muster concerning whether or not abortion is harmful to women.

Bringing the Debates Closer to Home
We all know that many things are wrong with this world. Families and communities are being torn apart by violence, crime, poverty, corruption, drugs, uncontrolled sex, and declining educational standards. We could fill these pages with statistics, but everybody knows that statistics can be manipulated to say what we want them to say. Most would be outdated by the time this book could reach your hands, and as I stated earlier, I'm not sure statistics do much to motivate anybody to action.

Even when we decide to get active, it is hard to know what to do. We all know about well-financed and powerful groups that exist to promote values that most Christians reject: values like homosexual rights, abortion on demand, euthanasia, sex without marriage or responsibility, the squelching of religious expression in the name of "tolerance," the promulgation of anti-Christian educational programs, and a host of legislative programs that claim to improve society but more often line the pockets or advance the personal agendas of their advocates. Sometimes these proposed solutions to our problems come from people who smugly reject "thousands of years of inherited wisdom, values, habit, custom, and insight and replace this heritage with their official utopian vision of the perfect society."[22] These people are found in every political party and in most localities. They "treat all social or moral traditions and conventions as arbitrary, rather than as venerable repositories of indispensable social, family, and religious values."[23] Often these people despise authority, especially religious or family authority, and they seek to replace this with laws that will bring in their own, often narrow, visions.[24]

I am uncomfortable writing words like these, even though they need to be written. I didn't want to write this chapter because it deals with controversy, and I hate both controversy and conflict. I don't like a good fight.[25] I am more comfortable trying to be a peacemaker than doing battle. I am distressed, sometimes even disgusted, by the name-calling, witch hunts, innuendo, character assassination, half-truths, and occasional violence that come from the conflicting camps, including the camps of Christians who follow the Prince of Peace.

In contrast, I deeply appreciate the efforts of those who speak out with conviction, state their positions articulately, organize campaigns to bring about change, run for political office, resist irrational extremism, and become advocates for their causes—especially when those causes are consistent with biblical values. Many Christians are part of movements to improve television programming, clean up the educational laxity and moral filth seen in some of our schools, lobby to change legislation, and work for the election of representatives who are sympathetic to the needs of families. Surely believers should be keeping well informed of social trends, getting involved with political and community issues, teaching family members to beware of the cultural influences that can undermine their values, and keeping tight control of television sets. The numbers of these activist people and concerned parents need to increase. It has been said that all it takes for evil to triumph is for good people to do nothing.

But to what extent will activism enable us to win battles against the secular values of our culture? Not much, according to Charles Colson, who believes that direct confrontation in the political realm rarely brings much change. Other Christians, of course, would disagree.

Instead of burying ourselves in politics, maybe individuals, families, and groups of believers should be more concerned about being salt and light in a dark world. That brings us back to the simple and profound question that President Clinton asked at the national prayer breakfast: How can anyone argue with a life well lived? Nothing in this chapter is of greater importance than the observation that family members, family life supporters, and those who fight for "family values" need to be characterized by lives that are pure, beyond reproach, and "well lived."

Maybe it won't stop revolutions or rock empires, but we need to instill values into lives that God can use to make an impact.

PART THREE

FAMILIES, COMMUNITIES, AND THE CHURCH

14

OUR WORLD, OUR COMMUNITY, AND OUR FAMILIES

WHEN our children were young, Julie and I took them to visit one of the Disney theme parks, where we climbed into a boat and rode through a long tunnel. As we rode, we were serenaded on both sides by animated figures colorfully dressed to represent different countries and appearing to sing "It's a Small World after All." I don't suppose our grandparents thought our world was small, but today we can jet to various countries all over the world with relative ease and without a lot of expense.

I've had more than my share of opportunities to visit other countries and to see how people live, build their marriages, and sometimes cope with a variety of family shocks. Before war tore Yugoslavia apart, for example, I visited the country and spent several days in the city of Osijek. It was clear to me that life was difficult for families in that riverfront community. I was invited to a Croatian wedding, had opportunity to visit in several homes, and met many new friends. Two years after my visit, when shells were falling on the city at the rate of one thousand every day, I agonized about my friends, saddened that their nation had disintegrated in a violent civil war.

When that war began, Ignjac and Marija Sokač, both in their late forties and the parents of eight children, were living in the small town of Beli Monastr, about ten miles from Osijek. War between the Serbs and the Croats put all of the townspeople under pressure, but the Sokač family had a special problem.

Ignjac Sokač was a Croatian who had grown up in a deeply

317

religious Catholic family. As a boy he had been sick much of the time, but his father kept the young boy alive. One day, the father and mother were invited to attend a Pentecostal church service, where they committed their lives to Christ in a new way and were saved. When Ignjac attended the church at age eighteen, he had a similar conversion experience. As his new faith permeated his life, his long-term illnesses left.

One day Ignjac rounded up some of the young Christian men from his church and went to visit another church, where a number of Christian young women attended. Marija was in the congregation and must have been surprised when the young visitor said that God had told him that she would be his wife. Marija talked to her pastor, who thought that the marriage might be the will of God and that the young woman should not resist.

Unlike her Croatian husband-to-be, Marija was Serbian. She came from a poor family and had moved from their village to find work. Like most Serbs, Marija had been raised in an Orthodox family and church; her family initially resisted her decision to leave their village church and worship with the Pentecostals. Marija had started attending a Bible study on the invitation of a co-worker who had an unusual and obvious joy that Marija found attractive. Soon Marija became a new believer too. After she met Ignjac, the two young people got married and settled down to raise a family.

A quarter century later, when the war broke out, the Serbs quickly overtook the area surrounding Beli Monastr, and the Sokačs faced a major family dilemma. In that part of the world, families stick together. When children grow up and marry, they stay within the same neighborhood as their parents and sometimes in the same house. But war shattered the Sokač family. The invading Serbs wanted some of the brothers in the army, and they had to decide what to do. One of the brothers joined the Serbian forces. The family's only married daughter went with her husband to Macedonia. The rest of the family fled to Osijek and joined thousands of other refugees entering that shell-shattered Croatian city. When they arrived, they lived for a time at the seminary where I had given lectures several years earlier. Two of the sons joined the Croatian army, and Marija Sokač faced a difficult tension: Because two of her sons were fighting with the Croats and another with the Serbs, her sons essentially were fighting each other.

Marija has another problem, one that is extremely painful for a person who lives in a culture in which family ties are very close. All of her relatives are nearby, but they are in Serbia. She cannot "go home" to visit them because she is suspect—married to a Croat, living in Croatia, and the mother of two sons who serve in the Croatian army. She is suspect in Croatia as well, where the police have checked on her, wanting to know why a Serb is living in their midst. This leaves Marija feeling tense because of the suspicion and because people set her apart as being different.

Today the Sokač family lives with several thousand others in a refugee camp. They've been there for three years and long to return to Beli Monastr, but they wonder if they would be welcome. In the meantime they wait. Their daughter Rahela says they are not bitter and often are reminded by Ignjac that the Lord will care for them and help their war-torn family to make the best of their difficult situation.[1]

Learning from Families in Different Countries

Most of us have families that are far different from the Sokač family. But rather than dismiss them as too different from us, we can learn valuable things from the Sokačs and families like them, families who face difficulties with strength and courage.

When you read these words, probably millions of families will be struggling as unwilling victims of social and political forces that they didn't create and never wanted. After the United Nations proclaimed an International Year of the Family, a U.N. official spoke of the "precarious situation" of families worldwide.[2] Many of these are families who have been impacted by the shocks of war, famine, political instability, riots, drought, severe economic hardships, and other influences beyond a family's control. Some of these are Christian families. Many have children whose young lives are enveloped in poverty and other forces that snuff out any rays of hope.

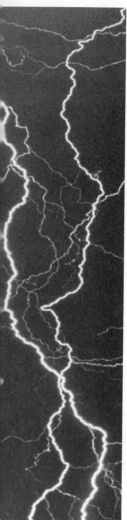

SOBERING FACTS ABOUT THE WORLD'S CHILDREN

In the United States:
- Every 32 seconds, a baby is born into poverty.
- Every 61 seconds, a baby is born to a teenage mother.
- Every 111 seconds, a baby is born at low birth weight.
- Every 13 minutes, we lose a baby to infant mortality.
- Every 2 1/2 hours, one of our children is murdered.

Around the World:
- Every day, almost 40,000 children under age five die (that equals 80 Boeing 747 airplanes filled with children and crashing every day with no survivors).
- Of the 600 million people who live in urban slums, 74 percent are under age 24.
- For every five live births, there are two abortions.
- Some estimates suggest that 100 million children (18 percent of children under age 15) live or work on the streets; Brazil alone has almost 7 million street children.
- Perhaps 300 million children under age fifteen are child laborers. India has an estimated 126 million; there are 5 million in Thailand. Why is this? Children are exploitable and docile. They work fast, don't tire easily, and can be cheated because they are less likely to detect this and have no recourse to get justice.
- Accurate figures are not possible, but some statistics estimate that as many as 10 million of the world's children are in the sex industry—child prostitution, pornography, sex for tourists. Some estimate 200,000 prostitutes under age twenty in Brazil, 150,000 in the United States. Of Thailand's one million prostitutes, 80 percent are under age sixteen.
- An estimated 130 million children have no access to primary school. Two-thirds of these are girls.

World figures are adapted from Bryant Myers, "State of the World's Children," *MARC Newsletter* 92-4 (December 1992): 3–4.

Displaced and Refugee Families

Try to imagine what it would be like if your city were overrun by an army of hoodlums who destroyed your house, took your valuables, beat your family members, and raped the women in your family, right before your eyes. Assume further that you lost your job, had no food, no medical care, and little reason to hope that things would get better. Then imagine that some foreigners, whose language you don't understand, took compassion on you

MAKING THE SHIFT FROM
ONE CULTURE TO ANOTHER

MASARU HORIKOSHI, M.DIV.
Minirth Meier New Life Clinics West
Coordinator, International
Services, Japan

Shinji Okamura came from Japan to the United States with his parents when he was eight years old. Now seventeen, Shinji has picked up a new language, English, and converses easily and fluently. At home, he speaks Japanese because that is the only language his parents understand. Shinji thinks and acts like an American, but he also thinks and acts like a Japanese. This has created some difficulties associated with cultural and identity issues. Shinji's situation is very common in the United States today.

Interestingly, we can find a similar situation in the Bible. Timothy, one of the apostle Paul's disciples, seems to have been well respected among Christians at that time. Acts 16 tells us that Timothy was a child of a mixed marriage and was growing up in a foreign city where idol worship was common. What was it like for him to grow up in a new culture and belong to the Christian community there? Did he face any cultural and value conflicts? (We know he faced the problem of circumcision.) How about his identity problems? How was he able to keep his faith?

We can learn several things from the life of Timothy and apply them to the life of Shinji and others like him. First, Timothy had a parent figure or mentor who was supportive and understanding. The apostle Paul appears to have been that person. Paul took Timothy on journeys, wrote him letters, encouraged him, and sometimes rebuked him. In Paul's second letter to Timothy, Paul called Timothy "my dear son" and mentioned that Timothy had cried in his presence. Paul appears to have been an emotionally safe person with whom Timothy could share his pains, struggles, and tears. Paul himself was bicultural, and perhaps this enabled him to understand, help, and mentor Timothy better than others could.

Second, Timothy's family, especially his mother and grandmother, influenced him significantly. Paul stated, "I have been reminded of your sincere faith, which first lived in your grandmother Lois and in your mother Eunice and, I am persuaded, now lives in you also." This indicates that the influences, positive or negative, from family members are inevitable.

Third, Timothy had a community that accepted him. He and his family probably belonged to the Christian subculture in the area.

The subculture probably protected him from a variety of obstacles, but at the same time, the subculture caused conflicts.

In order to help people like Shinji, we need to be concerned about these three areas: individual, family, and community. People trying to integrate themselves into another culture need a person with whom they will feel safe enough to share their own pains and struggles. They need a family that will not hinder their cultural adaptation. They need a group of people who will accept them and give them security.

How can you offer those qualities to people who are trying to integrate their lives in America? How can you become a mentor to a former refugee or an international student or a businessperson from another country? How can your family welcome the newcomers to our country? ◢◣

---

and took you away from your relatives and familiar surroundings and off to a place where the weather and customs were very different, the people ate different food, and almost everybody had religions that were very different from yours. Stretch your mind one step further and suppose that your children learned the language and customs of the new country very well, leaving you cut off from your own offspring and from almost everything that was familiar.

This describes the repeated shock waves that face hundreds of thousands of refugee and displaced families in the world today, many of whom live in the United States. These people face the normal stresses of parenthood, but their lives are made far more difficult because they must adjust to a new country, cope with persisting memories and flashbacks of torture and starvation, and try to raise children who are embracing the new culture.

These newcomers to America include thirty-one-year-old Joseph Dieujuste Kerizareth, who came from Haiti but who struggles to adjust and provide for his family because he can't find a job. His life is different from the life of Danh Hum Thi, a Cambodian mother who lives in the Bronx and who, after years of malnutrition in her native land, fed her children potato chips, candy, cookies, soda, and sugary cereals because she thought this must be how American children grow up "round and healthy." She is a single parent in unfamiliar surroundings and with limited knowledge of English. She works hard, coping alone to raise her kids, but surviving largely because of assistance from religious, social-service, and other agencies that try to help.[3]

Post-Communist Families

Far different are the families of people from Eastern European countries. Antonio Hristov, for example, grew up under a Communist regime, trying to live as a Christian. Now he is learning to adjust to the changes that are sweeping through his Bulgarian homeland.

Antonio's parents divorced when he was three months old, and he went to live with his father. Life in that home was difficult. When his father got drunk, he sometimes got violent, so Antonio went to live with his mother.

She was a Christian, and her son got involved in her church. Some of the young people wanted more enthusiasm in their worship, however, so they started a church of their own. A young man with limited theological education became the pastor, and the church began to grow—even to the point of starting three daughter churches, all of which continue to thrive.

Antonio wanted to attend Bible school, but Communist Bulgaria had no colleges like that. To study outside the country seemed impossible. All young men were required to serve two years in the military, and the Communist leaders condemned those who wanted to study in the West, even though many of these same leaders had sent their own sons and daughters abroad. Shortly after the fall of Communism in 1989, and surely because of the mercy and intervention of God, Antonio got permission to leave Bulgaria.

"How have families changed since the fall of Communism?" I asked when we talked recently. Antonio responded that some things are better but that people now feel less secure. They don't have money to buy essentials, and crime has risen. Some Bulgarian families don't have modern conveniences (his mother, for example, still does her washing by hand), and Western media influences appear to have contributed to increased immorality. Sex education is taboo in the schools, and sex is never mentioned in the church, but it dominates much of the media and the thinking and behavior of young Bulgarians.

"We need teachers," Antonio said in describing the future of Christian families. "We need people to teach sexual ethics, for example, but people who are sensitive to our culture. We don't need teachers who come to push their own methods but who don't have a clue about our culture and who don't seem to respect the fact that we are different from other countries."

Families Influenced by Culture

How sad and impoverished this world would be if families were all the same—or all like families in America. How narrow would be our perspective and how limited our understanding if we knew families only like our own. When we accept and learn from people who are different, we are more aware of the greatness of God, who created people of such diversity. We are better able to appreciate the cultural heritage of our families and are capable of helping other families who are struggling and sometimes jolted by family shocks that are beyond our comprehension.[4]

Antonio's family, like all of the others discussed in this book as well as yours and mine, has been influenced by the culture where it exists. Every family has had its own set of experiences, and we all see ourselves, our problems, and our family traumas in ways that are influenced by our backgrounds and by where we have lived. For example, African American families perceive the world—including self-identity, racial pride, child-rearing practices, educational and school-related experiences, employment opportunities or lack of them, financial stresses, male-female relations, parental roles, and sexual behavior—through the lens of racial experience.[5] Our neighborhoods, communities, cultures, and the countries where we live all have an impact on how we build our families and deal with change. And wherever we live, politics and the government are likely to have an impact on our families.

Families and the Government

Criticizing politicians probably is as old as the history of governments. In democracies, we are free to speak openly against our

FAMILIES IN CENTRAL AMERICA

SERGIO MIJANGOS, M.A.
Dean of Students
Central America Seminary,
Guatemala
Coauthor of *Consejeria Cristina Efectiva*

When he came for counseling, Carlos was a high school senior. He had been a senior for three years, but he could never organize himself enough to graduate. Even though he was nineteen years old, he had difficulty keeping appointments, getting up on time, and even attending classes. Carlos sought counseling because of this lack of organization in his life.

Carlos belonged to the upper middle class. Both of his parents held full-time jobs. Carlos grew up with good moral principles but with a very poor sense of identity and discipline. Even though he had been raised in a two-parent home, he could identify with those who had lost their parents to divorce or to death.

Carlos's story is probably a good illustration of what is happening in many Central American families, where many children grow up without a father or with a father who is too busy. Children without role models within their homes lack discipline in the most basic areas.

These children become adults without direction, adults who get involved in unrewarding jobs. Many of them have grown up with a very frail sense of belonging and with confusion about their gender roles.

Some of these adolescents seek their identity in gangs, cults, or other destructive groups. Even though some are very intelligent, they do not know how to use that potential.

The adolescents also seem to have problems in relating to authority figures and to God. They seem to have difficulties conceptualizing a God who is present, involved in their lives, and caring for his children. It seems that many of their ideas about God come from what they incorporated from their parents.

People like Carlos are very common in Central America. Carlos profited from a substitute model he found in a counselor. When older, stable adults commit themselves to becoming substitute models and reparenting the younger generations, the emerging young adults have hope. This may be one of the ways in which mature Christians in any country can help young people and strengthen families. ✤

elected officials and free to turn them out of office whenever new elections are held. Many Christians seem to forget, however, that we also are called to pray for those in authority, to submit to their leadership.[6] We must recognize that God ultimately is in control, even of governments (Rom. 13:1-2; 1 Tim. 2:1-2).

None of this hides the fact, however, that families like yours and mine are being attacked and undermined by political and social forces that we cannot ignore. Our goal to avoid alarmist predictions of family disaster must not blind us to the well-documented antifamily agendas of Planned Parenthood, the National Education Association, the American Civil Liberties Union, the National Organization for Women, and other organizations that war against the family. We must not bury our heads in the sand and ignore the accumulating evidence that many (certainly not all) government and political officials, from all political persuasions, are talking about family values but are working to undermine the very values that they proclaim so eloquently in their public speeches.

In his analysis of the shocking forces that put families under siege, George Grant writes some thought-provoking words: "Institutions that have traditionally provided stability, strength, and solace to families in times of crisis—our churches, private associations, and community organizations—have been systematically undermined. Their values have been attacked, their methods have been challenged, and their reputations have been distorted—more often than not at the hands of our own government and social engineers under its aegis. Amazingly, this assault was initiated under the pretense of *helping* us, not hurting us. Not only has it hurt us, we have paid for the injury ourselves."[7]

Grant documents the increased spending for social programs during the past thirty-five years and argues that these programs have neither solved the social ills of society nor led to improvements. "Though the grandiose failure of the modern government-sponsored engineers has been glaringly obvious for more than a decade—fully documented with reams of empirical data—their desire to utterly supplant and succeed the family remains undeterred. In fact, they are more powerful, more influential, and

CLINICAL ASSESSMENT WITH AFRICAN-AMERICAN FAMILIES

MICHAEL LYLES, M.D.
Rapha Adult Program
Charter Peachford Hospital
Contributor to *The Black Family*

The clinical assessment of African-American families in need remains a source of difficulty for mental health professionals. The family therapy literature is not always helpful because the bulk of it focuses on socioeconomically deprived families rather than on the total spectrum of families who come for therapy. With the ubiquity of stereotyped images of racial minorities in the media, it becomes difficult for therapists, regardless of race, to be totally free of subtle preconceptions about black family life.

Therapists working with racial minorities must become aware of their own racial and cultural stereotypes and how these may affect assessment and treatment. Thera-pists who refuse to examine their "blind spots" are at risk of defining adaptive responses of culturally different families as deviant as well as ignoring the pathology inherent in patterns of behavior that they hold to be consistent with the culture. Therapists who consider themselves familiar with a culture are especially cautioned to look for blind spots and to recognize that families who seek treatment are in fact more prone to have problems that are not culturally explained.

Misconceptions and stereotypes that focus only on cultural deficits and structural pathology can impede the formation of a thera-peutic alliance between therapist and family. Ultimately these false impressions not only can obstruct therapeutic progress but also can lead to the premature termination of therapy.

---

more determined than ever before. Their organizations, institutions, and endowments have recently entered into a whole host of lucrative new partnerships with government at all levels."[8]

Sometimes the political and social assault on the family is blatantly obvious, but more often the attack is subtle, characterized by what has been called *incrementalism*. This is a neutral-sounding word that means making small and gradual progression toward a specified goal. In the political realm, it involves making changes in the laws so that long-standing values are slowly dropped and replaced with standards that are politically correct and often detrimental to families.[9]

All of this can leave us feeling helpless and defensive, wondering how we can protect our families against the onslaughts that come from our own society. There is no easy answer or precise formula for resisting, although Christians know the power of prayer, and many choose to be active politically as well. Others are convinced that "the best response we can make to the subverters of the family and the perverters of freedom is the inculcation of godly virtue, of moral ethics, of Christian character," in ourselves, our children, our businesses, our professional organizations. Then we need "the dissemination of those values throughout the whole of society."[10]

As a Christian, I doubt that we can make much progress with a human-based, character-building approach that ignores God. Still, there are hopeful signs. Three out of every four Americans agree that the country is in "a moral and spiritual decline." At present the pendulum is swinging away from self-expression and toward self-discipline, according to a *Newsweek* cover story. That same article ends with the conclusion that "in the end, it's not the laws we pass but the lives we live."[11]

How we best live, however, depends on our individual values and ethics. When we build our lives on pluralism and relativism, we continue with the same moral and spiritual decline that characterizes any culture that forsakes biblical teaching. If the new interest in spirituality moves us closer to a biblically based spirituality, we can have much greater hope for moral stability in our families, communities, and whole societies.

Healthy and Unhealthy Communities

After completing a major survey of young people throughout the country, researchers looked at the towns and small cities where the young people lived. The researchers found that in some communities there was a high likelihood of teens engaging in the at-risk behaviors—like heavy alcohol use, sexual activity, delinquent behavior—that we mentioned in an earlier chapter. In other communities these activities were much less common.

FAMILIES AND GOVERNMENT

GARY BAUER, J.D.
President, Family Research Council
Author of *Our Journey Home: What Parents Are Doing to Preserve Family Values*

Telling the truth about families and government can be dangerous. Just ask Dan Quayle and little Joey Ford. Everyone remembers Vice President Quayle's Commonwealth Club speech about the link between family breakdown and civil disorder—the famous "Murphy Brown" speech. It came soon after the Los Angeles riots and reflected the germinating public awareness that fatherless homes can lead to blood-drenched streets. For the vice president, that speech led to ridicule.

For Joey Ford, a similar speech led indirectly to death. Ford was a thirteen-year-old honor student who lived in the suburbs of Washington, D.C. The week after the L.A. riots, he spoke from the pulpit of Three Way Deliverance Church. Joey talked to the congregation about violence and drugs and urged them to remember that the answer to these problems and every other was salvation through Jesus Christ. Minutes later, while Joey and his family drove home, he was killed by a single bullet fired in the middle of a shoot-out between rival drug gangs.

The nation is slowly coming around to the point of view expressed by Dan Quayle and Joey Ford. The former vice president has returned to the Commonwealth Club to restate his thesis to standing ovations. Joey's ovation should consist of his fellow Americans refusing to forget him or the thousands of other promising young men, black and white, who are victims of our national amnesia about family and faith as the keys to self-government. Joey Ford not only gave voice to the meaning of "saving" families; he gave his very life.

Armed with these facts, the researchers found twenty-eight communities where kids engaged in high-risk behaviors and twenty-eight communities in which the risk behaviors were lower. The researchers called these towns unhealthy and healthy communities. They then studied them more carefully to see if they differed in any significant ways. They did.[12]

Communities and Young People

When young people have problems, we tend to blame the kids, tell them to take responsibility, to just say no, and to grow up. If they have problems, we assume they have only themselves to blame. There is some truth in this idea. Young people do need to take responsibility for their actions and learn self-control.

But communities need to take responsibility as well. Urban gang wars or high pregnancy rates in poor neighborhoods both show that communities have an influence on the problems that develop. It's hard to grow up in towns and neighborhoods that do not provide the values, norms, and opportunities that help young people develop healthy habits so they can stay out of trouble.

Communities and Families

I have a friend who thinks he knows why gangs develop and why young people have problems. "It's the breakdown of the family," he told me after church one Sunday. "The parents aren't doing their job. If the mothers would stay home and care for their kids, the fathers took some authority at home, and the parents wouldn't get divorced, then this country would be a whole lot better."

Most researchers agree that a strong, healthy family often insulates young people from risky behaviors and helps them develop the backbone that enables them to cope. It is true that caring, stable, loving families are the best protectors and nurturers of children. But my friend seems naively oblivious to the practical challenge of how we get parents to change their behaviors or how we teach families to be healthy.

The researchers concluded that all parts of the community must play a role if we are to protect young people, including those who do not have ideal family lives. The mayor of Minneapolis agreed when he called for the building of "nurturing communities"—neighborhoods with parks, libraries, services, recreational facilities, and supportive neighbors who provide stability for families in stress and shock. Families don't need to be controlled by their communities, but they all can benefit from community support. Trying to carry all the responsibilities of family building and shock control is a burden most families cannot and should not have to bear alone.[13]

Families and Schools

Everybody knows that schools can create more problems than they solve and can contribute to family disruption, especially when schools ignore parents and struggle with tight budgets. In contrast to the schools in unhealthy communities, however, the schools in healthy communities had caring and supportive staff members, academically motivated students, help for students who had difficulties, and an open partnership between the school and the parents.

More recent research shows that when parents are interested and involved with schools and when schools welcome and encourage parental involvement, grades go up and behavior problems go down. Sadly, some schools discourage parental partnerships, especially as students get older, and many parents are too busy, unwilling, or distrustful of the schools, so they stay away. Involvement of parents is greater when schools and families are willing to be flexible with schedules, creative in working together, and able to develop personal relationships between teachers and parents.[14]

Of special interest are the community differences in the availability of after-school clubs, Scout troops, youth programs, sports teams, and involvement with music. When budgets are short, school boards tend to cut the extras and "get back to the basics." In contrast, the research found that, if anything, extracurricular activities need "increased support and commitment from communities so that young people won't be idle in front of the television or hanging out on the street corner or in a shopping mall. These programs are as essential as more formal education and contribute to it."[15]

School, community, and church-sponsored programs tend to reduce the impact of bad peer influences, give positive role models, and often involve parents and other community volunteers in helping kids. The list on the next page summarizes ways in which parents can work with communities for the benefit of everybody's children.

Researchers aren't sure of the reasons, but young people in healthy communities feel less negative peer pressure, perhaps because healthy communities provide so much for young people to do. As a result they are less likely to encourage each other to get into trouble.

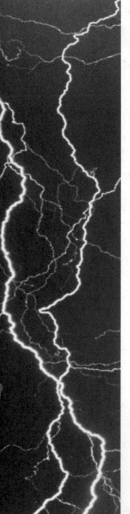

PARENTS AND COMMUNITIES

Parents should not be made scapegoats for all the problems of children in a society that hinders or fails to help in the process of child rearing. Caring and supportive parents are very important, but their involvement does not automatically make a difference in the health and well-being of the young people in the community. To work with the community to make a difference, parents can

- recognize each person's responsibility for the welfare of all young people; parenting does not stop at our own front doors
- avoid the trap of abandoning their children as they move through adolescence
- actively get their children involved in community (and church) opportunities that are consistent with the family's values and support others who wish to get involved as well
- become directly involved by coaching, chaperoning, or leading some of the activities in which their children are interested
- volunteer to help in organizations or activities in which their children are not involved
- advocate for and support schools, youth-serving organizations, and other groups that provide constructive outlets for young people of different ages
- make home a comfortable place for teenagers and their friends
- take advantage of opportunities to be with teenagers and their friends when driving them to and from activities and events
- insist that the community (and church) and its various groups provide a variety of activities for all types of young people
- understand the importance of their own family influence on their children's own internalized values

Adapted from Dale A. Blyth and Eugene C. Roehlkepartain, *Healthy Communities, Healthy Youth* (Minneapolis: Search Institute, 1993): 55.

Families and Churches

One study found that 70 percent of young people in the healthy communities were involved in a church at least once a month, compared to 50 percent of the young people from the unhealthy communities. When congregations raise youth programs to a high level of importance and when churches find ways to include young people in their ministries, the churches and the communities both are healthier.

Christ Presbyterian Church is an example. Not far from the University of Wisconsin in Madison, members of the church made long-term commitments to a group of sixth-grade students at a local public school. Every Monday night, the kids have a home-cooked meal and get tutoring from church members who are committed to helping their young friends get through high school and on to college. The program is interracial and intergenerational, involving a group of Christians who want to know "what would happen if you just stayed with a group of kids no matter what?" Thus far, the kids and the volunteers have built relationships that involve love, mentoring, and encouragement. The kids' grades have gone up, their teachers have been supportive, and church leaders have watched how the experience has enriched the lives and families of many of the volunteer tutors.[16] The Christ Presbyterian program shows how community involvement can have an impact on adults as well as on people under twenty.

Sometimes, of course, community involvement is harmful to families. Even in the suburbs, neighborhoods can be unfriendly places. People with demanding jobs or busy schedules need time to retreat and be with their families rather than rushing off to be involved with community programs. But these can also be excuses for not being involved.

When we cut ourselves off from our communities and completely withdraw into our homes, we stifle all opportunities for evangelism, often become narrower and more self-centered in our thinking, and miss opportunities to make a difference in the lives of our neighbors. Even when we go into our houses and shut the doors, the community still makes a difference. Individuals and families are influenced by the people in the neighborhoods where they live, the social norms of their communities, the expectations that come from their places of worship, the types of television and leisure activities that take up their free time, the laws of the places where they live, the political decisions of their governments, and numerous other influences. No person is an island. If one person in your world changes in some way, then you are likely to be influenced.

This does not mean that we are like rudderless rafts, bobbing about on a sea of winds over which we have no control. It does mean, however, that we cannot understand and improve families or anticipate and deal with family shocks unless we are aware of the roles and influences of other people. Families need other families.

We can learn from families with experiences that differ from our own, even from families who normally live far away. Every year we invite two or three international families to have Christmas dinner with our family. Most of these have been student families from different cultures. Over the years our family has been enriched immeasurably by these times together.

Our families can be enriched as well when we participate in community activities, get involved with schools and with the political process, and work with others to make our own communities healthier and friendlier to families.

No community influence, however, can match the healthy church in its potential to strengthen homes and enable us to resist the family shocks that continual change brings into our lives. But even the church works in different ways, from culture to culture, to have an impact on families.

J O S E P H   &   S U N E E T H A

First comes love, then comes marriage
Next comes a baby in a baby carriage.

Maybe you have never heard this old couplet. It describes the
normal order of things in most American marriages: First
comes love, then comes marriage.

That's not how it works in countries like India. Indian young
people often turn the selection of their spouse over to
somebody else and go on with other things while they wait for
what is known as an arranged marriage. This is how Joseph
and Suneetha found each other.

Joseph, a Biola University graduate who was working for a
year in the United States, was twenty-two years old when his
Christian parents came for a visit from their home in
Hyderabad, a bustling city in south central India. "It is time for
you to get married," his parents told him during the visit.

They expressed a concern that he would not be able to find
an Indian girl in the U.S., especially one who is a committed
Christian and who would be willing to return to India. Joseph
knew that because he is the oldest son, it is his responsibility
to live near his parents and care for them as they grow older.
Like his countrymen, Joseph has always considered this a
privilege and a responsibility that he is glad to assume.

Joseph agreed, therefore, that his parents should return to

Hyderabad and find him a bride. He had only one request: He
wanted to be kept informed of the bride-searching process.
Most Indian young couples do not meet each other until
shortly before the wedding, so Joseph's request was unusual
and maybe a reflection of the American influence on his life.

Back in India Joseph's parents started their search. Often
parents know other parents who have marriage-eligible
children, but frequently they contact a marriage arranger.
Among Hindus, this person, known as a *pandit,* is often a
priest, sometimes one who spends his whole life as a specialist
in arranging marriages. Christians turn to the church for help
from the pastor, an older woman in the church, or a family
member. Joseph's parents talked with their relatives and
people in their church and finally contacted the mother's
younger brother, who helped them find almost a dozen young
women who might be possible wives for Joseph.

Proverbs reminds us that "he who finds a wife finds what is
good," but how does one find a wife of noble character (Prov.
18:22; 31:10)? Among India's Hindus, where there are many
different languages and castes, the pandit looks for brides
among people of the same language group, the same caste,
sometimes the same subcaste, and usually somebody in the
same geographical area as the prospective groom. Often the
match is made between distant relatives, but that wasn't true
with Joseph.

Everyone in Joseph's family and the church agreed that he
needed a wife who was attractive, educated, with a background
similar to Joseph's family, and clearly a dedicated believer. One
day Joseph's cousin had been visiting in another town and
spotted Suneetha in a church service. He found out who she
was and made a special trip to tell Joseph's parents that the girl
in the church might make a good bride for their son. That's
how the name of her parents was added to the list of those who
received a visit from Joseph's mother and father. The purpose
of these parental meetings (almost always initiated by the
parents of the male) was to discuss a possible marriage
between their children. Sometimes the visiting parents meet

the girl briefly; often they do not, but they may look at a photograph.

Because Joseph's parents had agreed to keep him informed, they let him know about their search. When Joseph returned to India for a family celebration, he and his parents visited the families whose daughters had passed the initial screening. They traveled to a nearby city, and in one day they met the families of five prospective wives. In one of the homes, Joseph asked the four parents (his and hers) if he could talk in private to the girl. This was a peculiar request in that culture, but the parents agreed. The two young people talked for almost ten minutes. Joseph turned this into a brief interview in which he asked a few questions about the woman's priorities. Afterward, the visiting family went home and compared notes.

The parents had tried to keep their preference hidden, but Joseph knew which girl they preferred, and he felt the same: It was Suneetha, the young woman whom the cousin had seen earlier in church. At that point the parents could have arranged the marriage and started the wedding plans, but their son was not quite ready to have the process move ahead. He wanted to look at the girl at least one more time, and he had a suggestion for arranging this additional meeting.

Joseph had returned to India to help his father celebrate the Indian custom of *shastipurti,* meaning "completion of sixty" years. At the celebration, visitors talk about the man's achievements, sometimes the parents renew their marriage vows, and everybody participates in the festive occasion, planned and paid for by the oldest son. Joseph had spent a year following his graduation from Biola working to raise money for this birthday party. Once Joseph's father turned sixty, it was Joseph's responsibility to care for his parents until they died.

As the family prepared for the shastipurti celebration, Joseph asked if his parents could invite Suneetha and her parents to be part of the half day of festivities. Normally this is not done, but once again the parents agreed, and the two young people were able to look at each other across the crowded room. At one point they even were able to take a brief walk during which Joseph asked a few more questions. If they married and moved to Georgia, where he was working on a graduate degree in computer science, would Suneetha be willing to come with him to the States and then return to India? Joseph knew that many Indian young woman often refused to return to India once they had lived in the States. Would she be willing to leave her government job as an electrical engineer and become a housewife who would have babies and take care of Joseph's parents? Was she free of any other possible marriage commitments? Would she be willing to marry Joseph?

After talking for less than half an hour, Suneetha agreed to marry Joseph. They told their parents, announced the engagement the following Sunday, and were married shortly thereafter.

In our culture, where love comes first and marriage comes second, very often divorce comes next. Not so in India. Joseph believes that most marriages in India are strong, even though in India the marriage comes first and then the love.

Joseph noted that the divorce rate is much lower in India than it is in the States. For one reason, divorce is frowned on in India and carries more of a social stigma than it does here. Furthermore, in many respects the marriage of a young man and a young woman is really a marriage of their families. Each family member fills a specific role, and often this takes pressure off the couple so they need not handle all of their problems and make all decisions alone. For example, because of the nature of their families, Joseph now has a major responsibility for ensuring that his wife's younger sister finds a husband. This extended family support helps people handle the pressures of life and marriage more easily.

Are arranged marriages better than love marriages? When Joseph and I discussed his marriage, my Indian friend suggested that both marriage arrangements could be effective, but for his family and Suneetha's the arranged relationship is best.

15

THE CHURCH AND THE FAMILY

JONATHAN, now in his midthirties, was raised in a nominally religious family and sent to Sunday school as a child. He participated in church youth programs while he was growing up and got involved in parachurch activities as a teenager. In college, Jonathan went to an evangelical church near campus and resisted the partying lifestyles of the other students. After graduation, he settled into a job with a large engineering firm, married a woman from a fine Christian family, and after a couple of years they had the first of their three children.

But Jonathan is mad at God.

To outsiders, Jonathan and his wife have an ideal family, but their marriage has traveled a rocky road from the start. He likes reading, sports, and kicking off his shoes to relax at home. His wife, intellectually his equal, doesn't like to read and prefers to relax by watching a good movie in a neat house. Sports bore her, but she is an impeccable and tightly structured homemaker who always has a to-do list waiting when her husband returns from work. After almost ten years of marriage, he doesn't look forward to coming home at night, and his wife gives little indication that she is glad to see him walk through the door.

The couple have been to counselors, attended marriage seminars, read books together, and talked several times with their pastor. Both are trying hard to help matters improve, and both agree that things are better now than they have ever been. Even so, Jonathan is angry because God hasn't given him the ideal marriage and family life that he wants. After a lifetime of involvement in churches, he has stopped going because everything Christian, including the people, seems so phony. He hasn't been reading the Bible lately, especially since he started to work on a master's degree, and he sees no point in praying since God doesn't seem to have paid much attention or done anything to improve the marriage. Recently Jonathan dropped out of his men's accountability group, claiming that he was too busy to attend. His fellow group members challenged that explanation and suggested that he really wanted to avoid the responsibility of being accountable to a group of guys who know him well.

There still is hope for Jonathan and his family, although he has set himself adrift from his best sources of help and strength. He has cut loose from God, from the church, and from a supportive group of believers who still are available, willing to give support and mutual accountability.

How Should the Family Relate to the Church?

Rodney Clapp, an insightful writer, argues that people in our society place their highest value on autonomy and independence. We treasure self-reliance, and when we face problems, we conclude, in the words of a very old song, "I can handle this thing all by myself. There's no help wanted." Clapp uses more technical words: "In our society, we have been prone to imagine that we can live privately and individually as Christians with or without the social support of the church."[1]

That's Jonathan's perspective. It's an independent way of thinking, and it extends to our views of families.

In a book published several years ago, two writers identified six characteristics of what we have come to call the traditional family. (See list on next page.) Despite the fact that this model is mostly Western and less than two centuries old—we saw this earlier—many people like to think that the traditional nuclear family is *the* biblical family.

Clapp's Critique of the Church

Rodney Clapp and others suggest, however, that this conclusion comes when we read twentieth-century thinking into the biblical text. Traditional families, as we know them, are consistent with biblical teaching and have served us well, at least until recently. But historically and in different cultures, families have taken various shapes and forms. If we assume that traditional families are the only really biblical families, then we must face the fact that there are no biblical families in the Bible.

CHARACTERISTICS OF TRADITIONAL FAMILIES

1. Family life is eminently attractive, and the home, as a private refuge from the harsh public world, is a major focus of family life.
2. The traditional family has a heightened concern for children, particularly for their formation and education.
3. The family is a source of personal values and identity for both sexes.
4. Romantic love is the major motive for marriage.
5. Spouses are intensely affectionate and respectful to one another.
6. The woman is paramount in the home, which is her special domain.

Adapted from Brigitte and Peter L. Berger, *The War over the Family* (Garden City, N.Y.: Doubleday, 1983), 101–2. The Bergers call these characteristics of "the bourgeois family" rather than marks of "the traditional family."

In their admirable determination to preserve family values against all the antifamily forces, Christians have tended to glorify the traditional nuclear family. Many among us defend it against all criticisms, publish alarmist predictions about its impending collapse, and resist suggestions that in the next century our views about Christian families may differ from our views of Christian families today. We proclaim that our traditionalist views of the family are taken directly from the Bible, and we are uncomfortable if anybody suggests otherwise.

The 1970s gave rise to some bold new assumptions about the family. Many people concluded, for example, that two-parent families aren't needed, that family disruption causes no harm to children, that personal freedom and self-expression are more important than family commitments, and that families should be defined broadly, as "two or more persons who live together and call themselves a family." In previous pages we have seen how assumptions like these have created turmoil in many homes and upheaval in many lives, especially in the lives of children.

Clapp agrees that Christians must resist these destructive assumptions. But we also must move away from thinking that Christian families should be independent havens where a mother and father withdraw with their children into isolated little cocoons that are cut off from everybody else. Of course, some family functions must take place behind closed doors. The intimacy of sexual intercourse between husband and wife is private and personal. Many of the responsibilities of child rearing, nurturing, disciplining, and the bonding of a child with his or her parents are best handled within the confines of a biological family. Jesus affirmed the existence and importance of biological families. He did not expect the nuclear family to be denied or eliminated. He knew the importance of parents caring for their children and of older children caring for their parents. He experienced the refreshment of getting away from the crowds and into the confines of a stable home. He never married, and he never had children, but he was very pro-family.

For Christ, however, the family of believers took precedence over the family of biological relatives. Entrance into that broader family requires a second birth. For those who follow Jesus, "the critical blood, the blood that most significantly determines their identity and character, is not the blood of the biological family. It is the blood of the lamb."[2] That lamb died so that all who put their faith in him will become a part of his eternal family (John 3:16; Rom. 8:14-17; Eph. 2:8, 13). When Jesus walked on earth, he claimed his disciples (his fellow believers) and not his blood relatives as his first family (Matt. 12:46-50).[3]

This does nothing to deny the importance of our individual families. But if Christians see the wider and more inclusive role of the family of God, we might agree with two declarations that Clapp states in his book. These are worth considering seriously because they give a broader, probably more biblically valid view of families than the traditional-family model that many Christians embrace and defend.

The first declaration—admittedly controversial—states, "The family is not God's most important institution on earth. The

CHURCHES AND FAMILIES

CHARLES SELL, TH.D.
Trinity Evangelical Divinity School
Author of *Family Ministry*

The church and the family, both God's institutions, need each other. *That the family needs the church* is well recognized; family-life specialists constantly plead with church leaders to help families. They point out that the church is in the best position to do preventative work since it usually has all family members and can readily teach and counsel about family matters. In that way it can head off problems.

That the church needs the family is not so readily recognized. Ministering to families is not something the church should do merely because families need it but because the church needs it.

For one thing, fortifying people's morals, an obvious task of the church, is closely tied to family health. Infidelity, sex outside marriage, divorce, and honoring and caring for parents are moral issues. People will not only need to be told not to commit adultery, but they also will need to be taught how to commit to a marriage. Classes and seminars on marriage, for example, are not just efforts to make people happy; they are attempts to keep them morally and spiritually healthy, which is the business of the church.

Families are also connected to one of the most recognized goals of the church: discipling. Parents, not Sunday school teachers or youth workers, are the major disciplers of the church's children. Studies show that Christian education programs are relatively ineffective unless at least one of the parents of the child is a Christian. In other words, the family is an agency of Christian education. Training people to be godly parents is not just family ministry; it is church ministry.

Experts in systems theory also confirm how churches and families cannot be separated. They show, for example, how trouble in a church leader's family, even though concealed from others, can still have a substantially negative impact on the life of the congregation. Many congregations are now aware that their own success and health are connected to the strength of their families.

Counseling, seminars, classes, and intergenerational events to develop marriages and families are not options; they are essential parts of the church's ministry.

If you want stronger families, build a stronger church.

If you want a stronger church, build stronger families. ◣◣

family is not the social agent that most significantly shapes and forms the character of Christians. The family is not the primary vehicle of God's grace and salvation for a waiting, desperate world."[4]

Clapp's second declaration is more positive: "The church is God's most important institution on earth. The church is the social agent that most significantly shapes and forms the character of Christians. And the church is the primary vehicle of God's grace and salvation for a waiting, desperate world."[5]

Think again about Jonathan's determination to save his marriage and fix his family on his own, apart from the church. By withdrawing into his own family cluster, Jonathan has taken the difficult tasks of building a marriage and nurturing kids, and made the challenge much harder than it otherwise would be. He has taken the whole load of family building and put it on his own shoulders. Little wonder that so many families collapse under this burden.

"Outside the church, isolated from it, individual families [like Jonathan's] are simply caught in competing cultural currents," Rodney Clapp writes. In contrast,

> The church is a kind of ark—providing a place to stand, companionship with others of like mind and imagination, and a rudder to guide in a society that has otherwise lost direction.
>
> On this ark, furthermore, individual Christians can sail with hope and some safety back into the troubled waters of their own biological families. For even though we have for nearly two centuries attempted to sentimentalize the family, it is still [for many people] a dangerous place.
>
> Because of the awesome power of family ties, the sentimental family can destroy the very people it wants to love. Family ties can be powerfully supporting, holding us up, drawing us to safety after a misstep. But the ties that bind us in unity can also bind us in captivity. They can be stifling, oppressive, destructive. . . . Family loyalty can become ultimate loyalty. . . . Then family ties bind destructively rather than constructively.[6]

FAMILY VALUES
IN BELGIUM

JEF DE VRIESE, M.A.
General Coordinator, Center for
Pastoral Counseling
Belgian Bible Institute and
Evangelical Theological Faculty
Coauthor of *Doeltreffende
Pastorale Counseling*

Did you know that a legalistic
Catholic theology in Belgium
results in excellent family values?
And are you puzzled by the fact
that Protestantism in Holland
produces a lower sense of
belonging together as a family
than Catholicism in Belgium does?

In Belgian families the influence
of parents on their children is
tremendous. Children are brought
up with a deep sense of belonging
to the family and of being
responsible for contributing to its
well-being. Even adults and
married children are pressured by
their parents, who impose their
views and values on the next
generation. But children in Holland
are raised to be more independent. They are free to leave their
parents at the age of eighteen.
They make their own decisions
and rules.

In Belgium this family pattern
has resulted in an ongoing protection of Christian family values

among Catholics. In Holland, however, Christian values often fade
from one generation to the next,
and good family values are lost.

The impact of the Belgian
parents stimulates family life but
hinders the spreading of the
gospel of grace. The lack of
parental impact in Holland opens
opportunities to expose the gospel
to unbelieving children from a
non-Christian background, but it
hinders the reproduction of
Christian family values in the next
Christian generation.

Families in the two countries I
know best raise some questions
about families everywhere. Is
traditionalism really better able to
influence people than the gospel
of grace? Can churches and
Christian counseling give more
attention to programs that help
families influence the next
generations even if the culture
discourages this? Is there a way
by which healthy spiritual traditionalism is beneficial to Christian
family values? Churches can help
Christian families understand and
demonstrate the gospel of grace
while we pass on strong Christian
values to our children and coming
generations.

This is heavy stuff that boils down to this: *Families will not be strong and healthy unless they are tied to the church.*

Churches Can Help or Hinder

Perhaps this family-church tie can be seen most clearly in African American congregations. The local church has been heralded as the most enduring institution within the African American community. It has been called a major social support system, a strong stimulus for social change, a significant source of status, a beacon of hope, and a social equalizer where people of all socioeconomic, occupational, and educational levels join together as equal members to worship and serve. For people who feel oppressed, the African American church gives respect and acceptance. For people who struggle to save their children from the streets, the church provides alternate friends, meaningful activities, and distinct role models. For people who feel like second-class citizens, the black church is the one institution that is owned, controlled, managed, supported, and patronized primarily by African American people.[7]

All churchgoers know, however, that many congregations are far from ideal builders of families or supporters of family values. Churches fail families in at least three ways: through their politics, their pathologies, and their programs.

Politics and the Church

In his book *The War against the Family,* Canadian writer William D. Gairdner wrote lengthy chapters on the antifamily activities of some educators, feminists, homosexuals, politicians, and court officials. Near the end of the book was a chapter titled "Blessing Our Trespasses: The Church vs. the Family." Gairdner argued that "almost all the rapid and debilitating changes in modern church thinking . . . are resoundingly anti-family. The church, which should be defending this value-generating and value-perpetuating primal structure called the family, is participating in contemporary social decay." The book quotes a bishop who explained that the mission of the church is to build the kingdom of God on earth, and "the means to the mission is politics."[8]

Gairdner writes mostly about liberal, mainstream Protestant

churches and the activist, left-leaning element in the Roman Catholic church, but he suggests that more conservative Christians are also in danger of getting distracted by their involvement in politics. Sometimes even the best churches lose their first love and get caught up in political activism.

In their attempts to bolster and enhance family values, should Christians get involved in the political process? Few issues are likely to arouse more debate and stimulate more disagreement. Conservative Christian leaders may disagree on specifics, but they all sense a need to be involved in the political process. Undoubtedly, their actions have had an impact in stemming some of the antifamily forces in the society.[9]

In contrast, equally conservative believers, like Charles Colson, write about Lenin's conclusion that the best way to neutralize the impact of the church was to get it involved in politics.[10] The declining impact of the politically active liberal church would seem to support this conclusion. Few evangelical Christians have been as close to the seat of political power as was Colson when he worked for Richard Nixon. Yet in his impressive book about the church, Colson argues that recent history has demonstrated that "on virtually every issue where we've launched a frontal assault on the culture, we've lost."[11] Jesus resisted attempts to get him into political action and seemed to suggest that a life well lived could have more impact than a political battle well fought (Matt. 5:13-16; 1 Pet. 2:11-12).

On one issue probably most of us will agree: While individual Christians may be—and many should be—involved in different levels of political activism, we who are in the church must not let our concern about family values and antifamily political trends so engulf our thinking that we forget our primary tasks of going into the world to make disciples and to build wholly devoted followers of Jesus Christ. A church that marches to political drumbeats, even drumbeats that promote family values, is in danger of ignoring and hurting the families in its midst.

Pathology and the Church

During our lifetimes, most of us hear many sermons about the church and what it should be like. When I hear these messages,

I often feel uncomfortable because most churches are far from the ideals that we hear about in sermons or read about in books. Stated bluntly, too many churches are pathological: abusive, manipulative, and legalistic. Many are divided into feuding factions, and some are headed by self-centered, incompetent, unhealthy church leaders. Unhealthy churches can't make healthy families.

Sociologist and cult expert Ronald Enroth recently turned his attention to "churches that abuse." In a sobering book filled with heart-rending stories of families who were harmed by their churches, Enroth described how legalism, authoritarian leadership, rigid control, excessive discipline, spiritual intimidation, suppression of dissent, overemphasis on experience, and harsh denunciation of outsiders all can have a devastating impact on families. A central theme of Enroth's argument is that spiritual abuse can take place anywhere, even "in the context of doctrinally sound, Bible preaching, fundamental, conservative Christianity. All that is needed for abuse is a pastor accountable to no one and therefore beyond confrontation."[12]

All of the blame cannot rest on the pastor, however. Almost all of us know of pastoral ministries and sometimes pastoral families that have been torn apart by gossip, conflict, and some of the most vicious forms of verbal attack and factionalism. Many pastors and their families have tried to stand firm in the midst of these ecclesiastical earthquakes but have been powerless to stop the gales that have blown them from their pulpits and out of their communities. One of Satan's most effective techniques is to divide believers and have them at odds with one another. Churches beset by battles can be poisonous environments for families.

Equally disturbing, perhaps, are churches that turn religion into an unhealthy addiction, often fueled by insecure and manipulative church leaders who preach messages that are of partial validity at best. The list on the next page shows some of the characteristics of a toxic faith system. When family members get trapped in these kinds of churches, they are pulled away from their family responsibilities at home. The church makes demands that are all-consuming, and the church leader becomes a self-centered, powerful, authoritarian taskmaster.

TOXIC AND HEALTHY FAITH

TOXIC FAITH

1. Leaders or members claim to have special abilities, calling, or insights from God.
2. The leader is dictatorial and authoritarian.
3. There is an "us versus them" mentality, and all believers are expected to fall in line and do what they are told.
4. The leader is addicted to power and purges the system of any who question the system or its teachings.
5. Church members are expected to give overwhelming service even to the detriment of their families.
6. The church claims to free people from their problems, but many are physically ill, emotionally distraught, and spiritually dead.
7. Communication is from the top down and from the inside out.
8. The system is characterized by rules and regulations that further the empire of the leader.
9. There is no objective accountability.
10. People who disagree are given labels like "traitors" or "malcontents" to dehumanize and discount objectors.

HEALTHY FAITH

1. Leaders or members claim to be members of the body of Christ; these members are brothers and sisters with different spiritual gifts but equal access to God through the Scriptures.
2. The leader seeks to be a servant.
3. There is an attitude that all of us are sinners saved by God's grace, called to serve in different places and in different roles.
4. The leader seeks to encourage and build up others and is not threatened by questions.
5. Church members are encouraged to balance their church activities and home responsibilities.
6. People are free to serve in accordance with their spiritual gifts and balanced with their family obligations. They tend to be spiritually alive.
7. Communication is more often from the bottom up, and two-way interaction is common and encouraged.
8. The system is not bogged down with rules. Believers are encouraged to obey Scripture, and the leader is humble and not an empire builder.
9. There are clear and open accountability relationships with others.
10. There is no labeling.

Adapted from Stephen Arterburn and Jack Felton, "Ten Characteristics of a Toxic Faith System," chapter 6, in *Toxic Faith: Understanding and Overcoming Religious Addiction* (Nashville: Nelson, 1991).

Healthy churches with good pastors do exist, and many work in partnership with families to bring spiritual growth, biblical-theological knowledge, loving accountability, encouragement, and help in times of need. Healthy churches serve families, giving them places from which they can reach out to serve others in their congregations, their communities, and the world. Healthy churches will have unhealthy and unstable people in them, but the healthy church offers love and a willingness to embrace even those who otherwise would be seen as misfits. The pastors of these churches will not be perfect, but they will acknowledge that they are servants called by God to use the gifts he has given to encourage, enlighten, enable, and be examples to others so that they can be servants too.

Programs and the Church

The church has been defined as the community made up of those who believe in God as revealed in the Scriptures and who unite for worship and service to him.[13] The church is comprised of people who have servant attitudes and diverse spiritual gifts. The believers may be led by a spiritual leader, but that person is also a member of the body and not one who dominates others.

Good churches often have well-planned programs to reach communities and to nurture and disciple believers within the local congregation. Sometimes, however, these programs are so numerous and so time consuming that people are pulled away from their families, often leaving children or spouses feeling neglected because a family member's time commitment to the church leaves little time for his or her family.

Clearly we need balance so that we can fulfill our duties as parents, children of our elderly fathers and mothers, members of our nuclear and extended families, and faithful servants of Christ within the family of believers. In these hyperbusy times, this is a hard balance to reach. Often we need the wisdom and encouragement of our family members and fellow believers to help us strike a balance. And we need to keep aware of the subtle influences that can make our lives unbalanced or overly busy so that we are committed to doing more than we have time to do and to accomplishing tasks that are inconsistent with our divinely given spiritual gifts.

Ministry Families

Some time ago, an older pastor came to me in tears, talking about one of his grown children who had forsaken the church and was living a life far away from God. My visitor pulled a New Testament from his pocket and read from 1 Timothy 3:4-5, verses that describe the qualifications of a church leader: "He must manage his own family well and see that his children obey him with proper respect. (If anyone does not know how to manage his own family, how can he take care of God's church?)"

Christian leaders must not be guilty of neglecting or mismanaging their own families. In their commitment to ministry and to the often overwhelming responsibilities of caring for a congregation, it is easy for pastors and other leaders to be engulfed in their work for the Lord and to leave the work of bringing up children and managing the household to their spouses. In trying to meet deadlines, to discharge their duties, and to satisfy the expectations of church members, Christian leaders can forget that being a parent and a spouse is every bit as much a "work for the Lord" as preparing sermons or doing marriage counseling. A friend once said it this way: "The church can always get another pastor, but my kids can't get another dad."

I do not mean to suggest that people in ministry must have perfect families if they are to stay in ministry. If that were the case, we would have a lot of empty pulpits. Some Christian leaders put their children and their spouses under a lot of pressure to be model Christians, and this causes tension in everybody. Others feel the glare of living a fishbowl existence with all the church members watching. Some, like my pastor friend, are distraught when their grown children react against these pressures and reject the church or when they choose to turn from the values of their parents and go a different way.

Church leaders have a duty to care for their families, to be considerate of their spouses, to be self-controlled, and to teach their children to be obedient and respectful. However, we live in a culture where many influences pull kids away from the values and beliefs of their parents. A major achievement of the devil is to undermine a ministry or ministry family by pulling away one or more of the kids. At times like these, we need to give encouragement, support, and prayer rather than criticism. We need to remember that the prodigal sons and daughters who turn away very often come back eventually. We must also remember that the only Father who is perfect understands the pain of those whose children forsake their roots: "For the Lord has spoken: 'I reared children and brought them up, but they have rebelled against me'" (Isa. 1:2). I pointed out this verse to the pastor who wanted to talk with me about his sons. Even God's kids have rebelled.

Those of us who are not pastors or employed in ministry situations can be aware of the special pressures that Christian workers face. Many are lonely, unappreciated, underpaid, insecure in their positions, constantly under pressure, and inundated by an ever-gushing pipeline of things that need to be done. Often people in ministry—pastors, missionaries, Christian musicians, youth workers, and others—feel inadequate, fear failure, worry about rejection. Many are cut off from anyone with whom they can talk confidentially and not feel rejected, even if they talk honestly. Many pastors' spouses have similar tensions, but they also have unique frustrations of their own. These can lead to marital tensions, depression, poor self-esteem, and other problems.[14]

None of this is meant to paint a picture of despair and misery. Ministry can be exciting and fulfilling, but we need to recognize that pastoral families are not exempt from family shocks. We who benefit from the ministries of others can pray for our leaders, encourage them, and do what we can to reduce the stress. Some of the most frazzled pastors with the most pressured families are those whose congregations assume that the pastor should do everything. If this describes your church, you might consider ways in which you can help others take off some of the pressure.

Building Better Families by Molding Better Young People

Josh McDowell is a crusader, not the kind of crusader who marches with posters or engages in obstructionist tactics.[15] In-

MARRIAGE IN THE MINISTRY

STUART BRISCOE AND
JILL BRISCOE
Elmbrook Church, Waukesha,
Wisconsin
Authors of *Marriage Matters*

Simon Barjonas had only one ambition: to be a fisherman. Then Jesus walked into his life and challenged him to catch men instead of fish. Simon wondered. Should he follow the Lord's challenge? Simon decided to accept his master's call to the ministry.

Then Simon went home and told his wife. She was flabbergasted! What would it mean? How would they pay the bills and care for the kids and her ailing mother? But after a little time she knew that Simon's decision was right, even if he hadn't consulted her first. Both of them recognized a privilege when they saw one. Was anything more significant than being the agent of eternal change in people's lives? Ministry was a privilege, not a punishment. So off went Simon, and she stayed at home.

It wasn't easy. Simon reminded the Lord of the sacrifice that he had made. Jesus was understanding but pointed out that they were in eternal business. He knew better than anybody else did that ministry involves sacrifice.

But that didn't mean that Simon's marriage was a sacrificial lamb. He believed that his wife was a "weaker vessel" who needed to be cared for. So he didn't ignore her needs or neglect his marriage. But Simon's wife knew that she and Simon were "heirs together." This saved her from selfishness and bitterness because she had a ministry too. Later in life they ministered together as a team. Marriage and ministry are friends, not foes.

---

stead, he sees a need, does research to get the facts, determines what can be done to bring change, rallies others to a cause, and does something to make a difference. Several years ago, he enlisted the partnership of thousands of churches to help teenagers resist sexual temptations before marriage. More recently he has turned his attention to helping kids make right choices.

McDowell is employed by a Christian parachurch organization, Campus Crusade for Christ, but his goal has always been to work with churches to strengthen pastoral leaders and to find ways to help young people develop solid values. Like many parents, Josh and Dottie McDowell have noticed that young people today have no real concept of truth, morality, or what makes something right or wrong. For many kids, including kids who are raised in good churches, truth has become a matter of expediency, and morality is no more than a reflection of one's individual preference. Church leaders are among those who have watched in anguish as young people have abandoned the values of their parents and slid into the valueless void of their contemporaries.

To get a picture of what young people really think about right and wrong, McDowell's associates launched a Church Youth Survey that obtained responses from 3,795 young people from thirteen denominations. Some of the findings were distressing. Fifty-five percent reported that they had fondled breasts or had intercourse at least once before they were eighteen years old, but 51 percent could not state that such activity was morally unacceptable. Fifty percent said they were stressed out, 36 percent had cheated on an exam, and 23 percent had tried to hurt somebody intentionally. Half the kids said they were confused about how to tell right from wrong, although 74 percent indicated that they were looking for answers.

In response to these findings, McDowell has launched a Right from Wrong campaign, which seeks to provide a blueprint "for countering the culture and rebuilding the crumbling foundations that begin at home, expand to the church, and ultimately affect our community." Working in partnership with churches, this campaign "helps families take a Daniel-like stand in a Babylonian-type culture."[16] The goal is to help young people distinguish right from wrong and increase their future effectiveness as husbands, wives, and parents.

Right and Wrong, Church and Family
If Christian young people don't embrace biblical values or know how to distinguish right from wrong, how can we hope for solid family relationships in the future? We have seen what relativistic do-what-seems-right-or-feels-good values have done to families

FAMILIES IN MINISTRY—
ARE WE STILL HAVING FUN?

H. B. LONDON, JR., B.D.
Vice President, Ministry
Outreach/Pastoral Ministries
Focus on the Family

Our church was sending our family to Hawaii for a vacation. Bev and I had already been to Hawaii, so for months before we left on the trip we were telling the boys how much fun it would be. Well, the travel day from Portland to Maui was mixed with plane delays, terrible weather, on-edge emotions, and a stalled rental car. Our youngest son, Bryan, could tell we were all just about at the end of our rope. Somewhat sheepishly, especially since we had built up the family excursion with such high expectations, Bryan asked, "Dad, are we still having fun?"

That's a question many families in ministry are asking. As I talk to families in ministry, I always remind them of the three Cs, which will help keep the potential for fun and fulfillment, even amid the pressures of the minister's home.

1. *Compassion.* Compassion shows a constant concern for the other members of the family. Compassion feels with the other person, celebrates when the person is victorious, and supports when the person is defeated. We must learn to forgive one another and to stand up for one another. The ministry home should be a sanctuary: a safe, forgiving, loving place to come home to.

2. *Communication.* Communication involves the ability not only to speak but also to ask *big* questions. When turmoil invades the home, it is most often because of misunderstandings that come from jumping to conclusions rather than talking. For instance, when something upsets you, ask, Why is this happening? How have I contributed to the problem? Is my reaction Christlike? When we find the answers to those questions, we have pretty well found the solution.

3. *Commitment.* Joshua said to those who surrounded him, "As for me and my household, we will serve the Lord" (Josh. 24:15). In other words, we will not compromise; we will not give in to the pressures of the world. How important it is for ministry families to live as God has ordained us to live. Our most remembered sermon will be *the one we lived.* The commitment we make is to the lordship of Jesus Christ and to those he has given us to love even as he loves them.

How did you do? In this form of family and personal evaluation, making straight Cs is as good as it gets!

and to the whole society. We know that many homes are not teaching solid values and that even when parents do have this commitment, many feel overwhelmed and confused about how to instill objective standards of right and wrong. When churches work together with each other and in partnerships with parents, they can teach moral guidelines and the values that form the foundations for healthy families.

People from the president down are concerned about what we can do to help young people face their futures. Reports, proposals, and community coalitions continue to address the problems of young people, but almost all of these discussions ignore the religious community. Most of the public-policy initiatives are about school reform, neighborhood revitalization, parent education, and the improvement of social services. There is an irony in this, according to a report from the Search Institute, because evidence suggests that church congregations have more potential than schools or youth agencies for addressing the problems of young people.[17]

Churches Teaching Teens
Only half of the teenagers involved in churches report that they learn a lot at church or that their congregations have done a good or excellent job in giving them a sense of purpose in life. Even so, when kids who are active in church are compared with those who are not active, the church kids score lower in all the at-risk issues like alcohol use, sexual activity, drug use, or suicide attempts.

According to the Search researchers, apart from the family, no other institution comes close to the church in helping kids deal with the present and prepare for the future. Churches provide some things that are unique.

1. *Contact.* The church is probably the only institution in society in which a majority of youth participate voluntarily.
2. *Access to families.* "Through a dynamic ministry with parents, congregations can enhance parents' abilities to be responsible sources of support, control, and values for young people."

3. *Intergenerational contact.* Church may be one of the few places where many young people have contact with principled, caring adults.

4. *Emphasis on service.* "According to an Independent Sector survey, youth are about twice as likely to learn about their volunteer activities through their religious congregations (62 percent) than any other organization, including schools (34 percent)."

5. *Nurturing values and decision-making skills.* Schools and community organizations shy away from discussing and shaping values, but congregations—some linked to the Right from Wrong campaign—can nurture positive values and help shape the choices that young people face.

6. *Nurturing social competencies and leadership.* By giving young people leadership and responsibility in the congregation, religious organizations cultivate social competence, teach leadership skills, and create relevant, caring youth programs where young people can ask tough questions and get mutual support.[18]

The Bottom Line Is Positive

"Restoring and redeeming the family, then, does not begin with the nation or with the family itself. It begins with the church."[19]

No church is perfect. We all know that. When everything is considered, however—when we look at the family problems in our homes, see how many good social programs have failed to make much difference, and consider the church's potential for making changes—we are likely to move to one conclusion. At the bottom line, the church is a positive force for improving family life. Indeed, the church of Jesus Christ is *the* most significant force and our greatest hope for strengthening homes and building better families.

I hope Jonathan reaches that conclusion too—before it's too late.

I wish Jonathan could meet Joseph and Suneetha. Although their story is set in a culture different from our own, it demonstrates how the couple gain strength and guidance by looking to the larger families of church and community to help them. The Indian couple never assume that they have to make it on their own. They know that they can count on the other people to help them stay strong. We independent-minded Americans can learn from other cultures and begin to recognize how the church and the family must work together to strengthen families in the midst of earthshaking changes.

Part Four

FAMILIES ON THE EDGE OF THE TWENTY-FIRST CENTURY

16

LOOKING TO THE FUTURE

THIS world is in the midst of cataclysmic change, change so sweeping and so pervasive that nobody can resist it or be unmoved by its power and impact. It is change that repeatedly rattles individuals and sends shock waves through families. It is disruptive and revolutionary change that threatens to strip away our values, tear apart our religious beliefs, undermine our economic and emotional stability, and radically alter our ways of living—like it or not. It is change that already has begun to inundate us with cascading landslides of data, rocketing down an information superhighway that most of us don't understand and have no idea how to handle.

This theme has been woven through the pages of this book. Like cliff dwellers who must beware of earthquakes that can damage or destroy their homes, we who stand on the edge of the twenty-first century need to be strong and firmly grounded lest our families, careers, beliefs, lifestyles, and worldviews collapse from the current onslaught of diversity and innovation.

While this change rumbles around me, however, sometimes I feel as if I'm removed from it all, standing on the outside, looking in. I know that the world is in the midst of upheaval and that "the United States is going through a time of tremendous instability, perhaps the most serious ever outside the Civil War."[1] I agree with those who criticize Christians and others for burying their heads in the sand, giving yesterday's answers to questions nobody is asking today, proclaiming that we need to go back to antiquated family living arrangements that would be hard to apply in practice. I applaud the statement that individuals, families, and churches must "anticipate, understand and adjust to change, or be left standing in front of a mirror talking religiobabble . . . to ourselves."[2]

Still, I feel as if I'm on the sidelines, where it seems safer. You may feel as if you are there with me. We want to make a difference, but we don't have a clue about what to do. We accept the reality of change and know that many families today are different from families in the past, but we go on as we always have, assuming that we will survive the aftershocks and not crumble.

The Challenge

Watching from the sidelines, I was interested to read the words of a *USA Today* writer who observed that recent voters have not been happy with their elected officials or with many of the trends that are being encouraged throughout the society. The government, for example, has spent the better part of a generation trampling on values and traditions that glued "Americans together for two centuries," according to writer Tony Snow.[3]

"The feds tried to replace old-fashioned faith with a new politics of meaning," but they have succeeded only in bringing forth a horde of absurdities.[4]

"We now pay for a welfare system that annihilates families. The penal code excuses murderers while imprisoning people who add an extra bedroom too near the nests of spotted owls.

"The federal government goes after cities that erect créches at Christmastime while forcing taxpayers to fund [so-called art that blasphemes Christ.] The wars on poverty, racism, drugs and other evils failed because they absolved individuals of direct responsibility for the outcomes."[5]

Snow describes the work of researchers who examined the scripts of prime-time television for the past twenty years and could not find any that attested "the importance of faith, the power of prayer and the possibility of miracles. The traditional religious messages were replaced by television's social gospel and cautionary tales about the need to question religious authority."[6]

It is odd, Snow continued, that the "establishment" and molders of public opinion choose to ignore the fact that 125 million Americans attend religious services every week. There is a failure to recognize that *"every successful reform wave in American history has pushed society forward while pulling people together."*[7]

Reform does not come from those who stand on the sidelines.

Across the Atlantic, Sir Fred Catherwood, one-time vice president of the European Parliament, recently wrote in a similar vein. "British society has gone badly wrong," he argued in an article that could equally apply to the U.S. "You don't just have to look at the terrible statistics. People have started to look back to the good old days—not so long ago—when the streets were safe, everyone had a job, most people had a home, children stayed in school, the family stayed together and we all looked forward to better times."[8]

"We look back today because we dare not look forward," the writer continued. "We live in a violent, greedy, rootless, cynical and hopeless society, and we don't know what's to become of it all."[9] As a result, apprehensive apathy abounds amidst half-hearted efforts to find hope or meaning in pleasure seeking, New Age spirituality, or the assumed activities of angels.

How, then, do we live in the midst of change, building healthy families, experiencing personal fulfillment, actively reaching out to others, and growing in spiritual maturity without collapsing? What can we do to resist the temptation to withdraw to the sidelines, watching the changes with apprehensive apathy but content to stay uninvolved? How do we resist the morals-slashing impact of big government and irresponsible television that push society apart but do little to pull us together? How can we avoid the fears of the future and the temptation to look back when we need to be moving forward with confidence?

These are tough questions that cannot be answered by people who try to remove or dismiss God. If he is the almighty being that we sing about in our churches and read about in our Bibles, then God won't be threatened, surprised, or shaken by change. Even in the midst of the most devastating family shock, faith in Christ can sustain us, give us hope, and point with certainty to the future. Ask Scott and Janet Willis.

This Is What We've Been Prepared For

Their church was filled to capacity one November day recently. Squeezed into the basement, overflow crowds watched the service upstairs on closed-circuit television. Others, unable to get into the building, stood in silence and listened on speakers outside. Church members, neighbors, relatives, and friends of the family were there. Members of the news media moved around, recording the events for a nation of strangers, many of whom had sent cards, letters, and donations. Fellow staff members had come from the Dawes School, where Scott Willis was a teacher. Young members of the Mount Greenwood Mustangs youth wrestling club were there, wearing their green team jackets and sometimes glancing uncomfortably toward their part-time wrestling coach who sat in the front, facing the row of gold and white caskets.[10]

A few days earlier, Rev. Duane "Scott" Willis and his wife, Janet, loaded their six children—ages thirteen years to only eleven months—into the family minivan and started the short trip north to see one of their older sons in Milwaukee. A car in front of the Willises' vehicle swerved to avoid a piece of metal on the road, but Scott wasn't able to do the same. As he ran over the object, it pierced the gas tank of the minivan, suddenly engulfing it in flames. Scott jammed on the brakes, and he and Janet leaped out, their hands already burned severely. Thirteen-year-old Ben was able to unbuckle his seat belt and stagger from the flames, but he died a few hours later of intensive burns. None of the others escaped.

Two days after the accident, Scott and Janet Willis held a press conference in the hospital before leaving for the funeral of their six children. Burned, bandaged, still sedated, and numbed by the tragedy, they thanked the rescue workers and hospital personnel. Then the parents talked about what had happened.

Immediately following the accident, when Janet Willis looked back at their vehicle enveloped in flames, she began screaming, "No!"

But her husband touched her shoulder, saying, "Janet, this is what we've been prepared for."

Mrs. Willis told the room full of reporters, "And he was right.

He said, 'Janet, it was quick, and they're with the Lord.' And he was right. . . . We belong to him. My children belong to him. He's the giver and taker of life and he sustains us."

Scott added that he and his wife don't take a short view of life. "We take the long view," he said, "and that includes eternal life. As believers, we know that one day we will be reunited."

Reporters learned that the grieving couple had spent more time consoling doctors and nurses than the other way around. They had talked openly with the medical staff and later greeted long lines of visitors who came to express condolences before the service in that packed church.

"The sad thing in this is that so many people don't want to believe [the family's] faith is real," the Reverend Don Voegtlin told the crowd as he led the memorial service. "This is real, and what a wonderful, wonderful thing that God has preserved their faith."

After the service, a friend of the family agreed. Twenty-five-year-old Ken Thompson had wrestled with one of the older Willis children and knew of the Willises' faith. "I only wish I had that perspective, because I hurt right now," Thompson said following the service.

But the Willis family hurts too, and they will continue to grieve. "We cry every day," they told a radio interviewer several weeks after their tragedy. They have a faith that sustains them and friends who give support, but their grief is real and so is their pain.

In the coming years, life will not be easy for the Willis family, including their three older children. They will look back, relish their memories, and find comfort in the ancient text of the Bible. They will feel loneliness, emptiness, sadness, and maybe a flood of other emotions, but I doubt that Scott and Janet Willis will join those who keep looking back because they dare not look ahead. Jolted by family shock that most of us cannot begin to imagine, they will adjust to the change in their lives, knowing that "this is what we've been prepared for" and moving into the future with steady assurance because they are not coping alone. Their faith in a living God and the loving support of caring friends enables them to meet the abrupt changes in their lives and move on.

Back to the Future

Earlier in this book, we considered nine influences that shape our families and our lives: experiences and incidents from the past, events and pressures in the present, the worldviews that determine how we see things, the dreams and expectations we have for the future, the decisions and choices we make, the stages and transitions in our families, our racial and cultural uniquenesses, the constant changes that our families encounter, and the sovereign hand of God in all that happens. Each of these nine threads is woven into our lives and our families; each has been woven throughout the pages of this book. Each has a role in helping us handle family shock and in giving us hope as we move into the new century.

Beginning Assumptions

To apply all of this in practical ways and in our own lives and families, we must start with some assumptions that are so simple and obvious that I hesitate to mention them:

- No one person can do everything
- No one person can know everything
- No one person can read everything
- No one person can control everything

Almost everybody would agree with these statements, but I wonder if others like me, individuals or people in families, live as if these statements are false. I know I can't *do* everything, but I take on too many responsibilities anyway. Then I'm surprised when my family, my spiritual life, my work, my sense of well-being, and sometimes my health suffer as a result. Certainly I can't *know* everything, but I don't want to lose touch with what's going on, so I push myself constantly to keep learning. Often that means buying books that I genuinely want to read and have every intention of reading. But I know I can't *read* everything, so why do I kid myself into believing that the mile-high to-be-read pile of books and magazines actually will get read? And why do I feel uncomfortable when I'm not in complete control of my circumstances, my family, my life, or my career? I know I can't *control* everything.

It is possible for me to be honest about these issues because I'm not alone. Many of us agree that we can't do, know, read, or control everything, but we keep trying, maybe thinking that this effort will give us a greater ability to face the storms of life and to cope effectively with change. Certainly there is nothing wrong with being active, learning, reading, and seeking to take control of events in our lives and families. But it is healthier when we also recognize our limitations.

Some people are more energetic than others, more challenged by novelty, better able to adapt and ride the waves of change to gain new mastery over their futures. But there are limits to the amount of change and newness that even the most energetic person or hyperactive family can absorb and handle.

To cope most effectively and to grow most fully, we should keep reminding ourselves that God is in control and that people and families must deal with change together. When we work as teams, we can deal more effectively with harmful influences from the past, set goals and priorities to deal with change in the present, and equip ourselves to move confidently and less fearfully into the future.

Dealing with the Past

Individuals and families stand more firmly against future family shocks and coming waves of change when they have dealt honestly with the past. This involves facing and freely talking about disruptive past experiences, incidents, embarrassments, or tensions that may have pulled apart family relationships or caused pain and shame in a family member. Sometimes we deal with the past by forgiving relatives who have caused hurt, asking others to forgive us, and doing what we can to bring reconciliation within the family.

Dealing with the past has been the theme of countless books, twelve-step programs, and recovery workshops, many of which suggest that we can find healing only with the help of God and the support of others. For those who have had painful and difficult backgrounds, these recovery experiences can be helpful.

The past has a more positive side, however. This involves remembering our roots, reflecting on good times together, looking at old photographs and family mementos, and acknowledging the influences of our parents and others who weren't perfect but who made contributions to each of our lives and families. Occasionally we all need to reflect on our racial and ethnic backgrounds, the richness that may have come from the countries of our ancestors, the diversities—and sometimes the extra stresses—that come into our families because we have older relatives, baby boomers, teenagers, or little kids in our families. The biblical writers frequently recited stories from the past. Maybe it is healthy for us to do the same.

Setting Family Goals and Priorities

If you have a family, why did you start one? What are your specific goals for your family? Ideally, especially in times of rapid change and periodic shock, the home should be a place where family members find and learn some values and facts about life. The home should be a place where we find

1. security and safety, not abuse, criticism, and turmoil
2. moral standards that are clear, practical, respectful of other human beings, built on the Scriptures, and not the jellylike, wishy-washy, situation ethics that let each person decide what is right or wrong for oneself
3. skills that are needed to relate to other people, handle stress, manage money, and develop lifestyles that are fulfilling and not self-centered or hedonistic
4. a serving mentality that involves all family members in reaching beyond the nuclear or extended family to give to others, to touch lives, and to show that we care about the tormented, shaken world in which we live
5. a healthy sexuality that gives accurate information and guidelines for maximum sexual fulfillment within the bonds of marriage and the guidelines of Scripture
6. spiritual knowledge so that family members know God

and have an accurate knowledge and understanding of
his attributes and impact in their lives

7. clear self-identity, self-esteem, and self-worth that give a
feeling of being significant, affirmed, and accepted.
This sense of worth does not deny that we are all
sinners, but it affirms that all of us are created by God.
He loves us and sent his Son to die to pay the penalty
for our sins. As a result, we are free to ask him to
forgive us, to know that he will do this, and to expect
that he will adopt us as his own children.

This list of goals is basic, ideal, and probably incomplete.
Maybe few families succeed in all seven areas—providing security, standards, skills for living, a servant mentality, healthy sexuality, spiritual growth, and self-identity—but by aiming for these
basics, we can build families that will stand firm in the midst of a
changing society.

Preparing for the Future by Taking Action in the Present

When Alvin Toffler wrote about handling change, he seemed to
suggest two broad strategies for coping. We can reduce the
amount of novelty and innovation that comes into our lives, and
we can increase our abilities to cope and adapt. Some of Toffler's
suggestions for accomplishing this and his "strategies for survival" in a world of rapid change may not have been practical. But
he proclaimed that we don't have to mope about, wringing our
hands in despair, standing like helpless victims of change without
hope or determination to resist. Instead, we can take action to
move toward family goals in the present, knowing that this will
determine, in large part, how we cope with continual change,
anticipate family shocks, prepare for the unexpected, and move
confidently into the future.

Accepting What Cannot Be Changed

When Scott and Janet Willis buried their six children, they knew
that their family would never be together again in this world as
they had been together in the past. They knew what we all must

concede at times: The healthiest way to deal with some unexpected events or family shocks is to accept what cannot be changed.

This isn't easy, especially when we desperately want a miracle and when acceptance means that our hopes and dreams for the future have to be abandoned. The Christian believes that God ultimately is in control and that he permits even tragedies to come into our lives and families. But acceptance often takes time, struggle, and the patient support of caring friends.

Choosing How to Respond

"The future does not depend so much on the dreams that we dream or the plans that we conceive. The future depends more on the choices that we make." I'm not sure where I first heard that idea, but it expresses a basic principle for families facing the future. Mothers and fathers who choose to spend time with their children, adults who choose to care for their older relatives, people who choose to set priority time and give attention to their families—these are people who, in the present, largely determine what their families and lives will be like in the future.

I have a friend who is intelligent, gifted, personable—and in prison. We have talked often about his life, most frequently during visiting hours behind the locked doors of the facilities where he has spent so much time. He has dreams and hopes for the future, but he is discouraged and "on hold" with his life because of the ways he behaves in the present. When he encounters unexpected and frustrating change, he seems to respond in one of three ways: He withdraws, refusing to go to work, or when he isn't in jail, running away. He resists, expressing his frustration with his fists. Or he turns sour, feeling bitter about the events and people in his life, angry with "the system," depressed with his lot in life. Every one of these reactions gets him into more trouble.

In his more poignant moments, my friend admits that he can't make it on his own. He needs God, and he needs other people who can hold him rigidly accountable. But he doesn't submit to anybody, so his present choices continue to lead him into the incarcerations that are shaping and stealing away his future.

BABY BOOMERS AND FAMILIES

TIMOTHY E. CLINTON, ED.D.
Executive Vice President, American Association of Christian Counselors
Coauthor of *Baby Boomer Blues*

In the eyes of his friends John has attained much. A highly successful businessman, he enjoys a position of community respect. He is an active member of a local church, and most who know him describe him as a devout Christian, loving husband, and patient father.

But the man who sat in my office did not resemble this profile of control and confidence. As he spoke, tears formed in his eyes. "Tim, I need to stop. I just can't keep up the pace. My head has been killing me, I'm feeling a lot of pressure, and to top it off, things are not going well at home. What's the matter with me? At times I feel so exhausted and unbelievably guilty for not spending more time with my family. The kids are growing so fast. I need help."

No generation has worked so hard and gained so much as the baby-boomer generation. Too often, however, boomers have sacrificed what matters most on the altar of attainment. They have sacrificed people they love. How, then, do we respond?

1. *Slow down.* Life is a journey, not a destination. Psalm 46:10 highlights this truth in a profound way. Read it and ask yourself, "When was the last time I was 'still'?" Remember that God is doing his work in you. You have exactly enough time in each day to accomplish everything God wants for you.

2. *Restore margin in your life.* Margin is the opposite of overload. If we have lost one thing in our fast-paced lives, it is margin. We must learn to build in a wider space between ourselves and our limits.

3. *Count the cost.* Life will trash your trophies. Ask yourself this question: "Is what I am doing really worth the ultimate cost?"

4. *Invest in and enjoy the finer things in life—now.* In a recent CNN/*Time* poll, 89 percent of the people polled said they would spend more time with their families if they could. Remember Matthew 6:31. What really matters to any dying person is the people they loved, and the people who loved them.

5. *Give to others.* Ours is a taking generation, but many people are discovering the awesome power in the act of giving. It is refreshing, therapeutic, and personally enriching to give and to be of value to others.

6. *Accept and rely on the omnipotent and sovereign God.* God desires us. That's why he sent his Son, Jesus. Remember his ways are higher than ours.

In many ways my friend is not unusual. Most of us are not locked behind the bars of a state prison, but we easily can be imprisoned by our choices, our actions, or our procrastinations. Over the years I have watched hundreds of students. The ones who get their diplomas are those who set goals and work toward them diligently. If they stumble, they get up and keep going. If they choose to quit, that decision has a bearing on their future lives and careers.

Stories of determination do not always have happy endings—consider the people who train for years to qualify for the Olympics but who never win a medal. But the principle still applies: To prepare for the future, to build healthy families, and to stand firm in the midst of change, we must decide on our goals, make careful choices, and then take action, all with the help of God and with encouragement from others.

Getting the Right Mind-set

Not long ago I had a birthday and passed a significant milestone in my progress toward old age. A friend, barely in his thirties, gave me a card on which he had written these words by Tryon Edwards:

> *Age does not depend upon years,*
> *but upon temperament and health.*
> *Some men are born old; and some never grow so.*

Our attitudes, values, perceptions, and worldviews largely determine both how we handle the changes that come with age and how we cope with the accelerated changes that come from society and impact our families.

Every psychology student has heard about self-fulfilling prophecies—the idea that what we expect is often what happens. It isn't always that simple, of course, but when we expect that our children will get hooked on drugs or drop out of school, expect that our marriages will grow stronger (or fail), expect that we will grow healthy families despite the forces that pull against family stability, then we often find that what we expected is what comes to be. Perhaps when we develop a negative mind-set about our families, we begin to act in accordance with our expectations, and our actions help to bring about the very catastrophe that we most feared.

It would be unkind and unfair to imply that family pain and tension comes directly from the negative attitudes in some family members. But it is accurate to conclude that what we think in our minds often contributes to what eventually comes to pass.

Dreaming and Envisioning the Future

When one of the Disney theme parks was opened some months after Walt Disney's death, an impressed visitor reportedly expressed his appreciation to one of the park's designers. "It is sad that Mr. Disney did not live to see this," the visitor said.

"Oh, but he did see it," the designer replied. "That's why the park is here."

Some people are visionaries, and a few are like Walt Disney: In their minds they can anticipate the future, imagine the possibilities, and then work to bring the dream into reality.

We need visionaries like that for the family—realistic people who understand change, who know the difficulties of building healthy families in a rapidly changing world. We need visionaries who see possibilities that others miss and who refuse to be sidetracked by the prophets of family doom. Robert Kennedy once described people who see things as they are and ask, Why? In contrast, he said, "I dream of things that never were and say, Why not?"

We need family visionaries who look to the future and say, Why not? We need idealists who are leaders with their dreams high in the sky but with their feet planted firmly on the ground.

What will these visionaries see, and what will they find ways to build? We don't know until we hear about their visions, but perhaps we will see a future, not far distant, with

- marriages in which faithfulness and commitment are priorities that guide behavior and strengthen relationships
- marriages with clear communication, mutual respect, a

willingness to allow each other to develop his or her potential, and mutually satisfying sexual pleasure

- families with humor, compassion, genuine friendship, and freedom from violence, ridicule, or conflict
- homes in which parents are teachers and mentors, giving their children solid spiritual and cultural roots, teaching their children values for making decisions, admitting their own mistakes, and slowly relinquishing control so that their children have freedom to build stable marriages and families of their own
- families who maintain contact with their extended family members, who are actively involved in a local church, and who reach out to their and communities in acts of caring, support, and Christian love
- families who do not ignore the political and social forces that threaten to tear society apart but who resist these forces in ways that show respect, determination, and clear, informed thinking
- families who maintain lifestyles that reflect a walk with Jesus Christ, who place worship as a high priority, who are committed to growing in the knowledge of the Scriptures, who show the world that the Christ-honoring family is the core of a socially stable society

Perhaps future visionaries will foresee the development of a cadre of family leaders who are willing to inspire and guide others so that they can anticipate and cope with incessant change, keep abreast of relevant data on the information highway, design and conduct relevant family research, plan strategies to foresee and deal with future change so that others can be taught to be strategizers and change agents as well. These family visionaries can teach family members how to be more effective in their homes, stimulate family education in churches and colleges, encourage family ministries worldwide, and assist churches in building caring bodies of believers who are involved in doing good to all people, especially to those who belong to the family of believers (Gal. 6:10).

Family visionaries must be realistic enough to find ways to help families who struggle with interpersonal tension, domestic conflict, financial pressures, persistent failure, incessant physical pain, or emotional agitation. These visionaries will find ways to develop the most effective family counseling and other forms of caregiving and intervention so that broken families are healed and potential family problems are avoided and prevented. We need visionaries who have hearts of compassion and sensitivity, melted by a spiritual warmth and an openness to the guiding influence of the Holy Spirit, who alone can guide us to ways of strengthening faltering families. We need, as well, sensitive, spiritually alert men and women with solid minds to help the rest of us learn more about families. We need these men and women to learn from careful biblical scholarship, solid research, clinical cases, the events of history, debates in the universities, and the perspectives of families from other countries and cultures.

I hope that these family visionaries—some of whom will read these words—can pull us beyond our myopic debates about conflicting roles, gender issues, or parent-teen disagreements in nuclear families and help us to see how the nuclear, extended, and Christian families of men and women, boys and girls, old and young, can reach out—shoulder to shoulder—to change the world through evangelism, compassion, education, scholarship, therapy, and creative thinking. Some of us may be the brunt of television jokes about the families, but we also must be among the few in society with families that work with perspectives that can build solid families that stand firm in an earthquake-rumbling environment of change.

The builders of family dreams need to start right away. They need to think about the future but also show us how all of this can work in our individual lives and homes. It is there that family building takes place. It is there that we work toward goals, accepting what cannot be changed but going on, making choices, forming healthy mind-sets and expectations, and dreaming dreams for our own families.

Critics who read these paragraphs will dismiss this as pie-in-the-sky optimism that describes the impossible. "We can't expect anything like that as we move into the new millennium," they will proclaim. But the best dreams are the ones that cause some to criticize and to say it can't be done but inspire others to move toward goals that even visionary leaders cannot see except dimly through the fog.

Some men and women look into the future and don't see many possibilities or don't see very far. Others have almost limitless vision that can see potential nobody today can imagine for the family. Some visionary needs to find a way to bring those other visionaries together to pray, plan, and mobilize a movement that, under God, can show the world that healthy families are not dead but that they form the foundation of future stability for the nation and for the world.

17

CELEBRATE THE FAMILY

EVEN Mike Royko was at a loss for words. The seasoned, sometimes humorous, and often stinging newspaper columnist seemed overwhelmed by the murder of yet another young person who came from a dysfunctional family and lived in a gang-infested urban neighborhood. Society finds more than enough targets for blame, Royko suggested in one of his columns: parents, the courts, social-service agencies, gangs, politicians, gun laws, drugs, bloody movies and television, rap music, schools, the economy, racism, and our violent society. Royko wrote about the weaknesses in the legal system, the political system, and the media. He also wrote about parents.

The boy whose death sparked the newspaper column was a trigger-happy gang member who had shot others and lost his own life in gang-related violence. His father was a criminal, and his mother was a drug user who naively told police that her son really was "a nice kid who needs some counseling." These two should not have had children, Royko wrote:

> But how do you stop them? Tie her tubes? Snip his organs? No, because that's unconstitutional and will remain so unless we become a totalitarian state. Refuse to support them by withholding welfare? That would be legal, but it would punish children. . . . Snatch the children away at the first sign of family neglect or abuse? And do what with them? There aren't enough foster homes for even a fraction of the

goofed-up ghetto kids; we'd have to build the world's biggest chain of orphanages. So, realistically, not hysterically, what do we do about teenage mothers and thug fathers, third- and fourth-generation welfare illiterates? Darned if I know. I guess we do what we've been doing: conduct studies, then wring our hands and worry."[1]

We watch families struggle, see people abused, feel sad about people who get killed, and point fingers at others and at ourselves, Royko said at the end of his column. "Then we can wait a few days for a new shocking headline and start all over again."[2] In the meantime we wring our hands and worry.

Pessimism like this is common today. Several recent polls agree that Americans are more pessimistic than ever. One survey found 71 percent dissatisfied with the way things are going in the country, and evidence suggests that this negativism is not limited to any one part of the world. When a professional journal published a survey of world trends following the collapse of Communism, the author concluded that "despite an occasional bubble of temporary euphoria, if present trends continue, the '90s seem destined to be remembered as a decade of despair."[3]

This attitude has pervaded the church and probably has led to some of the pessimistic books that have been mentioned earlier. When former cabinet member Bill Bennett was having lunch with a friend recently, he asked a thought-provoking question, "Tell me, can you name one positive trend in our culture?" While the friend groped for an answer, Bennett broke the silence. "All my friends respond the same way," he said. "They can't find anything encouraging."[4]

How, then, do we react? Many people, Christians included, start looking for somebody to blame. We often deal with tough problems in society and in our families by pointing the finger, shaking our fists, and hurling insults. We see this in political campaigns, but it's not limited to men and women who run for office. During the months that I spent writing this book, I read innumerable articles, research studies, and critiques of the family. I read facts that, to say the least, were disturbing. The United States, for example, has a higher child poverty rate than any developed nation in the world—four times greater than Western Europe; the social conditions of children in America have declined steadily since 1970, according to UNICEF. Nine out of ten murders of children in the rich countries occur in the U.S. Within a recent five-year period, the number of children in foster care has doubled, and almost half of these kids are under the age of five. The United States has made divorce quicker and easier than in any other Western nation with the exception of Sweden. And the number of families headed by single mothers has skyrocketed. Certainly there is reason for pessimism, for trying to assign blame, and for the what's-the-use-nobody-knows-what-to-do attitude that Mike Royko reflects in his newspaper articles.

Signs of Hope
But I am not pessimistic. I am buoyed by two simple and related conclusions.

We Need God
First, *we are finally coming to recognize that the family problems in our society cannot be solved on a human level.* From this it does not follow that we wring our hands in despair or sit back and do nothing. Of course, we take every possible action to strengthen families, encourage family members, and bolster values that enable families to function effectively. History has shown us, however, that our effectiveness in rescuing families from destruction and building better families is limited when God is left out.

Prevailing attitudes in society have moved us toward self-focused independence and away from God. Might this have something to do with the fact that family conditions have become worse? Concerned and intelligent people have tried almost every program imaginable to make things better, but with a few exceptions, family relations have deteriorated at all levels of society. When we realize our weakness, however, we are forced to turn to God for help. That is cause for hope.

Surprisingly, many people in our secular society seem inclined to agree. A recent *Newsweek* survey found that three out of every four adults who responded thought that the United States is in moral and spiritual decline. "Nobody today lives by the rules we

were raised on," one suburban mother said. "What ever happened to decency and respect?"[5] Part of the answer, the magazine
suggested, is that development of good character comes from
living in communities—family, neighborhood, religious, and
civic institutions pulling together—where virtue is encouraged,
rewarded, and not diminished. Communities with these kinds of
values have become fewer.

Some media, professional, and public figures take delight in
criticizing those who advocate the values that have guided people
for centuries. Many dismiss the emphasis on family values as
self-serving political prattle from Christians on the "religious and
political right" who are assumed to be intolerant, mean-spirited,
divisive, rigid, and bigoted. Those who launch these verbal attacks sometimes select extreme examples from among our numbers and sweep all believers together.[6] While these critics
proclaim their own tolerance and concern for individual rights,
however, they fail to recognize that their attacks demonstrate the
very bias that they claim to see in those who stand for more
traditional values.

We who stand committed to building better families can ham-
mer back with verbal attacks, but we can choose a better way. A soft
answer is what turns away wrath. An exemplary life is what coun-
teracts the self-centered individualism of many who attack families.
A presentation of the facts is what moves many who try to argue
that we need new family forms for postmodern living. We don't
have to beat people with arguments, Bible verses, alarmist predictions, or noisy rhetoric. We can simply present the facts:

- Christian marriages tend to be stronger and last longer.
- Kids who attend church are more likely to resist drugs
  and sex.
- Crime is less in neighborhoods where churches and
  communities band together to help one another.
- Children from intact families are psychologically
  healthier as teenagers and as adults as a result of
  growing up in stable families without divorce.
- Couples who attend church on a regular basis are more

satisfied with their marriages and have more satisfying sex than couples who do not attend church.

- Children in two-parent families do better in school and are less likely to be poor.
- Suicide is less common in people who live as part of intact families, and it is less common among Christians.
- Religion tends to be good for your health.
- Kids with caring fathers are better adjusted kids—and adults.
- When young people don't live together before the marriage, they have stronger marriages.
- Three decades of research has demonstrated that for children, two-parent families are preferable to single-parent families and stepfamilies.

Families Are Forever

This brings us to a second conclusion. *Family issues must be seen within a broader eternal perspective.* When God put us in this world, he set us into families. When he sent his Son, Jesus Christ, to redeem the world, the Father chose to have him born into a family and to be raised there. The Bible never gives any indication that families—nuclear-biological and extended families—are passé.

Even secular writers are beginning to see that the nuclear family "is not dead, and it will be alive in the years ahead."[7] The authors of an article in *Family Relations* wrote that it is time for scholars to stop "bashing the nuclear family." The article argues that despite recent changes in the ways we view the family (views that are "not bold at all compared with those of the 19th century"), we should stop spending time and energy debating the status of nuclear families and the threats to their existence; instead, we should be expending our best efforts in "helping all families to better cope and adapt to changes in a modern world."[8]

Throughout the Bible and throughout history, families have had to cope with and adapt to change. Some of these changes came from outside the home, but many resulted from the actions of family members themselves. In the Garden of Eden, for example, Adam told God that the apple had been eaten because of "the woman you put here with me." That comment probably didn't lead to smooth marital communication at home after Adam and Eve were expelled from the Garden. When they become parents of two children, the first married couple saw the first sibling rivalry, which was so intense that it ended in murder. Years later, young Joseph knew about sibling rejection and about sexual temptation. Still later, the esteemed King David had marital problems so intense that his wife despised him (2 Sam. 6:16). Then came David's well-known affair with Bathsheba and the king's grief over the death of more than one son. Tamar experienced rape—abuse within her own bedroom from one of her own relatives. Sarah, Hannah, and Elizabeth all struggled with infertility. Across the pages of Scripture, issues like these were acknowledged honestly, but the family was never dismissed as a failure or declared defunct.

Looking at this world from God's eternal perspective, we are able to conclude that the problems families face are "light and momentary" (2 Cor. 4:17). Believing that God is sovereign and ultimately in control, we can keep going and know that we are not forsaken even when family problems are intense. When the focus of our lives is too much on the here and now, we can be overwhelmed with pessimism. We can reduce this sense of despair if we take a broader perspective. To echo one of the psalms, when family problems come and pessimism is rampant, some trust in social programs, money, self-help books, or seminars, but we trust in the name of the Lord our God (Ps. 20:7).

Without God, we have no hope for the family.

It follows, then, that prayer must be a crucial response to the needs of families. My wife sometimes tells people, "We raised our kids on our knees." There is no other way. There is no better way.

We can take action, however, as individuals in our own nuclear families and as members of communities, cultures, and especially churches.

Partnerships

After nearly twenty years on the job, Cleo Terry recently quit. A lot of people were surprised.

When she started her career as a caseworker, Terry was glad to be working for the state, helping abused and neglected children who had been victimized by harmful family situations.[9] In time she became a supervisor, a trainer, a manager, and then a regional administrator. Eventually she was appointed executive deputy director of her state's department of children and family services. As the number of abused and needy children began to grow, however, the state did not provide funds for the agency to hire more caseworkers. Everybody got busier, and then the inevitable happened. Two or three children "fell through the cracks" and were returned to their incompetent mothers, who abused the children severely. One little girl even died. The newspapers published accounts of these tragic stories, and the state agency was smeared with high-profile negative publicity.

Determined to prevent this from happening again, Cleo Terry left her desk in the state office building and went to observe and help out at a state-run emergency shelter for mistreated children. The woman was shocked. She met an eight-year-old who didn't know his name and a nine-month-old whose panhandling mother placed him in the road to stop motorists.

When a family of seven children arrived, Terry watched as they were split apart and sent one by one to various foster homes. Finally only two were left in the shelter's waiting room, a nine-year-old boy and his baby brother. The boy held on to the baby and rocked him tenderly. Then Terry watched as the baby was taken from the little boy's arms while he cried uncontrollably.

"I knew they were going to get us," the nine-year-old said, referring to the state social workers. "Last week they got my cousins. Two weeks ago they got our neighbors. I knew they were going to get us." Suddenly Cleo Terry understood that the fear of being removed from the home was something these children lived with "the same way they live with guns and gangs and drugs."[10]

Back in her office, Terry concluded that her department was not doing what was right. Tearing apart families wasn't right, but neither was it right to keep young people in abusive homes where they risked getting hurt. "At some point we've got to reduce the number of kids coming in," she concluded.[11] That can't be done by mammoth government-run bureaucracies like the one she was helping to direct. As families get less able to care for their kids, the government agencies are getting bigger and less efficient as they suffocate under ever-increasing caseloads.

So Cleo Terry quit her state job. She went to work with a not-for-profit, community-based organization that tries to reduce family stress, teach parenting skills, and gear their programs to local community needs rather than imposing solutions from the top. Terry and many like her know that there are no simple solutions to complex problems, but they realize that community efforts, especially those that involve churches, will be more effective than many of the well-intentioned social programs that have been tried and found to fail.[12]

Mission executive Bryant Myers has reached a similar conclusion.[13] Global solutions to problems of poverty, poor health, or crop failure are never as effective as the grassroots initiatives of the community people who understand their circumstances and can work together to bring change, Myers has concluded. Few people believe in big, global approaches to bring social change or in the ability of outsiders to deliver solutions to problems. Of course, it is futile to give education and job training if the people can find no jobs that guarantee decent wages. Certainly it is difficult to develop community programs if people have no funds to run the programs. But when families and communities work together, the projects are owned by people in the neighborhoods and are more likely to work than those that are imposed by some outside agency.

I realize that these words present a political perspective that some won't accept. I also realize that human beings are imperfect, that many come from families in which they never learned to trust, and that many don't know how to cooperate, give, or follow through when they make a promise or agree to participate in community programs. Affluent people can hire somebody else to handle their problems. People who are less affluent, who are poorly educated, or who wrestle with special family needs must look for help from overburdened government workers. Few are blessed by running into somebody like Scott, who gives encouragement to the Martinez family, like Patricia Yauch and her Ameritech co-workers who have helped Lue Ella Edwards build her

FAMILY RELATIONSHIPS AND BUSY LIVES

TED W. ENGSTROM, LL.D.
President Emeritus, World Vision
Author of *The Fine Art of Mentoring*

The most important part of God's creation is people—individuals—you and me. Relationships are what life is all about. No matter how high our spiritual calling, the basis of our effectiveness is the love we have for each other in the mystical body called the church. If we look for a measure of our effectiveness, we need to check out the love life within our family.

At a Managing Your Time seminar that my colleague Ed Dayton and I conducted, a Christian executive shared his frustration that his work consumed so much of his time and energy that his family suffered. He indicated that no matter how hard he tried, he arrived home each evening full of the day's problems. He tried the suggestion of leaving his worries on a "worry tree" in the front yard. It didn't work.

Finally, he sensed the Lord was telling him he was approaching his worry in the wrong way. Rather than empty his mind of his concerns, he saw that he should fill it with thoughts of his family. His drive home was about five miles. He picked out conspicuous landmarks along the way and associated them with specific members of his family. As he passed each one, he tried to imagine what that family member would have been doing that day, what special concerns he or she would have, or what the family member would like to discuss with him that evening.

By the time he walked up the front path, his mind was full of his family. Now the cries of "Dad's home!" began to take on new significance. When he arrived at the door, he really *was* home, and the family knew it. 🔹

---

girls' club, like the Jochims, who give to other parents whose daughters have Rett syndrome, or like Jonathan's friends, who wait for the day when he will see that he needs to get help from the church.

Partnerships like this and ongoing contacts with extended family and fellow believers can combine to give practical support and the encouragement to keep going.

How Can We Prepare?

Following a weekend retreat to plan future directions for his church, a colleague dropped by my office and told me what had happened. Apparently it was a good gathering, but one topic kept surfacing and dominating the discussions: Everybody is too busy.

How can busy people build better families? How do we come to the end of a book like this and reach conclusions that can apply to the families in our country and to our own individual families? We know that simple answers or never-fail formulas do not exist, but perhaps we can focus our conclusions on four words: living, learning, modeling, and giving.

Living: Taking a Fresh Look at Our Lives

In the introduction to a recent book, Stephen R. Covey and his coauthors begin with these words: "If you were to pause and think seriously about the 'first things' in your life—the three or four things that matter most—what would they be?"[14] I took the challenge and jotted four things in the margin. You may want to do the same.

As I read further, I was challenged to realize that the things I say matter most often are issues that get pushed aside by the other activities of my busy life. Covey argues that too many of us have lives that are run by the clock and not by the compass. We are so busy rushing to meet time deadlines that we've lost sight of where we are going. The values that we cherish too often get overpowered by the projects and activities that keep pushing to control our lives.

In describing what he calls "the urgency addiction," Covey observes, "People expect us to be busy, overworked. It's become a status symbol in our society: if we're busy, we're important; if we're not busy, we're almost embarrassed to admit it. Busyness is where we get our security. It's validating, popular, and pleasing. It's also a good excuse for not dealing with the first things in our lives."[15]

None of us needs to be sent on guilt trips with reminders that we're too busy to deal adequately with the first things in our lives, like our families. Periodically, however, we all need to stop and ask where our lives are going and whether we want to keep living as we are living. That kind of reflection often is done best with other people who can help us reset priorities and do what we can to change our lifestyles.

If we don't make these periodic course corrections, most of our lives will be consumed with new technologies and new things to do so that our families get pushed aside.

SELECTING SELF-HELP BOOKS AND SEMINARS

1. Remember, brochures and book descriptions are designed to sell products or seminars, so read with caution.
2. Ask yourself, Who has written the book, and what are his or her qualifications? Are these qualifications convincing enough for you to spend your time or energy learning from these sources?
3. Ask yourself, Who is sponsoring the seminar, or who has published the book? Often that is a clue to what you might expect. A book by a respected Christian publisher, for example, is more likely than a secular book to give suggestions that are consistent with Scripture.
4. Try to get an evaluation from somebody whose opinion you respect and who has read the book or attended the seminar you are considering.
5. Look for endorsements on the brochures or book cover. Well-known people whose names appear in publicity often have not had time to become completely familiar with what they endorse, but their reputations are on the line, and they are not likely to give their names to something unless they agree at least in general.
6. Try to determine if the proposed self-help materials actually change people. Most research suggests that these materials can give encouragement and genuine help, but they don't always bring lasting change, especially in people who are too distraught to read a book or apply what they learn.
7. In general, be open to learning, be cautious, and be realistic about how much you will change.

Learning: Keeping Our Minds Alive and Growing
How is the mind related to the family?

We all know people whose minds seem to dry up. They leave school and stop learning. They slide into routine ways of doing things and never allow themselves to be challenged in ways that help them change and grow. In contrast are people who have inquiring minds that always seem alive and willing to learn.

Most of us fit between these two extremes. We have limited time for learning, and we don't always have the energy or inclination to be reading self-help books or going off to seminars. But we do this occasionally, and we learn new ways to enrich our marriages, improve parenting skills, relate to our older relatives or adult children, and build our families. The list on the previous page gives some guidelines for selecting helpful books and learning opportunities.

Often these learning experiences enable us to anticipate and prevent problems before they arise. Relationship experts Les and Leslie Parrott have a training program built around their book *Saving Your Marriage before It Starts.*[16] This is an example of preventive learning that helps couples handle relationships better and avoid family problems that could come later.

As you think about ongoing learning, try to keep these thoughts in mind.

Families do have strengths. With so much emphasis on what is wrong, we forget sometimes that many things are right about our families. Try this exercise: Jot down what is good about your family. Then ask your family members to do the same, and share your answers. You will find encouragement in pondering the positives and in building on the strengths that already exist in your family.

Families can help each other. Earlier we mentioned the benefits of parents talking with other parents whose children are a little older. Often a different perspective can be very helpful. Everybody knows about families that help each other in times of crisis, and we need to remember that many people still live in neighborhoods where families help families. Learning to build better families doesn't always require a seminar.

Families need the church. No institution parallels the church in helping in times of crisis, knowing the family members as they grow through the stages of life, and giving support and encouragement. The church is a place where family members can serve and reach out to others, and the church is a place where people can learn through sermons, seminars, classes, counseling, and other ministries to families.

Family learning is not just for married couples or parents. Do you remember the Johansons, the people with the three adopted kids who like to eat at McDonald's? Except for the baby, they are all involved in children's ministries. As we talked, the Johansons shared a dream. "Our churches have good ministries for men, women, couples, singles, teens, and children," they said, "but they offer few places where the family as a whole is the center of ministry." This couple was suggesting that sometimes the best learning takes place when the whole family is together. Family therapists work with whole families. Perhaps churches and individuals need to think more creatively about how families can all learn together.

I have a friend who suggests that the key to a healthy family is the authenticity of the parents who have learned what it is to live by the Spirit of the law rather than by the letter of the law.[17] Perhaps this also is a key to learning how to build better families.

Giving: Reaching Out beyond Our Families

When we face busy days and never-ending pressures, many of us like to think of home as a haven where we can retreat, rest, and get away from the demands of other people. But our families will dry up if we allow our homes to be sanctuaries that we rarely leave. To be healthy, suggests Rodney Clapp, the family needs a purpose or a mission beyond itself. "What will make a family exciting, what will make it worthy of our commitment and take us through the dry times, is common commitment to a mission bigger than our family."[18]

One evening last year, a few days before Christmas, our doorbell rang. When we answered it, we found the pastor of our church with his wife, his four kids, and a foster daughter from a dysfunctional home. They sang a Christmas carol, handed us a homemade Christmas ornament, and went on their way.

As we closed the door, I thought about what these children were learning—about making music and Christmas ornaments, giving to people in the neighborhood, and reaching out as a foster family to include a young woman who may never have seen anything like this. I doubt that the parents had given much thought to what the caroling was teaching their children, but by this simple holiday activity, a family was reaching out and being strengthened as a result.

Modeling: Learning and Teaching by Example
Who are the heroes in your life—the individuals or families whose examples have inspired you or your family?

Look at the question from the opposite perspective: What individuals or families are watching you and holding you up as a model of a healthy family?

During the years when I was a professor, we had hundreds (maybe thousands) of students into our home for meals, discussions, coffee breaks, graduation parties, holiday celebrations, and informal chats. Julie and I didn't think much about it at the time, but during those visits, many students apparently were watching us. Some have told us what they learned as we interacted with each other or with our kids. Some of these students had rarely seen a family that functions.

We have never been perfect—no family is—but without intending to do so, we have been models for others to watch. It is likely that you and your family also are models, even if you never entertain visitors in your home. Even if we reach no further, our children learn how to parent and how to relate by watching us.

Maybe we need to put more emphasis on looking for good models and for being good models.

When the Going Gets Tough

Before his recent election to Congress, Steve Largent was a football player, a very good football player. When he completed his fourteenth season with the National Football League, Largent had set a number of impressive records: 100 touchdowns, 819 interceptions, 177 consecutive games with a reception, 13,089 yards gained. He was selected as the Seattle Seahawks' most valuable player five times and was voted by his peers to play in seven Pro Bowls.

When Largent was a biology student at the University of Tulsa, he had an outstanding football career and was selected by the

EXPERTS OR ELDERS?

LARRY CRABB, PH.D.
Founder and Director, Institute for Biblical Counseling
Author of *Finding God* and *God of My Father*

Our culture has reduced itself to two groups: experts and followers. Seminars, books, and thriving churches sometimes give the impression that a few experts know what the rest of us need to know—and we'd better listen.

A married man made a habit of visiting a pornography store. Under conviction, he finally confessed to his wife what he had done. Together, they came to me. She was enraged. She called him the most pathetic man she had ever known. He played the part well. He turned to me in tears and begged me to help him. I felt required to have the "expertise" to diagnose and treat his sexual addiction.

Instead, I spoke about vision. I shared my (often frustrating and failure-ridden) pursuit of godliness. I told him how deeply I longed to become an elder, not an expert in psychology; a mentor, not a manager of other people's lives. The change in his life has been dramatic.

He asked what my vision was for my life. Without pausing, I replied, "To one day utter a sentence in the powerful energy of Christ."

Fathers in families do not need as much expert guidance as they may think. They need a deeper, richer walk with Christ, a walk that will provoke others to ask them questions about the quality of their lives. That's what an elder, a true mentor is: one whose life puzzles people enough to ask questions, giving him or her the opportunity to say something about the reality of God. ❧

---

alumni board as one of the top eight graduating seniors in his class. The Houston Oilers picked him in the fourth round of the draft, but he was traded to Seattle because the Houston coaches didn't think he had the skills or potential to be a great pass receiver. The young professional persevered, however. He committed himself to hard work and focused his attention on the task of being the best he could be. When times were tough in the NFL, he was determined to keep going. He didn't quit.

The first of the four Largent children was born when Steve was in the midst of his illustrious football career. Two years after Kyle's birth, daughter Casie made her appearance, followed by two more boys, Kelly and Kramer. All were healthy except Kramer, who was born with spina bifida and went into the first of his several surgeries within twenty-four hours after his birth.

"We were devastated," Largent responded when I asked how he and his wife, Terry, responded to the news of their son's birth defect. "Your mind goes into high gear" at a time like that. "Typically your worst fears are never realized, but you think of all the things your child won't be able to do." From the beginning, however, the parents never hesitated in their determination to help their little boy develop as much and as normally as he could. His dad describes him as being bright, active, independent, and a can-do kid. Kramer doesn't quit, and in working with him, his parents don't quit either.

Kramer's siblings have the same attitude. Before the new baby came home from the hospital, his sister and two brothers made a poster to welcome him into their family. It said: KRAMER, WE HOPE YOU CAN CATCH FROGS WITH US.

During the years when Steve Largent was a star among the football fans of Seattle, he often visited hospitals or called kids to bring encouragement and to say that they were important. His family had supported a child in Ecuador through Compassion International, and Steve had even visited with poor families in South America. With Kramer's arrival, however, the father found that he was able to give this encouragement and show compassion with a lot more ease, sympathy, and understanding. For the family, Kramer has been a blessing in disguise: a young man (age nine when these words were written) who has helped to draw his family closer together.

The Largents, like the Jochims, whom we met in an earlier chapter, have built a stronger family because they haven't quit.

Sue Rutz raises her kids as a single mom and hasn't quit.

Lue Ella Edwards saw her little girl die as the result of gang violence, but this grieving mother decided to start her girls' club. When the going was tough, Lue Ella Edwards didn't quit.

Grethel Beyah raised her nine kids and then worked on her own degree. She didn't quit.

Adrián was trapped in his drug habit, but people helped him get turned around. They didn't quit.

That pastor whose grown son had rejected the church and led his father to think about resigning from the ministry decided to keep going. He didn't quit.

I know a young man who wants to get married but who recently broke his engagement. It was clear that he and his intended wife were not in agreement about their values and spiritual commitment. When he is tempted to turn to somebody who is less than God's best for him and when he is tempted to stop looking for a soul mate with whom he can fully bond, he needs friends who can tell him, "Don't quit."

Only God knows how many people want families but struggle with infertility, are trying to adopt but can't seem to get a child, or are struggling because of a hard-to-control preschooler or a wayward teenager whose behaviors seem to be getting worse. God alone knows about all who are frustrated in their singleness because no marriage partner has come, feel trapped in a marriage that seems to be failing, or grieve because a family is being torn apart by sickness, physical or mental disability, or death. How many who have read this book are trying to build a family ministry in the church and are hitting a brick wall of resistance, are involved in the political process and not seeming to have much of an influence, or face discouragement in their efforts to help young women avoid abortion? Maybe your struggles or family-related frustrations are not listed in this book, but they continue to persist.

Please don't quit. Remember that God in his sovereignty and wisdom can take your frustrations and your efforts and turn them into something beautiful.

Many years ago, Ignacy Paderewski, the great Polish pianist, composer, and statesman was almost ready to begin one of his recitals on a concert tour. Waiting in the audience was an eight-year-old boy who slid out of his seat and headed for the stage before his parents could stop him. The young man seated himself at the piano and began playing the only piece of music he knew: "Chopsticks."

The disapproving audience scowled at this brash young lad

who had dared to desecrate the music hall with these jarring sounds. At that exact moment, Paderewski entered from the side of the stage. Quietly the master musician slid up behind the boy, reached his long arms out to the keyboard to the right and left of the two small hands, and began to improvise on the "Chopsticks" theme. Suddenly the simple melody, played imperfectly, took on a sound of beauty, blessed with the master's approval and engulfed with the master's touch. The audience burst into enthusiastic applause.

Everybody noticed that Paderewski had whispered into the boy's ear when the skilled hands first touched the keyboard. He said two words that encouraged the young man to keep going.

"Don't quit!"

Suggestions for Further Reading

James and Phyllis Alsdurf, *Battered into Submission: The Tragedy of Wife Abuse in the Christian Home* (Downers Grove, Ill.: InterVarsity, 1989).

Gary Bauer, *Our Journey Home* (Dallas: Word, 1992).

Michael A. Braun, *Second-Class Christians? A New Approach to the Dilemma of Divorced People in the Church* (Downers Grove, Ill.: InterVarsity, 1989).

Debra Bridwell, *The Ache for a Child* (Wheaton, Ill.: Victor, 1994).

Stuart and Jill Briscoe, *Marriage Matters: Growing through the Differences and Surprises of Life Together* (Wheaton, Ill.: Harold Shaw, 1994).

Dave Carder, Earl Henslin, John Townsend, Henry Cloud, and Alice Brawand, *Secrets of Your Family Tree* (Chicago: Moody, 1991).

Wm. Lee Carter, *Family Cycles* (Colorado Springs: NavPress, 1993).

Rodney Clapp, *Families at the Crossroads* (Downers Grove, Ill.: InterVarsity, 1993).

William L. Coleman, *Eight Things Not to Say to Your Teen* (Minneapolis: Bethany, 1994).

———, *You and Your Aging Parents* (Grand Rapids: Discovery House, 1994).

Jim Conway, *Adult Children of Legal or Emotional Divorce* (Downers Grove, Ill.: InterVarsity, 1990).

Jim and Sally Conway, *Moving On after He Moves Out* (Downers Grove, Ill.: InterVarsity, 1994).

James Dobson and Gary L. Bauer, *Children at Risk* (Dallas: Word, 1990).

Paul Faulkner, *Achieving Success without Failing Your Family* (West Monroe, La.: Howard, 1994).

William D. Gairdner, *The War against the Family* (Toronto, Canada: Stoddart, 1992).

George Grant, *The Family under Siege* (Minneapolis: Bethany, 1994).

Rebecca Merrill Groothuis, *Women Caught in the Conflict* (Grand Rapids: Baker, 1994).

Janis Long Harris, *What Good Parents Have in Common* (Grand Rapids: Zondervan, 1994).

Earl R. Henslin, *Man to Man* (Nashville: Nelson, 1993).

———, *You Are Your Father's Daughter* (Nashville: Nelson, 1994).

Greg Johnson and Mike Yorkey, *Faithful Parents, Faithful Kids* (Wheaton, Ill.: Tyndale, 1993).

Jay Kesler, *Grandparenting* (Ann Arbor, Mich.: Servant, 1993).

Grace Ketterman, *Parenting the Difficult Child* (Nashville: Nelson, 1994).

Teresa A. Langston, *Parenting without Pressure* (Colorado Springs: NavPress, 1994).

Kevin Leman, *Bringing Up Kids without Tearing Them Down* (Colorado Springs: Focus on the Family, 1995).

———, *Keeping Your Family Together When the World Is Falling Apart* (Colorado Springs: Focus on the Family,1993).

———, *Living in a Stepfamily without Getting Stepped On* (Nashville: Nelson, 1994).

Margie M. and Gregg Lewis, *The Hurting Parent* (Grand Rapids: Zondervan, 1988).

Lynda Gianforte Mansfield and Christopher H. Waldmann, *Don't Touch My Heart: Healing the Pain of an Unattached Child* (Colorado Springs: Pinon, 1994).

Cleveland McDonald and Philip M. McDonald, *Creating a Successful Christian Marriage,* 4th ed., (Grand Rapids: Baker, 1994).

Josh McDowell and Bob Hostetler, *Right from Wrong* (Dallas: Word, 1994).

Robert S. McGee, *Father Hunger* (Ann Arbor, Mich.: Servant, 1993).

David L. McKenna, *When Our Parents Need Us Most* (Wheaton, Ill.: Harold Shaw, 1994).

Douglas McMurry and Everett L. Worthington, Jr., *Value Your Mate* (Grand Rapids: Baker, 1993).

David R. Miller, *Counseling Families after Divorce: Wholeness for the Broken Family* (Dallas: Word, 1994).

Bob Moeller, *For Better, For Worse, For Keeps* (Sisters, Ore.: Multnomah, 1993).

James Osterhaus, *Family Ties Don't Have to Bind* (Nashville: Nelson, 1994).

Les Parrott III, *Helping the Struggling Adolescent* (Grand Rapids: Zondervan, 1993).

———and Leslie Parrott, *Saving Your Marriage before It Starts* (Grand Rapids: Zondervan, 1995).

Dennis Rainey, *Lonely Husbands, Lonely Wives* (Dallas: Word, 1989).

Lawrence O. Richards, *The Parenting Bible, NIV* (Grand Rapids: Zondervan, 1994).

Lyn Rose, *Mom's Diary* (West Monroe, La.: Howard, 1994).

Lillian B. Rubin, *Families on the Fault Line: America's Working Class Speaks about the Family, the Economy, Race, and Ethnicity* (New York: HarperCollins, 1994).

Jayne E. Schooler, *The Whole Life Adoption Book* (Colorado Springs: NavPress, 1993).

Buddy Scott, *Relief for Hurting Parents* (Nashville: Nelson, 1989).

Seven Promises of a Promise Keeper (Colorado Springs: Focus on the Family, 1994).

Beth Sterling, *The Thorn of Sexual Abuse: The Gripping Story of a Family's Courage and One Man's Struggle* (Grand Rapids: Revell, 1994).

Nancy L. Swihart and Ken R. Canfield, *Beside Every Great Dad* (Wheaton, Ill.: Tyndale, 1993).

Laura Sherman Walters, *There's a New Family in My House!* (Wheaton, Ill.: Harold Shaw, 1993).

Linda Weber, *Mom, You're Incredible* (Colorado Springs: Focus on the Family, 1994).

E. James Wilder, *Rite of Passage* (Ann Arbor, Mich.: Servant, 1994).

Everett L. Worthington, Jr., *Hope for Troubled Marriages* (Downers Grove, Ill.: InterVarsity, 1993).

———, *I Care about Your Marriage* (Chicago: Moody, 1994).

———, and Douglas McMurry, *Marriage Conflicts* (Grand Rapids: Baker, 1994).

H. Norman Wright, *Communication: Key to Your Marriage* (Ventura, Calif.: Regal, 1995).

———, *Family Is Still a Great Idea* (Ann Arbor, Mich.: Servant, 1992).

———, *Marriage Counseling* (Ventura, Calif.: Regal, 1995).

———, *So You're Getting Married* (Ventura, Calif.: Regal, 1995).

NOTES

Chapter 1: Coping with Change

1. Alvin Toffler, *Future Shock* (New York: Random House, 1970).
2. Ibid., 34.
3. Ibid., 211.
4. Ibid.
5. Faith Popcorn, "The Armored Cocoon," *Psychology Today* 28 (January/February 1995): 36.
6. Amy Saltzman, *Downshifting: Reinventing Success on a Slower Track* (New York: HarperCollins, 1991).
7. Alvin Toffler, *The Third Wave* (New York: William Morrow and Company, 1980), 17, 19.
8. Karl Menninger, with Martin Mayman and Paul Pruyser, *The Vital Balance* (New York: The Viking Press, 1963), 204–5.

Chapter 2: Nine Influences That Shape Our Families

1. See, for example, 2 Kings 18:3-7; 21:19-20; 22:2.
2. I have discussed worldviews, including their influence on counseling, in Gary R. Collins, *The Biblical Basis of Christian Counseling for People Helpers* (Colorado Springs: NavPress, 1993).
3. Robert Coles, *The Call of Service: A Witness to Idealism* (Boston: Houghton Mifflin, 1993), 81–85.
4. Ibid.
5. Ibid., 85.
6. Everett L. Worthington, Jr., *Marriage Counseling: A Christian Approach to Counseling Couples* (Downers Grove, Ill.: InterVarsity, 1989), chapter 4. Different writers have given different numbers of stages, although most suggest between six and eight. Sociologist Evelyn Duvall, perhaps the first to propose family life cycles, suggested eight stages: (1) Married couples (without children); (2) Childbearing families (when the oldest child is between birth and 30 months); (3) Families with preschool children (when the oldest is between 2 and 6 years); (4) Families with school children (when the oldest child is between 6 and 13 years); (5) Families with teenagers (when the oldest child is between 13 and 20); (6) Families as launching centers (between the time when the first child goes until the last leaves); (7) Middle-aged parents (from empty nest to retirement); and (8) The aging family (until both spouses die). For

399

further discussion, see Goldenburg and Goldenburg, *Family Therapy,*
3rd. ed. (Pacific Grove, Calif.: Brooks/Cole, 1991), 14–32.
7. For an anecdotal look at some sandwich-generation families, see "The
Sandwich Generation," *Ebony* (December 1993): 68–74.
8. James H. Bray and E. Mavis Hetherington, "Families in Transition:
Introduction and Overview," *Journal of Family Psychology* 7 (1993): 3–8.
This article introduces a special section of the magazine on families in
transition.
9. P. Hines, "The Life Cycle of Poor Black Families," in *The Changing Family
Life Cycle,* ed. B. Carter and M. McGoldrick (Boston: Allyn & Bacon,
1989).
10. Monica McGoldrick, "Ethnicity, Cultural Diversity, and Normality," in
Normal Family Processes, ed. Froma Walsh, 2d ed. (New York: Guilford,
1993), 331–33.
11. For an overview of the baby-boomer generation, including baby-boomer
families and how they can be reached and counseled, see Gary R. Collins
and Timothy E. Clinton, *Baby Boomer Blues: Understanding and
Counseling Baby Boomers and Their Families* (Dallas: Word, 1992). The
book includes discussion of baby busters. Of special interest is Wade
Clark Roof, *A Generation of Seekers: The Spiritual Journeys of the Baby
Boom Generation* (New York: HarperCollins, 1993). For a discussion of
Generation X, see Andres Tapia, "Reaching the First Post-Christian
Generation," *Christianity Today* 38 (September 12, 1994): 18–23; and
William Mahedy and Janet Bernardi, *A Generation Along: Xers Making a
Place in the World* (Downers Grove, Ill.: InterVarsity, 1994).
12. Den Dychtwald and Joe Flower, *Age Wave: The Challenges and
Opportunities of an Aging America* (Los Angeles: Jeremy P. Tarcher,
1989).
13. Gene A. Getz, *The Measure of a Family* (Ventura, Calif.: Regal, 1976), 13.

Chapter 3: What Is a Family?
1. Lance Morrow, "But Seriously, Folks . . . ," *Time* (1 June 1992): 29–31.
The former vice president wrote about this incident in Dan Quayle,
"Murphy and Me," in *Standing Firm* (New York: HarperCollins, 1994),
317–29.
2. Barbara Dafoe Whitehead, "Dan Quayle Was Right," *Atlantic* 271, no. 4
(April 1993): 47–84. The quotation is from the cover of the magazine.
3. Kathleen Gough, "The Origin of the Family," *Journal of Marriage and the
Family* (November 1971): 760.
4. For further discussion of the changing definition of the family, see Teresa
Marciano and Marvin B. Sussman, "The Definition of the Family Is
Expanding"; and Bryce J. Christensen, "The Definition of Family Should
Remain Limited" both in *The Family in America: Opposing Viewpoints,* ed.
Viqi Wagner and Karin Swisher (San Diego: Greenhaven, 1992), 40–54.
See also Irene Levin and Jan Trost, "Understanding the Concept of
Family," *Family Relations* 41 (1992): 348–51.

5. Adapted from William J. Doherty, "Private Lives, Public Values: The New Pluralism—A Report from the Heartland," *Psychology Today* (May/June 1992): 32–38.
6. Ibid.
7. Dennis K. Orthner, "The Family Is in Transition," in *The Family in America,* ed. Wagner and Swisher, 25–32.
8. Some observers would challenge statements like these. In a thoughtful book, Os Guinness argues that there is much talk about "traditional values" in our society. This might account for what people check on survey questionnaires. But many who talk about traditional values are "stronger in rhetoric than in reality." See Os Guinness, *The American Hour* (New York: Free Press, 1993), 47.
9. Doherty, "Private Lives, Public Values," 35.
10. The families that are described throughout this book are real families, and in most cases—like in the story of Gus—I have used real names, with the family members' permission. On occasion, I have changed the names and details about real families to protect their privacy.
11. "The American Family: There Is No Normal," *Life, Collector's Edition: Getting to the Heart of the American Family* 15, no. 5A, (1992): 4.
12. Stephanie Coontz, *The Way We Never Were: American Families and the Nostalgia Trap* (New York: Basic, 1993).
13. David Popenoe, "The Family Is in Decline," in *Family in America,* ed. Wagner and Swisher, 18. We should note that writers criticize definitions such as this as being too narrow. By using narrow definitions, some people—including politicians and policy makers—have argued that the traditional family is fading and have used this to justify very broad and liberalized views of future family life.
14. This was not true of all classes or geographical locations. Among many working-class people, the women went off to work too. In Glasgow, children sometimes were chained up all day to keep them from harm and mischief when no adults were around to watch them.
15. I understand that this is controversial, and I respect the fact that some readers will disagree.
16. H. Norman Wright, *Family Is Still a Great Idea* (Ann Arbor, Mich.: Servant, 1992).
17. For information about Rett syndrome or about parent support groups, contact the International Rett Syndrome Association, Inc., 9121 Piscataway Road, #2B, Clinton, MD 20735, or the Rett Syndrome Association of Illinois, 930 E. Northwest Highway, Mt. Prospect, IL 60056, phone (708) 342-9105.

Chapter 4: Families on the Fault Line

1. William D. Gairdner, *The War against the Family: A Parent Speaks Out on the Political, Economic, and Social Policies That Threaten Us All* (Toronto: Stoddart, 1992).
2. Ibid., xii–xiii.

3. The four books cited in this paragraph are Larry Burkett, *What Ever Happened to the American Dream?* (Chicago: Moody, 1993); William Bennett, *The De-Valuing of America: The Fight for Our Culture and Our Children* (Colorado Springs: Focus on the Family, 1994); George Grant, *The Family under Siege: What the New Social Engineers Have in Mind for You and Your Children* (Minneapolis: Bethany, 1994); and Vincent Ryan Ruggiero, *Warning: Nonsense Is Destroying America* (Nashville: Nelson, 1994).

4. Michael Novak, *The Spirit of Democratic Capitalism* (New York: Simon & Schuster, 1982).

5. G. Steiner, *The Futility of Family Policy* (Washington, D.C.: Brookings Institute, 1981); David Popenoe, *Disturbing the Nest: Family Change and Decline in Modern Societies* (New York: Aldine de Gruyter, 1988); L. Hodgkinson, *Unholy Matrimony: The Case for Abolishing Marriage* (London: Columbia Books, 1988); M. Bane, *Here to Stay: American Families in the Twentieth Century* (New York: Basic Books, 1976); H. Norman Wright, *Family Is Still a Great Idea* (Ann Arbor, Mich.: Servant, 1992). Self-help books include William B. Berman, Dale R. Doty, and Jean Huff Graham, *Shaking the Family Tree: Use Your Family's Past to Strengthen Your Family's Future* (Wheaton, Ill.: Victor, 1991); Michael J. McManus, *Marriage Savers: Helping Your Friends and Families Stay Married* (Grand Rapids: Zondervan, 1993); and Kevin Leman, *Keeping Your Family Together When the World Is Falling Apart* (Colorado Springs: Focus on the Family, 1993).

6. George Barna, *The Future of the American Family* (Chicago: Moody, 1993), 18.

7. Cited by David Popenoe, "The Family Is in Decline," in *The Family in America: Opposing Viewpoints,* ed. Viqi Wagner and Karin Swisher (San Diego: Greenhaven, 1992), 20.

8. Many of the conclusions and statistics from this section are adapted from Steven K. Wisensale, "Toward the 21st Century: Family Change and Public Policy," *Family Relations* 41 (October 1992): 417–22.

9. California Assembly Human Services Committee, *The Changing American Family to the Year 2000: Planning for Our Children's Future* (Sacramento: California General Assembly, 1987).

10. F. Levy and R. Michel, *The Economic Future of American Families* (Washington, D.C.: Urban Institute, 1991).

11. Myron Magnet, "The American Family, 1992," *Fortune* (10 August 1992): 45.

12. From *Running in Place: How American Families Are Faring in a Changing Economy and an Individualistic Society* (Washington, D.C.: Child Trends, Inc., 1994).

13. Scott W. Henggeler, Robert Cohen, and James J. Edwards, "Family Stress As a Link in the Association between Television Viewing and Achievement," *Child Study Journal* 21 (1991): 1–10.

14. Linda Stone Fish and Janet L. Osborn, "Therapists' Views of Family Life: A Delphi Study," *Family Relations* 41 (1992): 409–16.

15. Barbara Ehrenreich, "The American Family vs. the American Dream," *Networker* 16 (September/October 1992): 55–60. See also Michael R. Frone, Marcia Russell, and M. Lynne Cooper, "Prevalence of Work-Family Conflict: Are Work and Family Boundaries Asymmetrically Permeable?" *Journal of Organizational Behavior* 13 (December 1992): 723–29.

16. Children's Defense Fund, *Welfare and Teen Pregnancy: What Do We Know? What Do We Do?* (Washington, D.C., 1986). See also Colin McMahon, "Babies Born into Peril: When Kids Have Kids," the first article of a five-part series on "Saving Our Children," *Chicago Tribune,* 22 May 1994.

17. Robert S. McGee, *Father Hunger* (Ann Arbor, Mich.: Servant, 1993). See also Richard Louv, "The Crisis of the Absent Father," *Parents* (July 1993): 54–58; Tamar Lewin, "Father's Vanishing Act Called Common Drama," *New York Times National* (4 June 1990): A18; Steve Johnson, "Some Young Dads Have to Grow into Fatherhood," *Chicago Tribune,* 23 May 1994; and David Blankenhorn, *Fatherless America* (New York: Basic Books, 1994). An article in *USA Today,* 27 October 1994, began with this heading: "37% of U.S. kids live away from their fathers. And that spells trouble."

18. Saul D. Binder, "What If Government Programs Had to Compete for Our Tax Dollars?" *Success Stories: News of Note from Success National Bank* (One Marriott Drive, Lincolnshire, Ill. 60069: April 1994): 2–3.

19. My wife and I have good friends who joined with other parents to question and challenge some materials used in their local public schools. The parents were dismissed as troublemaking "right-wing fundamentalists"—a catchy term that is used to dismiss religious people, regardless of their theologies, if they object to the "professional expertise" and often biased views of some educators. The attitudes of our culture toward religious belief are discussed insightfully by Stephen L. Carter, *The Culture of Disbelief: How American Law and Politics Trivialize Religious Devotion* (New York: Basic Books, 1993). See also William J. Bennett, *The De-Valuing of America: The Fight for Our Culture and Our Children* (Colorado Springs: Focus on the Family, 1994).

20. Merton and Irene Strommen, *Five Cries of Grief: One Family's Journey to Healing after the Tragic Death of a Son* (New York: HarperCollins, 1993). The story of Dave's death and the quotations are taken, with permission, from the Strommens' book.

21. James H. Bray and E. Mavis Hetherington, "Families in Transition: Introduction and Overview," *Journal of Family Psychology* 7 (July 1993): 3–8.

22. There is abundant research to show that, compared with the nonreligious, religious people have better mental and physical health. This, in turn, has a positive influence on families. Some of this research is

summarized by Susan S. and David B. Larson, "Warning: Research Shows Religion is Good for Your Mental Health," *Christian Counseling Today* 1 (October 1993): 26–29.

23. Fish and Osborn, "Therapists' Views," *Family Relations:* 409–16.

24. This is one finding of research by David Elkind, reported in *Ties That Bind: The New Family Imbalance* (Cambridge, Mass.: Harvard University Press, 1994).

25. These statistics are reported by Dennis K. Orthner, "The Family Is in Transition," in *Family in America,* ed. Wagner and Swisher, 25–32.

26. Pauline Boss, "Primary of Perception in Family Stress Theory and Measurement," *Journal of Family Psychology* 6 (December 1992): 113–119.

Chapter 5: Undergirding the Family

1. A *Chicago Tribune* article (17 July 1994) titled "Hot Air on the Air" noted that about twenty radio stations every month move to a talk-show format, "offering a varied menu of erudition, insight and thoughtfulness with bombast, half-truths and flapdoodle. It is provocative, profitable and quintessentially American." But the article seemed to agree with President Clinton that talk radio is the irritant of our age and a "constant unremitting drumbeat of negativism and cynicism."

2. Robert Coles, "Moral Purpose and the Family," *Family Therapy Networker* 11 (November/December 1987): 45–52.

3. My thinking in this paragraph has been stimulated by a book by D. Waters and E. Lawrence, *Competence, Courage and Change: A New Approach for Family Therapy* (New York: Norton, 1993).

4. Adapted from Bruce A. Chadwick and Tim Heaton, *Statistical Handbook on the American Family* (Phoenix: Oryx Press, 1992), 53.

5. Tom Peters and Nancy Austin, *A Passion for Excellence: The Leadership Difference* (New York: Random House, 1985), 419.

6. Paul Faulkner, *Achieving Success without Failing Your Family* (West Monroe, La.: Howard, 1994).

7. "Lynn Minton Reports: Fresh Voices: Two Readers Find Each Other—Right Here," *Parade* (24 July 1994): 9.

8. Ibid.

9. Barbara Ehrenreich, "Oh, *Those* Family Values," *Time* 144 (18 July 1994): 62.

10. Stephen Chapman, "Concern for Family Provokes Backlash from Some Feminists," *Chicago Tribune,* 24 July 1994.

11. L. Gordon, *Heroes of Their Own Lives* (New York: Viking, 1988), 17.

12. Froma Walsh, ed., *Normal Family Processes,* 2nd ed. (New York: Guilford, 1993), 10, 17, 55.

13. Ibid., 58–59.

14. Ted W. Engstrom with Robert C. Larson, *A Time for Commitment* (Grand Rapids: Zondervan, 1987).

15. David B. Larson, Susan S. Larson, and John Gartner, "Families,

Relationships, and Health," in *Behavior and Medicine,* ed. Danny Wedding (St. Louis: Mosby, 1990), 135–46.

16. "Parents Flee, but Baby-sitters Stay," *Chicago Tribune,* 25 September 1994.

17. "The Coming Apart of America," *Chicago Tribune,* 24 July 1994.

18. Walsh, *Normal Family Processes,* 59.

19. David B. Larson, "Religious Involvement," in *Family Building: Six Qualities of a Strong Family,* ed. George Rekers (Ventura, Calif.: Regal, 1985), 121–47.

20. Rowland Croucher, "The Family: At Home in a Heartless World," *Grid,* a publication of World Vision Australia (fall 1994).

Chapter 6: Marriage and the Family

1. This conclusion is argued and documented by Paul C. Glick, "American Families: As They Are and Were," *Sociology and Social Research* 74, no. 3 (April 1990): 139–45.

2. On the contrary, the apostle Paul argues that it is good to stay unmarried and that there are significant benefits to singleness (1 Cor. 7:8, 38-40). Jesus Christ, God's Son, was the most spiritually and psychologically balanced person who ever lived on earth, and he was not married.

3. Genesis 2:18; Hebrews 13:4.

4. Robert H. Coombs, "Marital Status and Personal Well-Being: A Literature Review," *Family Relations* 40 (January 1991): 97–102. The quotation is from page 97. The research summary that follows is adapted from Coombs's article.

5. Ibid., 101.

6. Ibid., 100–101.

7. Ibid.

8. Willard F. Harley, Jr., *His Needs, Her Needs* (Old Tappan, N.J.: Revell, 1986), 11.

9. Kevin Leman, *Keeping Your Family Together When the World Is Falling Apart* (Colorado Springs: Focus on the Family, 1993), 128.

10. Dennis Rainey, *Lonely Husbands, Lonely Wives* (Dallas: Word, 1989), chapter 2.

11. John Gottman, "What Makes Marriage Work?" *Psychology Today* 27, no. 2 (March/April 1994): 38–43, 68. This article was excerpted from Gottman's book *Why Marriages Succeed or Fail* (New York: Simon & Schuster, 1994).

12. Linda C. Robinson and Priscilla W. Blanton, "Marital Strengths in Enduring Marriages," *Family Relations* 42 (January 1993): 38–45.

13. Genesis 2:24; Malachi 2:16; Ephesians 5:25-31.

14. C. Swensen and G. Trahaug, "Commitment and the Long-Term Marriage Relationship," *Journal of Marriage and the Family* 47 (1987): 939–45.

15. K. Hahlweg, D. Revenstorf, and L. Schindler, "Effects of Behavioral Marital Therapy on Couples' Communication and Problem-Solving Skills," *Journal of Consulting and Clinical Psychology* 52 (1984): 553–66.

16. This and several other conclusions in this section are from research by

Tamara Golsman Sher and Donald H. Baucom, "Marital Communication: Differences among Maritally Distressed, Depressed, and Nondistressed-Nondepressed Couples," *Journal of Family Psychology* 7 (1993): 148–53.

17. Lawrence J. Crabb, Jr., *The Marriage Builder* (Grand Rapids: Zondervan, 1982).

18. John 17:15-21.

19. John 3:16; Ephesians 2:11-16; Colossians 1:19-22.

20. John 17:15, 20-23. For a further discussion of this, see Gilbert Bilezikian, *Christianity 101* (Grand Rapids: Zondervan, 1993), chapter 7.

21. Ephesians 5:21-33.

22. Galatians 5:22-23.

23. Smalley, "Five Secrets," 110–11.

Chapter 7: Sex, Gender, and the Family

1. Genesis 19:1-5.

2. Stephen A. Hayner has summarized these attitudes and outlined the biblical teachings on sex in his article "What Dr. Ruth Couldn't Tell You," *Discipleship Journal* 11, no. 4 (July/August 1991): 22–25. See also David Wyrtzen, "Healthy Sexuality: The Biblical Perspective," *Christian Counseling Today* 2, no. 3 (summer 1994): 50–53.

3. Mark Clements, "Sex in America Today," *Parade* (7 August 1994): 4–6.

4. This information is taken from a newspaper report of a University of Chicago study of sexuality: Peter Gorner, "Sex Study Shatters Kinky Assumptions," *Chicago Tribune,* 6 October 1994.

5. James Patterson and Peter Kim, *The Day America Told the Truth* (New York: Prentice-Hall, 1992), 83–84.

6. Matthew 19:4-6; 1 Corinthians 7:1-9; 1 Thessalonians 4:1-8. This and the following paragraph are adapted from Gary Collins, *Christian Counseling: A Comprehensive Guide* (Dallas: Word, 1988), 250.

7. Proverbs 5:1-8; 1 Corinthians 6:9-10; Ephesians 5:3-7; Colossians 3:5-6; 1 Thessalonians 4:3.

8. Allan Bloom, *The Closing of the American Mind* (New York: Simon & Schuster, 1987), 120, 143.

9. Colin McMahon, "Babies Born into Peril," *Chicago Tribune,* 22 May 1994.

10. Ibid.

11. Ibid.

12. Cited by David Brader, "The One Simple Fact Everyone Agrees On: Kids Need Two Parents," *Chicago Tribune,* 22 June 1994.

13. One of the readers of the manuscript for this book wrote in the margin, "It is interesting that Mr. Clinton did not speak directly to the real moral issue, which is whether one is going to be sexually active before marriage. The president's statement could easily be followed by a commercial for abortion."

14. Jason DeParle, "Big Rise in Births Outside Wedlock," *New York Times National,* 14 July 1993.

15. Robert Wright, "Our Cheating Hearts," *Time* 144, no. 7 (15 August 1994): 44–52.
16. In one sense we *are* inclined to be moral because we are created in God's image with a moral conscience. When we fell into sin, however, our original goodness was disrupted and so was our natural inclination to be moral.
17. Wright, "Cheating Hearts."
18. Ibid.
19. Grant L. Martin, "Relationship, Romance, and Sexual Addiction in Extramarital Affairs," *Journal of Psychology and Christianity* 8 (winter 1989): 5–25. For an excellent discussion of this issue, see Henry A. Virkler, *Broken Promises: Understanding, Healing and Preventing Affairs in Christian Marriage* (Dallas: Word, 1992).
20. Patricia Hersch, "Sex and the Boomers' Babies," *The Family Therapy Networker* 17, no. 2 (March/April 1993): 25.
21. Ibid., 25–27, 70.
22. George Barna, *The Future of the American Family* (Chicago: Moody, 1993), 131–34.
23. Ibid.
24. Ibid.
25. Shervert H. Frazier, *Psychotrends* (New York: Simon & Schuster, 1994), 106. The Wisconsin study is by Larry Bumpass and James Sweet, "National Estimates of Cohabitation: Cohort Levels and Union Stability," paper no. 2 in the National Survey of Families and Households (Center for Demography and Ecology, University of Wisconsin: n.d.), cited in Barna, *American Family,* 134.
26. Cited by Harriet Meyer, "Fighting the Teen Pregnancy War," *Chicago Tribune,* 16 August 1994. Meyer correctly notes that the two cited studies have some procedural errors, but these do not negate the conclusion that people who are abused sexually experience long-term consequences.
27. Stanton L. and Brenna B. Jones, *How and When to Tell Your Kids about Sex* (Colorado Springs: NavPress, 1994).
28. Sol and Judith Gordon, *Raising a Child Conservatively in a Sexually Permissive World* (New York: Simon & Schuster, 1983).
29. Ibid.
30. Lynne Marek, "I'm Going to Wait: Teens Promise to Abstain from Sex as Part of a Growing Movement," *Chicago Tribune,* 29 July 1994.
31. These figures, and many of the facts in the following discussion, are taken from Andres Tapia, "Abstinence: The Radical Choice for Sex Ed," *Christianity Today* 37, no. 2 (8 February 1993): 24–29.
32. Richard Whitmire, "Effective Sex Ed Teaches Knowledge, Abstinence," *Houston Post,* 24 January 1994.
33. Tony Campolo, "Sex Ed's Failure Rate," *Christianity Today* 37, no. 2 (8 February 1993): 22.
34. Stanley R. Graham, "What Does a Man Want?" *American Psychologist* 47, no. 7 (July 1992): 837–41.

35. Ibid.
36. James C. Dobson, "Masculinity and Femininity: More Ambiguous Than Ever," *Focus on the Family* (September 1991): 4–5.
37. Robert Lewis and William Hendricks, *Rocking the Roles: Building a Win-Win Marriage* (Colorado Springs: Navpress, 1991).
38. *20/20,* ABC News, 29 January 1993.
39. Stanley J. Grenz, "Don't take the bait: The best time to fight temptation is before it strikes," *Discipleship Journal* 12, no. 6 (November/December 1992): 42.
40. Joe Maxwell, "Lean on Me," *New Man* 1, no. 1 (July/August 1994): 38–42.
41. Consider these words from the psalmist: "I am still confident of this: I will see the goodness of the Lord in the land of the living. Wait for the Lord; be strong and take heart and wait for the Lord" (Ps. 27:13-14).

Chapter 8: Parenting and the Family

1. Jerry Adler, "Kids Growing Up Scared," *Newsweek* (10 January 1994): 43.
2. David Elkind, "Waah!! Why Kids Have a Lot to Cry About," *Psychology Today* 25 (May/June 1992): 80.
3. B. Gunter and M. Svennevig, *Behind and in Front of the Screen: Television Involvement with Family Life* (London: John Libby, 1987).
4. See, for example, Robert Lichter, Linda Lichter, and Stanley Rothenberg, *Prime Time: How TV Portrays American Culture* (Washington, D.C.: Regnery Publishing, 1994); Jennings Bryant, ed., *Television and the American Family* (Hillsdale: Lawrence Erlbaum Associates, 1990); Stewart Cohen, "Television in the Lives of Children and Their Families," *Childhood Education* 70 (winter 1993–94): 103–4; Gordon L. Berry and Joy K. Asamen, ed., *Children's Television: Images in a Changing Sociocultural World* (Newbury Park, Calif.: Sage, 1993); and Robert H. Knight, "Cultural Pollution: The Pernicious Effects of TV Sex and Violence," *Family Policy* 7 (August 1994). See also Michael Medved, *Hollywood vs. America: Popular Culture and the War on Traditional Values* (New York: HarperCollins-Zondervan, 1992).
5. James Dobson and Gary L. Bauer, *Children at Risk: The Battle for the Hearts and Minds of Our Kids,* rev. ed. (Dallas: Word, 1994).
6. This conclusion is based on a study done at the University of Virginia cited by William R. Mattox, Jr., "Two-Career Parents Spend Too Little Time with the Family," *The Family in America: Opposing Viewpoints,* ed. Viqi Wagner and Karin Swisher (San Diego: Greenhaven, 1992): 183–90. The same book contains contrasting viewpoints by Robin Parker, "Working Mothers Benefit the Family," and Juli Loesch Wiley, "Working Mothers Harm the Family": 141–51.
7. Edith Williams and Norma Radin, "Paternal Involvement, Maternal Employment, and Adolescents' Academic Achievement: An 11-year Follow-up," *American Journal of Orthopsychiatry* 63 (April 1993): 306–12.
8. The figures in this paragraph are all cited by Mattox, "Two-Career Parents."

9. Carol Hymowitz, "Unrealistic Standards," *Wall Street Journal* (5 August 1991). Cited by Gary Burtless and Robert J. Samuelson, "Two-Career Parents Have Enough Time to Spend with the Family," *Family in America,* 191–97.

10. Peter L. Benson, *The Troubled Journey: A Portrait of 6th–12th Grade Youth* (Minneapolis: Search Institute, 1993). For more information about Search Institute publications, write Thresher Square West, Suite 210, 700 South Third Street, Minneapolis, MN 55415.

11. Dale A. Blyth and Eugene C. Roehlkepartain, "Working Together," *Search Institute Source* 8 (May 1992).

12. Cited by E. E. LeMasters and J. DeFrain, *Parents in Contemporary America* (Belmont, Calif.: Wadsworth, 1989), 72.

13. Ibid., 24–25.

14. Many of these books are listed in Suggestions for Further Reading, beginning on page 395 of this book.

15. Linda Weber, *Mom, You're Incredible!* (Colorado Springs: Focus on the Family), 1994; Grace Ketterman, *Mothering* (Nashville: Nelson, 1990); Earl R. Henslin, *You Are Your Father's Daughter* (Nashville: Nelson, 1994); Earl R. Henslin, *Man to Man: Helping Fathers Relate to Sons and Sons Relate to Fathers* (Nashville: Nelson, 1994); E. James Wilder, *Rite of Passage: How to Teach Your Son about Sex and Manhood* (Ann Arbor, Mich.: Servant, 1994); Greg Johnson and Mike Yorkey, *Faithful Parents, Faithful Kids* (Wheaton, Ill.: Tyndale, 1993); Nancy L. Swihart and Ken R. Canfield, *Beside Every Great Dad* (Wheaton, Ill.: Tyndale, 1993); and Robert S. McGee, *Father Hunger* (Ann Arbor, Mich.: Servant, 1993).

16. For a summary of opinions about the American mother and the American father, see chapters 7 and 8 of LeMasters and DeFrain, *Parents in Contemporary America.* For an example of a popular article about fatherhood, see Richard Louv, "The Crisis of the Absent Father," *Parents* (July 1993).

17. For more information see Claudia Wallis, "Life in Overdrive" (a cover story on attention deficit disorder), *Time* 144 (18 July 1994): 42–50; and Grant L. Martin, *The Hyperactive Child: What You Need to Know about Attention Deficit Disorder—Facts, Myths, and Treatment* (Wheaton, Ill.: Victor Books, 1992).

18. If you appreciate the writings of priest-counselor-spiritual leader Henri J. M. Nouwen, you will learn from his book *The Return of the Prodigal Son: A Story of Homecoming* (New York: Doubleday, 1992). Hurting parents might be helped by Buddy Scott, *Relief for Hurting Parents: What to Do and How to Think When You're Having Trouble with Your Kids* (Nashville: Nelson, 1989); and Margie M. Lewis, with Gregg Lewis, *The Hurting Parent: Help for Parents of Prodigal Sons and Daughters* (Grand Rapids: Zondervan, 1988).

19. "Blaming mom and dad," from Ann Landers' column of 11 February 1994.

Chapter 9: Single People and the Family

1. Ben is not his real name.
2. For a thoughtful consideration of how adoption into an earthly family parallels adoption into God's family, see David V. Anderson, "When God Adopts," *Christianity Today* 37 (19 July 1993): 36–39.
3. William Barclay, *Letters to the Galatians and Ephesians* (Edinburgh: Saint Andrew Press, 1962): 202.
4. Ibid., 204.
5. Ibid., 199.
6. Quoted by Rowland Croucher, "The Family: At Home in a Heartless World," *Grid,* a publication of World Vision Australia (Autumn 1994): 1–3.
7. Ibid.
8. Leslie N. Richards and Cynthia J. Schmiege, "Problems and Strengths of Single-Parent Families: Implications for Practice and Policy," *Family Relations* 42 (1993): 3.
9. Katha Pollitt, "Bothered and Bewildered," *New York Times,* 22 July 1993.
10. Steven L. Nock, "The Family and Hierarchy," *Journal of Marriage and the Family* 50 (November 1988): 957–66.
11. Richards and Schmiege, "Problems and Strengths," 277–85.
12. M. Lindblad-Goldberg, J. Dukes, and J. Lasley, "Stress in Black, Low-income, Single-parent Families: Normative and Dysfunctional Patterns," *American Journal of Orthopsychiatry* 58 (1988): 104–20, cited in *Normal Family Processes,* ed. Froma Walsh, 2d ed. (New York: Guilford, 1993), 371.
13. Richards and Schmiege, "Problems and Strengths," 277–85.
14. E. E. LeMasters and J. DeFrain, *Parents in Contemporary America* (Belmont, Calif.: Wadsworth, 1989), 204–205.
15. Grethel Beyah's story is told by Joyce Kelly, "To the Tenth Degree," *Chicago Tribune,* 20 March 1994.
16. Ibid.
17. Ibid.
18. Ibid.
19. Peter L. Benson and Eugene C. Roehlkepartain, "Single-Parent Families," *Search Institute Source* (Minneapolis: Search Institute, 1993), 3.
20. Ibid. See also the Search Institute Publication, *Youth in Single-Parent Families.*
21. Richards and Schmiege, "Problems and Strengths."
22. Ibid., 281.
23. I am grateful to Scott, one of my former students, for sharing this story, and I am grateful to the Martinez family for their cooperation. To protect their privacy and identity, we all agreed that details should be changed and that I should not use real names—except for the name of Scott Thelander.
24. According to the Martinez family, *guero* is a nonderogatory slang term for somebody who is white.

25. Paul Cromwell, Dorothy Taylor, and Wilson Palacios, "Youth Gangs: A 1990s Perspective," *Juvenile and Family Court Journal* 43 (1992): 25–31.
26. James D. Virgil and Steven Chong Yun, "Vietnamese Street Gangs in Southern California," *Gangs in America,* ed. Ronald Huff (Newbury Park, Calif.: Sage, 1990), 156.

Chapter 10: Divorce and the Family

1. For other references to what God hates, see Isaiah 61:8; Amos 5:21; and Zechariah 8:17. The statement "I hate divorce" is found in Malachi 2:16.
2. Melinda Blau, "Getting through the Fire: Negotiating the Hurdles of Co-parenting," *Family Therapy Networker* 18 (May/June, 1994): 34–39. This article is adapted from Blau's book, *Families Apart: Ten Keys to Successful Co-parenting* (New York: Putnam, 1994).
3. George Barna, *The Future of the American Family* (Chicago: Moody, 1993). Barna describes how misunderstanding and "illogical mathematics" have led to the erroneous figure that half of all marriages end in divorce.
4. Kathryn Robinson, "Which Side Are You On? Increasingly, Therapists Are Taking a Stand in the Divorce Debate," *Family Therapy Networker* 18 (May/June 1994): 18–30.
5. Ibid.
6. Robert J. Garber, "Long-Term Effects of Divorce on the Self-Esteem of Young Adults," *Journal of Divorce and Remarriage* 17 (1992): 131–37.
7. E. Mavis Hetherington, Tracy C. Law, and Thomas G. O'Connor, "Divorce: Challenges, Changes, and New Chances," *Normal Family Processes,* ed. Froma Walsh, 2d ed. (New York: Guilford, 1993), 208–34.
8. James H. Bray and E. Mavis Hetherington, "Families in Transition: Introduction and Overview," *Journal of Family Psychology* 7 (1993): 3–8.
9. P. R. Amato and B. Keith, "Parental Divorce and the Well-Being of Children: A Meta-Analysis," *Journal of Marriage and Family* 53 (1986): 26–46; and Darin R. Featherstone, Bert P. Cundick, and Larry C. Jensen, "Differences in School Behavior and Achievement between Children from Intact, Reconstituted, and Single-Parent Families," *Family Therapy* 20 (1993): 37–48. For an in-depth study of children of divorce, see Judith Wallerstein and Sandra Blakeslee, *Second Chances* (New York: Ticknor & Fields, 1989).
10. Barna, *Future of the American Family,* 84.
11. Bryan Neighbors, Rex Forehand, and Lisa Armistead, "Is Parental Divorce a Critical Stressor for Young Adolescents? Grade-Point Average As a Case in Point," *Adolescence* 27 (1992): 639–45.
12. Deborah A. Dawson, "Family Structure and Children's Health and Well-Being: Data from the 1988 National Health Interview Survey on Child Health," *Journal of Marriage and Family* 53 (1991): 573–84.
13. Phyllis Bronstein, JoAnn Clauson, Miriam Frankel Stoll, and Craig L. Abrams, "Parenting Behavior and Children's Social, Psychological, and

Academic Adjustment in Diverse Family Structures," *Family Relations* 42 (1993): 268–76.

14. Ibid. See also, Heather Monroe Blum, Michael H. Doyle, and David R. Offord, "Single-Parent Families: Child Psychiatric Disorder and School Performance," *Journal of the American Academy of Child and Adolescent Psychiatry* 27 (1988): 214–19; Herbert W. Marsh, "Two-Parent, Stepparent, and Single-Parent Families: Changes in Achievement, Attitudes, and Behaviors During the Last Two Years of High School," *Journal of Educational Psychology* 82 (1990): 327–40; and Lynne A. Hall, Diana N. Curley, Barbara Sachs, and Richard J. Kryscio, "Psychosocial Predictors of Maternal Depressive Symptoms, Parenting Attitudes, and Child Behavior in Single-Parent Families," *Nursing Research* 40 (1991): 214–20.

15. Cited in "Breaking the Divorce Cycle," *Newsweek* (13 January 1992): 48–53; see also Carin Rubenstein, "The Children of Divorce As Adults," *Psychology Today* 13 (January 1980): 74.

16. Nicholas Zill, Donna Ruane Morrison, and Mary Jo Coiro, "Long-Term Effects of Parental Divorce on Parent-Child Relationships, Adjustment, and Achievement in Young Adulthood," *Journal of Family Psychology* 7 (1993): 91–103.

17. Karl Pillemer and J. Jill Suitor, "'Will I Ever Escape My Child's Problems?' Effects of Adult Children's Problems on Elderly Parents," *Journal of Marriage and Family* 53 (August 1991): 585–94; and Jane E. Myers and Novella Perrin, "Grandparents Affected by Parental Divorce: A Population at Risk?" *Journal of Counseling and Development* 72 (September/October 1993): 62–66.

   According to a report from the American Association of Retired Persons (AARP), grandparents who become parents to their grandchildren experience more than financial and emotional stresses. Many find that laws and benefits extended to parents do not extend to grandparents who are raising children. From Glen Elsasser, "Second-Time Parenting Not so Grand," *Chicago Tribune,* 11 September 1994.

18. Quoted by Barbara Dafoe Whitehead, "Dan Quayle Was Right," *Atlantic Monthly* 271, no. 4 (April 1993): 82.

19. Christopher A. Hall, "Holy Health: An Interview with David Larson," *Christianity Today* 36 (23 November 1992): 22.

20. Howard Wineberg and James McCarthy, "Separation and Reconciliation in American Marriages," *Journal of Divorce & Remarriage* 20 (1993): 21–42.

21. David G. Myers, *The Pursuit of Happiness: Who Is Happy and Why* (New York: Morrow, 1992), 173–74.

22. Jack and Carole Mayhall, "Keeping Your Marriage Afloat," *Discipleship Journal* 13 (May/June 1993): 42–47.

23. Kay Pasley, David C. Dollahite, and Marilyn Ihinger-Tallman, "Bridging

the Gap: Spouse and Stepparent Roles in Remarriage," *Family Relations* 42 (1993): 315–22.

24. For an excellent Christian discussion of counseling single people and people contemplating remarriage, see Everett L. Worthington, Jr., *Counseling before Marriage* (Dallas: Word, 1990). See also Emily B. and John S. Visher, "Remarriage Families and Stepparenting," *Families in Transition,* ed. Froma Walsh, 235–53.

25. Jeanne Zornes, "Ten Ways to Help a Friend Who's Single Again," *Discipleship Journal* 13 (May/June 1993): 54–55.

26. See, for example, H. Wayne House, ed., *Divorce and Remarriage: Four Christian Views* (Downers Grove, Ill.: InterVarsity, 1990). For a briefer treatment see H. Wayne House, "The Bible and Divorce: Three Views," *Discipleship Journal* 13 (May/June 1993): 33–40.

27. Eleanor E. Maccoby, Christy M. Buchanan, Robert H. Mnookin, and Sanford M. Dornbusch, "Postdivorce Roles of Mothers and Fathers in the Lives of Their Children," *Journal of Family Psychology* 7 (1993): 24–38.

28. Edward Kruk, "The Disengaged Noncustodial Father: Implications for Social Work Practice with the Divorced Family," *Social Work* 39 (1994): 15–25.

29. Claire Berman, "When Children of Divorce Become Parents," *Parents Magazine* (July 1992): 82–84, 159–67.

30. Vincent is not his real name, but I'll use this because I don't want to cause him any embarrassment—even though it is unlikely that he will ever read this chapter.

Chapter 11: Families in the Midst of Grief and Loss

1. George Papajohn and Byron P. White, "Families Who Defy the Odds," *Chicago Tribune,* 18 December 1994.

2. See D. Waters and E. Lawrence, chapter 1, "The Family As Hero," in *Competence, Courage and Change: A New Approach to Family Therapy* (New York: Norton, 1993).

3. Ibid., 11.

4. Susan H. McDaniel, Jeri Hepworth, and William J. Doherty, "A New Prescription for Family Health Care," *Family Therapy Networker* 17 (January/February 1993): 19–29, 62.

5. John S. Rolland, "Mastering Family Challenges in Serious Illness and Disability," *Normal Family Processes,* ed. Froma Walsh, 2d ed. (New York: Guilford, 1993), 452.

6. Books geared to understanding and helping the elderly and their adult children include Lissy Jarvik and Gary Small, *Parentcare: A Commonsense Guide for Adult Children* (New York: Crown, 1988); Donna Cohen and Carl Eisdorfer, *Seven Steps to Effective Parent Care: A Planning and Action Guide for Adult Children with Aging Parents* (New York: Tarcher/Putman, 1993); and Angela Heath, *Long-Distance Caregiving: A Survival Guide for Far Away Caregivers* (Lakewood, Colo.: American Source Books, 1993).

7. Cited by Jacob Climo, *Distant Parents* (New Brunswick, N.J.: Rutgers University Press, 1992).

8. Lillian B. Rubin, *Families on the Fault Line: America's Working Class Speaks about the Family, the Economy, Race, and Ethnicity* (New York: HarperCollins, 1994), 234.

9. Ibid.

10. Ibid.

11. Ibid. Quotation is by Mark B. Katz, professor of history at University of Pennsylvania on the back cover.

12. Peter L. Benson, Anu R. Sharma, L. P. Roehlkepartain, and Eugene C. Roehlkepartain, *Growing Up Adopted: A Portrait of Adolescents and Their Families* (Minneapolis: Search Institute, 1994).

13. Ibid.

14. For a moving, informative, and interesting account of one family that learned to accept and later adopt a foster child, see Lynda Gianforte Mansfield and Christopher H. Waldmann, *Don't Touch My Heart: Healing the Pain of the Unattached Child* (Colorado Springs: Pinon Press, 1994).

15. E. E. LeMasters and J. DeFrain, *Parents in Contemporary America* (Belmont, Calf.: Wordsworth, 1989), 227–29.

16. Tori DeAngelis, "Homeless Families: Stark Reality of the 90s," *APA Monitor* 25 (May 1994): 1, 38.

17. Randy Alcorn, "Will Work for Food," *Discipleship Journal* 12 (November/December 1992): 73–78.

18. Adapted from H. Norman Wright, "Blessed Are Those Who Mourn," *Christian Counseling Today* 2 (fall 1994): 10–15. See also H. Norman Wright, *Recovering from the Losses of Life* (Grand Rapids: Revell, 1991).

Chapter 12: Abusive and Dysfunctional Families

1. George Papajohn, "Robert: Executed at 11," *Chicago Tribune,* 2 September 1994.

2. Ibid.

3. "How to Stop Growing Child Murders," *Chicago Tribune,* 4 September 1994.

4. The photograph illustrates the article by Ronald Henkoff, "Kids Are Killing, Dying, Bleeding," *Fortune* (10 August 1992): 62.

5. Kathleen McCarthy, "More Research Is Needed on Coping with a Child's Murder," *APA Monitor* 25 (July 1994): 54.

6. Quotation by Foster W. Cline in "Neglected, Abused, Deadly," *(Colorado Springs) Gazette Telegraph,* 23 January 1994.

7. Some of this is cited by Grant L. Martin, *Counseling for Family Violence and Abuse* (Waco, Tex.: Word, 1986).

8. Quoted in "Neglected, Abused, Deadly."

9. James M. Gaudin, Jr., Norman A. Polansky, Allie C. Kilpatrick, and Paula Shilton, "Loneliness, Depression, Stress, and Social Supports in Neglectful Families," *American Journal of Orthopsychiatry* 63 (October 1993): 597–605.

10. See *The Counseling Psychologist,* (October 1994) devoted to wife abuse. Two good Christian sources are by James and Phyllis Alsdurf, *Battered into Submission: The Tragedy of Wife Abuse in the Christian Home* (Downers Grove, Ill.: InterVarsity, 1989); and Grant L. Martin, *Counseling for Family Violence and Abuse* (Waco, Tex.: Word, 1986).

11. Anna Quindlen, "Now We All Know: O.J.'s Not a Hero, He's a Wife-Beater," *Chicago Tribune,* 22 June 1994.

12. "Living in Families," *Royal Bank Letter* (September/October 1994).

13. The history is summarized briefly by Richard J. Gelles, in R. L. Hampton, T. P. Gullotta, G. R. Adams, E. H. Potter, and R. P. Weissberg, ed. *Family Violence: Prevention and Treatment* (Newbury Park, Calif.: Sage, 1993).

14. See, for example, Hilary Wilce, "Turned Off by Violence: People in the U.S. Against Violent Television Programs," *Times Educational Supplement:* 25 February 1994, 19; and Stephen Cvengros, "Reality Overdose: Violence in News, Too, Is Shaping Young Minds," *Chicago Tribune,* 3 April 1994.

15. These issues are discussed in detail in books such as V. B. Van Hasselet, R. L. Morrison, A. S. Bellack, and M. Hersen, eds., *Handbook of Family Violence* (New York: Plenum, 1988); and R. T. Ammerman and M. Hersen, eds., *Assessment of Family Violence: A Clinical and Legal Sourcebook* (New York: Wiley, 1992). For an excellent Christian perspective see Grant L. Martin, *Counseling for Family Violence and Abuse* (Waco, Tex.: Word, 1986).

16. Leonard P. Edwards, "Reducing Family Violence: The Role of the Family Violence Council," *Juvenile & Family Court Journal* 43 (1992): 1–9.

17. This is discussed in R. J. Gelles and M. A. Straus, *Intimate Violence* (New York: Simon & Schuster, 1988).

18. For an authoritative and informative Christian perspective on ACOAs, see Sandra D. Wilson, *Counseling Adult Children of Alcoholics* (Dallas: Word, 1989). The drawing by the thirteen-year-old appears on page 19 of Wilson's book.

19. Something similar happens in schools where a teacher begins to pick on one of the students and everybody else in the class follows the teacher's lead.

20. Andrew Vachss, "You Carry the Cure in Your Own Heart," *Parade* (28 August 1994): 4–6.

21. Some of these conclusions are summarized by Lisa H. Jaycox and Rena L. Repetti, "Conflict in Families and Child Adjustment," *Journal of Family Psychology* 7 (1993): 344–55. The authors of this research conclude that while conflict between parents often is harmful to the children, an overall climate of conflict and tension in the home is even more disruptive, especially with girls.

22. "Renewing the Family Values Debate," editorial in the *Chicago Tribune,* 21 September 1994.

23. Adapted from "Living in Families," *Royal Bank Letter* (September/October 1994).

24. Timothy J. Zwart has given a concise summary of these traits, and I have followed his outline in the next several paragraphs. See "How Children Grow Up: Breaking the Cycle of Family Dysfunction," *Pine Rest Today* ([Box 165, 300 68th Street SE, Grand Rapids, MI 49501-0165] summer 1992): 1–4.

25. Ibid.

Chapter 13: Families on the Battlefield: Radical Feminism, Gay Rights, and Abortion

1. I am grateful to Moody Bible Institute president Joseph Stowell, who told this story in a sermon presented at Willow Creek Community Church, South Barrington, Illinois, 25 August 1994.

2. See William J. Bennett, *The De-Valuing of America: The Fight for Our Culture and Our Children* (Colorado Springs: Focus on the Family, 1994); and William J. Bennett, ed., *The Book of Virtues* (New York: Simon & Schuster, 1994).

3. Katherine Kersten, "How the Feminist Establishment Hurts Women: A Christian Critique of a Movement Gone Wrong," *Christianity Today* 38, no. 7 (20 June 1994): 20. For a more detailed treatment of the same issue, see Christina Hoff Sommers, *Who Stole Feminism: How Women Have Betrayed Women* (New York: Simon & Schuster, 1994).

4. *The Gallup Poll Monthly* (January 1994): 40.

5. Kersten, "Feminist Establishment," 22–24.

6. Quoted by Ellen Snortland in the *Los Angeles Times* and cited by James Dobson in *Focus on the Family Newsletter* (July 1992).

7. Ibid.

8. Cited by William D. Gairdner, *The War against the Family* (Toronto: Stoddart, 1992), 295.

9. George Grant, *Grand Illusions: The Legacy of Planned Parenthood* (Brentwood, Tenn.: Wolgemuth and Hyatt, 1990).

10. For a balanced evangelical Christian critique of the history of feminism, current feminism, and the issues facing contemporary women, see Rebecca Merrill Groothuis, *Women Caught in the Conflict: The Culture War between Traditionalism and Feminism* (Grand Rapids: Baker, 1994).

11. Perhaps we can place people on a continuum that looks like this:

Radical	Biblical	Biblical	Radical
Traditionalism	Traditionalism	Feminism	Feminism
	_____	_____	_____	_____	

Most of us could place ourselves someplace on this line. Others might place us at a point different from where we would place ourselves.

12. Larry Kramer, *Reports from the Holocaust* (New York: Penguin, 1989).

13. Review of *Stranger at the Gate: To Be Gay and Christian in America,* by Mel White, *Christianity Today* 38, no. 7 (June 20, 1994): 35–37.

14. Joseph Berger, "Letter to the Editor," *(Toronto) Globe and Mail,* 26 February 1992.

15. Stanton L. Jones and Mark A. Yarhouse, "Homosexuality: What We Know

for Sure," *Christian Counseling Today* 2, no. 3 (summer 1994): 34–38. Jones has also written a compassionate and biblically sensitive article on how Christians should respond to homosexuals in Stanton L. Jones, "The Loving Opposition: Our Response to the Homosexual Crisis—Speaking the Truth in a Climate of Hate," *Christianity Today* 37 (19 July 1993): 18–25. For a summary of research arguing that homosexuality is biological, see Chandler Burr, "Homosexuality and Biology," *Atlantic* 271, no. 3 (March 1993): 47–65. But be sure to see the letters to the editor in the June 1993 *Atlantic,* where even some of the researchers cited in Burr's article claim their data was misrepresented.

16. Jones and Yarhouse, 35. See also Gordon Muir, "Homosexuals and the 10% Fallacy," *Wall Street Journal,* 31 March 1993.

17. For a good discussion of the change issue, see Bob Davies and Lori Rentzel, *Coming Out of Homosexuality: New Freedom for Men and Women* (Downers Grove, Ill.: InterVarsity, 1993).

18. Chuck Colson, "Neither Busybodies nor Bigots," *Jubilee* (March 1993): 7.

19. For a discussion of both sides of the birth-control issue, see *Christianity Today* (11 November 1991), which carried several articles under the theme "Is Birth Control Christian?"

20. Betsy Powell, "'Pro-Life' Getting Bum Rap," *San Juan Star* 11 August 1994, originally published in the *San Francisco Examiner.*

21. David Hanley, "A Case of Post-Abortion Stress," *Christian Counseling Today* 2 (fall 1994): 26–31; see also Jeanette Vought, *Post-Abortion Trauma: 9 Steps to Recovery* (Grand Rapids: Zondervan, 1991).

22. Gairdner, *War against the Family,* 6.

23. Ibid.

24. Ibid.

25. In contrast to William J. Bennett, who titles a chapter "Why I Like a Good Fight," in his book *The De-Valuing of America.*

Chapter 14: Our World, Our Community, and Our Families

1. I am grateful to Bill Smith, my former research associate, who has visited Osijek on several occasions. Bill first told me about the Sokač family and obtained the material that I have used to start this chapter. I am grateful, in addition, to Rahela Sokač who sent information about her family and shared details in a lengthy telephone conversation from Croatia.

2. The International Year of the Family was 1994. A description of how some were using this U.N. declaration to strengthen family life is given by Peter Frieberg, "APA, U.N. Focus on World's Families," *APA Monitor* 25 (February 1994): 38–39.

3. Susan Chira, "Culture Shock: Cambodians Struggle to Raise Kids," *New York Times News Service* (1994).

4. Two very different resources can help us understand families abroad. For an in-depth treatment, see Helene Tremblay, *Families of the Word: Family Life at the Close of the 20th Century,* vol. 1 (New York: Farrar, Straus and Giroux, 1988). Much briefer and more accessible is a special issue of

Focus on the Family magazine (July 1994) with the theme "Families around the World."

5. Nancy Boyd-Franklin, "Race, Class, and Poverty," in *Normal Family Processes,* ed. Froma Walsh (New York: Guilford, 1993), 361–76.

6. This should be seen in parallel to the model set by Peter and John in Acts 4:18-20. They recognized that when obeying political leaders puts us at odds with obeying God, we must obey God rather than man.

7. George Grant, *The Family under Siege: What the New Social Engineers Have in Mind for You and Your Children* (Minneapolis: Bethany, 1994), 16.

8. Ibid. A major purpose of Grant's book is to document this last statement.

9. For ongoing reports of family-threatening political events and legislation in the United States, see the publications of the Family Research Council, 700 13th St., NW, Suite 500, Washington, DC 20005

10. Grant, *Family under Siege,* 271–72.

11. Howard Fineman, "The Virtuecrats," *Newsweek* 123 (13 June 1994): 36.

12. The conclusions that follow are adapted from two publications, both written by Dale A. Blyth and Eugene C. Roehlkepartain: "Working Together: A New Study Highlights What Youth Need from Communities," *Search Institute Source* 8 (May 1992): 1–3; and *Healthy Communities, Healthy Youth: How Communities Contribute to Positive Youth Development* (Minneapolis: Search Institute, 1993).

13. Blyth and Roehlkepartain, "Working Together," 2.

14. Eugene C. Roehlkepartain and Peter L. Benson, "Connecting Schools and Families," *Search Institute Source* 10 (October 1994).

15. Blyth and Roehlkepartain, "Working Together," 3.

16. Dale Buss, "Close Encounters across Cultures," *Christianity Today* 38 (12 December 1994): 15–16.

Chapter 15: The Church and the Family

1. Rodney Clapp, *Families at the Crossroads: Beyond Traditional and Modern Options* (Downers Grove, Ill.: InterVarsity, 1993), 157, 165.

2. Ibid., 79.

3. Ibid., 166.

4. Ibid., 67–68.

5. Ibid.

6. Ibid., 85–86.

7. These conclusions are drawn from A. Billingsley, *Black Families in White America* (Englewood Cliffs, N.J.: Prentice-Hall, 1989); N. Boyd-Franklin, *Black Families in Therapy: A Multisystems Approach* (New York: Guilford, 1989); and Donelda A. Cook, "Research in African-American Churches: A Mental Health Counseling Imperative," *Journal of Mental Health Counseling* 15 (July 1993): 320–33.

8. William D. Gairdner, *The War against the Family* (Toronto: Stoddart, 1992). 498–99.

9. Leaders like James Dobson, Jerry Fawell, and Pat Robertson demonstrate this perspective. Dobson's books are well known. Jerry

Falwell's most developed statement on the family is his well-written book *The New American Family: The Rebirth of the American Dream* (Dallas: Word, 1992). For an introduction to the Christian Coalition, see Ralph Reed, *Politically Incorrect: The Emerging Faith Factor in American Politics* (Dallas: Word, 1994).

10. Charles Colson, with Ellen Santilli Vaughn, *The Body: Being Light in Darkness* (Dallas: Word, 1992), 237.

11. Ibid., 366.

12. Ronald M. Enroth, *Churches That Abuse* (Grand Rapids: Zondervan, 1992), 189. See also Ronald Enroth, *Recovering from Churches That Abuse* (Grand Rapids: Zondervan, 1994).

13. Gilbert Bilezikian, *Christianity 101* (Grand Rapids: Zondervan, 1993), 177.

14. Psychologist Louis McBurney, along with his wife, Melissa, has spent his whole professional career helping burned-out and troubled pastors and their spouses. For an excellent overview of ministry families, the stresses they face and the ways in which they can be helped, see Louis McBurney, *Counseling Christian Workers* (Waco, Tex.: Word, 1986).

15. I am not suggesting that these methods are wrong or ineffective, although I question the actions of some of my fellow believers who use violence in an effort to stop violence. My point here is that McDowell's approach is different.

16. These words are taken from a brochure titled "Are They Making Right Choices?" distributed by Word publishing. The book that forms the basis of the Right from Wrong campaign is Josh McDowell and Bob Hostetler, *Right from Wrong: What You Need to Know to Help Youth Make Right Choices* (Dallas: Word, 1994).

17. "Congregations as Partners in Positive Youth Development," *Search Institute Source* 10 (March 1994). See also, "The Faith Factor: What Role Can Churches Play in At-Risk Prevention?" *Search Institute Source* 8 (February 1992).

18. "Congregations as Partners," 2, 4.

19. Clapp, *Families at Crossroads,* 47.

Chapter 16: Looking to the Future

1. David Aikman, "The State of the World," *World Christian* 11 (September/October 1994): 19.

2. Rick Thompson, "God's World: Facing Up to Change," *World Christian* 11 (September/October 1994): 9.

3. Tony Snow, "Counterpoints: Religious Right Leads Way to Reuniting Country," *USA Today,* 14 November 1994.

4. Ibid.

5. Ibid.

6. Ibid.

7. Ibid., italics added.

8. The quotatations are taken from an article by Fred Catherwood in

Evangelicals Now (September 1994), summarized by J. I. Packer, "Fear of Looking Forward," *Christianity Today* 38 (12 December 1994): 13.

9. Ibid., italics added.

10. The story of Scott and Janet Willis is told by Michael A. Lev, "Couple Held On to God in Tragedy," *Chicago Tribune,* 11 November 1994.

Chapter 17: Celebrate the Family

1. Mike Royko, "Who's to Blame? The Obvious Targets," *Chicago Tribune,* 12 September 1994.

2. Ibid.

3. David Beisel, "Looking for Enemies, 1990–1994," *The Journal of Psychohistory* 22 (summer 1994): 1.

4. Charles Colson, "The Upside of Pessimism," *Christianity Today* 38 (15 August 1994): 64.

5. Howard Fineman, "The Virtuecrats," *Newsweek* 123 (13 June 1994).

6. Whatever one's religious or political persuasion, we must be very careful that we are not guilty of doing to the critics of family values what some of these critics do to us. We must not erect caricatures of our critics or select the extreme examples and hurl counterattacks that assume all of those who disagree with us are the same.

7. Jay D. Schvaneveldt and Margaret H. Young, "Strengthening Families: New Horizons in Family Life Education," *Family Relations* 41 (1992): 385–89.

8. Ibid.

9. The story of Terry Cleo is told in Andrew Gottesman, "DCFS Aide Quits: Sees Better Way to Aid Kids," *Chicago Tribune,* 14 September 1994.

10. Ibid.

11. Ibid.

12. Ibid.

13. Bryant Myers, "Beyond Management by Objectives," *MARC Newsletter* 92 (June 1992): 3–4.

14. Stephen R. Covey, A. Roger Merrill, and Rebecca R. Merrill, *First Things First* (New York: Simon & Schuster, 1994), 11.

15. Ibid., 35.

16. Les Parrott III and Leslie Parrott, *Saving Your Marriage before It Starts* (Grand Rapids: Zondervan, 1995).

17. I am grateful to Nancy Moelk from Pittsburgh, who jotted these words on a piece of paper during a conference where we were both participants.

18. Rodney Clapp, *Families at the Crossroads: Beyond Traditional and Modern Options* (Downers Grove, Ill.: InterVarsity, 1993), 163.

INDEX